Why
Does
He Do
That?

DISCARD

INSIDE THE
MINDS OF
ANGRY AND
CONTROLLING
MEN

Why
Does
He Do
That?

Lundy Bancroft

G. P. PUTNAM'S SONS
New York

The names, identifying characteristics, and other relevant details of the anecdotal cases in this book have been modified to protect the privacy of these individuals. This book is not intended as a substitute for advice from a trained counselor, therapist, or other mental health professional. If you are currently in counseling or therapy, check with your mental health provider before altering or discontinuing your therapeutic regimen.

While the author has made every effort to provide accurate telephone numbers and Internet addresses at the time of publication, neither the publisher nor the author assumes any responsibility for errors or for changes that occur after publication.

G. P. Putnam's Sons
Publishers Since 1838
a member of
Penguin Putnam Inc.
375 Hudson Street
New York, NY 10014

Library of Congress Cataloging-in-Publication Data

Bancroft, Lundy.
   Why does he do that? : inside the minds of angry and
controlling men / Lundy Bancroft.
      p.   cm.
   Includes index.
   ISBN 0-399-14844-2
     1. Abusive men—United States—Psychology.
2. Wife abuse—United States.   3. Family violence—United States.
4. Victims of family violence—United States.   I. Title.
HV6626.2.B255   2002   2001048850
362.82'92'0973—dc21

Printed in the United States of America
10 9 8 7 6 5 4 3 2 1

This book is printed on acid-free paper. ∞

Book design by Mauna Eichner

10/02

Acknowledgments

I HAVE HAD MANY, many teachers along my path to understanding the mentality and behavior of abusive men. Before I can name names, however, I need to thank above all the hundreds of female partners and ex-partners of my clients who have shared their stories with me and who have thereby shed light on the denial and distortions running through my clients' accounts of events. The survivors of abuse have been my greatest educators; if we could hear their voices much more, and the voices of the abusers and their allies much less, the world would move rapidly to eliminate the chronic mistreatment that so many women currently face in their intimate relationships.

My early colleagues at Emerge have a unique responsibility for setting me on the course that has brought me here: David Adams, Susan Cayouette, Ted German, Magueye Seck, Chuck Turner, Charlene Allen, and Jim Ptacek. In addition to being such a pleasure to work with, this group provided me with indispensable intellectual support and stimulation; I hope I was able to return some reasonable part of what they offered me.

Equally important to the growth of my understanding of abusive men, and of their impact on their partners and children, was Carole Sousa, who simultaneously educated us at Emerge and kept us honest. Her criticisms of our blind spots were often annoying, mostly because of how right they were. No single person has contributed more to the understandings that I am now sharing. I need further to thank Carole for generously reviewing the manuscript for this book and marking her comments (important ones, as usual) with dozens of sticky tabs. Her suggestions have strengthened this book in critical ways.

Other important influences on my insight into controlling and angry men and the destructive trail they leave behind them include Lonna Davis, Pam Whitney, Isa Woldeguiorguis, Susan Schechter, Sarah Buel, Jim Hardeman, Janet Fender, and Brenda Lopez. I would also like to express my appreciation to Jeff Edleson, Claire Renzetti, Jackson Katz, Peter Jaffe, Barbara Hart, Bonnie Zimmer, Elaine Alpert, Joan Zorza, Jennifer Juhler, Stephanie Eisenstat, Range Hutson, Scott Harshbarger, and Maureen Sheeran for their contributions to my learning about abuse and oppression and for their professional support and encouragement. Kate O'Kane contributed by providing me with a beautiful and relaxing place to write during the day.

I also need to acknowledge how much I have learned from my clients themselves over the years, but it would not be appropriate for me to thank them, since without their abuse of women the writing of this book would be unnecessary.

I am grateful to Gillian Andrews, Carlene Pavlos, Jay Silverman, Steve Holmes, Catherine Benedict, Gail Dines, Carrie Cuthbert, and Kim Slote for their combination of personal support and intellectual/professional stimulation and assistance over the years. Gillian and Gail in particular have both kept after me for years to write this book, and it is largely due to their continued prodding that it is finally here; Gillian also provided invaluable comments and suggestions on the manuscript. My family, too, has been loving and supportive (and tolerant) during the time-consuming and sometimes stressful writing process; I love you and thank you more than I can say for carrying me along.

I owe tremendous gratitude to my agent, Wendy Sherman, who not only found a home for this book but also played a major role in forming the original concept and guiding its direction. A writer could not be in better hands. My appreciation also goes to Deb Futter at Doubleday, who led me to Wendy. My editor at Putnam, Jeremy Katz, has had unshakable faith in this project from the beginning and has helped me through several moments of anxiety or hesitation. It fell to Jeremy to let my wagonloads of text dump down upon him so that he could stir it all around and figure out how to shape it into a presentable whole. I also wish to express appreciation to other people at Putnam who supported and worked on this book, including AnnMarie Harris, Denise Silvestro, Marilyn Ducksworth, and Brenda Goldberg.

Finally, I want to express my deep gratitude to three people who don't know me but whose work has inspired and sustained me for years: Bruce Cockburn, Mercedes Sosa, and Linda Hogan. Perhaps our paths will yet cross.

Lundy Bancroft
Winter 2002

To the thousands of courageous women,

many of them survivors of abuse themselves,

who have created and sustained the movement

against the abuse of women, and to the many

men who have joined this struggle as allies.

Contents

PART I

The Nature of Abusive Thinking

PART II

The Abusive Man in Relationships

PART III

The Abusive Man in the World

PART IV

Changing the Abusive Man

Note on Terminology

IN REFERRING TO angry and controlling men in this book, I have chosen to use in most cases the shorter terms *abusive man* and *abuser*. I have used these terms for readability and not because I believe that every man who has problems with angry or controlling behaviors is abusive. I needed to select a simple word I could apply to any man who has recurring problems with disrespecting, controlling, insulting, or devaluing his partner, whether or not his behavior also involves more explicit verbal abuse, physical aggression, or sexual mistreatment. Any of these behaviors can have a serious impact on a woman's life and can lead her to feel confused, depressed, anxious, or afraid. So even if your partner is not an abuser, you will find that much of what is described in the pages ahead can help to clarify for both of you the problems in your relationship and what steps you can take to head in a more satisfying, supportive, and intimate direction. If you are not sure whether your partner's behavior should be called *abuse* or not, turn to Chapter 5, which will help you sort out the distinctions.

At the same time, remember that even if your partner's behavior doesn't fit the definition of abuse, it may still have a serious effect on you. Any coercion or disrespect by a relationship partner is an important problem. Controlling men fall on a *spectrum* of behaviors, from those who exhibit only a few of the tactics I describe in this book to those who use almost all of them. Similarly, these men run a gamut in their attitudes, from those who are willing to accept confrontation about their behaviors and strive to change them, to those who won't listen to the woman's perspective at all, feel completely justified, and become highly retaliatory if she attempts to stand up for herself. (In fact, as we see in Chapter 5, one of the best ways to tell how deep a man's control problem goes is by seeing how he reacts when you start demanding that he treat you better. If he accepts your grievances and actually takes steps to change what he does, the prospects for the future brighten somewhat.) The level of anger exhibited by a controlling man also shows wide variation, but unfortunately it doesn't tell us much in itself about how psychologically destructive he may be or how likely he is to change, as we will see.

In addition, I have chosen to use the terms *he* to refer to the abusive person and *she* to the abused partner. I selected these terms for convenience and because they correctly describe the great majority of relationships in which power is being abused. However, control and abuse are also a widespread problem in lesbian and gay male relationships, and the bulk of what I describe in this book is relevant to same-sex abusers.

Why
Does
He Do
That?

Introduction

I HAVE BEEN WORKING WITH angry and controlling men for fifteen years as a counselor, evaluator, and investigator, and have accumulated a wealth of knowledge from the two thousand or more cases with which I have been involved. I have learned the warning signs of abuse and control that a woman can watch out for early in a relationship. I've come to know what a controlling man is *really* saying, the meaning that is hidden behind his words. I've seen clues to recognizing when verbal and emotional aggression are heading toward violence. I've found ways to separate out abusive men who are faking change from those who are doing some genuine work on themselves. And I have learned that the problem of abusiveness has surprisingly little to do with how a man *feels*—my clients actually differ very little from nonabusive men in their emotional experiences—and everything to do with how he *thinks*. The answers are inside his mind.

However, as delighted as I am to have had the opportunity to gain this insight, *I am not one of the people who most needs it*. The people who can best benefit from knowledge about abusers and how they think are *women*, who can use what I have learned to help themselves recognize when they are being controlled or devalued in a relationship, to find ways to get free of abuse if it is happening, and to know how to avoid getting involved with an abusive man—or a controller or a user—next time. The purpose of this book is to equip women with the ability to protect themselves, physically and psychologically, from angry and controlling men.

To prepare for writing this book, I first generated a list of the twenty-

one questions that women most often ask me about their abusive partners, questions such as:

> *"Is he really sorry?"*
> *"Why do so many of our friends side with him?"*
> *"Is he going to hit me some day?"*

and many others. I then built my explanations around these concerns, to
make sure that women would be able to look here to find the information
they urgently need. You will find these twenty-one questions highlighted
as you go through this book; you might want to flip through the pages for a
moment now just to grab a quick glimpse of where I have addressed the
issues that are most pressing for you.

Another central goal of mine is to offer assistance to each woman
who is struggling with how she is being treated in a relationship, regardless of what label she may put on her partner's behavior. Words like *control* and *abuse* can be loaded ones, and you may not feel that they fit your
particular circumstances. I have chosen to use the term *abusers* to refer to
men who use a wide range of controlling, devaluing, or intimidating behaviors. In some cases I am talking about physical batterers and at other
times about men who use or insult their partners but never frighten or intimidate them. Some of the men I describe in the pages ahead change
moods so drastically and so often that a woman could never feel sure *what*
they are like, much less attach a label. Your partner may be arrogant, or
may play mind games, or may act selfishly over and over again, but his better aspects may make you feel that he is miles away from being an
"abuser." Please don't let my language put you off; I have simply chosen
the word *abuser* as a shorthand way of saying "men who chronically make
their partners feel mistreated or devalued." You can adopt a different term
if you know one that fits your partner better. But whatever style of mistreatment your partner uses, rest assured that you will find in these pages
the answers to many questions that have perplexed you.

If the person you are involved with is the same sex as you are, you have
a place here too. Lesbians and gay men who abuse their partners exhibit
much of the same thinking, and most of the same tactics and excuses,
that abusive heterosexual men do. In this book I have used the term *he* for

the abuser and *she* for the abused partner to keep my discussions simple and clear, but abused lesbians and gay men are very much in my thoughts, right alongside of abused straight women. Of course, you will need to change the gender language to fit your relationship, for which I apologize in advance. You will also find a section in Chapter 6 where I speak specifically about the similarities and differences in same-sex abusers.

Similarly, this book includes stories of men from a very wide range of racial and cultural backgrounds. Although the attitudes and behaviors of controlling and abusive men vary somewhat from culture to culture, I have found that their similarities greatly outweigh their differences. If your partner is a person of color or an immigrant, or if you are a member of one of these groups yourself, you will find that much of what this book discusses, or perhaps all of it, fits your experience quite well. While I have not specified race or ethnicity in the cases I describe in these pages, roughly one-third of the abusers whose stories I tell are men of color or men from nations outside of North America. I further discuss some specific racial and cultural issues in Chapter 6.

My Experience Working with Angry and Controlling Men

I began counseling abusive men individually and in groups in 1987, while working for a program called Emerge, the first agency in the United States to offer specialized services for men who abuse women. For roughly the next five years I worked almost exclusively with clients who were coming to the program voluntarily. They generally attended under heavy pressure from their female partners, who were either talking about leaving the relationship or had already done so. In many cases, the woman had gone to court to seek a restraining order legally barring the man from the home and in many cases ordering him to stay away from the woman altogether. The men's main motivation for seeking counseling was the hope of saving their relationships. It was common for them to feel some guilt or discomfort about their abusive behavior, but they simultaneously believed strongly in the validity of their excuses and justifications, so their feelings of remorse would not have been enough in themselves to have kept them in my program. In those early years, the clients I worked with were men who used far more verbal and emotional abuse than physical violence, although most of them had been physically intimidating or assaultive on at least a few occasions.

During the 1990s the legal system became much more involved than it had been in the past in responding to domestic abuse, with the result that court-mandated clients started at first to trickle and then to pour in the doors of our program. These men often had a much greater propensity for physical violence than our earlier clients, sometimes involving the use of weapons or vicious beatings resulting in the hospitalization of their partners. Yet we observed that in other ways these men were generally not significantly different from our verbally abusive clients: their attitudes and excuses tended to be the same, and they used mental cruelty side by side with their physical assaults. Equally important was that the female partners of these battering men were largely describing the same distresses in their lives that we were hearing about from women who had been psychologically abused, showing us that different forms of abuse have similar destructive impacts on women.

Throughout my years of working with controlling and abusive men, my colleagues and I have been strict about always speaking to the woman whom our client has mistreated, whether or not the couple is still together. (And if he has started a new relationship, we talk with his current partner as well, which is part of how we became aware of the ways in which abusive men continue their patterns from one relationship to the next.) It is through these interviews with women that we have received our greatest education about power and control in relationships. The women's accounts also have taught us that abusive men present their own stories with tremendous denial, minimization, and distortion of the history of their behaviors and that it is therefore otherwise impossible for us to get an accurate picture of what is going on in an abusive relationship without listening carefully to the abused woman.

Counseling abusive men is difficult work. They are usually very reluctant to face up to the damage that they have been causing women, and often children as well, and hold on tightly to their excuses and victim blaming. As you will see in the pages ahead, they become attached to the various privileges they earn through mistreating their partners, and they have habits of mind that make it difficult for them to imagine being in a respectful and equal relationship with a woman.

I am sometimes asked: Why work with abusive men if it is so hard to get them to change? The reasons are several. First, if even one man out of a ten-person group makes substantial and lasting changes, then my time and energy have been invested well, because his partner and his children will experience a dramatic change in the quality of their lives. Second, I believe in holding abusers accountable for their actions. If they attend an abuser program they can at least be called to task for the harm they have done, and I have hope (and see the signs) that cultural values can change over time if people find that men who chronically mistreat and degrade women are being made answerable. Third, and probably most important, is that I consider the woman that my client has mistreated to be the person I am primarily serving, and I make contact with her at least every few weeks. My goal is to give her emotional support, help her learn about counseling and legal services that exist for her in her community (usually for free), and help her get her mind untangled from the knot that her abusive partner has tied. I can make it more difficult for him to manipulate her, and I may be able to warn her of underhanded maneuvers that he is planning or of escalation that I'm observing. As long as I stay focused on the woman and her children as those who are most deserving and in need of my assistance, I can almost always make a positive contribution, whether or not my abusive client decides to seriously face his own problem. (In Chapter 14, I describe what actually goes on inside a counseling program for abusive men, and I explain how a woman can determine whether or not a particular program is being run properly.)

In recent years, through my work as a child abuse investigator and as a custody evaluator for various courts, I have come to interact in a new way with families affected by abusive men. I share some of the insights I have gained through these experiences in Chapter 10, which examines the experiences of children who are exposed to abusive men—usually their fathers or stepfathers—and the ways in which some abusers continue their patterns of controlling and intimidating behavior through custody actions in the family courts.

How to Use This Book

One of the prevalent features of life with an angry or controlling partner is that he frequently *tells you what you should think* and tries to get you to doubt or devalue your own perceptions and beliefs. I would not like to see your experience with this book re-create that unhealthy dynamic. So the primary point to bear in mind as you read the pages ahead is to listen carefully to what I am saying, but always to think for yourself. If any part of what I describe about abusers doesn't match your experience, cast it aside and focus on the parts that do fit. You might even put the book down from time to time and ask yourself, "How does this apply to *my* relationship? What are my own examples of how a controlling or cruel man thinks and behaves?" If you come upon sections that don't speak to you—because you don't have children, for example, or because your partner is never physically frightening—just skip ahead to the pieces that can help you more.

Some women will find that being alone with this book is too difficult because it awakens feelings and realizations that are overwhelming. I encourage you to reach out for support from trusted friends and family as you go along. While reading this book is likely to be clarifying for you, it may also awaken an awareness that can be painful or distressing.

If you can't find someone whom you know to talk to—or even if you can—call the abuse hotline in your area. If you need a listing near where you live in the United States or Canada, call the National Abuse Hotline at (800) 799-7233, and they will give you your local program information (in almost any language imaginable). For many other options for assistance, look in the "Resources" section at the back of this book. Again, don't be stymied by the word *abuse;* the hot line staff is there to listen to you and to help you think about any relationship in which you are being treated in a way that is making you feel bad.

I understand how uncomfortable it can be to take the leap of talking with people you care about regarding the mistreatment you are experiencing in your relationship. You may feel ashamed of having a partner who sometimes behaves in unkind or bullying ways, and you may fear that people will be critical of you for not leaving him right away. Or you might have the opposite concern: that people around you are so fond of your partner that you question whether they will believe you when you describe how mean or abusive he can be. But, regardless of these anxieties, it is essential *not* to stay isolated with your distress or confusion about what is happening in your relationship. Find someone whom you can trust—it might even be a person you have never considered opening up to before—and unburden yourself. This is probably the single most critical step you can take toward building a life that is free from control or abuse.

If your partner's controlling or devaluing behavior is chronic, you no doubt find yourself thinking about him a great deal of the time, wondering how to please him, how to keep him from straying, or how to get him to change. As a result, you may find that you don't get much time to think about *yourself*—except about what is wrong with you in his eyes. One of my central reasons for writing this book is, ironically, to help you think about him *less*. I'm hoping that by answering as many questions as possible and clearing away the confusion that abusive behavior creates, I can make it possible for you to escape the trap of preoccupation with your partner, so that you can put yourself—and your children if you are a mother—back in the center of your life where you belong. An angry and controlling man can be like a vacuum cleaner that sucks up a woman's mind and life, but there are ways to get your life back. The first step is to learn to identify what your partner is doing and why he does it, which is what the pages ahead will illuminate. But when you have finished diving deeply into the abuser's mind, which this book will enable you to do, it is important to rise back to the surface and from then on *try to stay out of the water as much as you can.* I don't mean that you should necessarily leave your partner—that is a complex and highly personal decision that only you can make. But whether you stay or go, the critical decision you can make is to stop letting your partner distort the lens of your life, always forcing his way into the center of the picture. You deserve to have your life be about *you;* you are worth it.

The Nature
of Abusive
Thinking

1

The Mystery

<small>LISTEN TO THE VOICES OF THESE WOMEN:</small>

He's two different people. I feel like I'm living with Dr. Jekyll and Mr. Hyde.

He really doesn't mean to hurt me. He just loses control.

Everyone else thinks he's great. I don't know what it is about me that sets him off.

He's fine when he's sober. But when he's drunk, watch out.

I feel like he's never happy with anything I do.

He's scared me a few times, but he never touches the children. He's a great father.

He calls me disgusting names, and then an hour later he wants sex. I don't get it.

He messes up my mind sometimes.

The thing is, he really understands me.

Why does he do that?

THESE ARE THE WORDS of women who are describing their anxiety and inner conflict about their relationships. Each of these women knows that something is wrong—very wrong—but she can't put her finger on what it is. Every time she thinks she's got her partner figured out, that she finally understands what is bothering him, something new happens, something changes. The pieces refuse to fit together.

Each of these women is trying to make sense out of the roller-coaster ride that her relationship has become. Consider Kristen's account:

> When I first met Maury, he was the man I had dreamed of. It seemed too good to be true. He was charming, funny, and smart, and best of all, he was crazy about me. I opened up to him about hard things I'd been through over the previous few years, and he was so much on my side about it all. And he was so game for *doing* things—whatever I wanted to do, he was up for it. The first year or so that we were together was great.
>
> I can't say exactly when things started to change. I think it was around the time we started living together. It started with him saying he needed more space. I felt confused, because before that it had always seemed like *he* was the one who wanted to be together every second.
>
> Then he began to have more and more criticisms and complaints. He would say that I talk on and on and that I'm self-centered. Maybe I am—it's true that I talk a lot. But earlier it had seemed like he couldn't hear enough about me. He started to say that I wasn't doing anything with my life. I know he has big ambitions, and maybe he's right that I should be more that way, but I'm happy with what I have. And then it was my weight. It started to seem like all the time he was saying that I needed to work out more, that I wasn't watching what I ate. That hurt the most, to tell you the truth. He seemed to want sex less and less often, and if I ever tried to be the one to initiate love-making, forget it.
>
> We're still together, but I have a feeling he's going to leave me. I just can't seem to live up to what he needs. I'm trying, but he doesn't think so. And now when he's really angry or frustrated, he says things that cut me down. A few days ago he said, "You're a lazy bitch, just looking for a man to live off of like your mother." I don't get that; I've contributed a lot. I haven't worked the last two years since our baby

was born, but I'm getting ready to go back to work soon. I don't think he really meant it, but still . . .

He says I've changed a lot, but I'm not always so sure it's me. Sometimes for a few days he seems like the guy I fell in love with, and I get hopeful, but then he slips away again into being so unhappy with me. I set him off somehow, but I don't know what I'm doing wrong.

Kristen was troubled by several questions. What had happened to the man she had loved so much? Why was he always putting her down? What could she do to stop his explosions? Why did he think *she* was the one who had changed?

Other women tell stories that are quite distinct from Kristen's, but they feel just as confused as she does. Here is what Barbara describes:

Fran is kind of quiet and shy. But he's cute as a button, and I got a crush on him the day I met him. I had to really go after him; it was hard to draw him out. We would go out and have great talks, and I couldn't wait to see him again. But three weeks would go by, and he'd say he hadn't been feeling well, or his sister was in town, or whatever. A couple of times he forgot dates we had.

Well, he finally opened up. It turned out he'd been really hurt before. He'd been cheated on a lot, and women had done some pretty mean things to him. He was afraid to get close again.

Little by little, he came around, but I was definitely the pursuer. I tried to show him that I wasn't like other women he'd been with. I'm not flirtatious. I don't show my body off to other men; I'm just not that style. But Fran wouldn't believe it. He would always say that I was making eyes at a man at the next table, or that I was checking someone out who walked past us. I feel bad for him, he's so insecure. His mother cheated on his father when he was growing up, so I guess that's made it even worse.

I was eager to get married, because I thought then he'd feel secure that I was his, but he was very reluctant to commit. When we finally did tie the knot, he was more trusting for a while, but then the jealousy came back, and it's never left. I've asked him off and on for years to go see a therapist, but he gets really mad and says there's nothing wrong with him.

A few days ago we went to a birthday party for a friend of his, and I had this great conversation with his friend's brother. It was nothing but talking—I mean, the guy isn't even cute. Well, suddenly Fran was saying that we had to go home because he had a bad head-ache. On the drive home, it turned out the real reason was jealousy. He started yelling at me, saying he was sick of me humiliating him in front of other people, "strutting your stuff," and on and on. He was pounding his fist on the dashboard, and two or three times he shoved me up against the car door. Each time that I told him it wasn't true he would go through the roof, so I stopped saying that. Our children were sitting in the backseat; it scared the daylights out of them.

At my age, it's hard to think about leaving him. Starting all over now seems so hard. I just wish he would get some help.

Barbara was struggling with issues different from Kristen's. Why couldn't Fran trust her, and why was he isolating her from other people? Why couldn't he see that he had a problem, and get help? Was he going to hurt her badly some day? Would her life ever get better?

At first look, Maury and Fran sound nothing like each other: One is young, popular, energetic, and assertive; the other is socially awkward, passive, and easily hurt. Fran is physically violent sometimes, whereas Maury is not. But are they as different as they seem? Or do they both ac-tually have the same set of issues under the surface, driving their behav-ior? These are some of the questions for which we will find answers in the chapters ahead.

Consider one more account, from Laura:

Paul is a great guy. We dated for about six months, and now we've been living together for several more. We're engaged. I feel so bad for him. His ex-wife accused him of abusing her, and it's a total lie. He made one mistake, which is that he cheated on her, and she is deter-mined to get him back for that. She will stop at nothing. Now she is even saying that he was *violent,* claiming he slapped her a few times and broke her things. That's ridiculous! I've been with him for over a year now, and I can tell you, he's *nothing* like that. Paul has never even raised a hand to me. In fact, he's tried to help me get my life together and has been really there for me. I was in a bad place when I met him, I was depressed and I was drinking too much, and I'm doing so much better now, because of him. I hate that bitch for accusing him of those things. We're going to work together on getting custody of his kids, because she's out of control.

Laura wondered how Paul's ex-wife could accuse such a delightful man of abuse. She was so angry about it that she didn't notice several warning signs about her own relationship with Paul.

If Kristen, Barbara, and Laura were to sit down together and compare notes, they might decide that their partners couldn't be more different. The personalities of the three men seem miles apart, and their relationships follow very separate paths. Yet Maury, Fran, and Paul actually have far more in common than meets the eye. Their moodiness, their excuses, their outlook, are all bubbling from the same source. And all three are abusive men.

THE TRAGEDY OF ABUSE

Abuse of women in relationships touches an unimaginable number of lives. Even if we leave aside cases of purely verbal and mental abuse and just look at physical violence, the statistics are shocking: 2 to 4 million women are assaulted by their partners *per year* in the United States. The U.S. Surgeon General has declared that attacks by male partners are the *number one cause of injury* to women between the ages of fifteen and forty-four. The American Medical Association reports that *one woman out of three* will be a victim of violence by a husband or boyfriend at some point in her life. The emotional effects of partner violence are a factor in more than one-fourth of female suicide attempts and are a leading cause of substance abuse in adult women. Government statistics indicate that 1,500 to 2,000 women are murdered by partners and ex-partners per year, comprising more than one-third of all female homicide victims, and that these homicides almost always follow a history of violence, threats, or stalking.

The abuse of women sends shock waves through the lives of children as well. Experts estimate that 5 million children per year witness an assault on their mothers, an experience that can leave them traumatized. Children exposed to violence at home show higher rates of school behavior and attention problems, aggression, substance abuse, depression, and many other measures of childhood distress. Abuse of women has been found to be a cause of roughly one-third of divorces among couples with children and one-half of divorces where custody is disputed.

As alarming as this picture is, we also know that physical assaults are just the beginning of the abuse that women may be subjected to. There are millions more women who have never been beaten but who live with repeated verbal assaults, humiliation, sexual coercion, and other forms of psychological abuse, often accompanied by economic exploitation. The scars from mental cruelty can be as deep and long-lasting as wounds from punches or slaps but are often not as obvious. In fact, even among women who have experienced violence from a partner, half or more report that *the man's emotional abuse is what is causing them the greatest harm.*

The differences between the verbally abusive man and the physical batterer are not as great as many people believe. The behavior of either style of abuser grows from the same roots and is driven by the same thinking. Men in either category follow similar processes of change in overcoming their abusiveness—if they do change, which unfortunately is not common. And the categories tend to blur. Physically assaultive men are also verbally abusive to their partners. Mentally cruel and manipulative men tend to gradually drift into using physical intimidation as well. In this book you will meet abusers on a spectrum, ranging from those who never use violence to those who are terrifying. The extent of their common ground may startle you.

One of the obstacles to recognizing chronic mistreatment in relationships is that most abusive men simply don't *seem* like abusers. They have many good qualities, including times of kindness, warmth, and humor, especially in the early period of a relationship. An abuser's friends may think the world of him. He may have a successful work life and have no problems with drugs or alcohol. He may simply not fit anyone's image of a cruel or intimidating person. So when a woman feels her relationship spinning out of control, it is unlikely to occur to her that her partner is an abuser.

The symptoms of abuse are there, and the woman usually sees them: the escalating frequency of put-downs. Early generosity turning more and more to selfishness. Verbal explosions when he is irritated or when he doesn't get his way. Her grievances constantly turned around on her, so that everything is her own fault. His growing attitude that he knows what is good for her better than she does. And, in many relationships, a mounting sense of fear or intimidation. But the woman also sees that her partner is a human being who can be caring and affectionate at times, and she loves him. She wants to figure out why he gets so upset, so that she can help him break his pattern of ups and downs. She gets drawn into the complexities of his inner world, trying to uncover clues, moving pieces around in an attempt to solve an elaborate puzzle.

The abuser's mood changes are especially perplexing. He can be a different person from day to day, or even from hour to hour. At times he is aggressive and intimidating, his tone harsh, insults spewing from his mouth, ridicule dripping from him like oil from a drum. When he's in this mode, nothing she says seems to have any impact on him, except to make him even angrier. Her side of the argument counts for nothing in his eyes, and everything is her fault. He twists her words around so that she always ends up on the defensive. As so many partners of my clients have said to me, "I just can't seem to do anything right."

At other moments, he sounds wounded and lost, hungering for love and for someone to take care of him. When this side of him emerges, he appears open and ready to heal. He seems to let down his guard, his hard exterior softens, and he may take on the quality of a hurt child, difficult and frustrating but lovable. Looking at him in this deflated state, his partner has trouble imagining that the abuser inside of him will ever be back. The beast that takes him over at other times looks completely unrelated to the tender person she now sees.

Sooner or later, though, the shadow comes back over him, as if it had a life of its own. Weeks of peace may go by, but eventually she finds herself under assault once again. Then her head spins with the arduous effort of untangling the many threads of his character, until she begins to wonder whether she is the one whose head isn't quite right.

To make matters worse, everyone she talks to has a different opinion about the nature of his problem and what she should do about it. Her clergyperson may tell her, "Love heals all difficulties. Give him your heart fully, and he will find the spirit of God." Her therapist speaks a different language, saying, "He triggers strong reactions in you because he reminds you of your father, and you set things off in him because of his relationship with his mother. You each need to work on not pushing each other's buttons." A recovering alcoholic friend tells her, "He's a rage addict. He controls you because he is terrified of his own fears. You need to get him into a twelve-step program." Her brother may say to her, "He's a good guy. I know he loses his temper with you sometimes—he does have a short fuse—but you're no prize yourself with that mouth of yours. You two need to work it out, for the good of the children." And then, to crown her increasing confusion, she may hear from her mother, or her child's schoolteacher, or her best friend: "He's mean and crazy, and he'll never change. All he wants is to hurt you. Leave him now before he does something even worse."

All of these people are trying to help, and they are all talking about the same abuser. But he looks different from each angle of view.

The woman knows from living with the abusive man that there are no simple answers. Friends say: "He's mean." But she knows many ways in which he has been good to her. Friends say: "He treats you that way because he can get away with it. I would never let someone treat *me* that way." But she knows that the times when she puts her foot down the most firmly, he responds by becoming his angriest and most intimidating. When she stands up to him, he makes her pay for it—sooner or later. Friends say: "Leave him." But she knows it won't be that easy. He will promise to change. He'll get friends and relatives to feel sorry for him and pressure her to give him another chance. He'll get severely depressed, causing her to worry whether he'll be all right. And, depending on what style of abuser he is, she may know that he will become dangerous when she tries to leave him. She may even be concerned that he will try to take her children away from her, as some abusers do.

How is an abused woman to make a sensible picture out of this confusion? How can she gain enough insight into the causes of his problem to know what path to choose? The questions she faces are urgent ones.

FIVE PUZZLES

Professionals who specialize in working with abusive and controlling men have had to face these same perplexing issues at work. I was a codirector of the first counseling program in the United States—and perhaps in the world—for abusive men. When I began leading groups for abusers fifteen years ago, they were as much of a mystery to me as they are to the women they live with. My colleagues and I had to put a picture together from the same strange clues faced by Kristen, Barbara, and Laura. Several themes kept confronting us over and over again in our clients' stories, including:

HIS VERSION OF THE ABUSE IS WORLDS APART FROM HERS.

A man named Dale in his mid-thirties gave the following account when he entered my group for abusive men:

> My wife Maureen and I have been together for eleven years. The first ten years we had a good marriage, and there was no problem with abuse or violence or anything. She was a great girl. Then about a year ago she started hanging around with this bitch she met named Eleanor who really has it in for me. Some people just can't stand to see anyone else happy. This girl was single and was obviously jealous that Maureen was in a good marriage, so she set out to wreck it. Nobody can get along with Eleanor, so of course she has no relationships that last. I just had the bad luck that she ran into my wife.
>
> So this bitch started planting a lot of bad stuff about me in Maureen's head and turning her against me. She tells Maureen that I don't care about her, that I'm sleeping with other girls, all kinds of lies. And she's getting what she wants, because now Maureen and I have started having some wicked fights. This past year we haven't gotten along at all. I tell Maureen I don't want her hanging around with that girl, but she doesn't listen to me. She sneaks around and sees her behind my back. And, look, I'm not here to hide anything. I'll tell you straight out, it's true that two or three times this year I finally couldn't take all the accusations and yelling anymore, and I've hauled off and slapped her. I need help, I'm not denying it. I have to

learn to deal with the stress better; I don't want her to get me arrested. And maybe I can still figure out how to persuade Maureen not to throw a great thing away, because at the rate we're going we'll be broken up in six months.

I always interview the partner of each of my clients as soon as possible after he enrolls in the program. I reached Maureen by phone several days later, and heard her account:

Dale was great when I first met him, but by the time we got married something was already wrong. He had gone from thinking I was perfect to constantly criticizing me, and he would get in such bad moods over the littlest things. I wouldn't be able to figure out how to get him to feel better. Only a couple of months after the wedding he shoved me for the first time, and after that some explosion would happen about two or three times a year. Usually he would break something or raise a fist, but a few times he shoved me or slapped me. Some years he didn't do it at all, and I would think it was all over, but then it would happen again—it sort of came in waves. And he was always, always, putting me down and telling me what to do. I couldn't do anything right.

Anyhow, about a year ago I made a new friend, Eleanor. She started telling me that what Dale was doing was abuse, even though he had never punched me or injured me, and that I hadn't done anything to deserve it. At first I thought she was exaggerating, because I've known women that got it so much worse than me. And Dale can be really sweet and supportive when you least expect it. We've had a lot of good times, believe it or not. Anyhow, Eleanor kind of opened my eyes up. So I started standing up to Dale about how he talks to me, and told him I was thinking of moving out for a while. And what's happened is that he's gone nuts. I swear, something has happened to him. He's backhanded me twice in the last eight months, and another time he threw me over a chair and my back went out. So I finally moved out. For now I'm not planning to get back with him, but I guess it depends partly on what he does in the abuser program.

Notice the striking contrasts. Dale describes the first ten years of his marriage as abuse-free, while Maureen remembers put-downs and even physical assaults during those years. Maureen says that Eleanor helps and supports her, while Dale sees her as corrupting Maureen and turning her against him. Dale says that they are still together, while Maureen reports that they have already broken up. Each one thinks the other has developed a problem. How can their perceptions clash so strongly? In the chapters ahead, we will explore the thinking of abusive men to answer the question of why Dale's view contains such serious distortions.

HE GETS INSANELY JEALOUS, BUT IN OTHER WAYS HE SEEMS ENTIRELY RATIONAL.

In a group session one day, a young client named Marshall was recounting a confrontation with his partner that had occurred in the previous week:

> My wife and I had plans to meet in the lobby of the building where she works to go out for lunch. I was waiting around near the elevators, and when she finally came out I saw that she'd been alone on the elevator with this good-looking guy. He had a look on his face, and she did too, I can't really describe it, but I could tell something was up. I said, "What was that all about?," and she pretended like she didn't know what I was talking about. That really pissed me off, and I guess I kind of blew up at her. I may have gotten a little louder than I should have. I was mad, though, and I was saying, "You were making it with that guy on the elevator, weren't you? Don't lie to me, you slut, I'm not a fool." But she kept on playing dumb, saying she doesn't even know him, which is a crock.

Marshall was extremely jealous, but I had worked with him long enough to know that he wasn't crazy. He was lucid and logical in group, had a stable work history and normal friendships, and showed no signs of living in a world of fantasy or hallucination. He simply did not have symptoms of the type of serious mental illness that could convince a man that

his wife could have sex in an elevator, fully clothed and standing up, between floors of a busy office building. Marshall had to know that his accusation wasn't true. And when I confronted him, he admitted it.

Given that even very jealous abusers turn out to have a reasonable
grasp on reality, why do they make these insane-seeming accusations?
Is there something about acting crazy that they enjoy? What does this
behavior accomplish for them? (I answer these questions in Chapter 3,
where we consider the issue of *possessiveness*.)

HE SUCCEEDS IN GETTING PEOPLE
TO TAKE HIS SIDE AGAINST HER.

Martin, a man in his late twenties, joined my abuser group while also
seeing an individual therapist. He told me the first day that he was confused
about whether he had a problem or not, but that his long-time girlfriend
Ginny was preparing to break up with him because she considered him
abusive. He went on to describe incidents of insulting or ignoring Ginny
and of deliberately causing her emotional pain "to show her how it feels
when she hurts me." He also admitted to times of humiliating her in front
of other people, being flirtatious with women when he was mad at her, and
ruining a couple of recent important events in her life by causing big scenes.
He justified all of these behaviors because of ways he felt hurt by her.

As a routine part of my assessment of Martin, I contacted his private
therapist to compare impressions. The therapist turned out to have strong
opinions about the case:

THERAPIST: I think it's a big mistake for Martin to be attending your
abuser program. He has very low self-esteem; he believes anything bad
that anyone says about him. If you tell him he's abusive, that will just
tear him down further. His partner slams him with the word *abusive*
all the time, for reasons of her own. Ginny's got huge control issues,
and she has obsessive-compulsive disorder. She needs treatment. I
think having Martin in your program just gets her what she wants.

BANCROFT: So you have been doing couples counseling with them?

THERAPIST: No, I see him individually.

BANCROFT: How many times have you met with her?

THERAPIST: She hasn't been in at all.

BANCROFT: You must have had quite extensive phone contact with her, then.

THERAPIST: No, I haven't spoken to her.

BANCROFT: You haven't spoken to her? You have assigned Ginny a clinical diagnosis based only on Martin's descriptions of her?

THERAPIST: Yes, but you need to understand, we're talking about an unusually insightful man. Martin has told me many details, and he is perceptive and sensitive.

BANCROFT: But he admits to serious psychological abuse of Ginny, although he doesn't call it that. An abusive man is not a reliable source of information about his partner.

What Martin was getting from individual therapy, unfortunately, was an official seal of approval for his denial, and for his view that Ginny was mentally ill. How had he shaped his therapist's view of his partner to get her to adopt this stance? How can abusers be so adept at recruiting team members in this way, including sometimes ones with considerable status or influence, and why do they want to? (These questions are the focus of Chapter 11, "Abusive Men and Their Allies.")

DURING SOME INCIDENTS HE SEEMS TO LOSE CONTROL,
BUT CERTAIN OTHER CONTROLLING BEHAVIORS
OF HIS APPEAR VERY CALCULATED.

Several years ago, a young man named Mark came to one of my abuser groups. When a client joins the program, I set behavioral goals with him as soon as possible. I often begin by asking, "What are the top three or four complaints your partner has about you?" Mark's response was:

One of the things Eileen gets on me about the most is that she says I ignore her. She says I make her a low priority and always want to do other things instead of be with her, so she feels like she's nothing. I like to have time to myself a lot, or to relax and watch television. I guess I kind of tune her out.

Based on Mark's account, I wrote near the top of his Behavior Plan: **"Spend more time with Eileen. Make her a higher priority."**

Eileen was very difficult to reach by phone, but three weeks later she finally called me, with a surprising story to tell:

A few weeks before Mark started your program, I told him that I needed a total break from the relationship. I just couldn't take it anymore, the yelling and the selfishness. He won't even let me sleep. So I didn't even want to talk to him for a while; I had to have time away to get myself together. I reassured him that the relationship wasn't over, and we'd work on getting back together in a couple of months, after a breather.

Then, a couple of weeks later, he called me and said that he had enrolled in an abuser program. He said that his counselor wants him to spend more time with me and had written it on his sheet, and that the program told him that being with me was part of how he needed to work on his issues. I wasn't ready for that yet at all, but I also didn't want to interfere with his program. So I started seeing him again. I want whatever is going to work best to help him change. I could have used a little more time apart, to tell you the truth, but if that's what your program recommends . . .

Mark had succeeded in twisting the abuser program to suit his own purposes. I explained to Eileen what had happened and apologized for the way my program had added to the many difficulties she already had with him. The high degree of manipulativeness that Mark used is not uncommon among abusive men, unfortunately. How can abusers be capable of such calculation yet at other times appear to be so out of control? What's the connection? The answers can be found in Chapter 2, where we examine the excuses that abusive men use to justify their behavior.

SOMETIMES HE SEEMS TO BE REALLY CHANGING,
BUT IT TENDS TO VANISH.

Carl was a twenty-six-year-old man who had been arrested repeatedly for domestic assaults and had finally served a few months in jail. He said to me in a group session:

> Going to jail was the last straw. I finally got it that I have to stop blaming my problems on everybody else and take a look at myself instead. People in jail said the same thing to me: If you don't want to be back in here, get real with yourself. I have a bad temper, and kind of a mean streak to tell you the truth, and I have to deal with it. I don't want to be back inside for anything.

At the end of each counseling session, Carl would make comments such as, "I can see that I've really got to work on my attitude" and "I learned a lot tonight about how excuses keep me from changing." One night he looked at me and said, "I'm really glad I met you, because I think if I wasn't hearing the things you are saying, I would be headed straight back to being locked up. You're helping me get my head on straight."

I reached Carl's girlfriend, Peggy, by telephone and began to ask her about the history of Carl's problem with abusiveness. She sounded noticeably distracted and uncomfortable. I suspected strongly that Carl was listening to the conversation, so I made an excuse to wrap it up soon. However, when Carl was at my group the next week, I left my co-leader in charge of the session and slipped out to give Peggy another call, to see if she would feel freer to talk. This time she gave me an earful:

> Carl comes home from your program in a rage every week. I'm afraid to be around the house on Wednesday nights, which is when he has his group session. He says the program is total bullshit, and that he wouldn't have to be sitting there getting insulted by you people if I hadn't called the police on him, and he says that I know the fight that night was my fault anyhow. He says he especially hates that guy Lundy. A few nights ago I told him to stop blaming it on me that he has to go to counseling, and he slammed me up against the doorjamb

and told me if I didn't shut up he'd choke me. I should call the police, but he'd get sent away for two years this time because he's on
parole, and I'm afraid that would be enough to get him to kill me
when he got out.

Peggy then went on to describe the history of beatings she had suffered at Carl's hands before he went to jail: the black eyes, the smashed
furniture, the time he had held a knife to her throat. He invariably had
blamed each attack on her, no matter how brutal his abuse or how serious
her injuries.

After speaking with Peggy, I returned to the group session, where Carl
went through his usual routine of self-exploration and guilt. I of course
said nothing; if he knew Peggy had told me the truth, she would be in extraordinary danger. Soon after this, I reported to his probation officer that
he was not appropriate for our program, without giving the real reason.

Carl created the appearance of learning a great deal at each session,
and his comments suggested serious reflection on the issues, including
the effects of his abuse on his partner. What was happening each week inside his mind before he got home? How can an abuser gain such insight
into his feelings and still behave so destructively? And how does real
change happen? (We'll return to these questions in Chapter 14, "The Process of Change.")

THESE ARE JUST a very few of the many confounding questions that face
anyone—the partner of an abusive man, a friend, or a professional—who
is looking for effective ways to respond to abusive behavior. I came to realize, through my experience with over two thousand abusers, that the abusive man *wants* to be a mystery. To get away with his behavior and to avoid
having to face his problem, he needs to convince everyone around him—
and himself—that his behavior makes no sense. He needs his partner
to focus on everything *except* the real causes of his behavior. To see the
abuser as he really is, it is necessary to strip away layer after layer of confusion, mixed messages, and deception. Like anyone with a serious problem, abusers work hard to keep their true selves hidden.

Part of how the abuser escapes confronting himself is by convincing you that *you* are the cause of his behavior, or that you at least share the blame. But abuse is not a product of bad relationship dynamics, and you cannot make things better by changing your own behavior or by attempting to manage your partner better. Abuse is a problem that lies entirely within the abuser.

Through years of direct work with abusers and their partners, I found that the realities behind the enigmatic abuser gradually came out into the bright light forming a picture that increasingly made sense to me. The pages ahead will take you through the pieces that I watched fall into place one by one, including:

- Why abusers are charming early in relationships but don't stay that way

- What the early warning signs are that can tip you off that you may be involved with an abusive or controlling man

- Why his moods change at the drop of a hat

- What goes on inside his mind and how his thinking causes his behavior

- What role alcohol and drugs play—and don't play—in partner abuse

- Why leaving an abusive man doesn't always solve the problem

- How to tell whether an abuser is really changing—and what to do if he isn't

- How friends, relatives, and other community members can help to stop abuse

- Why many abusive men seem to be mentally ill—and why they usually aren't

We will explore answers to these questions on three levels. The first level is the abuser's thinking—his attitudes and beliefs—in daily interactions. The second is his learning process, through which his thinking began to develop early in his life. And the third involves the rewards he reaps from controlling his partner, which encourage him to use abusive behavior over and over again. As we clear away the abusive man's smoke screen with these understandings, you will find that abusiveness turns out to be far less mysterious than it appears at first.

Inside the abuser's mind, there is a world of beliefs, perceptions, and responses that fits together in a surprisingly logical way. His behavior *does* make sense. Underneath the facade of irrationality and explosiveness, there is a human being with a comprehensible—and solvable—problem. But he doesn't want you to figure him out.

The abuser creates confusion because he has to. He can't control and intimidate you, he can't recruit people around him to take his side, he can't keep escaping the consequences of his actions, unless he can throw everyone off the track. When the world catches on to the abuser, his power begins to melt away. So we are going to travel behind the abuser's mask to the heart of his problem. This journey is critical to the health and healing of abused women and their children, for once you grasp how your partner's mind works, you can begin reclaiming control of your own life. Unmasking the abuser also does *him* a favor, because he will not confront—and overcome—his highly destructive problem as long as he can remain hidden.

The better we understand abusers, the more we can create homes and relationships that are havens of love and safety, as they should be. Peace really does begin at home.

2

The Mythology

He's crazy.

He feels so bad about himself. I just need to build up his self-image a little.

He just loses it.

He's so insecure.

His mother abused him, and now he has a grudge against women and he takes it out on me.

I'm so confused. I don't understand what's going on with him.

IN ONE IMPORTANT WAY, an abusive man works like a magician: His tricks largely rely on getting you to look off in the wrong direction, distracting your attention so that you won't notice where the real action is. He draws you into focusing on the turbulent world of his feelings to keep your eyes turned away from the true cause of his abusiveness, which lies in how he *thinks*. He leads you into a convoluted maze, making your relationship with him a labyrinth of twists and turns. He wants you to puzzle over him, to try to figure him out, as though he were a wonderful but broken machine for which you need only to find and fix the malfunctioning parts to bring it roaring to its full potential. His desire, though he may not admit it even to himself, is that you wrack your brain in this way so that you won't notice the patterns and logic of his behavior, the consciousness behind the craziness.

To further divert your gaze, he may work to shape your view of his past partners to keep you from talking to them directly and to prepare you to disbelieve them should you happen to hear what they say. If you could follow the thread of his conduct over a series of relationships, you would find out that his behavior isn't as erratic as it looks; in fact, it follows a fairly consistent pattern from woman to woman, except for brief relationships or ones he isn't that serious about.

Above all, the abusive man wants to avoid having you zero in on his abusiveness itself. So he tries to fill your head up with excuses and distortions and keep you weighed down with self-doubt and self-blame. And, unfortunately, much of the society tends to follow unsuspectingly along behind him, helping him to close your eyes, and his own, to his problem.

The mythology about abusive men that runs through modern culture has been created largely by the abusers themselves. Abusive men concoct explanations for their actions which they give to their partners, therapists, clergypeople, relatives, and social researchers. But it is a serious error to allow abusers to analyze and account for their own problems. Would we ask an active alcoholic to tell us why he or she drinks, and then accept the explanation unquestioningly? This is what we would hear:

"I drink because I have bad luck in life."

"I actually don't drink much at all—it's just a rumor that some people have been spreading about me because they don't like me."

"I started to drink a lot because my self-esteem was ruined by all these unfair accusations that I'm alcoholic, which I'm not."

When we hear these kinds of excuses from a drunk, we assume they are exactly that—excuses. We don't consider an active alcoholic a reliable source of insight. So why should we let an angry and controlling man be the authority on partner abuse? Our first task, therefore, is to remove the abusive man's smoke and mirrors, and then set about watching carefully to see what he is really doing.

A BRIEF EXERCISE

In my public presentations on abuse, I often begin with a simple exercise. I ask the audience members to write down everything they have ever heard, or ever believed, about where an abuser's problem comes from. I invite you to close this book for two or three minutes now and make a similar list for yourself, so that you can refer to it as we go along.

I then ask people to call out items from their lists, and I write them on the blackboard, organizing them into three categories: one for myths, one for partial truths, and one for accurate statements. We usually end up with twenty or thirty myths, four or five half-truths, and perhaps one or two realities. The audience members squint at me and fidget in their seats, surprised to discover that the common beliefs about the causes of abuse contain several dollops of fantasy and misconception for each ounce of truth. If you find as you go through this chapter that your own list turns out to contain mostly myths, you are not alone.

For the partner of an abusive or controlling man, having all of these mistaken theories pulled out from under you at once can be overwhelming. But for each stick that we pull out of the structure of misconception about abusive men, a brick is waiting to take its place. When we're finished, your partner will find it much harder than before to throw you off balance and confuse you, and your relationship will make sense to you in a way that it hasn't before.

THE MYTHS ABOUT ABUSERS

1. He was abused as a child.

2. His previous partner hurt him.

3. He abuses those he loves the most.

4. He holds in his feelings too much.

5. He has an aggressive personality.

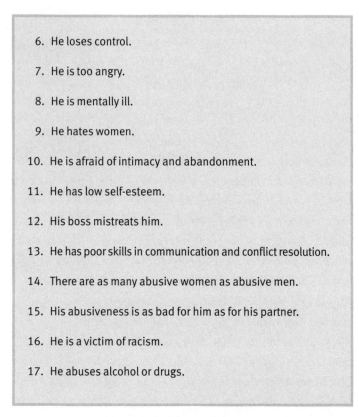

6. He loses control.

7. He is too angry.

8. He is mentally ill.

9. He hates women.

10. He is afraid of intimacy and abandonment.

11. He has low self-esteem.

12. His boss mistreats him.

13. He has poor skills in communication and conflict resolution.

14. There are as many abusive women as abusive men.

15. His abusiveness is as bad for him as for his partner.

16. He is a victim of racism.

17. He abuses alcohol or drugs.

MYTH #1:

He was abused as a child, and he needs therapy for it.

The partners of my clients commonly believe that the roots of the man's abusiveness can be found in mistreatment that he suffered himself, and many professionals share the same misconception. I hear explanations along the lines of:

> *"He calls me all those horrible things because that is what his mother used to do to him."*

> *"His father used to get angry at him and beat him with a belt, so now if I get angry at all, he just freaks out and starts throwing things around the house. He says it's because deep down, he's really scared of my anger."*

"His stepmother was a witch. I've met her; she's vicious. So now he really has this thing against women."

QUESTION 1:
IS IT BECAUSE HE WAS ABUSED AS A CHILD?

Multiple research studies have examined the question of whether men who abuse women tend to be survivors of childhood abuse, and the link has turned out to be weak; other predictors of which men are likely to abuse women have proven far more reliable, as we will see. Notably, men who are violent toward other *men* are often victims of child abuse—but the connection is much less clear for men who assault women. The one exception is that those abusers who are brutally physically violent or terrifying toward women often do have histories of having been abused as children. In other words, a bad childhood doesn't cause a man to become an abuser, but it can contribute to making a man who is abusive especially dangerous.

If abusiveness were the product of childhood emotional injury, abusers could overcome their problem through psychotherapy. But it is virtually unheard of for an abusive man to make substantial and lasting changes in *his pattern of abusiveness* as a result of therapy. (In Chapter 14, we'll examine the differences between psychotherapy and a specialized abuser program, because the latter sometimes can bring good results.) He may work through other emotional difficulties, he may gain insight into himself, but his behavior continues. In fact it typically gets worse, as he uses therapy to develop new excuses for his behavior, more sophisticated arguments to prove that his partner is mentally unstable, and more creative ways to make her feel responsible for his emotional distress. Abusive men are sometimes masters of the hard-luck story, and may find that accounts of childhood abuse are one of the best ways to pull heartstrings.

For some abusive men, the blame-the-childhood approach has an additional reason for being appealing: By focusing on what his mother did wrong, he gets to blame a woman for his mistreatment of women. This explanation can also appeal to the abused woman herself, since it makes sense out of his behavior and gives her someone safe to be angry at—since getting angry at *him* always seems to blow up in her face. The wider society, and the field of psychology in particular, has often jumped on this bandwagon instead of confronting the hard questions that partner abuse raises. Abuse of women by men is so rampant that, unless people can somehow make it women's own fault, they are forced to take on a number of uncomfortable questions about men and about much of male thinking. So it may seem easier to just lay the problem at the feet of the man's mother?

My clients who have participated extensively in therapy or substance-abuse recovery programs sometimes sound like therapists themselves—and a few actually have been—as they adopt the terms of popular psychology or textbook theory. One client used to try to lure me into intellectual debates with comments such as, "Well, your group follows a cognitive-behavioral model, which has been shown to have limitations for addressing a problem as deep as this one." An abusive man who is adept in the language of feelings can make his partner feel crazy by turning each argument into a therapy session in which he puts her reactions under a microscope and assigns himself the role of "helping" her. He may, for example, "explain" to her the emotional issues she needs to work through, or analyze her reasons for "mistakenly" believing that he is mistreating her.

An abusive man may embellish his childhood suffering once he discovers that it helps him escape responsibility. The National District Attorney's Association Bulletin reported a revealing study that was conducted on another group of destructive men: child sexual abusers. The researcher asked each man whether he himself had been sexually victimized as a child. A hefty 67 percent of the subjects said yes. However, the researcher then informed the men that he was going to hook them up to a lie-detector test and ask them the same questions again. Affirmative answers suddenly dropped to only 29 percent. In other words, abusers of all varieties tend to realize the mileage they can get out of saying, "I'm abusive because the same thing was done to me."

Although the typical abusive man works to maintain a positive public image, it is true that some women have abusive partners who are nasty or intimidating to *everyone*. How about that man? Do his problems result from mistreatment by his parents? The answer is both yes and no; it depends on *which* problem we're talking about. His hostility toward the human race may sprout from cruelty in his upbringing, but he abuses women because he has an abuse problem. The two problems are related but distinct.

I am not saying that you should be unsympathetic to your partner's childhood suffering. An abusive man deserves the same compassion that a nonabusive man does, neither more nor less. But a nonabusive man doesn't use his past as an excuse to mistreat you. Feeling sorry for your partner can be a trap, making you feel guilty for standing up to his abusiveness.

I have sometimes said to a client: "If you are so in touch with your feelings from your abusive childhood, then you should know what abuse feels like. You should be able to remember how miserable it was to be cut down to nothing, to be put in fear, to be told that the abuse is your own fault. You should be *less* likely to abuse a woman, not more so, from having been through it." Once I make this point, he generally stops mentioning his terrible childhood; **he only wants to draw attention to it if it's an excuse to stay the same, not if it's a reason to change.**

> **MYTH #2:**
> He had a previous partner who mistreated him terribly, and now he has
> a problem with women as a result. He's a wonderful man,
> and that bitch made him get like this.

As we saw with Fran in Chapter 1, an abuser's bitter tale of emotional destruction by a past wife or girlfriend can have a powerful impact on his current partner. In the most common version of this story, the man recounts how his ex-partner broke his heart by cheating on him, perhaps with several different men. If you ask him how he found out, he answers that "everybody" knew about it or that his friends told him. He also may say, "I caught her cheating myself," but when you press him on what he actually *saw*, it often turns out that he saw nothing, or that he saw her talking to some guy or riding in his car late at night, "so I could tell."

He may describe other wounds he received from a previous partner: She tried to control him; she wouldn't let him have any freedom; she expected him to wait on her hand and foot; she turned their children against him; she even "had him arrested" out of vindictiveness. What he is describing usually are his *own* behaviors, but he attributes them to the woman so that he is the victim. He can gain sympathy from his new partner in this fashion, especially because so many women know what it is like to be abused—unfortunately—so they can connect with his distress.

The abusive or controlling man can draw a rich set of excuses from his past relationships. For controlling his current partner's friendships and for accusing her of cheating on him: "It's because my ex-partner hurt me so badly by cheating on me so many times, and that's why I'm so jealous and can't trust you." For throwing a tempter tantrum when she asks him to clean up after himself: "My ex-partner controlled my every move, and so now it makes me furious when I feel like you're telling me what to do." For having affairs of his own or keeping other love interests going on the side: "I got so hurt last time that now I am really afraid of committing, so I want to keep having involvements with other people." He can craft an excuse to fit any of his controlling behaviors.

I recommend applying the following principle to assertions that an angry or controlling man makes about past women in his life:

IF IT IS AN EXCUSE FOR MISTREATING YOU, IT'S A DISTORTION.

A man who was genuinely mistreated in a relationship with a woman would not be using that experience to get away with hurting someone else.

Consider the reverse situation for a moment: Have you ever heard a woman claim that the reason why she is chronically mistreating her male partner is because a previous man abused her? I have never run into this excuse in the fifteen years I have worked in the field of abuse. Certainly I have encountered cases where women had trouble trusting another man after leaving an abuser, but there is a critical distinction to be made: Her past experiences may explain how she *feels*, but they are not an excuse for how she *behaves*. And the same is true for a man.

When a client of mine blames a past relationship for his cruel or controlling behavior in the present, I jump in with several questions: "Did your ex-partner ever say that she felt controlled or intimidated by you? What was her side of the story? Did you ever put your hands on her in anger, or did she ever get a restraining order?" By the time he has finished providing his answers, I usually can tell what happened: He abused that woman too.

It is fine to commiserate with a man about his bad experience with a previous partner, but the instant he uses her as an excuse to mistreat you, stop believing *anything* he tells you about that relationship and instead recognize it as a sign that he has problems with relating to women. Track down his ex-partner and talk with her as soon as possible, even if you hate her. An abuser can mistreat partner after partner in relationships, each time believing that the problems are all the woman's fault and that he is the real victim.

Whether he presents himself as the victim of an ex-partner, or of his parents, the abuser's aim—though perhaps unconscious—is to play on your compassion, so that he can avoid dealing with his problem.

MYTH #3:
He's abusive because he feels so strongly about me.
People cause those they care about most deeply the most pain.

Excuses along these lines crop up frequently in my groups for abusive men. My clients say to me, "No one else gets me upset like she does. I just go out of my head sometimes because I have such strong feelings for her. The things she does really hurt me, and nobody else can get under my skin like that." Abusers can use this rationalization successfully with their partners, friends, and relatives. There is a grain of truth to it: People we love *can* cause us deeper pain than anyone else. But what does this have to do with abuse?

The abuser would like us to accept the following simple but erroneous formula:

"FEELINGS CAUSE BEHAVIOR."

"When people feel hurt, they lash out at someone else in retaliation. When they feel jealous, they become possessive and accusatory. When they feel controlled, they yell and threaten." Right?

Wrong. Each human being deals with hurt or resentment in a unique way. When you feel insulted or bullied, you may reach for a chocolate bar. In the same circumstance, I might burst into tears. Another person may put his or her feelings quickly into words, confronting the mistreatment directly. Although our feelings can influence how we wish to act, our choices of how to behave are ultimately determined more by our *attitudes* and our *habits*. We respond to our emotional wounds based on what we believe about ourselves, how we think about the person who has hurt us, and how we perceive the world. Only in people who are severely traumatized or who have major mental illnesses is behavior governed by feelings. And only a tiny percentage of abusive men have these kinds of severe psychological problems.

There are other reasons not to accept the "love causes abuse" excuse. First, many people reserve their *best* behavior and kindest treatment for their loved ones, including their partners. Should we accept the idea that these people feel love less strongly, or have less passion, than an abuser does? Nonsense. Outside of my professional life, I have known many couples over the years who had passion and electricity between them and who treated each other well. But unfortunately there is wide acceptance in our society of the unhealthy notion that passion and aggression are interwoven and that cruel verbal exchanges and bomblike explosions are the price you pay for a relationship that is exciting, deep, and sexy. Popular romantic movies and soap operas sometimes reinforce this image.

Most abusive men have close relationships with people other than their wives or girlfriends. My clients may feel deep fondness for one or both of their parents, a sibling, a dear friend, an aunt or uncle. Do they abuse their other loved ones? Rarely. It isn't the love or deep affection that causes his behavior problem.

> **MYTH #4:**
> He holds in his feelings too much, and they build up until
> he bursts. He needs to get in touch with his emotions and learn to express
> them to prevent those explosive episodes.

My colleagues and I refer to this belief as "The Boiler Theory of Men." The idea is that a person can only tolerate so much accumulated pain and frustration. If it doesn't get vented periodically—kind of like a pressure cooker—then there's bound to be a serious accident. This myth has the ring of truth to it because we are all aware of how many men keep too much emotion pent up inside. Since most abusers are male, it seems to add up.

But it doesn't, and here's why: *Most of my clients are not unusually repressed.* In fact, many of them express their feelings more than some nonabusive men. Rather than trapping everything inside, they actually tend to do the opposite: They have an exaggerated idea of how important their feelings are, and they talk about their feelings—and act them out—all the time, until their partners and children are exhausted from hearing about it all. An abuser's emotions are as likely to be too big as too small. They can fill up the whole house. When he feels bad, he thinks that life should stop for everyone else in the family until someone fixes his discomfort. His partner's life crises, the children's sicknesses, meals, birthdays—nothing else matters as much as his feelings.

It is not *his* feelings the abuser is too distant from; it is his *partner's* feelings and his *children's* feelings. Those are the emotions that he knows so little about and that he needs to "get in touch with." My job as an abuse counselor often involves steering the discussion *away* from how my clients feel and toward how they *think* (including their attitudes toward *their partners' feelings*). My clients keep trying to drive the ball back into the court that is familiar and comfortable to them, where their inner world is the only thing that matters.

For decades, many therapists have been attempting to help abusive men change by guiding them in identifying and expressing feelings. Alas, this well-meaning but misguided approach actually feeds the abuser's selfish focus on himself, which is an important force driving his abusiveness.

Part of why you may be tempted to accept "The Boiler Theory of Men" is that you may observe that your partner follows a pattern where he becomes increasingly withdrawn, says less and less, seems to be bubbling gradually from a simmer to a boil, and then erupts in a geyser of yelling, put-downs, and ugliness. It looks like an emotional explosion, so naturally you assume that it is. But the mounting tension, the pressure-cooker buildup of his feelings, is actually being driven by his lack of empathy for *your* feelings, and by a set of attitudes that we will examine later. And he explodes when he gives himself permission to do so.

> **MYTH #5:**
> He has a violent, explosive personality.
> He needs to learn to be less aggressive.

Does your partner usually get along reasonably well with everyone else except you? Is it unusual for him to verbally abuse other people or to get in physical fights with men? If he does get aggressive with men, is it usually related somehow to you—for example, getting up in the face of a man who he thinks is checking you out? The great majority of abusive men are fairly calm and reasonable in most of their dealings that are unrelated to their partners. In fact, the partners of my clients constantly complain to me: "How come he can be so nice to everyone else but he has to treat me like dirt?" If a man's problem were that he had an "aggressive personality," he wouldn't be able to reserve that side of himself just for you. Many therapists have attempted over the years to lead abusive men toward their more sensitive, vulnerable side. But the sad reality is that plenty of gentle, sensitive men are viciously—and sometimes violently—abusive to their female partners. The two-sided nature of abusers is a central aspect of the mystery.

The societal stereotype of the abuser as a relatively uneducated, blue-collar male adds to the confusion. The faulty equation goes: "Abusive equals muscle-bound caveman, which in turn equals lower class." In addition to the fact that this image is an unfair stereotype of working-class men, it also overlooks the fact that a professional or college-educated man has roughly the same likelihood of abusing women as anyone else. A successful businessperson, a college professor, or a sailing instructor may be less likely to adopt a tough-guy image with tattoos all over his body but still may well be a nightmare partner.

Class and racial stereotypes permit the more privileged members of society to duck the problem of abuse by pretending that it is someone else's problem. Their thinking goes: "It's those construction-worker guys who never went to college; it's those Latinos; it's those street toughs—they're the abusers. Our town, our neighborhood, isn't like that. We're not macho men here."

But women who live with abuse know that abusers come in all styles and from all backgrounds. Sometimes the more educated an abuser, the more knots he knows how to tie in a woman's brain, the better he is at getting her to blame herself, and the slicker is his ability to persuade other people that she is crazy. The more socially powerful an abuser, the more powerful his abuse can be—and the more difficult it can be to escape. Two of my early clients were Harvard professors.

Some women are attracted to the tough-guy image, and some can't stand it. Take your pick. There are ways to tell whether a man is likely to turn abusive, as we will see in Chapter 5, but his gentle or macho personality style is not one of them. (But do beware of one thing: If a man routinely intimidates people, watch out. Sooner or later, he will turn his intimidation on you. At first it may make you feel safe to be with a man who frightens people, but not when your turn comes.)

> **MYTH #6:**
> He loses control of himself. He just goes wild.

Many years ago, I was interviewing a woman named Sheila by telephone. She was describing the rages that my client Michael would periodically have: "He just goes absolutely berserk, and you never know when he's going to go off like that. He'll just start grabbing whatever is around and throwing it. He heaves stuff everywhere, against the walls, on the floor—it's just a mess. And he smashes stuff, important things sometimes. Then it's like the storm just passes; he calms down; and he leaves for a while. Later he seems kind of ashamed of himself."

I asked Sheila two questions. The first was, when things got broken, were they Michael's, or hers, or things that belonged to both of them? She left a considerable silence while she thought. Then she said, "You know what? I'm amazed that I've never thought of this, but he only breaks my stuff. I can't think of one thing he's smashed that belonged to him." Next, I asked her who cleans up the mess. She answered that she does.

I commented, "See, Michael's behavior isn't nearly as berserk as it looks. And if he really felt so remorseful, he'd help clean up."

QUESTION 2:
IS HE DOING IT ON PURPOSE?

When a client of mine tells me that he became abusive because he lost control of himself, I ask him why he didn't do something even worse. For example, I might say, "You called her a fucking whore, you grabbed the phone out of her hand and whipped it across the room, and then you gave her a shove and she fell down. There she was at your feet, where it would have been easy to kick her in the head. Now, you have just finished telling me that you were 'totally out of control' at that time, but you didn't kick her. What stopped you?" And the client *can always give me a reason.* Here are some common explanations:

"I wouldn't want to cause her a serious injury."

"I realized one of the children was watching."

"I was afraid someone would call the police."

"I could kill her if I did that."

"The fight was getting loud, and I was afraid neighbors would hear."

And the most frequent response of all:

*"Jesus, I wouldn't do **that**. I would never do something like that to her."*

The response that I almost never heard—I remember hearing it twice in fifteen years—was: "I don't know."

These ready answers strip the cover off of my clients' loss-of-control excuse. While a man is on an abusive rampage, verbally or physically, his mind maintains awareness of a number of questions: "Am I doing something that other people could find out about, so it could make me look bad? Am I doing anything that could get me in legal trouble? Could I get hurt myself? Am I doing anything that I myself consider too cruel, gross, or violent?"

A critical insight seeped into me from working with my first few dozen clients: **An abuser almost never does anything that he himself con-**

siders morally unacceptable. He may hide what he does because he thinks *other* people would disagree with it, but he feels justified inside. I can't remember a client ever having said to me: "There's no way I can defend what I did. It was just totally wrong." He invariably has a reason that he considers good enough. In short, **an abuser's core problem is that he has a distorted sense of right and wrong.**

I sometimes ask my clients the following question: "How many of you have ever felt angry enough at your mother to get the urge to call her a bitch?" Typically, half or more of the group members raise their hands. Then I ask, "How many of you have ever acted on that urge?" All the hands fly down, and the men cast appalled gazes on me, as if I had just asked whether they sell drugs outside elementary schools. So then I ask, "Well, why haven't you?" The same answer shoots out from the men each time I do this exercise: "But you can't treat your *mother* like that, no matter how angry you are! You just don't *do* that!"

The unspoken remainder of this statement, which we can fill in for my clients, is: "But you *can* treat your wife or girlfriend like that, as long as you have a good enough reason. That's different." In other words, the abuser's problem lies above all in his belief that controlling or abusing his female partner is *justifiable*. This insight has tremendous implications for how counseling work with abusers has to be done, as we will see.

When I was new to counseling abusive men, my own loss-of-control myth collided repeatedly with the realities contained in the stories of my early clients. Kenneth admitted that he used to dim the lights and then insist to Jennifer that nothing had changed, trying to make her feel crazy. (He also stands out in my mind for his outspoken criticisms of his group mates for their insensitivity toward their partners, despite his own actions.) James told me that he sometimes would hide something his partner was looking for, such as her pocketbook or car keys, wait for her to become frantic and frustrated looking for it, and then put it back out in plain view and insist that it had been there all along. Mario measured the distance from his house to the supermarket, and when his wife reported going out to shop during the day, he would check the odometer of her car to make sure she hadn't gone anywhere else.

One year my colleagues David and Carole were preparing a skit on abuse for a conference, and they decided to perform a rehearsal for their abuser group. Afterward, the group members rapid-fired their suggestions for improving the skit, directing them mostly at David: "No, no, you don't make excuses for why you're home late, that puts you on the defensive, you've got to turn it around on her, tell her you know she's cheating on you. . . . You're staying too far away from her, David. Take a couple of steps toward her, so she'll know that you mean business. . . . You're letting her say too much. You've got to cut her off and stick to your points." The counselors were struck by how aware the clients were of the kinds of tactics they use, and why they use them: In the excitement of giving feedback on the skit, the men let down their facade as "out-of-control abuser who doesn't realize what he's doing."

As we review the stories of my clients throughout this book, you will observe over and over the degree of consciousness that goes into their cruel and controlling actions. At the same time, I don't want to make abusive men sound evil. They don't calculate and plan out every move they make—though they use forethought more often than you would expect. It isn't that each time an abuser sweeps a pile of newspapers onto the floor or throws a cup against the wall he has determined ahead of time to take that course. For a more accurate model, think of an abuser as an acrobat in a circus ring who does "go wild" to some extent *but who never forgets where the limits are.*

When one of my clients says to me, "I exploded" or "I just lost it," I ask him to go step by step in his mind through the moments leading up to his abusive behavior. I ask, "Did you really 'just explode,' or did you actually decide at one point to give yourself the green light? Wasn't there a moment when you decided you 'had had enough' or you 'weren't going to take it anymore,' and at that instant you *gave yourself permission,* setting yourself free to do what you felt like doing?" Then I see a flicker of recognition cross my client's eyes, and usually he admits that there is indeed a moment at which he turns himself loose to begin the horror show.

Even the physically violent abuser shows self-control. The moment police pull up in front of the house, for example, he usually calms down immediately, and when the officers enter, he speaks to them in a friendly and reasonable tone. Police almost never find a fight in progress by the time they get in the door. Ty, a physical batterer who now counsels other men, describes in a training video how he would snap out of his rage when the police pulled up in front of the house and would sweet-talk the police, "telling them what *she* had done. Then they would look at her, and she'd be the one who was totally out of control, because I had just degraded her and put her in fear. I'd say to the police, 'See, it isn't me.'" Ty managed to escape arrest repeatedly with his calm demeanor and claims of self-defense.

MYTH #7:

He's too angry. He needs to learn anger-management skills.

A few years ago, the partner of one of my clients went through an ordeal where her twelve-year-old son (from a previous marriage) disappeared for more than forty-eight hours. For two days Mary Beth's heart was beating faster and faster as she drove around town looking for her son, made panicked phone calls to everyone she knew, and dropped her son's photograph at police departments, newspapers, and radio stations. She barely slept. Meanwhile her new husband, Ray, who was in one of my groups, was slowly building to a boil inside. Toward the end of the second day he finally burst out yelling at her, "I am so sick of being ignored by you! It's like I don't even exist! Go fuck yourself!"

When people conclude that anger causes abuse, they are confusing cause and effect. Ray was not abusive because he was angry; he was angry because he was abusive. Abusers carry attitudes that produce fury. A nonabusive man would not expect his wife to be taking emotional care of *him* during a crisis of this gravity. In fact, he would be focused on what he could do for her and on trying to find the child. It would be futile to teach Ray to take a time-out to punch pillows, take a brisk walk, or concentrate on deep breathing, because his thinking process will soon get him enraged again. In Chapter 3, you will see how and why an abuser's attitudes keep him furious.

When a new client says to me, "I'm in your program because of my anger," I respond, "No you're not, you're here because of your *abuse*." Everybody gets angry. In fact, most people have at least occasional times when they are *too* angry, out of proportion to the actual event or beyond what is good for their health. Some give themselves ulcers and heart attacks and hypertension. But they don't necessarily abuse their partners. In Chapter 3, we'll take a look at why abusive men tend to be so angry—and why at the same time their anger isn't really the main problem.

The abuser's explosive anger can divert your attention from all the disrespect, irresponsibility, talking over you, lying, and other abusive and controlling behaviors that he exhibits even at times when he *isn't* especially upset. Is it anger that causes such a high proportion of abusers to cheat on their partners? Does an abuser's rage cause him to conceal for years the fact that a former girlfriend went into hiding to get away from him? Is it a form of explosiveness when your partner pressures you into dropping your friendships and spending less time with your siblings? No. Perhaps his loudest, most obvious, or most intimidating forms of abuse come out when he's angry, but his deeper pattern is operating all the time.

MYTH #8:
He's crazy. He's got some mental illness that he should be medicated for.

When a man's face contorts in bitterness and hatred, he looks a little insane. When his mood changes from elated to assaultive in the time it takes to turn around, his mental stability seems open to question. When he accuses his partner of plotting to harm him, he seems paranoid. It is no wonder that the partner of an abusive man would come to suspect that he was mentally ill.

Yet the great majority of my clients over the years have been psychologically "normal." Their minds work logically; they understand cause and effect; they don't hallucinate. Their perceptions of most life circumstances are reasonably accurate. They get good reports at work; they do well in school or training programs; and no one other than their partners—and children—thinks that there is anything wrong with them. **Their *value system* is unhealthy, not their psychology.**

Much of what appears to be crazy behavior in an abuser actually works well for him. We already met Michael, who never broke his own stuff, and Marshall, who did not believe his own jealous accusations. In the pages ahead, you will encounter many more examples of the method behind the abuser's madness. You will also learn how distorted his view of his partner is—which can make him appear emotionally disturbed—and where those distortions spring from.

The most recent research shows that even in physically violent abusers the rate of mental illness is not high. Several of my brutal battering clients have had psychological evaluations, and only one of them was found to have a mental illness. At the same time, some of my clients whom I have believed to be truly insane have not necessarily been among the most violent. Research does indicate that the most extreme physical batterers— the ones who choke their partners to unconsciousness, who hold guns to their heads, who stalk and kill—have increased rates of mental illness. But there is no particular mental health condition that is typical of these severe batterers; they can have a range of diagnoses, including psychosis, borderline personality, manic depression, antisocial personality, obsessive-compulsive disorder, and others. (And, even among the most dangerous abusers, there are many who do not show clear psychiatric symptoms of any kind.)

How can all these different mental illnesses cause such similar behavioral patterns? The answer is, they don't. Mental illness doesn't cause abusiveness any more than alcohol does. What happens is rather that the man's psychiatric problem interacts with his abusiveness to form a volatile combination. If he is severely depressed, for example, he may stop caring about the consequences his actions may cause *him* to suffer, which can increase the danger that he will decide to commit a serious attack against his partner or children. A mentally ill abuser has two separate—though interrelated—problems, just as the alcoholic or drug-addicted one does.

The basic reference book for psychiatric conditions, the *Diagnostic and Statistical Manual of Mental Disorders (DSM-IV)*, includes no condition that fits abusive men well. Some clinicians will stretch one of the definitions to apply it to an abusive client—"intermittent explosive disorder," for example—so that insurance will cover his therapy. However, this diagnosis is erroneous if it is made solely on the basis of his abusive behavior; a man whose destructive behaviors are confined primarily or entirely to intimate relationships is an abuser, not a psychiatric patient.

Two final points about mental illness: First, I occasionally hear someone who is discussing a violent abuser say, "He must be delusional to think he can get away with this." But, unfortunately, it often turns out that he *can* get away with it, as we discuss in Chapter 12, so his belief is not a delusion at all. Second, I have received just a few reports of cases in which an abuser's behavior has improved for a while as a result of taking medication prescribed by a psychiatrist. His overall abusiveness hasn't stopped, but the most devastating or terrifying behaviors have eased. Medication is not a long-term solution, however, for two important reasons:

1. Abusers don't like to be medicated because they tend to be too selfish to put up with the side effects, no matter how much the improvement may benefit their partners, so they almost always quit the medication after a few months. The medication then can become another tool to be used in psychological abuse. For example, the abuser can stop taking his pills when he is upset with her, knowing that this will make her anxious and afraid. Or when he wants to strike out at her dramatically he may deliberately overdose himself, creating a medical crisis.

2. No medication yet discovered will turn an abuser into a loving, considerate, appropriate partner. It will just take the edge off his absolute worst behaviors—if it even does that. If your abusive partner is taking medication, be aware that you are only buying time. Take advantage of the (more) peaceful period to get support in your own healing. Begin by calling a program for abused women.

MYTH #9

He hates women. His mother, or some other woman, must have done something terrible to him.

The notion that abusive men hate women was popularized by Susan Forward's book *Men Who Hate Women and the Women Who Love Them*. Dr. Forward's descriptions of abusive men are the most accurate ones I have read, but she was mistaken on one point: Most abusers don't hate women. They often have close relationships with their mothers, or sisters, or female friends. A fair number are able to work successfully with a female boss and respect her authority, at least outwardly.

Disrespect for women certainly is rampant among abusive men, with attitudes toward women that fall on a continuum from those who can interact fairly constructively with most women (as long as they are not intimately involved with them) to men who are misogynists and treat most women they encounter with superiority and contempt. In general, I find that my clients' view that their partners should cater to their needs and are not worthy of being taken seriously does indeed carry over into how they view other females, including their own daughters. But, as we will see in Chapter 13, the disrespect that abusive men so often direct toward women in general tends to be born of their cultural values and conditioning rather than personal experiences of being victimized by women. Some abusive men use the *excuse* that their behavior is a response to such victimization because they want to be able to make women responsible for men's abuse. It is important to note that research has shown that men who have abusive mothers do not tend to develop especially negative attitudes toward females, but men who have abusive *fathers* do; the disrespect that abusive men show their female partners and their daughters is often absorbed by their sons.

So while a small number of abusive men do hate women, the great majority exhibit a more subtle—though often quite pervasive—sense of superiority or contempt toward females, and some don't show any obvious signs of problems with women at all until they are in a serious relationship.

> ## MYTH #10:
> He is afraid of intimacy and abandonment.

Abusive men are often jealous and possessive, and their coercive and destructive behaviors can escalate when their partners attempt to break up with them. Some psychologists have glanced quickly at this pattern and concluded that abusers have an extreme fear of abandonment. But *many people,* both male and female, are afraid of abandonment and may reel from panic, heartbreak, or desperation when being left by a partner. If a person's panicked reaction to being left could cause threats, stalking, or murder, our entire society would be a war zone. But postseparation homicides of intimate partners are committed almost exclusively by men (and there is almost always a history of abuse *before* the breakup). If fear of abandonment causes postseparation abuse, why are the statistics so lopsided? Do women have a much easier time with abandonment than men do? No, of course not. (We'll examine the real causes of the extreme behaviors some abusers use postseparation in Chapter 9.)

A close cousin of the abandonment myth is the belief that abusive men "are afraid of intimacy," which attempts to explain why most abusers mistreat only their partners and why most are male. According to this theory, the abuser uses his periodic cruelty to keep his partner from getting too close to him emotionally, a behavior which, in the language of psychologists, is called *mediating the intimacy*.

But there are several holes in this theory. First, abusive men usually have their worst incidents after a period of mounting tension and distance, *not* at the moments of greatest closeness. Some keep their emotional distance all the time so the relationship never gets close enough to trigger any fears of intimacy they might have, yet the abuse continues. Wife abuse occurs just as severely in some cultures where there is no expectation of intimacy between husbands and wives, where marriage has nothing to do with real emotional connection. And, finally, there are plenty of men who have powerful fears of intimacy who don't abuse or control their partners—because they don't have an abusive *mentality*.

MYTH #11:
He suffers from low self-esteem. He needs his self-image shored up.

QUESTION 3:
IS IT BECAUSE HE FEELS BAD ABOUT HIMSELF?

An abused woman tends to pour precious energy into supporting her abusive partner and massaging his ego, hoping against hope that if he is kept well stroked his next explosion might be averted. How well does this strategy work? Unfortunately, not very. You can't manage an abuser except for brief periods. Praising him and boosting his self-opinion may buy you some time, but sooner or later he'll jump back into chewing pieces out of you. When you try to improve an abuser's feelings about himself, his problem actually tends to get worse. An abusive man expects catering, and the more positive attention he receives, the more he demands. He never reaches a point where he is satisfied, where he has been given enough. Rather, he gets used to the luxurious treatment he is receiving and soon escalates his demands.

My colleagues and I discovered this dynamic through a mistake we made in the early years of abuse work. A few times we asked clients who had made outstanding progress in our program to be interviewed on television or to speak to a group of high school students because we thought the public could benefit from hearing an abuser speak in his own words about his behaviors and his process of change. But we found that each time we gave a client public attention, he had a bad incident of mistreating his partner within a few days thereafter. Feeling like a star and a changed man, his head swelled from all the attention he had been given, he would go home and rip into his partner with accusations and put-downs. So we had to stop taking our clients to public appearances.

The self-esteem myth is rewarding for an abuser, because it gets his partner, his therapist, and others to cater to him emotionally. Imagine the privileges an abusive man may acquire: getting his own way most of the time, having his partner bend over backward to keep him happy so he won't explode, getting to behave as he pleases, and then on top of it all, he gets *praise* for what a good person he is, and everyone is trying to help *him* feel better about himself!

Certainly an abuser can be remorseful or ashamed after being cruel or scary to his partner, especially if any outsider has seen what he did. But those feelings are a *result* of his abusive behavior, not a cause. And as a relationship progresses, the abusive man tends to get more comfortable with his own behavior and the remorse dies out, suffocated under the weight of his justifications. He may get nasty if he doesn't receive the frequent compliments, reassurance, and deference he feels he deserves, but this reaction is not rooted in feelings of inferiority; in fact, the reality is almost the opposite, as we will see.

Think for a just a moment about how your partner's degrading and bullying behavior has hurt *your* self-esteem. Have you suddenly turned into a cruel and explosive person? If low self-esteem isn't an excuse for you to become abusive, then it's no excuse for him either.

> **MYTH #12:**
>
> His boss abuses him, so he feels powerless and unsuccessful.
> He comes home and takes it out on his family because
> that is the one place he can feel powerful.

I call this myth "boss abuses man, man abuses woman, woman abuses children, children hit dog, dog bites cat." The image it creates seems plausible, but too many pieces fail to fit. Hundreds of my clients have been popular, successful, good-looking men, not the downtrodden looking for a scapegoat for their inner torment. Some of the worst abusers I have worked with have been at the top of the management ladder—with no boss to blame. The more power these men have in their jobs, the more catering and submission they expect at home. Several of my clients have told me: "I have to order people around where I work, so I have trouble snapping out of that mode when I get home." So while some abusers use the "mean boss" excuse, others use the opposite.

The most important point is this one: In my fifteen years in the field of abuse, **I have never once had a client whose behavior at home has improved because his job situation improved.**

> **MYTH #13:**
>
> He has poor communication, conflict-resolution,
> and stress-management skills. He needs training.

An abusive man is not *unable* to resolve conflicts nonabusively; he is *unwilling* to do so. The skill deficits of abusers have been the subject of a number of research studies, and the results lead to the following conclusion: Abusers have normal abilities in conflict resolution, communication, and assertiveness *when they choose to use them.* They typically get through tense situations at work without threatening anyone; they manage their stress without exploding when they spend Thanksgiving with their parents; they share openly with their siblings regarding their sadness over a grandparent's death. But they don't *want* to handle these kinds of issues nonabusively when it involves their partners. You can equip an abuser with the most innovative, New Age skills for expressing his deep emotions, listening actively, and using win-win bargaining, and then he will go home and continue abusing. In the coming chapter, we'll see why.

MYTH #14:

There are just as many abusive women as abusive men.
Abused men are invisible because they are ashamed to tell.

There certainly are some women who treat their male partners badly, berating them, calling them names, attempting to control them. The negative impact on these men's lives can be considerable. But do we see men whose self-esteem is gradually destroyed through this process? Do we see men whose progress in school or in their careers grinds to a halt because of the constant criticism and undermining? Where are the men whose partners are forcing them to have unwanted sex? Where are the men who are fleeing to shelters in fear for their lives? How about the ones who try to get to a phone to call for help, but the women block their way or cut the line? The reason we don't generally see these men is simple: They're rare.

I don't question how embarrassing it would be for a man to come forward and admit that a woman is abusing him. But don't underestimate how humiliated a woman feels when she reveals abuse; women crave dignity just as much as men do. If shame stopped people from coming forward, no one would tell.

Even if abused men didn't want to come forward, they would have been discovered by now. Neighbors don't turn a deaf ear to abuse the way they might have ten or twenty years ago. Now, when people hear screaming, objects smashing against walls, loud slaps landing on skin, they call the police. Among my physically abusive clients, nearly *one-third* have been arrested as a result of a call to the police that came from someone other than the abused woman. If there were millions of cowed, trembling men out there, the police would be finding them. Abusive men commonly like to play the role of victim, and most men who claim to be "battered men" are actually the perpetrators of violence, not the victims.

In their efforts to adopt victim status, my clients try to exaggerate their partners' verbal power: "Sure, I can win a physical fight, but she is much better with her mouth than I am, so I'd say it balances out." (One very violent man said in his group session, "She stabs me through the heart with her words," to justify the fact that he had stabbed his partner in the chest with a knife.) But abuse is not a battle that you win by being better at expressing yourself. You win it by being better at sarcasm, put-downs, twisting everything around backward, and using other tactics of control—an arena in which my clients win hands down over their partners, just as they do in a violent altercation. Who can beat an abuser at his own game?

Men *can* be abused by other men, however, and women can be abused by women, sometimes through means that include physical intimidation or violence. If you are a gay man or lesbian who has been abused by a partner or who is facing abuse now, most of what I explain in this book will ring loud bells for you. The "he and she" language that I use obviously won't fit your experience, but the underlying dynamics that I describe largely will. We'll explore this issue further in Chapter 6.

> **MYTH #15:**
> Abuse is as bad for the man who is doing it
> as it is for his partner. They are both victims.

My clients get over the pain of the abuse incidents far, far faster than their partners do. Recall Dale from Chapter 1, who insisted to me that the first ten years of his marriage had gone swimmingly, while Maureen recounted ten years of insults and cruelty? Certainly abusing one's partner is not a healthy lifestyle, but the negative effects don't hold a candle to the emotional and physical pain, loss of freedom, self-blame, and numerous other shadows that abuse casts over the life of its female target. Unlike alcoholics or addicts, abusive men don't "hit bottom." They can continue abusing for twenty or thirty years, and their careers remain successful, their health stays normal, their friendships endure. As we'll see in Chapter 6, abusers actually tend to *benefit* in many ways from their controlling behaviors. An abuser can usually outperform his victim on psychological tests, such as the ones that are routinely required during custody disputes, because he isn't the one who has been traumatized by years of psychological or physical assault. No one who listens carefully to the tragic accounts of abused women and then sees the abusers each week at a counseling group, as my colleagues and I have done, could be fooled into believing that life is equally hard for the men.

> **MYTH #16:**
> He is abusive because he has faced so much societal discrimination
> and disempowerment as a man of color, so at home he needs to feel powerful.

I address this myth in detail in Chapter 6 under "Racial and Cultural Differences in Abuse," so here I offer only a brief overview. First, a majority of abusive men are white, many of them well educated and economically privileged, so discrimination couldn't be a central cause of partner abuse. Second, if a man has experienced oppression himself, it could just as easily make him *more* sympathetic to a woman's distress as less so, as is true for childhood abuse (see Myth #1). And in fact there are men of color among the most visible leaders in the United States in the movement against the abuse of women. So while discrimination against people of color is a terribly serious problem today, it should not be accepted as an excuse for abusing women.

> **MYTH #17:**
> The alcohol is what makes him abusive. If I can get him
> to stay sober, our relationship will be fine.

So many men hide their abusiveness under the cover of alcoholism or drug addiction that I have chosen to devote Chapter 8 to explore the issue of addiction in detail. The most important point to be aware of is this: Alcohol cannot create an abuser, and sobriety cannot cure one. The only way a man can overcome his abusiveness is by dealing with his abusiveness.

THE NATURE OF ABUSIVE THINKING

And you are not "enabling" your partner to mistreat you; he is entirely responsible for his own actions.

WE HAVE NOW COMPLETED our tour through a museum of myths about
abusive men. You may find it difficult to leave these misconceptions behind. I was attached to my own myths years ago, but the abusers themselves kept forcing me to look at the realities, even as they stubbornly
avoided doing so themselves. If you are involved with a man who bullies
you or cuts you down, perhaps you feel even more confused than you did
before reading this chapter. You may be thinking, "But if his problem
doesn't spring from these sources, where does it come from?"

So our next step is to carefully weave back together the tangled strands
we have just unraveled, to form a coherent picture. As we do so, you will
gradually find yourself relieved to leave these eye-bending distortions behind. An energizing clarity can then take their place, and the mystery that
abusers work so hard to create will vanish.

KEY POINTS TO REMEMBER

- An abusive man's emotional problems do not cause his
  abusiveness. You can't change him by figuring out what
  is bothering him, helping him feel better, or improving the
  dynamics of your relationship.

- Feelings do not govern abusive or controlling behavior; beliefs,
  values, and habits are the driving forces.

- The reasons that an abusive man gives for his behavior are
  simply *excuses*. There is no way to overcome a problem with
  abusiveness by focusing on tangents such as self-esteem,
  conflict resolution, anger management, or impulse control.
  Abusiveness is resolved by dealing with abusiveness.

- Abusers thrive on creating confusion, including confusion
  about the abuse itself.

- There is nothing wrong with you. Your partner's abuse
  problem is his own.

3

The Abusive Mentality

His attitude always seems to be: "You owe me."

He manages to twist everything around so that it's my fault.

I feel suffocated by him. He's trying to run my life.

Everyone seems to think he's the greatest guy in the world. I wish they could see the side of him that I have to live with.

He says he loves me so much. So why does he treat me like this?

CHRONIC MISTREATMENT gets people to doubt themselves. Children of abusive parents know that something is wrong, but they suspect the badness is inside of them. Employees of an abusive boss spend much of their time feeling that they are doing a lousy job, that they should be smarter and work harder. Boys who get bullied feel that they should be stronger or less afraid to fight.

When I work with an abused woman, my first goal is to help her to regain trust in herself; to get her to rely on her own perceptions, to listen to her own internal voices. You don't really need an "expert" on abuse to explain your life to you; what you do need above all is some support and encouragement to hold on to your own truth. Your abusive partner wants to deny your experience. He wants to pluck your view of reality out of your head and replace it with his. When someone has invaded your identity in this way enough times, you naturally start to lose your balance. But you can find your way back to center.

An abuser creates a host of misconceptions to get his partner to doubt herself and to make it possible for him to lead her down dead-end paths. Having dispelled those myths, we can now zero in on the roots of his steamrolling style. I believe you will recognize them.

The insights I share in the pages ahead have been taught to me primarily by the abused women themselves who are the experts on abuse. My other teachers have been my abusive clients, who lead us toward clarity each time that they accidentally reveal their true thinking.

REALITY #1:
He is controlling.

My client Glenn arrived angry and agitated for his group session one night. His words spilled out rapidly:

> Harriet started yelling at me on Friday afternoon and told me she is going to move out soon. Then she left for the whole weekend and took my two-year-old son with her. She really hurt me. So I decided to hurt her too, and I wanted to go after something that was really important to her, to show her what it's like. She had been working for a week on this college paper that she had put a lot of hours into and was going to hand in on Monday. She left it sitting right on top of her dresser, just asking for it. So I tore it up into little pieces. Then I ripped up a bunch of pictures of the three of us, and I left it all in a nice pile on the bed for her to come home to. I think she learned something from that.

Glenn was remarkably honest with me about his thought process and his motives, probably because of how justified he felt. He believed in his right to control his partner's actions; he expected his word to be the last word; and he did not accept defiance. He considered it his right to punish Harriet—in the most severe way he could think of—if she took steps to recover ownership of her life. He talked proudly of how he had "allowed" her various freedoms while they were together, as if he were her parent, and defended his right to remove her privileges when he thought the time had come.

Control comes in many different forms. A few of my clients have been so extremely controlling they could have passed for military commanders. Russell, for example, went so far as to require his children to do calisthenics each morning before school. His wife was not allowed to speak to *anyone* without his permission, and he would order her back to her room to change clothes in the morning if he didn't approve of her outfit. At dinnertime, he would sit back and comment like a restaurant reviewer on the strengths and weaknesses of what she had prepared and would periodically instruct her to go to the kitchen to get things for the children, as if she were a waitress.

Russell's style was at one end of the spectrum of controlling behavior, however. Most of my clients stake out specific turf to control, like an explorer claiming land, rather than trying to run *everything*. One abuser may be fanatical about having to win every argument but leave his partner alone about what she wears. Another man may permit his partner to argue with him about the children, for example, but if she refuses to let him change the TV station when he wants, watch out. (Dozens of my clients have thrown or smashed remote controls; the television is tightly controlled by many abusers.) One abuser will have a curfew for his partner, while another will allow his partner to come and go as she pleases—as long as she makes his meals and does his laundry.

THE SPHERES OF CONTROL

An abusive man's control generally falls into one or more of the following central spheres:

ARGUMENTS AND DECISION MAKING

An intimate relationship involves a steady flow of decisions to be made, conflicting needs to negotiate, tastes and desires to balance. Who is going to clean up the mess in the kitchen? How much time should we spend alone together and how much with other friends? Where do our other hobbies and interests fit into our priorities? How will we process and resolve annoyances or hurt feelings? What rules will we have for our children?

The mind-set that an abuser brings to these choices and tensions can make him impossible to get along with. Consider how challenging it is to negotiate or compromise with a man who operates on the following tenets (whether or not he ever says them aloud):

1. "An argument should only last as long as my patience does. Once I've had enough, the discussion is over and it's time for you to shut up."

2. "If the issue we're struggling over is important to me, I should get what I want. If you don't back off, you're wronging me."

3. "I know what is best for you and for our relationship. If you continue disagreeing with me after I've made it clear which path is the right one, you're acting stupid."

4. "If my control and authority seem to be slipping, I have the right to take steps to reestablish the rule of my will, including abuse if necessary."

The last item on this list is the one that most distinguishes the abuser from other people: Perhaps any of us can slip into having feelings like the ones in numbers one through three, but the abuser gives himself permission to *take action* on the basis of his beliefs. With him, the foregoing statements aren't feelings; they are closely held *convictions* that he uses to guide his actions. That is why they lead to so much bullying behavior.

PERSONAL FREEDOM

An abusive man often considers it his right to control where his partner goes, with whom she associates, what she wears, and when she needs to be back home. He therefore feels that she should be *grateful* for any freedoms that he does choose to grant her, and will say something in a counseling session like, "She's all bent out of shape because there's one sleazy girl I don't let her hang out with, when all the rest of the time I allow her to be friends with anyone she wants." He expects his partner to give him a medal for his generosity, not to criticize him for his oppressiveness. He sees himself as a reasonably permissive parent—toward his adult part-ner—and he does not want to meet with a lot of resistance on the occa-sions when he believes that he needs to put his foot down.

Sometimes this control is exercised through wearing the woman down with constant low-level complaints, rather than through yelling or barking orders. The abuser may repeatedly make negative comments about one of his partner's friends, for example, so that she gradually stops seeing her acquaintance to save herself the hassle. In fact, she might even believe it was her own decision, not noticing how her abuser pressured her into it.

Is the abusive man's thinking distorted? Certainly. A man's partner is not his child, and the freedoms he "grants" her are not credits to be spent like chips when the urge to control her arises. But his rules make sense to him, and he will fight to hang on to them.

PARENTING

If the couple has children, the abusive man typically considers himself the authority on parenting, even if he contributes little to the actual work of looking after them. He sees himself as a wise and benevolent head coach who watches passively from the sidelines during the easy times but steps in with the "correct" approach when his partner isn't handling the children properly. His arrogance about the superiority of his parenting judgment may be matched only by how little he truly understands, or pays attention to, the children's needs. No matter how good a mother his part-ner is, he thinks she needs to learn from *him,* not the other way around.

THE ABUSIVE MAN CLAIMS that his control is in his partner's best inter-est. This justification was captured by my client Vinnie:

> Olga and I were driving in a really bad neighborhood. We were argu-ing, and she got crazy the way she does and started trying to get out of the car. It was dark. This was the kind of place where anything could happen to her. I told her to stay in the car, that she wasn't get-ting out in a place like this, but she kept trying to push the door open. I couldn't get her to stop, so I finally had to slap her in the arm,

and unfortunately she hit her head against the window. But at least
that got her to settle down and stay in the car.

Does Vinnie really believe that he is abusing his partner for her own
good? Yes and no. To some extent he does, because he has convinced himself. But his real motivation is plain to see: Olga wants out of the car in order to escape Vinnie's control, and he wants to make sure she can't.

Unfortunately, an abuser can sometimes succeed at convincing people
that his partner is so irrational and out of control, that her judgment is so
poor, that she has to be saved from herself. Never believe a man's claim
that he has to harm his partner in order to protect her; only abusers think
this way.

When a man starts my program, he often says, "I am here because I
lose control of myself sometimes. I need to get a better grip." I always correct him: **"Your problem is not that you *lose* control of yourself, it's
that you *take* control of your partner. In order to change, you
don't need to *gain* control over yourself, you need to *let go* of control of her."** A large part of his abusiveness comes in the form of *punishments* used to retaliate against you for resisting his control. This is one of
the single most important concepts to grasp about an abusive man.

REALITY #2:
He feels entitled.

Entitlement is the abuser's belief that he has a special status and that it
provides him with exclusive rights and privileges that do not apply to his
partner. The attitudes that drive abuse can largely be summarized by this
one word.

To understand entitlement, we first need to look at how rights should
properly be conceived of in a couple or family.

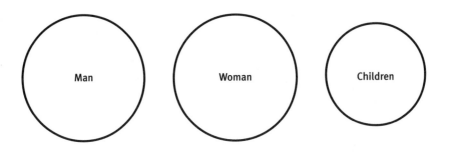

The man's rights and the woman's rights are the same size. They have the right to have their opinions and desires respected, to have a 50 percent say in decision making, to live free from verbal abuse and physical harm. Their children's rights are somewhat smaller but substantial none-theless; children can't have an equal say in decisions because of their limited knowledge and experience, but they do have the right to live free from abuse and fear, to be treated with respect, and to have their voices heard on all issues that concern them. However, an abuser perceives the rights of the family like this:

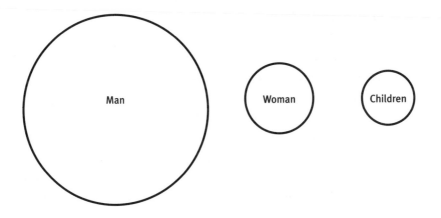

Not only are the rights of his partner and children diminished—with some abusers those little circles disappear altogether—but his rights are greatly inflated. My fundamental task as a counselor is to get the abusive man to *expand* his perception of his partner's and children's rights to their proper size and to *shrink* his view of his own rights down to where it belongs. The abusive man awards himself all kinds of "rights," including:

- Physical caretaking

- Emotional caretaking

- Sexual caretaking

- Deference

- Freedom from accountability

Physical caretaking is the focus of the more traditionally minded abuser. He expects his partner to make dinner for him the way he likes it, look after the children, clean the house, and perform an endlessly continuing list of additional tasks. He sees her essentially as an unpaid servant. He grouches, "I work my butt off all day, and when I come home I expect a little peace and quiet. Is that too much to ask for?" He seems to expect a soft chair, a newspaper, and a footstool. On the weekends he expects everything in the home to be taken care of so that he can watch sports or tinker with his car, go golfing or bird watching, or sleep. If she doesn't fulfill her myriad household responsibilities to his satisfaction, he feels entitled to dole out harsh criticism.

Although this style of abuser may seem out of date, he is alive and well. He did learn to use some prettier packaging for his regal expectations during the '80s and '90s, but the change is superficial. Fewer abusers look me in the eye nowadays and say, "I expect a warm, tasty dinner on the table when I come home," but they may still explode if it isn't there.

Interwoven with the abuser's overvaluation of his own work is the devaluation of his partner's labor. My clients grumble to me: "I don't know what the hell she does all day. I come home and the house is a mess, the children haven't been fed, and she's talking on the telephone. She spends her time watching soap operas." If she works outside the home—and few families can get by on one income—then he insists that her job is easy compared to his. Of course, if he attempts to do what she does—for example, if he is the primary parent for a while because he's unemployed and she's working—he does an abrupt about-face: Suddenly he declares that parenting and housekeeping are monumental and admirable tasks, requiring hours a day of rest for him to recuperate.

Emotional caretaking can be even more important than homemaking services to the modern abuser. Remember Ray, who swore at Mary Beth for "ignoring" him for two days while she looked for her missing son? His problem was that he believed that nothing—not even a missing child—should interfere with Mary Beth's duty to meet his emotional needs. Just as common as the abuser who blows up because dinner is late is the one who explodes because his partner gets tired of listening to him talk endlessly about himself, or because she wants to spend a little time doing something alone that she enjoys, or because she didn't drop everything to soothe him when he was feeling down, or because she failed to *anticipate* needs or desires he hadn't even expressed.

Abusive men often hide their high emotional demands by cloaking them as something else. My client Bert, for example, would be furious if his girlfriend Kirsten didn't get off the phone as soon as he came in the door. His excuse to tear into her would be "all the money she's wasting on the phone bill when she knows we can't afford it," but we noticed that the issue only arose when he wanted her attention. If she called England when he wasn't around, or if *he* spent an hour on the phone to his parents every Saturday morning, the expense was no big deal.

When I have new clients, I go to the board and draw a compass with the needle pointing straight up to a big N. "You want your partner to be this compass," I say to them, "and you want to be North. No matter where the compass goes, it always points in the same direction. And no matter where she goes, or what she's doing, or what's on her mind, you expect her to always be focused on you." My clients sometimes protest to me, "But that's what being in a relationship is about. We're *supposed* to focus on each other." But I notice that when he focuses on her, most of what he thinks about is what she can do for him, not the other way around. And when he doesn't feel like focusing on her at all, he doesn't bother.

An abuser can seem emotionally needy. You can get caught in a trap of catering to him, trying to fill a bottomless pit. But he's not so much needy as *entitled,* so no matter how much you give him, it will never be enough. He will just keep coming up with more demands because he believes his needs are your responsibility, until you feel drained down to nothing.

Sexual caretaking means that he considers it his partner's duty to keep him sexually satisfied. He may not accept having his sexual advances rejected, yet turn *her* down whenever he feels like it. Even her pleasure exists for his benefit: If she doesn't reach orgasm, for example, he may resent her for it because he wants the pleasure of seeing himself as a great lover.

Not all abusive men have great interest in sex. Some are too busy with outside relationships or use substances that diminish their sex drive. A few are gay, using their female partners for window dressing. Some of my clients can feel attracted to a woman only as part of a domination fantasy. This style of abuser loses interest in sex if his partner starts to assert herself as an equal human being deserving of respect, or he begins to coerce or assault her sexually. In short, he wants sex on his terms or not at all.

Deference refers to the abuser's entitlement to have his tastes and opinions treated as edicts. Once he has made the pronouncement that a certain movie is shallow, or that Louise was trying to seduce Jay at the picnic, or that Republicans don't know how to manage the economy, his partner is supposed to accept his view unquestioningly. It is especially important to him that she not disagree with him in front of other people; if she does, he may later yell at her, "You made me look like a fool, you're always out to show me up," and similar accusations. His unstated rule is that she is not to question his ideas.

Freedom from accountability means that the abusive man considers himself above criticism. If his partner attempts to raise her grievances, she is "nagging" or "provoking" him. He believes he should be permitted to ignore the damage his behavior is causing, and he may become retaliatory if anyone tries to get him to look at it. I had the following exchange with a man who was new to my program:

BANCROFT: Can you explain to me why you are joining this abuser group?

HANK: Well, I slapped my girl a few weeks ago, and now she says I can't come back in the house unless I get counseling.

BANCROFT: What led up to your abuse? Were you arguing?

HANK: Yes. And she accused me of having an affair! That really pissed me off!

BANCROFT: Well, *were* you having an affair?

HANK (Pause, a little startled by my question):   Well, yeah . . . but she had no proof! She shouldn't go saying things like that when she has no proof!

Hank reserved for himself the privilege of being critical of his partner, a privilege that he exercised a great deal. Complaints against him, including drawing any attention to how his behavior had hurt other people in the family, he was quick to stifle. In Hank's case, the retaliation took the form of a physical assault.

The abusive man's high entitlement leads him to have unfair and unreasonable expectations, so that the relationship revolves around his demands. His attitude is: "You owe me." For each ounce he gives, he wants a pound in return. He wants his partner to devote herself fully to catering to him, even if it means that her own needs—or her children's—get neglected. You can pour all your energy into keeping your partner content, but if he has this mind-set, he'll never be satisfied for long. And he will keep feeling that *you* are controlling *him*, because he doesn't believe that you should set any limits on his conduct or insist that he meet his responsibilities.

Many men feel specifically entitled to use violence. A recent study of college males studying psychology, published in 1997, found that 10 percent believed that it was acceptable to hit a female partner for refusing to have sex, and 20 percent believed that it was acceptable to do so if the man suspected her of cheating. Studies have found similar statistics regarding young men's belief that they have the right to force a female to have sex if they have spent a substantial amount of money on the evening's entertainment or if the woman started wanting sex but then changed her mind. These studies point to the importance of focusing on changing the entitled attitudes of abusers, rather than attempting to find something wrong in their individual psychology.

THE ABUSER'S OUTLOOK ON THE WOMAN'S ANGER

The abusive man's problem with anger is almost the opposite of what is commonly believed. The reality is:

YOUR ABUSIVE PARTNER DOESN'T HAVE A PROBLEM WITH *HIS* ANGER; HE HAS A PROBLEM WITH *YOUR* ANGER.

One of the basic human rights he takes away from you is the right to be angry with him. No matter how badly he treats you, he believes that your voice shouldn't rise and your blood shouldn't boil. The privilege of rage is reserved for him alone. When your anger does jump out of you—as will happen to any abused woman from time to time—he is likely to try to jam it back down your throat as quickly as he can. Then he uses your anger against you to prove what an irrational person you are. Abuse can make you feel straitjacketed. You may develop physical or emotional reactions to swallowing your anger, such as depression, nightmares, emotional numbing, or eating and sleeping problems, which your partner may use as an excuse to belittle you further or make you feel crazy.

Why does your partner react so strongly to your anger? One reason may be that he considers himself above reproach, as I discussed above. The second is that on some level he senses—though not necessarily consciously—that there is *power in your anger*. If you have space to feel and express your rage, you will be better able to hold on to your identity and to resist his suffocation of you. He tries to take your anger away in order to snuff out your capacity to resist his will. Finally, he perceives your anger as a *challenge* to his authority, to which he responds by overpowering you with anger that is greater than your own. In this way he ensures that he retains the exclusive right to be the one who shows anger.

THE ABUSER'S OWN ANGER

Once you grasp the nature of entitlement, the following concept about the abusive man becomes clear:

HE ISN'T ABUSIVE BECAUSE HE IS ANGRY;
HE'S ANGRY BECAUSE HE'S ABUSIVE.

The abuser's unfair and unrealistic expectations ensure that his partner can never follow all of his rules or meet all of his demands. The result is that he is frequently angry or enraged. This dynamic was illustrated on a recent talk show by a young man who was discussing his abuse of his present wife. He said that his definition of a good relationship was: "Never arguing and saying you love each other every day." He told the audience that his wife "deserved" his mistreatment because she wasn't living up to this unrealistic image. It wouldn't do any good to send this young man, or any other abuser, to an anger-management program, because his entitlements would just keep producing more anger. His attitudes are what need to change.

REALITY #3:

He twists things into their opposites.

Emile, a physically violent client with whom I worked, gave me the following account of his worst assault on his wife: "One day Tanya went way overboard with her mouth, and I got so pissed off that I grabbed her by the neck and put her up against the wall." With his voice filled with indignation, he said, "Then she tried to knee me in the balls! How would you like it if a woman did that to you?? Of course I lashed out. And when I swung my hand down, my fingernails made a long cut across her face. What the hell did she expect?"

QUESTION 4:

WHY DOES HE SAY THAT *I* AM THE ONE ABUSING *HIM*?

The abuser's highly entitled perceptual system causes him to mentally *reverse aggression and self-defense*. When Tanya attempted to defend herself against Emile's life-threatening attack, he defined her actions as violence toward *him*. When he then injured her further, he claimed he was defending himself against *her* abuse. The lens of entitlement the abuser holds over his eye stands everything on its head, like the reflection in a spoon.

Another client, Wendell, described an incident in which he stomped out of the house and slammed the door. "My wife Aysha nags at me for hours. I can only take so much of her complaining and telling me I'm no good. Yesterday she went on for a half hour, and I finally called her a bitch and took off." I asked him what Aysha was upset about, and he said he didn't know. "When she goes on like that I just tune her out." A few days later I spoke with Aysha about the incident, and she told me that she had indeed been yelling at Wendell for five or ten minutes. However, he had failed to tell me that he had launched a verbal assault when she first woke up that morning and had continued berating her all day: "He totally dominates arguments; he repeats himself like a broken record; and I'm lucky if I can get a word in. And his language is awful—he must have called me a 'bitch' ten times that day." She finally reached her limit and began standing up for herself forcefully, and that was when he stormed out for the evening.

Why does Wendell think that Aysha is the one who has been doing all the yelling and complaining? Because in his mind *she's supposed to be listening, not talking.* If she expresses herself at all, that's too much.

When I challenge my clients to stop bullying their partners, they twist my words around just as they do their partners'. They accuse me of having said things that have little connection to my actual words. An abuser says, "You're saying I should lie down and let her walk all over me" because I told him that intimidating his partner is unacceptable no matter how angry he is. He says, "So you're telling us that our partners can do anything they want to us, and we aren't allowed to lift a finger to defend ourselves" because his partner told him that she was sick of his friends trashing the house and that he should "clean up his goddamned mess," and I told him that was no excuse to call her a disgusting name. He says, "Your approach is that whatever she does is okay, because she's a woman, but because I'm the man, there's much stricter rules for me" because I pointed out *his* double standards and insisted that he should live by the same rules he applies to her.

The abusive man has another reason to exaggerate and ridicule his partner's statements (and mine): He wants to avoid having to think seriously about what she is saying and struggle to digest it. He feels entitled to swat her down like a fly instead.

REALITY #4:
He disrespects his partner and considers himself superior to her.

Sheldon's relationship with Kelly was over. He was required to enter my program because he had violated a restraining order but denied that he had ever been violent or frightening to Kelly. Now he was attempting to get custody of their three-year-old daughter, Ashley. He claimed that Kelly had never looked after Ashley from the time of her birth and had "never bonded with her." He added, "I don't consider her Ashley's mother. She's just a vessel, just a channel that Ashley came through to get into this world."

Sheldon had reduced Kelly to an inanimate object in his mind, a baby-producing machine. When he spoke of her, he twisted his face up in disgusted expressions of contempt. At the same time, he never sounded upset; he considered Kelly too far beneath him to raise his ire. He had the same attitude you might have if an annoying but harmless little dog were nipping at your heels. His tone of condescension indicated how certain he was of his superiority to Kelly.

As memorable as Sheldon's smug derision was, it was only a few notches worse than the common thinking of many abusive men. The abuser tends to see his partner as less intelligent, less competent, less logical, and even less *sensitive* than he is. He will tell me, for example, that she isn't the compassionate person he is. He often has difficulty conceiving of her as a human being. This tendency in abusers is known as *objectification* or *depersonalization*. Most abusers verbally attack their partners in degrading, revolting ways. They reach for the words that they know are most disturbing to women, such as *bitch, whore,* and *cunt,* often preceded by the word *fat.* These words assault her humanity, reducing her to an animal, a nonliving object, or a degraded sexual body part. The partners of my clients tell me that these disgusting words carry a force and an ugliness that feel like violence. Through these carefully chosen epithets—and my clients sometimes admit that they use the most degrading words they can think of—abusers make their partners feel both debased and unsafe.

Objectification is a critical reason why an abuser tends to get worse over time. As his conscience adapts to one level of cruelty—or violence—he builds to the next. By depersonalizing his partner, the abuser protects himself from the natural human emotions of guilt and empathy, so that he can sleep at night with a clear conscience. He distances himself so far from her humanity that her feelings no longer count, or simply cease to exist. These walls tend to grow over time, so that after a few years in a relationship my clients can reach a point where they feel no more guilt over degrading or threatening their partners than you or I would feel after angrily kicking a stone in the driveway.

Abuse and respect are diametric opposites: You do not respect some-one whom you abuse, and you do not abuse someone whom you respect.

REALITY #5:
He confuses love and abuse.

Here are comments my clients commonly make to me:

"The reason I abuse her is because I have such strong feelings for her. You hurt the ones you love the most."

"No one can get me as upset as she can."

"Yeah, I told her she'd better not ever try to leave me. You have no idea how much I love this girl!"

"I was sick of watching her ruining her life. I care too much to sit back and do nothing about it."

An abusive man often tries to convince his partner that his mistreat-ment of her is proof of how deeply he cares, but the reality is that abuse is the opposite of love. The more a man abuses you, the more he is demon-strating that he cares only about himself. He may feel a powerful desire to *receive* your love and caretaking, but he only wants to *give* love when it's convenient.

So is he lying when he says he loves you? No, usually not. Most of my clients do feel a powerful sensation inside that they call love. For many of them it is the only kind of feeling toward a female partner that they have ever had, so they have no way of knowing that it isn't love. When an abu-sive man feels the powerful stirring inside that other people call love, he is probably largely feeling:

- The desire to have you devote your life to keeping him happy with no outside interference

- The desire to have sexual access

- The desire to impress others by having you be his partner

- The desire to possess and control you

These desires are important aspects of what romantic love means to him. He may well be capable of feeling genuine love for you, but first he will have to dramatically reorient his outlook in order to separate abusive and possessive desires from true caring, and become able to really *see* you.

The confusion of love with abuse is what allows abusers who kill their partners to make the absurd claim that they were driven by the depths of their loving feelings. The news media regrettably often accept the aggressors' view of these acts, describing them as "crimes of passion." But what could more thoroughly prove that a man did *not* love his partner? If a mother were to kill one of her children, would we ever accept the claim that she did it because she was overwhelmed by how much she cared? Not for an instant. Nor should we. Genuine love means respecting the humanity of the other person, wanting what is best for him or her, and supporting the other person's self-esteem and independence. This kind of love is incompatible with abuse and coercion.

REALITY #6:
He is manipulative.

Let's examine the following interactions between an abusive man named David and his partner Joanne:

- David is yelling at Joanne, pointing his finger and turning red in the face. Joanne tells him he's too angry and she doesn't like it. He yells even louder, saying, "I'm not angry, I'm just trying to get my point across and you're not listening! Don't tell me what I'm feeling, I hate that! You're not inside me!"

- One day Joanne tells David that his outbursts are getting to her and she needs to take some time off from their relationship. David says, "What you are saying is that you don't love me anymore. I'm not sure you ever loved me. You don't understand how strong my feelings are for you," and he looks close to tears. The conversation shifts to Joanne reassuring David that she isn't abandoning him, and her complaints about his behavior get lost in the shuffle.

- On another occasion, Joanne brings up the fact that she would like to go back to school. David responds negatively, saying, "We can't afford it," and refuses to look after the children while she's at class. Joanne proposes a number of strategies for dealing with both money and child care, all of which David finds something wrong with. Joanne finally decides it's impossible to continue her education, but David then insists that he wasn't trying to talk her out of it. She winds up feeling that the decision not to go back to school is her own.

Few abusive men rely entirely on verbal abuse or intimidation to control their partners. Being a nonstop bully is too much work, and it makes the man look bad. If he is abusive all the time, his partner starts to recognize that she's being abused, and the man may feel too guilty about his behavior. The abuser therefore tends to switch frequently to manipulating his partner to get what he wants. He may also sometimes use these tactics just to get her upset or confused.

There are some signs of manipulation by abusers that you can watch for:

- *Changing his moods abruptly and frequently,* so that you find it difficult to tell who he is or how he feels, keeping you constantly off balance. His feelings toward *you* are especially changeable.

- *Denying the obvious about what he is doing or feeling.* He'll speak to you with his voice trembling with anger, or he'll blame a difficulty on you, or he'll sulk for two hours, and then deny it to your face. You know what he did—and so does he— but he refuses to admit it, which can drive you crazy with frustration. Then he may call you irrational for getting so upset by his denial.

- *Convincing you that what **he** wants you to do is what is best for you.* This way the abuser can make his selfishness look like generosity, which is a neat trick. A long time may pass before you realize what his real motives were.

- *Getting you to feel sorry for him,* so that you will be reluctant to push forward with your complaints about what he does.

- *Getting you to blame yourself, or blame other people, for what he does.*

- *Using confusion tactics in arguments,* subtly or overtly changing the subject, insisting that you are thinking or feeling things that you aren't, twisting your words, and many other tactics that serve as glue to pour into your brain. You may leave arguments with him feeling like you are losing your mind.

- *Lying or misleading you about his actions, his desires, or his reasons for doing certain things,* in order to guide you into doing what he wants you to do. One of the most frequent complaints I get from abused women is that their partners lie repeatedly, a form of psychological abuse that in itself can be highly destructive over time.

- *Getting you and the people you care about turned against each other* by betraying confidences, being rude to your friends, telling people lies about what you supposedly said about them, charming your friends and then telling them bad things about you, and many other divisive tactics.

In some ways manipulation is worse than overt abuse, especially when the two are mixed together. When a woman gets called "bitch," or gets shoved or slapped, she at least knows what her partner did to her. But after a manipulative interaction she may have little idea what went wrong; she just knows that she feels terrible, or crazy, and that somehow it seems to be her own fault.

REALITY #7:
He strives to have a good public image.

If you are involved with an abusive man, you may spend a lot of your time trying to figure out what is wrong with *you,* rather than what is wrong with *him.* If he gets along well with other people and impresses them with his generosity, sense of humor, and friendliness, you may wind up wondering, "What is it about me that sets him off? Other people seem to think he's great."

QUESTION 5:
HOW COME EVERYONE ELSE THINKS HE'S WONDERFUL?

Most abusive men put on a charming face for their communities, creating a sharp split between their public image and their private treatment of women and children. He may be:

- Enraged at home but calm and smiling outside

- Selfish and self-centered with you but generous and supportive with others

- Domineering at home but willing to negotiate and compromise outside

- Highly negative about females while on his own turf but a vocal supporter of equality when anyone else is listening

- Assaultive toward his partner or children but nonviolent and nonthreatening with everyone else

- Entitled at home but critical of other men who disrespect or assault women

The pain of this contrast can eat away at a woman. In the morning her partner cuts her to the quick by calling her a "brainless fat cow," but a few hours later she sees him laughing with the people next door and helping them fix their car. Later the neighbor says to her, "Your partner is so nice. You're lucky to be with him—a lot of men wouldn't do what he does."

She responds with a mumbled "Yeah," feeling confused and tongue-tied. Back at home, she asks herself over and over again, *"Why me?"*

DO ABUSIVE MEN HAVE SPLIT PERSONALITIES?

Not really. They are drawn to power and control, and part of how they get it is by looking good in public. The abusive man's charm makes his partner reluctant to reach out for support or assistance because she feels that people will find her revelations hard to believe or will blame her. If friends overhear him say something abusive, or police arrest him for an assault, his previous people-pleasing lays the groundwork to get him off the hook. The observers think, *He's such a nice guy, he's just not the type to be abusive. She must have really hurt him.*

The abuser's nice-guy front helps him feel good about himself. My clients say to me, "I get along fine with everyone but her. You should ask around about what I'm like; you'll see. I'm a calm, reasonable person. People can see that she's the one who goes off." Meanwhile, he uses the difficulties that she is having in her relationships with people—many of which may be caused by him—as further proof that she is the one with the problem.

One of the most important challenges facing a counselor of abusive men is to resist being drawn in by the men's charming persona. As they sit chatting and joking in their group meeting, cruelty and selfishness seem faraway. I find myself wondering the same thing the neighbors do: Could this guy really get that mean? And even after he admits to what he does, it's *still* hard to believe. This contrast is a key reason why abusers can get away with what they do.

Among my clients I have had: numerous doctors, including two surgeons; many successful businesspeople, including owners and directors of large companies; about a dozen college professors; several lawyers; a prominent—and very mellow-sounding—radio personality; clergypeople; and two well-known professional athletes. One of my violent clients had spent every Thanksgiving for the past ten years volunteering at his local soup kitchen. Another was a publicly visible staff member of a major international human rights organization. The cruelty and destructiveness that these men were capable of would have stunned their communities had they known.

Although these men usually keep their abusive side well hidden outside of the home, there is one situation in which it slips out: when someone confronts them about their abusiveness and sticks up for the abused woman, which happens to be my job. Suddenly, the attitudes and tactics they normally reserve for home come pouring out. The vast majority of women who say that they are being abused are telling the truth. I know this to be true because the abusers let their guard down with me, belying their denial.

REALITY #8:
He feels justified.

Several years ago, I had a client who began his first group session by declaring: "I am here because I'm a batterer." I was impressed with his ownership of his problem. However, the next week he softened his words to, "I'm here because I'm abusive," and the third week he stated, "I'm in the program because my wife thinks I'm abusive." Within a few more weeks he had quit coming, having comfortably wrapped himself back up in his justifications.

Abusers externalize responsibility for their actions, believing that their partners *make them* behave in abusive ways. Each of my clients predictably uses some variation of the following lines:

> *"She knows how to push my buttons."*
>
> *"She wanted me to go off, and she knows how to make it happen."*
>
> *"She pushed me too far."*
>
> *"There's only so much a man can take."*
>
> *"You expect me to just let her walk all over me. What would you do?"*

Many clients express guilt or remorse when they first begin attending counseling, but as soon as I start to press them to look at their histories of abusive behavior, they switch back to defending their actions. They don't mind glibly saying, "I know what I did was wrong," but when I ask them to describe their verbal or physical assaults in detail, they leap back to justifying.

Abusive men are masters of excuse making. In this respect they are like substance abusers, who believe that everyone and everything except them is responsible for their actions. When they aren't blaming their partners, they blame stress, alcohol, their childhood, their children, their bosses, or their insecurities. More important, they feel *entitled* to make these excuses; when I point out that other men under the same pressures choose not to be abusive, they tend to become irate or contemptuous.

Does this mean that abusers are psychopaths who lack any conscience that could cause them to feel guilt or responsibility? Generally not, although I have had a small number (perhaps 5 percent of my clients) who are. Most abusers *do* have a conscience about their behavior outside of the family. They may be willing to be answerable for their actions at work, at the club, or on the street. At home, however, their sense of entitlement takes over.

The abusive man commonly believes he can blame his partner for *anything* that goes wrong, not just his abusiveness. Did he just suffer a disappointment? She caused it. Is he embarrassed by a mistake he made? She should have prevented it. Is one of the children in a difficult period? She's a bad mother. Everything is someone else's fault, and "someone else" is usually her.

REALITY #9:
Abusers deny and minimize their abuse.

One of my areas of specialization is court-related work involving abusers who are physically violent or who abuse their children. I frequently encounter court personnel who say: "Well, she accuses him of abusing her, but he denies it." They then drop the matter, as if the man's denial closes the case. They also tell me: "He says she does the same things to him, so I guess they abuse each other." This kind of denial and cross-accusation tells us nothing about whether the woman is telling the truth. If the man is abusive, *of course* he is going to deny it, partly to protect himself and partly because his perceptions are distorted. *If he were ready to accept responsibility for his actions in relationships, he wouldn't be abusive.* Breaking through denial and minimization is one of the main tasks facing an abuse counselor. Most of the men in my groups admit to some abusive behavior—although they don't see it as abusive, of course—but they acknowledge only a small portion of what they have actually done, as I learn when I interview the abused partners.

When an abuser denies an incident immediately after it happens, he can set his partner's head spinning. Picture a woman who arises in the morning with her stomach still tied in a knot from an ugly blowout the night before. Her partner makes a face at her in the kitchen and says, "Why are you so grumpy today?"

She replies, "Why the hell do you think? You called me 'loser' right in front of the children, and then you yanked my towel off so they would laugh at me. Am I supposed to come down the stairs whistling a happy tune?"

"What are you *talking* about?" he gasps. "You're a fucking drama junkie. I was clear across the room from you when your towel fell off. You're going to blame that on me? You're nuts." And he walks off shaking his head.

A woman can feel that she is losing her mind—or develop actual psychiatric symptoms—if the obvious realities of her life, including abuse, are denied repeatedly by her partner. The certainty and authority in his voice, with his eyes twisted up to show how baffled he is, leave her questioning herself. "Did that really happen? Maybe it didn't. Maybe I do overreact to innocent things." The more serious the incidents he denies, the more her grip on reality can start to slip. And if outsiders start to notice her instability, the abuser can use their observations to persuade them that her revelations of abuse by him are fantasies.

The partners of this style of abuser ask me: "After an incident, it seems like he really believes the abuse didn't happen. Is he consciously lying?" The answer in most cases is yes. Most abusers do not have severe memory problems. He probably remembers exactly what he did, especially when only a short time has passed. He denies his actions to close off discussion because he doesn't want to answer for what he did, and perhaps he even wants you to feel frustrated and crazy. However, a small percentage of abusers—perhaps one in twelve—may have psychological conditions such as narcissistic or borderline personality disorder, in which they literally block any bad behavior from consciousness. One of the clues that your partner may have such a disturbance is if you notice him doing similar things to other people. If his denial and mind messing are restricted to you, or to situations that are related to you, he is probably simply abusive.

Denial and minimization are part of most destructive behavior patterns, whether they be alcohol abuse, gambling, or child abuse. Partner abuse is no exception.

REALITY #10:
Abusers are possessive.

New clients in my program sometimes look bewildered, as if I were giving a seminar on edible plants and they had wandered into the wrong room. They can hardly wait to speak, rising out of their seats to sputter at me: "But these are our *wives* and *girlfriends* you are talking about. Do you really mean to say that someone else can dictate what we do in our relationships?" They smile as they speak or shake their heads lightly, as if they feel compassion for my dull wits. They assume I somehow have failed to realize that these women are *theirs.*

The sense of ownership is one reason why abuse tends to get worse as relationships get more serious. The more history and commitment that develop in the couple, the more the abuser comes to think of his partner as a prized object. Possessiveness is at the core of the abuser's mind-set, the spring from which all the other streams spout; on some level he feels that he owns you and therefore has the right to treat you as he sees fit.

QUESTION 6:
WHY IS HE SO INSANELY JEALOUS?

For many abusers, possessiveness takes the form of sexual jealousy. This style of man monitors his partner's associations carefully, expects her to account for her whereabouts at all times, and periodically rips into her with jealous accusations, as Fran did in Chapter 1. Ironically, the most accusatory abusers are among the ones most likely to be cheating themselves; possessiveness and entitlement make the abuser feel that it is acceptable for him to have affairs, but not her.

An equally important reason for the extreme jealousy exhibited by so many abusive men is the desire to *isolate* their partners. In Chapter 1 we met Marshall, who did not believe his own hysterical accusations of infidelity against his wife. So what was driving his behavior? An abusive man who isolates his partner does so primarily for two reasons:

1. He wants her life to be focused entirely on his needs. He feels that other social contacts will allow her less time for him, and he doesn't accept that she has that right.

2. He doesn't want her to develop sources of strength that could contribute to her independence. Although it is often largely unconscious, abusive men are aware on some level that a woman's social contacts can bring her strength and support that could ultimately enable her to escape his control (as we saw with Dale and Maureen in Chapter 1). An abusive man commonly attempts to keep his partner completely dependent on him to increase his power.

Because of this mind-set, an abusive man tends to perceive any relationships that his partner develops, whether with males or females, as threats to him. You may try to manage this problem by giving him lots of reassurance that you still love him and are not going to cheat on him. But you will find that his efforts to isolate you don't lessen, because his fears that you might sleep with another man are actually only a small part of why he is trying to isolate you.

At the same time, jealous accusations and isolation are only one form that ownership can take. There are abusive men who do not try to control their partners' associations, but their underlying attitude of "You're mine to do with as I see fit" reveals itself in other ways. If your partner's sister criticizes him for bullying you, he may tell her: "What I do with my girl is none of your business." If you have children, he may start to treat all family members as his belongings. His anger may escalate dangerously when you attempt to break away from him. Keep the word *ownership* in mind, and you may begin to notice that many of your partner's behaviors are rooted in believing that you belong to him.

ABUSIVE MEN COME in every personality type, arise from good childhoods and bad ones, are macho men or gentle, "liberated" men. No psychological test can distinguish an abusive man from a respectful one. Abusiveness is not a product of a man's emotional injuries or of deficits in his skills. In reality, abuse springs from a man's early cultural training, his key male role models, and his peer influences. In other words, abuse is a problem of *values,* not of psychology. When someone challenges an abuser's *attitudes* and *beliefs,* he tends to reveal the contemptuous and insulting personality that normally stays hidden, reserved for private attacks on his partner. An abuser tries to keep everybody—his partner, his therapist, his friends and relatives—focused on how he *feels,* so that they won't focus on how he *thinks,* perhaps because on some level he is aware that if you grasp the true nature of his problem, you will begin to escape his domination.

KEY POINTS TO REMEMBER

- Abuse grows from attitudes and values, not feelings. The roots are ownership, the trunk is entitlement, and the branches are control.

- Abuse and respect are opposites. Abusers cannot change unless they overcome their core of disrespect toward their partners.

- Abusers are far more conscious of what they are doing than they appear to be. However, even their less-conscious behaviors are driven by their core attitudes.

- Abusers are *unwilling* to be nonabusive, not *unable.* They do not want to give up power and control.

- You are not crazy. Trust your perceptions of how your abusive partner treats you and thinks about you.

4

The Types of Abusive Men

I feel so bad for him; he's had a really hard life.

I'm lucky to be with him; he could get any woman he wants.

I'm really scared of what he may do to me some day.

I shouldn't argue with him, because I just come out feeling like an idiot.

He's very sensitive. I shouldn't complain so much; he's doing the best he can.

He says the reason he cheats on me so much is that he's a sex addict.

THE QUALITIES THAT MAKE UP an abusive man are like the ingredients in a recipe: The basics are always present, but the relative amounts vary greatly. One man may be so severely controlling that his partner can't make a move without checking with him first, and yet, oddly, he contributes substantially to the domestic work and child care. Another man may allow his partner to come and go as she pleases, even accepting her friendships with men, but there is hell to pay if she fails to wait on him hand and foot, or if she makes the mistake of asking him to clean up after himself. Still other abusers are less overtly controlling and entitled than either of these men but mind-twisting in the severity of their manipulations.

The tactics and attitudes of abusers can vary from country to country, from ethnic group to ethnic group, from rich man to poor man. Abusers from each culture have their special areas of control or cruelty. Middle-class white abusers, for example, tend to have strict rules about how a woman is allowed to argue. If she talks back to him, shows anger, or doesn't shut up when she is told to, he is likely to make her pay. My clients from Latin American cultures typically permit their partners to be more forceful and "mouthy" in a conflict than my white clients but can be highly retaliatory if their partners give any attention to another male. Abusers select the pieces of turf they wish to stake out, influenced in those choices by their particular culture and background. Each woman who is involved with an abusive or controlling man has to deal with his unique blend of tactics and attitudes, his particular rhythm of good times and bad times, and his specific way of presenting himself to the outside world. No one should ever tell an abused woman, "I know just what you're going through," because the experience of each woman is different.

Viewed from another angle, however, abuse *doesn't* vary that much. One man uses a little more of one ingredient and a little less of the other, but the overall flavor of the mistreatment has core similarities: assaults on the woman's self-esteem, controlling behavior, undermining her independence, disrespect. Each abused woman has times of feeling that a riptide is dragging her under the sea, and she struggles for air. *Confusion* has been part of the experience of almost every one of the hundreds of abused women I have spoken with. Whether because of the abuser's manipulativeness, his popularity, or simply the mind-bending contrast between his professions of love and his vicious psychological or physical assaults, every abused woman finds herself fighting to make sense out of what is happening.

Recognizing the nature of the abusive man's problem can be a first step out of the fog. In this chapter I introduce you to ten styles of abuse I have encountered among the two thousand men I have worked with. One—or more—of these profiles may jump out at you, so that you find yourself feeling: "There he is!" On the other hand, you might find instead that he does not fit neatly into any of these "types" but seems rather to draw bits of himself from each one. In that case, think of these profiles not as different men, but as the varying faces of one man. Either way, the descriptions can help you to put your finger on what your partner is up to.

The sections below describe each style of man *while he is being abusive.* I don't mean that he is like this all the time. In fact, men from any of

THE NATURE OF ABUSIVE THINKING

78

the categories below can turn kind and loving at any moment and stay in
that mode for days, weeks, or even months.

THE DEMAND MAN

The Demand Man is highly entitled. He expects his partner's life to revolve around meeting his needs and is angry and blaming if anything gets
in the way. He becomes enraged if he isn't catered to or if he is inconve-
nienced in even a minor way. The partner of this man comes to feel that
nothing she does is ever good enough and that it is impossible to make
him happy. He criticizes her frequently, usually about things that he thinks
she should have done—or done better—for him.

Is every highly demanding partner an abuser? No. There are specific
elements to the Demand Man's style:

1. He has little sense of give and take. His demands for emotional
   support, favors, caretaking, or sexual attention are well out of proportion to his contributions; he constantly feels that you owe him
   things that he has done nothing to earn.

2. He exaggerates and overvalues his own contributions. If he was
   generous one day back in 1997, you are probably still hearing
   about it today as proof of how wonderfully he treats you and how
   ungrateful you are. He seems to keep a mental list of any favors
   or kindnesses he ever does and expects each one paid back at a
   heavy interest rate. He thinks you owe him tremendous gratitude
   for meeting the ordinary responsibilities of daily life—when he
   does—but takes your contributions for granted.

3. When he doesn't get what he feels is his due, he punishes you for
   letting him down.

4. When he is generous or supportive, it's because he feels like it.
   When he isn't in the mood to give anything, he doesn't. He is positive or loving toward you when he feels the need to prove to
   himself or to others that he is a good person, or when there is

something that he is about to demand in return; in other words, it's about *him,* not you. The longer you have been with him, the more his generous-seeming actions appear self-serving.

5. If your needs ever conflict with his, he is furious. At these times he attacks you as self-centered or inflexible, turning reality on its head with statements such as, "All you care about is yourself!" He tends to work hard to convince outsiders of how selfish and ungrateful you are, speaking in a hurt voice about all the things he does for you.

At the same time, the Demand Man is likely to be furious if anything is demanded of *him.* Not only are you not supposed to demand any favors, you aren't even supposed to ask him to take care of his own obligations. If you ask him to clean up a mess *he's* left, he responds, "I'm not your fucking servant." If you ask him to pay money he owes you or to work more hours to help out with the household expenses, he says, "You're a typical woman, all you want from me is my money." If you complain to him of how rarely he is there for you, he'll say, "You are a needy, controlling bitch." He keeps twisting things around backward in these ways, so that any effort you make to discuss your needs or his responsibilities switches abruptly to being about *his* needs and *your* responsibilities.

The Demand Man is sometimes less controlling than other abusers as long as he is getting his needs met on his terms. He may allow you to have your own friendships or support you in pursuing your own career. But the effects on you of your partner's extreme entitlement can be just as destructive as severe control.

The central attitudes driving the Demand Man are:

- It's your job to do things for me, including taking care of my responsibilities if I drop the ball on them. If I'm unhappy about any aspect of my life, whether it has to do with our relationship or not, it's your fault.

> - You should not place demands on me at all. You should be grateful for whatever I choose to give.
>
> - I am above criticism.
>
> - I am a very loving and giving partner. You're lucky to have me.

MR. RIGHT

Mr. Right considers himself the ultimate authority on every subject under the sun; you might call him "Mr. *Always* Right." He speaks with absolute certainty, brushing your opinions aside like annoying gnats. He seems to see the world as a huge classroom, in which he is the teacher and you are his student. He finds little of value in your thoughts or insights, so he seeks to empty out your head and fill it up with *his* jewels of brilliance. When Mr. Right sits in one of my groups for abusive men, he often speaks of his partner as if she were in danger from her own idiocy and he needs to save her from herself. Mr. Right has difficulty speaking to his partner— or about her—without a ring of condescension in his voice. And in a conflict his arrogance gets even worse.

Mr. Right's superiority is a convenient way for him to get what he wants. When he and his partner are arguing about their conflicting desires, he turns it into a clash between Right and Wrong or between Intelligence and Stupidity. He ridicules and discredits her perspective so that he can escape dealing with it. Here is a conversation I had with a Mr. Right whom I worked with in one of my abuser groups:

BANCROFT: Pat, do you have any abusive behaviors to report from this past week?

PAT: Well, I did yell at Gwen once and called her "bitch." We were fighting about money, as usual.

BANCROFT: What was Gwen's perspective in the argument?

PAT: She thinks money grows on trees.

BANCROFT: Gwen said that money grows on trees?

PAT: Well no, not just like that. But that's how she acts.

BANCROFT: Let's try again. What was she saying in the argument?

PAT: She thinks we have enough money to get both of the children whole new sets of clothes. But we just bought all new stuff for them only a few weeks ago. And we just don't have it in the bank right now.

BANCROFT: Does Gwen agree that the last round of shopping was only a few weeks ago?

PAT: No, she says it was four months ago, at the beginning of the summer, which is a crock. I can remember that the summer was more than half over.

BANCROFT: So her memory is different from yours. Did she say why she thinks it was earlier?

PAT: Of course not, she's . . . Well, maybe she said something about how she remembers she paid the credit card bill for those clothes while the children were still in school. But she's wrong.

BANCROFT: Now, you said that the money simply isn't there. Gwen obviously thinks differently. Where does she think the money should come from?

PAT: I already told you, she wants me to be a magician who can just make it appear.

BANCROFT: But she must have been making points about it. What was she saying?

PAT: Oh, I don't know . . . She says we should sell our car and get a shit box, which would just end up costing us more in the long run, plus I don't want to deal with it.

BANCROFT: What do you drive now?

PAT: A Saab.

BANCROFT: Let me guess. She would like to trade the Saab in on a reliable car that has lower monthly payments, cheaper parts, and fewer repair bills.

PAT: Yeah, that's what I said, a shit box.

What Pat revealed in this exchange was that each time Gwen attempts to stand up for herself or put forth her views, he twists her statements to make them sound absurd. Notice how long it took me to drag out of him what Gwen's opinions actually were. Gwen naturally came out feeling stifled by Pat, as there was nothing she could do to get her views heard and taken seriously. Part of why Pat is convinced that Gwen is stupid is that he is so exaggeratedly certain of his own wisdom and clarity. Since she continues to disagree with him, he takes that as proof of her foolishness.

When Mr. Right decides to take control of a conversation, he switches into his Voice of Truth, giving the definitive pronouncement on what is the correct answer or the proper outlook. Abuse counselors call this tactic *defining reality.* Over time, his tone of authority can cause his partner to doubt her own judgment and come to see herself as not very bright. I notice how often I am speaking with the intelligent-sounding partner of one of my clients, only to have her say to me: "I'm not that smart." The abuser *wants* her to doubt her mental abilities in this way, so that he can control her better.

Besides knowing all about the world, Mr. Right is also an expert on your life and how you should live it. He has the answers to your conflicts at work, how you should spend your time, and how you should raise your children. He is especially knowledgeable about *your faults,* and he likes to inventory what is wrong with you, as if tearing you down were the way to improve you. He may seem to enjoy periodically straightening you out in front of other people to humiliate you, thereby establishing his unquestionable intellectual superiority.

When Mr. Right's partner refuses to defer to his sophisticated knowledge, he is likely to escalate to insulting her, calling her names, or mocking her with imitation. If he's still not satisfied that he has brought her down low enough, he may reach for bigger guns, such as ruining evening plans, leaving places without her, or saying bad things about her to other people. If he is physically assaultive, then this is the time he may throw things, raise fists, or attack violently. In short, Mr. Right finds some way to ensure that his partner regrets her insistence on having her own mind.

Mr. Right in some respects is a less violent and frightening version of the Drill Sergeant (see p. 86), but Mr. Right's control tends to be especially focused on telling his partner how to *think*. His partner feels suffocated by his control, as if he were watching her every move under a microscope.

Mr. Right tries to sanitize his bullying by telling me, "I have strong opinions" or "I like debating ideas." This is like a bank robber saying, "I'm interested in financial issues." Mr. Right isn't interested in debating ideas; he wants to impose his own.

The central attitudes driving Mr. Right are:

- You should be in awe of my intelligence and should look up to me intellectually. I know better than you do, even about what's good for you.

- Your opinions aren't worth listening to carefully or taking seriously.

- The fact that you sometimes disagree with me shows how sloppy your thinking is.

- If you would just accept that I know what's right, our relationship would go much better. Your own life would go better, too.

- When you disagree with me about something, no matter how respectfully or meekly, that's mistreatment of me.

- If I put you down for long enough, some day you'll see.

THE WATER TORTURER

The Water Torturer's style proves that anger doesn't cause abuse. He can assault his partner psychologically without even raising his voice. He tends to stay calm in arguments, using his own evenness as a weapon to push her over the edge. He often has a superior or contemptuous grin on his face, smug and self-assured. He uses a repertoire of aggressive conversational tactics at low volume, including sarcasm, derision—such as openly laughing at her—mimicking her voice, and cruel, cutting remarks. Like Mr. Right, he tends to take things she has said and twist them beyond recognition to make her appear absurd, perhaps especially in front of other people. He gets to his partner through a slow but steady stream of low-level emotional assaults, and perhaps occasional shoves or other "minor" acts of violence that don't generally cause visible injury but may do great psychological harm. He is relentless in his quiet derision and meanness.

The impact on a woman of all these subtle tactics is that either her blood temperature rises to a boil or she feels stupid and inferior, or some combination of the two. In an argument, she may end up yelling in frustration, leaving the room crying, or sinking into silence. The Water Torturer then says, "See, you're the abusive one, not me. You're the one who's yelling and refusing to talk things out rationally. I wasn't even raising my voice. It's impossible to reason with you."

The psychological effects of living with the Water Torturer can be severe. His tactics can be difficult to identify, so they sink in deeply. Women can find it difficult not to blame themselves for their reactions to what their partner does if they don't even know what to call it. When someone slaps you in the face, you know you've been slapped. But when a woman feels psychologically assaulted, with little idea why, after an argument with The Water Torturer, she may turn her frustration inward. How do you seek support from a friend, for example, when you don't know how to describe what is going wrong?

The Water Torturer tends to genuinely believe that there is nothing unusual about his behavior. When his partner starts to confront him with his abusiveness—which she usually does sooner or later—he looks at her as if she were crazy and says, "What the hell are you talking about? I've never done anything to you." Friends and relatives who have witnessed the couple's interactions may back him up. They shake their heads and say to each other, "I don't know what goes on with her. She just explodes at him sometimes, and he's so low-key." Their children can develop the impression that Mom "blows up over nothing." She herself may start to wonder if there is something psychologically wrong with her.

The Water Torturer is payback-oriented like most abusive men, but he may hide it better. If he is physically abusive, his violence may take the form of cold-hearted slaps "for your own good" or "to get you to wake up" rather than explosive rage. His moves appear carefully thought out, and he rarely makes obvious mistakes—such as letting his abusiveness show in public—that could turn other people against him or get him in legal trouble.

If you are involved with a Water Torturer, you may struggle for years trying to figure out what is happening. You may feel that you overreact to his behavior and that he isn't really so bad. But the effects of his control and contempt have crept up on you over the years. If you finally leave him, you may experience intense periods of delayed rage, as you become conscious of how quietly but deathly oppressive he was.

This style of man rarely lasts long in an abuser program unless he has a court order. He is so accustomed to having complete success with his tactics that he can't tolerate an environment where the counselors recognize and name his maneuvers and don't let him get away with them. He tends to rapidly decide that his group leaders are as crazy as his partner and heads for the door.

> **The central attitudes driving the Water Torturer are:**
>
> • You are crazy. You fly off the handle over nothing.
>
> • I can easily convince other people that you're the one who is messed up.
>
> • As long as I'm calm, you can't call anything I do abusive, no matter how cruel.
>
> • I know exactly how to get under your skin.

THE DRILL SERGEANT

The Drill Sergeant takes controlling behavior to its extreme, running his partner's life in every way that he can. He criticizes her clothing, tells her whether she can go out or not, interferes with her work. He wants her to have no one close to her, so he ruins her relationships with friends and relatives or simply forbids her to see them. He may listen to her phone calls or read her mail, or require the children to report on her activities any time he is away. If she isn't home by his appointed curfew at night, she is at risk for abuse. She feels like a little girl living with a tyrannical father, with no more freedom than an eight-year-old would have.

The Drill Sergeant is often fanatically jealous. He verbally assaults his partner with accusations that she is cheating on him or checking out other men and tosses crass and disturbing sexual terms into his tirades. He may augment his hateful remarks about his partner with hideous comments about females in general, such as, "All women are whores." The emotional experience of these verbal attacks can be similar to that of a sexual assault: The woman is left feeling violated, debased, and traumatized. At the same time, this style of abuser more often than not is out having affairs himself. It isn't fidelity he cares about; it's possession.

The Drill Sergeant is, unfortunately, almost sure to be physically violent sooner or later, probably beginning with threats and then eventually escalating to assault. If his partner stands up to him, such as by attempting to preserve any of her rights to freedom, his violence and threats are likely to escalate until she is hurt or terrified enough that she submits to his control. He is a risk to beat his partner up to the point of severe injury.

Getting away from the Drill Sergeant can be difficult. Since he monitors the woman's movements so closely, it is a challenge for her to get to a support group for abused women or to seek other kinds of support. Since he isolates her from people, she has to draw entirely on her own strength, and many days she may feel like she doesn't have much strength left. And since from time to time he is probably openly violent, she is forced to consider what the consequences of attempting to leave him could be, including whether he might try to kill her.

If your partner is a Drill Sergeant, your situation is a dangerous one. You may have to use some courage—as well as careful vigilance—to even get the opportunity to read this book. Perhaps you are hiding it under a mattress or reading it at someone else's house in quick bits. Don't give up. Many women have gone through this kind of captivity and have found a way to escape, even if it takes some time. The single most important thing to do is to seek opportunities to phone a hotline for abused women (see "Resources" in the back of this book). Call them to speak for five minutes if that's all you can safely do for now. Call every day if you can. The hot line is the beginning of the path to freedom.

You may be sorely tempted to have a secret affair, since your partner shows you so little kindness or tenderness. A positive sexual connection may be especially affirming for you, because of how sexually degrading the Drill Sergeant tends to be. But cheating on him can be deadly if he catches you. Consider holding off on seeing other men until you have gotten yourself safe.

The Drill Sergeant often has some psychological problems. Although mental health issues do not cause abusiveness, they can intensify a man's violent tendencies. If he sometimes seems to become convinced of things that are obviously not true, has trouble getting along with people in general, was severely abused or neglected as a child, or has other indications of mental illness, you need to take even greater caution.

To read more about dealing with dangerous abusers, see "The Terrorist" later in this chapter (p. 99) and "Leaving an Abuser Safely" in Chapter 9 (p. 225).

The central attitudes driving the Drill Sergeant are:

- I need to control your every move or you will do it wrong.

- I know the exact way that everything should be done.

- You shouldn't have anyone else—or any*thing* else—in your life besides me.

- I am going to watch you like a hawk to keep you from developing strength or independence.

- I love you more than anyone in the world, but you disgust me. (!!)

Mr. Sensitive

Mr. Sensitive appears to be the diametric opposite of the Drill Sergeant. He is soft-spoken, gentle, and supportive—when he isn't being abusive. He loves the language of feelings, openly sharing his insecurities, his fears, and his emotional injuries. He hugs other men. He may speak out about the absurdity of war or the need for men to "get in touch with their feminine side." Perhaps he attends a men's group or goes on men's retreats. Often he has participated extensively in therapy or twelve-step programs, or reads all the big self-help books, so he speaks the language of popular psychology and introspection. His vocabulary is sprinkled with jargon like *developing closeness, working out our issues,* and *facing up to hard things about myself.* He presents himself to women as an ally in the struggle against sex-role limitations. To some women, he seems like a dream come true.

So what's wrong with this picture? Nothing obvious yet. But this is exactly the problem: Mr. Sensitive wraps himself in one of the most persuasive covers a man can have. If you start to feel chronically mistreated by him, you are likely to assume that something is wrong with you, and if you complain about him to other people, they may think you must be spoiled: "You have the New Age man, what more do you want?"

The following dynamics are typical of a relationship with Mr. Sensitive and may help explain your feeling that something has gone awry:

1. You seem to be hurting his feelings constantly, though you aren't sure why, and he expects your attention to be focused endlessly on his emotional injuries. If you are in a bad mood one day and say something unfair or insensitive, it won't be enough for you to give him a sincere apology and accept responsibility. He'll go on and on about it, expecting you to grovel as if you had treated him with profound cruelty. (Notice the twist here: This is just what an abuser accuses his partner of doing to *him,* when all she is really looking for is a heartfelt "I'm sorry.")

2. When *your* feelings are hurt, on the other hand, he will insist on brushing over it quickly. He may give you a stream of pop-

psychology language ("Just let the feelings go through you, don't hold on to them so much," or "It's all in the attitude you take toward life," or "No one can hurt you unless you let them") to substitute for genuine support for your feelings, especially if you are upset about something *he* did. None of these philosophies applies when you upset him, however.

3. With the passing of time, he increasingly casts the blame on to you for anything he is dissatisfied with in his own life; your burden of guilt keeps growing.

4. He starts to exhibit a mean side that no one else ever sees and may even become threatening or intimidating.

Mr. Sensitive has the potential to turn physically frightening, as any style of abuser can, no matter how much he may preach nonviolence. After an aggressive incident, he will speak of his actions as "anger" rather than as "abuse," as though there were no difference between the two. He blames his assaultive behavior on you or on his emotional "issues," saying that his feelings were so deeply wounded that he had no other choice.

Many people reject the possibility that Mr. Sensitive could be an abuser. I ran into this disbelief one weekend when I was leading a training course on emotional recovery, as I periodically do. My workshops focus partly on the healing effects of crying and so tend to be attended by more women than men. The males who do come have included many of the most wonderful men it has been my good fortune to know, as well as a handful of the biggest manipulators. A few years ago, a participant named Deanna approached me anxiously before a workshop. She explained that an ex-partner of hers named Brad had called her a few days ahead of the workshop to tell her he was attending the same weekend. She was uncomfortable and told him that if he showed up she would leave. He promised not to bother her, though, and said he would not bring up their relationship in any way. He was coming with his new girlfriend, which eased Deanna's worries.

I spent some time talking with Brad as the workshop was starting, without mentioning Deanna, and he seemed likeable, kind, and—what can I say?—sensitive. However, I observed within a few hours that he was in fact speaking to other people about his past with Deanna and getting them riled up about her "running away from" their unresolved issues. On Sunday morning, he finally provoked a scene about their relationship in front of the full workshop, which was humiliating to Deanna.

The story does not end there. I called a break, and took Brad aside. I told him that it was my understanding that he had agreed not to raise these issues and that it had become obvious to me that he had come for the weekend with the intention of doing precisely what he had promised not to. I went on to point out that he had taken Deanna's weekend away from her and that I considered this kind of power move to be abuse, especially since it was directed at an ex-partner.

Saying the word *abuse* to an abusive person can be like lighting a tinderbox: When you name the unmentionable secret, he goes wild. Brad got loud, rolled his eyes at what a hysterical exaggerator he considered me to be, and adopted a victim stance, saying, "I *beg* you to stop this." Then came the most important part: He said in a screeching whine, "I have only put a hand on a partner once in my life, many years ago, and I just barely pushed her away from me like *this*"—and he shoved me hard by the shoulder—"after she called my mother a sick woman."

Well, why was Brad denying a history of assault (while actually admitting to one) when I hadn't said anything about violence? The possibility that he might be physically abusive had never occurred to me before, but it certainly did now. The signs were all there: bullying Deanna that weekend and then insisting it was for her own good; feeling entitled to ignore an important agreement; blaming his earlier girlfriend for his assault of her and minimizing it—the strength of the shove he gave me would have shaken up most women. I now doubted that the assaultive incident he had described was his only occasion of physically intimidating a woman.

At this point I required Brad to leave the workshop. I then had to deal with a mini-insurrection from some of the other workshop participants, who couldn't believe I was ejecting this gentle man who was so in touch with his feelings. He *cries* after all; how could he be abusive?

This "gentle man" style of abuser tends to be highly self-centered and demanding of emotional catering. He may not be the man who has a fit because dinner is late but rather erupts because of some way his partner failed to sacrifice her own needs or interests to keep him content. He plays up how fragile he is to divert attention from the swath of destruction he leaves behind him.

The central attitudes driving Mr. Sensitive are:

- I'm against the macho men, so I couldn't be abusive.

- As long as I use a lot of "psychobabble," no one is going to believe that I am mistreating you.

- I can control you by analyzing how your mind and emotions work, and what your issues are from childhood. I can get inside your head whether you want me there or not.

- Nothing in the world is more important than my feelings.

- Women should be grateful to me for not being like those other men.

THE PLAYER

The Player is usually good looking and often sexy. (But sometimes he just thinks he is.) In the early part of a relationship he seems head over heels in love and wants to spend as much time as possible in bed together. He is a pretty good lover. You may feel lucky that you have caught someone who knows how to turn you on and feel proud to be seen with him. Your self-opinion gets a nice boost.

After a while, though, a few things start to bother you. You notice that apart from sex his interest in you is waning, and even his sexual energy is dropping off a little. He seems to lock his eyes pretty hard onto women that walk by. He flirts with waitresses, clerks, or even friends of yours. Sexual undertones seem to run through most of his interactions with females, except for ones he finds completely unattractive. Rumors start to come back to you that he's been seen with this woman, that he is sleeping with that one, that he is pursuing another one but she isn't interested yet.

At first you discount these rumors as hurtful gossip, but after a while you start to wonder.

The Player often starts to stall on moving in together or agreeing to be exclusive, even though earlier he couldn't wait to get serious. He may say that he's been hurt or has a fear of commitment ("I'm just not ready"), but the real issue is that he doesn't want restrictions on his freedom. Much of his satisfaction in life comes from exploiting women and feeling like a sexual animal. Women around the Player seem to get angry *at each other* a lot, rather than at him, and sometimes get into physical confrontations. These tensions work out well for him, diverting attention from his infidelity and dishonesty. He sets up this dynamic with some combination of the following tactics:

1. He knows how to make each woman feel that she's the special one and yet at the same time keep her off balance, so that she never feels quite sure of where she stands with him.

2. He tells each one that the others are lying about their involvements with him because they are jealous of her, or because he turned them down, or because he used to be involved with them but isn't anymore.

3. He tells each one stories about how other women have mistreated him, or shares other bits of information—largely invented—to make previous, or current, women in his life sound conniving, vindictive, or addicted to substances.

4. He breaks up with women and gets back together with them, so that no one can keep track of what's going on.

5. He includes one or two women in his circle who feel unattractive, because he knows he can have more power over them, and manipulates them into hating the women who are seen as more attractive.

If this is your partner's style, you won't necessarily ever be sure whether he is really having sex with other women or if he just flirts because he enjoys the attention and likes you to feel threatened. He may hotly deny that he ever cheats and try to turn the tables by accusing you of being too suspicious. But even if he's telling the truth—which he probably isn't—his constant flirtatious behavior can be as damaging as actual affairs. Either way, he will damage your other relationships, because you will start to perceive any woman as a potential threat to you. If he has a history of hitting on women who are close to you, such as your sister or best friend, you can end up isolated from the women you care about most, because you're afraid he will have affairs with them unless you keep them away.

Chronic infidelity is abusive in itself, but the Player doesn't stop there. He is irresponsible, callous in dealing with his partner's feelings, and periodically verbally abusive. As the relationship progresses, he may start to go for long periods giving his partner next to no attention and barely speaking to her, so she feels shelved. He probably refuses to take responsibility for safe sex (such as using a condom), and he may have fathered children who he is not supporting. His abusiveness can escalate abruptly if he is confronted or caught in his infidelities, and he may turn physically frightening at this point. In a strange but dangerous twist, the Player sometimes hits his partner for catching *him* cheating rather than the reverse.

The Player's constant flirting and cheating help him to get away with other forms of mistreatment. His partner is likely to focus on her hurt feelings about his infidelities and pour effort into stopping him from straying and, in the process, lose sight of his pattern of abuse. When she asks me whether I think her partner will ever settle down and be faithful to her—if they get married, for example—I answer, "He may some day, but what you will have then is a faithful abuser." His promiscuity is a symptom of a deeper problem: He is incapable of taking women seriously as human beings rather than as playthings. With that mind-set, he'll be a destructive partner whether he cheats or not.

The Players I have worked with sometimes claim to suffer from "sex addiction," and join Sex and Love Addicts Anonymous (which they may discover is a good place to pick up women). But sex addiction doesn't cause dishonesty, verbal abusiveness, or intimidating behavior. The Player is not a sex addict at all. If he is addicted to anything, it's to the thrill of using women without regard for the effects on them.

The central attitudes driving the Player are:

- Women were put on this earth to have sex with men—especially me.

- Women who want sex are too loose, and women who refuse sex are too uptight. (!)

- It's not my fault that women find me irresistible. (This is a word-for-word quotation from a number of my clients.) It's not fair to expect me to refuse temptation when it's all around me; women seduce me sometimes, and I can't help it.

- If you act like you need anything from me, I am going to ignore you. I'm in this relationship when it's convenient for me and when I feel like it.

- Women who want the nonsexual aspects of themselves appreciated are bitches.

- If you could meet my sexual needs, I wouldn't have to turn to other women.

RAMBO

Rambo is aggressive with everybody, not just his partner. He gets a thrill out of the sensation of intimidating people and strives to handle all life situations by subtly or overtly creating fear. He has an exaggerated, stereotypical view of what a man is supposed to be, which goes hand in hand with seeing women as delicate, inferior, and in need of protection. Rambo often comes from a home or neighborhood where he was the target of violence himself and learned that the only way to feel safe is to be stronger, tougher, and less caring than everybody else. He has little patience for weakness, fragility, or indecision. Often he has a criminal record for violence, theft, drunk driving, or drug dealing.

Early in a relationship, Rambo is likely to be loving and kind to his partner, like most abusers. Because he lacks fear—or pretends to—he can make a woman feel safe and protected. This style of abuser can therefore be particularly appealing to a woman who comes from a violent home herself or to one *who is in the process of leaving another abusive relationship*. Rambo can make you feel as though his aggressiveness would never be directed toward you, because he loves you; he wishes to look after your safety as if you were his daughter. He enjoys the role of protector, feeling like a gallant knight. However, he lacks respect for women, and this disrespect, combined with his general violent tendencies, means that it is only a matter of time before he will be the one you need protection *from*.

Many highly "masculine" men are *not* Rambo. The notion that all macho men are likely to abuse women is based largely on class and ethnic prejudices, the same misconceptions that allow Mr. Sensitive or Mr. Right to skate by undetected. There are plenty of "tough guys" out there who are friendly to everyone and avoid aggressive interactions whenever possible but enjoy lifting weights, playing rough sports, hunting, and other aspects of stereotypical masculinity. They may be good fighters, but only in self-defense. It isn't macho that women need to watch out for. The danger signs are violence and intimidation toward anyone, and disrespect and superiority toward women.

Sometimes Rambo is a psychopath or sociopath, which can make him all the more emotionally abusive and in some cases physically abusive as well. Later we will take a look at psychopaths and other mentally disordered abusers.

The central attitudes driving Rambo are:

- Strength and aggressiveness are good; compassion and conflict resolution are bad.

- Anything that could be even remotely associated with homosexuality, including walking away from possible violence or showing any fear or grief, has to be avoided at any cost.

- Femaleness and femininity (which he associates with homosexuality) are inferior. Women are here to serve men and be protected by them.

- Men should never hit women, because it is unmanly to do so. However, exceptions to this rule can be made for my own partner if her behavior is bad enough. Men need to keep their women in line.

- You are a thing that belongs to me, akin to a trophy.

THE VICTIM

Life has been hard and unfair for the Victim. To hear him tell it, his intelligence has been chronically underestimated; he has been burned by people he trusted; and his good intentions have been misunderstood. The Victim appeals to a woman's compassion and desire to feel that she can make a difference in his life. He often tells persuasive and heart-rending stories about how he was abused by his former partner, sometimes adding the tragic element that she is now restricting or preventing his contact with his children. He maneuvers the woman into hating his ex-partner and may succeed in enlisting her in a campaign of harassment, rumor spreading, or battling for custody.

As a counselor of abusive men, I have dozens of times been in the position of interviewing a man's former partner and then speaking with the new one. The new partner usually speaks at length about what a wicked witch the woman before her was. I can't tell her what I know, much as I wish I could, because of my responsibility to protect the confidentiality and safety of the former partner. All I can say is: "I always recommend, *whenever* there are claims of emotional or physical abuse, that women talk to each other directly and not just accept the man's denial."

Women sometimes ask me: "But what if a man I am dating really was victimized by his former girlfriend? How can I tell the difference?" Here are some things to watch for:

1. If you listen carefully, you often can hear the difference between *anger* toward an ex-partner, which would not be worrisome in itself, and *disrespect* or *contempt*, which should raise warning flags. A man who has left a relationship with bitterness should nonetheless be able to talk about his ex-partner as a human being, with some understanding of what her side of the conflicts was and some ways he might have contributed to what went wrong. If he speaks in degrading or superior ways about her, or makes everything that went wrong in the relationship her fault, be careful, because it is likely that he was the abusive one.

2. Try to get him to talk about his own conduct in the relationship, especially around the time of the breakup. If he blames his own behavior on her, that's a bad sign.

3. Be particularly careful with a man who claims to have been the victim of physical violence by a previous female partner. The great majority of men who make such claims are physical abusers. Ask him for as much detail as you can about the violent incidents, and then try to talk to her or seek out anyone else who could give you a different perspective on what happened. Watch for warning signs of abusiveness (see Chapter 5).

4. Pay attention to how he talks and thinks about abused women. A genuine male victim tends to feel sympathy for abused women and support their cause. The Victim, on the other hand, often says that women exaggerate or fabricate their claims of abuse or insists that men are abused just as much as women are.

The Victim may adopt the language of abuse victims, claiming, for example, that his ex-partner was "focused on power and control," disrespected him, and always had to have her own way. In a few years, he will be using similar reality-inversion language about you—unless, of course, you kowtow to him to his satisfaction.

The Victim is highly self-centered in relationships. Everything seems to revolve around his wounds, and he keeps himself at the center of attention. If you have children, he tries to get them to feel sorry for him as well.

He seems forever to be telling you: "You don't understand me, you don't appreciate me, you hold my mistakes over my head." Yet you sense that the dynamic is actually the other way around. If you stand up to him about these distortions, he tells you that you are abusing him or says, "You just can't tolerate my standing up to your bullying." This recurring inversion of reality is similar to what happens with Mr. Sensitive, but without the introspective psychology, gentle man, or recovering alcoholic routines. If you leave him, you risk his seeking custody of your children, presenting himself to the court as the victim of your abuse and of your efforts to turn the children against him.

Often the Victim claims to be victimized not only by you but also by his boss, his parents, the neighbors, his friends, and strangers on the street. Everyone is always wronging him, and he is always blameless.

When the Victim joins an abuser group, his story tends to go like this: "I put up with my partner's mistreatment of me for years, and I never fought back or even tried to defend myself. But I finally couldn't take it anymore, and I started to give her back a little taste of what she was doing to me. So now I've been labeled abusive. Women are allowed to do those things and nobody cares, but as soon as a man does it he's a pariah."

This line of reasoning many times develops into a discussion of how men are the victims of women *overall* in society, because women run the world. This is a startling distortion, given which gender actually dominates almost all legislatures, police departments, judgeships, businesses, and so on ad nauseam. When I point out this reality to the Victim, he describes a kind of paranoid fantasy in which women are behind the scenes secretly pulling the strings, largely by getting men to feel sorry for them. His capacity for turning things into their opposites in this way is a central cause of his abusiveness.

If you are involved with the Victim and want to escape his abuse, you may find that you feel guilty toward *him,* despite his treatment of you, and have difficulty ending the relationship as a result. You may feel that because his life has been so hard, you are reluctant to add to his pain by abandoning him. You may worry that he won't take care of himself if you leave, that he will wither away from depression, won't eat or sleep, or might even try to kill himself. The Victim knows how to present himself as helpless and pathetic so that you will find it harder to take your own life back.

The central attitudes driving the Victim are:

- Everybody has done me wrong, especially the women I've been involved with. Poor me.

- When you accuse me of being abusive, you are joining the parade of people who have been cruel and unfair to me. It proves you're just like the rest.

- It's justifiable for me to do to you whatever I feel you are doing to me, and even to make it quite a bit worse to make sure you get the message.

- Women who complain of mistreatment by men, such as relationship abuse or sexual harassment, are anti-male and out for blood.

- I've had it so hard that I'm not responsible for my actions.

THE TERRORIST

I worked for a few months with an abused woman named Gloria who was wondering how much longer she would be alive. Her husband, Gerald, would glare at her, drum his fingers methodically on the table, and say: "You have six months left. Things better shape up around here. Six months." Her head would swim and her heart would race with fear, and she would plead with him to tell what exactly he planned to do to her at the end of that period. And he would answer, with maybe just a hint of a cold smile: "Just wait and see, just wait and see. Six months, Gloria." Gerald had never laid a hand on Gloria in the five years they had been together, but she was terrified. She started working with me on making an escape plan to run away with their two-year-old son.

The Terrorist tends to be both highly controlling and extremely demanding. His worst aspect, however, is that he frequently reminds his partner that he could physically rip her to pieces or even kill her. He doesn't necessarily beat her, however; some abusers know how to terrorize their partners with threats, strange veiled statements, and bizarre behaviors. One of my violent clients cut an article out of the newspaper about a woman who had been murdered by her husband, and he taped it up on the refrigerator. Another man responded to his partner's announcement that she was leaving him by spilling the blood of an animal in front of the house. Another client would take out his gun when he was angry at his partner but would insist that he was just going to clean it and that it had nothing to do with her.

Unlike most other abusers, the Terrorist often seems to be sadistic: He gets enjoyment out of causing pain and fear and seems to find cruelty thrilling. He is likely to have been severely abused as a child, which generally is not true of other abusers. However, *you cannot help him to heal.* This may be difficult to accept, since the hope of helping him overcome his problems may be what gets you through the terror of living with him. The Terrorist's problems are much too deep for a partner to solve, as they involve a complex weave of serious psychological problems with the typical destructive nature of an abuser. You need to focus instead on getting yourself safe. The Terrorist's top goal is to paralyze you with fear so that you won't dare think of leaving him or cheating on him. The great majority of abusers who make lethal threats against their partners never carry them out, but that still leaves many who do. The trauma of living with this kind of terror can be profound and can make it extremely difficult for you to think clearly about strategies for escaping to safety. However, *most women **do** manage to get out.* The critical first step is to seek confidential help as soon as possible. Begin by calling an abuse hotline as soon as you safely can (see "Resources"). There are more suggestions in Chapter 9.

When a woman does leave the Terrorist, he may stalk or threaten her, and this dangerous harassment can continue for a long time. If the couple has children, he may attempt to get custody or unsupervised visitation, so that he can terrorize or control her through the children. He also may use information he has about her, such as where she works or where her parents live, to track her and to threaten her loved ones. *It is essential that friends, relatives, courts, and communities understand the realities of these risks and give the woman the most complete support and protection possible, while simultaneously taking steps to hold the abuser accountable.* It may be possible to stop the Terrorist from escalating to murder, but only if he gets a strong message that stalking and threatening an ex-partner is unacceptable, that he is responsible for his own actions, and that the community is prepared to jail him if his threatening behavior does not stop immediately. Actions short of these are often insufficient.

Chapter 10 contains more information for a woman who is involved in a custody or visitation battle with an abuser or for those who are concerned that one may start.

The central attitudes driving the Terrorist are:

- You have no right to defy me or leave me. Your life is in my hands.

- Women are evil and have to be kept terrorized to prevent that evil from coming forth.

- I would rather die than accept your right to independence.

- The children are one of the best tools I can use to make you fearful.

- Seeing you terrified is exciting and satisfying.

THE MENTALLY ILL OR ADDICTED ABUSER

This last category is not actually separate from the others; an abusive man of any of the aforementioned styles can also have psychiatric or substance-abuse problems, although the majority do not. Even when mental illness or addiction is a factor, it is not the *cause* of a man's abuse of his partner, but it can contribute to the severity of his problem and his resistance to change. When these additional problems are present, it is important to be aware of the following points:

1. Certain mental illnesses can increase the chance that an abuser will be dangerous and use physical violence. These include paranoia, severe depression, delusions or hallucinations (psychosis), obsessive-compulsive disorder, and antisocial personality disorder (known as psychopathy or sociopathy). These psychiatric conditions also make it next to impossible for an abuser to change, at least until the mental illness has been brought under control through therapy and/or medication, which can take years. Even if the mental illness is properly treated, his *abusiveness* won't necessarily change.

2. An abuser's reactions to going on or off medication are unpredictable. A woman should take extra precautions for her safety at such a time. Abusers tend to go off medication before long—I have had few clients who were consistent and responsible about taking their meds in the long term. They don't like the side effects, and they are too selfish to care about the implications of the mental illness for their partners or children.

3. The potential danger of a mentally ill abuser has to be assessed by looking at the severity of his psychiatric symptoms *in combination with* the severity of his abuse characteristics. Looking at his psychiatric symptoms alone can lead to underestimating how dangerous he is.

4. Antisocial personality disorder is present in only a small percentage of abusers but can be important. Those who suffer from this condition lack a conscience and thus are repeatedly involved in behaviors that are harmful to others. Some signs of this condition include: (a) He started getting into illegal behavior when he was still a teenager; (b) his dishonest or aggressive behavior involves situations unrelated to his partner, rather than being restricted to her; (c) he periodically gets into trouble at workplaces or in other contexts for stealing, threatening, or refusing to follow instructions and is likely to have a considerable criminal record by about age thirty, though the offenses may be largely minor ones; (d) he is severely and chronically irresponsible in a way that disrupts the

lives of others or creates danger; and (e) he tends to cheat on women a lot, turn them against each other, and maintain shallow relationships with them. The psychopath's physical violence is not necessarily severe, contrary to the popular image, but he may be very dangerous nonetheless. Antisocial personality disorder is very difficult to change through therapy, and there is no effective medication for treating it. It is highly compatible with abusiveness toward women.

5. Those who suffer from narcissistic personality disorder have a highly distorted self-image. They are unable to accept that they might have faults and therefore are unable to imagine how other people perceive them. This condition is highly compatible with abusiveness, though it is present in only a small percentage of abusive men. Clues to the presence of this disorder include: (a) Your partner's self-centeredness is severe, and it carries over into situations that don't involve you; (b) he seems to relate everything back to himself; and (c) he is outraged whenever anyone criticizes him and is incapable of considering that he could ever be anything other than kind and generous. This disorder is highly resistant to therapy and is not treatable with medication. The abuser with this disorder is not able to change substantially through an abuser program either, although he sometimes makes some minor improvements.

6. Many abusers who are not mentally ill want women to think that they are, in order to avoid responsibility for their attitudes and behavior.

Substance abuse, like mental illness, does not cause partner abuse but can increase the risk of violence. Like the mentally ill abuser, the addicted abuser doesn't change unless he deals with his addiction, and even that is only the first step. Chapter 8 examines the role that substances play in partner abuse.

The attitudes driving the mentally ill or addicted batterer are the same as those of other abusers and will likely follow the pattern of one of the nine styles described above. In addition, the following attitudes tend to be present:

> • I am not responsible for my actions because of my psychological or substance problems.
>
> • If you challenge me about my abusiveness, you are being mean to me, considering these other problems I have. It also shows that you don't understand my other problems.
>
> • I'm not abusive, I'm just ____ (alcoholic, drug addicted, manic-depressive, an adult child of alcoholics, or whatever his condition may be).
>
> • If you challenge me, it will trigger my addiction or mental illness, and you'll be responsible for what I do.

Although I have focused on the emotionally abusive styles of these different kinds of abusers, any of them may also use physical violence, including sexual assault. Although the Terrorist and the Drill Sergeant are especially likely to become dangerous, they are not the only ones who may do so. Many abusers occasionally use physical violence or threats as a way to intimidate you when they feel that their power or control over you is slipping; violence for them is a kind of "trump card" they use when their normal patterns of psychological abuse are not getting them the degree of control they feel entitled to. If you are concerned about how dangerous your partner may be, see "Is He Going to Get Violent?" in Chapter 6 and "Leaving an Abuser Safely" in Chapter 9.

KEY POINTS TO REMEMBER

• Tremendous variation exists among abusive styles. Your abusive partner may be of a type I haven't encountered yet, but that doesn't make him any less real. Many men are mixtures of different aspects.

- An abuser may change so much from day to day that he couldn't belong to *any* type. This style of abuser is so unpredictable that his partner can never make sense out of what she is living with.

- An abuser of any type can have days when he turns loving, attentive, and thoughtful. At these times, you may feel that his problem has finally gone away and that the relationship will return to its rosy beginning. However, abuse always comes back eventually unless the abuser has dealt with his abusiveness.

The Abusive
Man in
Relationships

5

How Abuse Begins

I don't understand what's gone wrong. We used to be so close.

I don't know if there's something wrong with him or if it's me.

He really cares for me. He wants to spend every second together.

My friends complain that they never see me anymore.

"THE GARDEN OF EDEN"—that's what I call the beginning of a relationship with an abuser. For the first few weeks or months, or longer, the woman is walking on air. Remember Kristen and Maury, whom we met in Chapter 1? Maury was dazzling—entertaining, interesting, energetic—and Kristen was smitten. One of the things she liked most about him was how crazy he was about *her*. He pursued her avidly, seemed to like everything about her, and couldn't get enough. She felt as though she had stepped into a top-40 love song, the kind where "Everything Is Perfect Now That I've Met You." This pattern is common in abusive relationships; an abusive man is often unusually good at expressing an intensity of caring early in a relationship and can make you feel *so* special and chosen—as if you were the only person who could ever matter so much to him.

Not every abusive man falls head over heels so quickly the way Maury did. Fran, whom we also got to know in Chapter 1, was quiet and withdrawn early on, and Barbara was the pursuer. She was drawn powerfully to him because of his sweetness and sensitivity and for the challenge of drawing him out. What a triumph it was when she finally got him to open up and then won him over! Sadness and mistrust were gnawing at his heart, she could see that, but she saw herself healing him, like a tender nurse. She was excited by her confident belief that she could bring out the person he was capable of being.

The idyllic opening is part of almost every abusive relationship. How else would an abuser ever have a partner? Women aren't stupid. If you go out to a restaurant on a giddy first date and over dessert the man calls you a "selfish bitch" and sends your water glass flying across the room, you don't say: "Hey, are you free again next weekend?" There has to be a hook. Very few women hate themselves so thoroughly that they will get involved with a man who is rotten from the very start—although they may feel terrible about themselves *later*, once the abuser has had time to destroy their self-image step by step.

THE POWER OF THOSE WONDERFUL EARLY MONTHS

The partners of my clients have described to me the many ways in which the glowing beginning of a relationship with an abusive man can serve to entrap a woman, including:

- Like any love-struck person, she runs around telling her friends and family what a terrific guy he is. After talking him up so much, she feels embarrassed to reveal his mistreatment when it begins, so she keeps it to herself for a long time.

- She assumes that his abusiveness comes from something that has gone wrong inside of him—what else is she to conclude, given how wonderful he was at first?—so she pours herself into figuring out what happened.

- She has a hard time letting go of her own dream, since she thought she had found a wonderful man.

- She can't help wondering if she did something wrong or has some great personal deficit that knocked down their castle in the sky, so she tries to find the key to the problem inside of herself.

QUESTION 7:
WHEN HE IS SO GOOD EARLY ON,
IS HE PLANNING TO BE ABUSIVE LATER?

One of the questions about abuse that I am asked most frequently is: When an abusive man is being charming at the beginning of a relationship, is he already thinking ahead to abusing the woman? Does he have it all planned out? Is he deliberately hooking her emotionally so he can be cruel to her later? The answer is usually no. The abuser doesn't picture himself yelling, degrading her, or hurling objects at her. As he falls in love, he dreams of a happy future of conjugal bliss, just as the woman does.

So, if he isn't laying plans to hurt her, what *is* going on in his mind? First, he is gazing longingly at the image he holds of the future, where the woman meets all of his needs, is beautiful and sexy at all times of the day and night, has no needs of her own, and is in awe of his brilliance and charm. He desires a woman who will cater to him and never complain about anything he does or darken his day with frustrations or unhappiness about her own life.

The abusive man doesn't expose these self-focused fantasies to his new partner. In fact, he is largely unaware of them himself. So she has no way of knowing that he is looking more for a personal caretaker than for a partner. In fact, abusers tend to use the language of mutuality during the dating period:

"We are going to be really good for each other."

"I want to be with you all the time."

"I really want to be there for you."

"You can stop working for now so that you can finish school, and we can live off of my income."

"I'll help you study for that medical assistant exam, so that you can get that promotion."

He may truly believe his own promises, because he wants to see himself as a generous and thoughtful partner, one who does not use or disrespect women. Later, when he begins to control the woman and take advantage of her, he will find ways to convince himself that it's not happening or that it is her fault. Abuse is not his goal, but *control* is, and he finds himself using abuse to gain the control he feels he has a right to.

On the other hand, a certain number of my clients are consciously manipulative from the outset. A man of this style smiles knowingly at me, assuming that every man uses the same ploys, and says, "Of course you have to charm the ladies and listen to them blabber on and on, they like that. You talk the nice talk a little, you take them dancing. You know how it is." But even this man is generally not calculating to abuse the woman later. He creates the kind of relationship he wants through charm and dishonesty and expects to continue in that mode for good. Manipulation feels clean and satisfying to this style of abuser, while degrading language and physical intimidation do not. When he does start to tear her down or frighten her later, he will blame it on her, probably thinking of her as a "bitch" for not allowing him to lie and manipulate his way through life. And he doesn't consider manipulation abusive.

An Abuser Is Neither a Monster Nor a Victim

We arrive now at two of the most important concepts regarding abusive men. First:

An abuser is a human being, not an evil monster, but he has a profoundly complex and destructive problem that should not be underestimated.

The common view of abusive men as evil, calculating brutes can make it difficult for a woman to recognize her partner's problem. She tends to think: *My partner really cares about me and has a good side to him. He has feelings; he's not a sadist. He couldn't be an abuser.* She doesn't realize that he can have all these positive qualities and still have an abuse problem.

At the other end of the spectrum we find an equally common—and equally misleading—view of abusers: the abuser as a man whose gentle humanity is just barely hidden under his abusive surface and who can be transformed by love, compassion, and insight. One morning he will wake up to realize how hurtful he has been and will renounce his cruelty, particularly if he has the love of a good woman. This outlook is portrayed and supported in popular songs, movies, romantic novels, and soap operas. The painful reality is that bringing about change in abusers is difficult. An abusive man has to bury his compassion in a deep hole in order to escape the profound inherent aversion that human beings have to seeing others suffer. He has to adhere tightly to his excuses and rationalizations, develop a disturbing ability to insulate himself from the pain he is causing, and learn to enjoy power and control over his female partners. It is unrealistic to expect such a complex structure, one that takes fifteen or twenty years to form, to vanish like steam. Yet women are often pressured by friends, family, or professionals to "give him a chance to change" and "have a little faith in people."

The second critical understanding is:

AN ABUSER'S BEHAVIOR IS PRIMARILY CONSCIOUS—
HE ACTS DELIBERATELY RATHER THAN BY ACCIDENT OR BY
LOSING CONTROL OF HIMSELF—BUT THE UNDERLYING THINKING
THAT DRIVES HIS BEHAVIOR IS LARGELY NOT CONSCIOUS.

An abuser learns manipulative and controlling behavior from several sources, including key male role models, peers, and pervasive cultural messages (see Chapter 13). By the time he reaches adulthood, he has integrated manipulative behavior to such a deep level that he acts largely on automatic. He knows what he is doing but not necessarily why. Consider the following call I received from Kelsea, the partner of a client:

> Lance wanted me to go skiing with him this weekend, but I really didn't feel like it because I'd had an exhausting week and wanted to spend time with my friends. When I said no, he dove into criticizing me. He said the reason why I've never become a good skier is that I won't stick with it, that I'm not willing to give things a chance and work at them, that I'm lazy and that's why I never get good at anything, and so forth. It felt awful . . . But, you know, I think in a way he's right—maybe I should be more disciplined about learning to ski.

Where was Lance's stream of put-downs coming from? Was he really concerned that Kelsea was letting herself down? No. A man doesn't tear down his partner's self-esteem out of a desire to help her. The real issue concerned what Lance wanted for himself: He wanted Kelsea to keep him company for the weekend because he didn't feel like going skiing alone. He resented her choice to make her friendships central in her life—a common theme with abusive men—and believed that it was her duty to be by his side and focus on him. He was hammering her with whatever put-downs he could think of in order to bully her into going (and was having some success in getting her to doubt herself). When some members of his abuser group challenged him about his behaviors at his next session, his real motives and attitudes became apparent; much of my work as a counselor involves helping abusive men to become conscious of, and face up to, their real reasons for choosing to behave as they do.

EARLY WARNING SIGNS

When women hear how charming abusers can be—or when they experience it directly—they feel at a loss. They ask, "Does this mean there is no way to avoid an abusive relationship? How can I tell whether I should worry about my new partner?" Fortunately, most abusers put out warning signals before their abuse goes into full gear. The signs to watch for should be part of every girl's education before she starts dating.

QUESTION 8:
HOW CAN I TELL IF A MAN I'M SEEING WILL BECOME ABUSIVE?

The following warning flags mean that abuse could be down the road, and perhaps not far:

• *He speaks disrespectfully about his former partners.*

A certain amount of anger and resentment toward an ex-partner is normal, but beware of the man who is very focused on his bitterness or who tells you about it inappropriately early on in your dating. Be especially cautious of the man who talks about women from his past in degrading or condescending ways or who characterizes himself as a victim of abuse by women. Be alert if he says that his previous wife or girlfriend falsely accused him of being abusive; the great majority of reports of abuse are accurate. When you hear that another woman considers him abusive, *always* find a way to get her side of the story. Even if you end up not believing her, you will at least know the behaviors to watch out for in him, just in case. Be cautious also of the man who admits to abusing a former partner but claims that the circumstances were exceptional, blames it on her, or blames it on alcohol or immaturity.

Be cautious of the man who says that you are nothing like the other women he has been involved with, that you are the first partner to treat him well, or that earlier women in his life have not understood him. You will be tempted to work doubly hard to prove that you aren't like those other women, and one foot will already be in the trap. It won't be long before he is telling you that you are "just like the rest of them." His perceptual system ensures that no woman can be a good woman while she is involved with him.

A few men have the opposite approach, which is to glorify and elevate their former partners so that you feel like you can never quite compete. If he starts to lament the fact that you aren't as sexy, athletic, domestic, or successful as the women who went before you, I can assure you that you won't measure up any better later, no matter how hard you try. He wants to feel one up on you so that he can have the upper hand.

Notice whether he seems to accept any responsibility for what went wrong in his previous relationships. If everything was always the women's fault, you will soon be to blame for all difficulties in this new relationship.

- *He is disrespectful toward you.*

Disrespect is the soil in which abuse grows. If a man puts you down or sneers at your opinions, if he is rude to you in front of other people, if he is cutting or sarcastic, he is communicating a lack of respect. If these kinds of behaviors are a recurring problem, or if he defends them when you complain about how they affect you, control and abuse are likely to be in the offing. Disrespect also can take the form of idealizing you and putting you on a pedestal as a perfect woman or goddess, perhaps treating you like a piece of fine china. The man who worships you in this way is not seeing *you*; he is seeing his fantasy, and when you fail to live up to that image he may turn nasty. So there may not be much difference between the man who talks down to you and the one who elevates you; both are displaying a failure to respect you as a real human being and bode ill.

- *He does favors for you that you don't want or puts on such a show of generosity that it makes you uncomfortable.*

These can be signs of a man who is attempting to create a sense of indebtedness. My client Alan, for example, spent much of his first two years with Tory helping her brother fix his car, helping her sister paint her new apartment, and transporting her father to medical appointments. When Tory's family started to become upset about how Alan was treating her, Alan was able to convince her that her relatives had taken advantage of him and were now turning against him unfairly. He said, "Now that they don't need my help anymore they want to get me out of the way so they can have you to themselves." Alan succeeded in getting Tory to feel sorry for him, thereby driving a wedge between her and her family that endured for years until she saw through Alan's manipulation.

A man named Robert combined these first two warning signs: He told Lana that his ex-wife had falsely accused him of violence in order to keep him from seeing his boys. He said, "If a woman tells the family court that she wants the father's visits to be supervised, they give it to her automatically." Lana's heart naturally went out to him. But two things happened that made her uneasy. First, Robert called after a snowstorm and offered to shovel her driveway. She said, "Oh, please don't," because she wasn't sure how serious she felt about him and didn't want to lead him on. When she got off the train from work that afternoon, she found her driveway completely cleared. Second, Lana happened by coincidence to have a female friend who was divorcing an abuser, and she learned from her friend that the family court required extensive evidence of violence in order to consider imposing supervised visitation on the father. She found herself wondering what Robert's ex-wife might have to say.

- *He is controlling.*

At first it can be exciting to be with a man who takes charge. Here's a typical story from the partner of one of my clients:

Our first few dates were exciting and fun. I remember him arriving at my house with our evening all planned out. He'd say, "We're going to the Parker House for a drink, then we're having a Chinese dinner, and then I've got tickets for a comedy club." It would all have to go according to plan. At first I loved the way he would design what he wanted to do with me. But then I started to notice that he rarely considered what *I* might want to do. We kept going out to things that he enjoys, like hockey games. I enjoy the hockey games, too, but it's not my top interest. And after a few months, he started to get annoyed if I wasn't in the mood to do what he wanted.

Control usually begins in subtle ways, far from anything you would call abuse. He drops comments about your clothes or your looks (too sexy or not sexy enough); is a little negative about your family or one of your good friends; starts to pressure you to spend more time with him or to quit your job or to get a better job that pays more; starts to give too much advice about how you should manage your own life and shows a hint of impatience when you resist his recommendations; or begins to act bothered that you don't share all of his opinions about politics, personal relationships, music, or other tastes.

• *He is possessive.*

Jealous behavior is one of the surest signs that abuse is down the road. Possessiveness masquerades as love. A man may say: "I'm sorry I got so bent out of shape about you talking to your ex-boyfriend, but I've never been so crazy about a woman before. I just can't stand thinking of you with another man." He may call five times a day keeping track of what you are doing all the time or insist on spending every evening with you. His feelings for you probably *are* powerful, but that's not why he wants constant contact; he is keeping tabs on you, essentially establishing that you are his domain. Depending on what kind of friends he has, he also may be trying to impress them with how well he has you under his thumb. All of these behaviors are about *ownership,* not love.

Jealous *feelings* are not the same as behaviors. A man with some insecurities may naturally feel anxious about your associations with other men, especially ex-partners, and might want some reassurance. But if he indicates that he expects you to give up your freedom to accommodate his jealousy, control is creeping up. Your social life shouldn't have to change because of his insecurities.

A man's jealousy can be flattering. It feels great that he is wildly in love with you, that he wants you so badly. But a man can be crazy about you without being jealous. Possessiveness shows that he doesn't love you as an independent human being but rather as a guarded treasure. After a while, you will feel suffocated by his constant vigilance.

• *Nothing is ever his fault.*

He blames something or someone for anything that goes wrong. As time goes by, the target of his blame increasingly becomes you. This style of man also tends to make promises that he doesn't keep, coming up with a steady stream of excuses for disappointing you or behaving irresponsibly, and perhaps taking serious economic advantage of you in the process.

• *He is self-centered.*

In the first few months of a relationship, the abuser's self-centeredness is not always apparent, but there are symptoms you can watch for. Notice whether he does a lot more than his share of the talking, listens poorly when you speak, and chronically shifts the topic of conversation back to himself. Self-centeredness is a personality characteristic that is highly resistant to change, as it has deep roots in either profound entitlement (in abusers) or to severe early emotional injuries (in nonabusers), or both (in narcissistic abusers).

• *He abuses drugs or alcohol.*

Be especially careful if he pressures you to participate in substance use with him. Although substances do not cause partner abuse, they often go hand in hand. He may try to hook you into believing that you can help him get clean and sober; substance abusers are often "just about" to quit.

• *He pressures you for sex.*

This warning sign is always important, but even more so for teenagers and young adult men. Not respecting your wishes or feelings regarding sex speaks of exploitativeness, which in turn goes with abuse. It also is a sign of seeing women as sex objects rather than human beings. If he says you need to have sex with him to prove that you truly love and care for him, give him his walking papers.

• *He gets serious too quickly about the relationship.*

Because so many men are commitment-phobic, a woman can feel relieved to find a partner who isn't afraid to talk about marriage and family. But watch out if he jumps too soon into planning your future together without taking enough time to get to know you and grow close, because it can mean that he's trying to wrap you up tightly into a package that he can own. Take steps to slow things down a little. If he won't respect your wishes in this regard, there is probably trouble ahead.

• *He intimidates you when he's angry.*

Intimidation, even if it appears unintentional, is a sign that emotional abuse is on the way—or has already begun—and is a warning flag that physical violence may eventually follow. Any of the following behaviors should put you on alert:

- He gets too close to you when he's angry, puts a finger in your face, pokes you, pushes you, blocks your way, or restrains you.

- He tells you that he is "just trying to make you listen."

- He raises a fist, towers over you, shouts you down, or behaves in any other way that makes you flinch or feel afraid.

- He makes vaguely threatening comments, such as, "You don't want to see me mad" or "You don't know who you're messing with."

- He drives recklessly or speeds up when he's angry.

- He punches walls or kicks doors.

- He throws things around, even if they don't hit you.

The more deeply involved you become with an intimidating man, the more difficult it will be to get out of the relationship. Unfortunately, many women believe just the opposite: They think, *Well, he does scare me a little sometimes, but I'll wait and see if it gets worse, and I'll leave him if it does.* But getting away from someone who has become frightening is much more complicated than most people realize, and it gets harder with each day that passes. Don't wait around to see.

- *He has double standards.*

Beware of the man who has a different set of rules for his behavior than for yours. Double standards are an important aspect of life with an abuser, as we will see in Chapter 6.

- *He has negative attitudes toward women.*

A man may claim early in a relationship that he views you in a light different from that in which he sees women in general, but the distinction won't last. If you are a woman, why be involved with someone who sees women as inferior, stupid, conniving, or only good for sex? He isn't going to forget for long that you're a woman.

Stereotyped beliefs about women's sex roles also contribute to the risk of abuse. His conviction that women should take care of the home, or that a man's career is more important than a woman's, can become a serious problem, because he may punish you when you start refusing to live in his box. Women sometimes find it challenging to meet men who *don't* have restrictive beliefs about women's roles, particularly within certain cultural or national groups, but the effort to meet such men is an important one.

- *He treats you differently around other people.*

Adult abusers tend to put on a show of treating their partners like gold when anyone is watching, reserving most of their abuse for times when no one else will see. In teenage abusers the opposite is often true. He may be rude and cold with her in front of other people to impress his friends with how "in control" and "cool" he is but be somewhat nicer when they are alone together.

- *He appears to be attracted to vulnerability.*

One way that this warning sign manifests itself is in cases of men who are attracted to women (or girls) who are much younger than they are. Why, for example, does a twenty-two-year-old man pursue a sixteen-year-old adolescent? Because he is stimulated and challenged by her? Obviously not. They are at completely different developmental points in life with a dramatic imbalance in their levels of knowledge and experience. He is attracted to *power* and seeks a partner who will look up to him with awe and allow him to lead her. Of course, he usually tells her the opposite, insisting that he wants to be with her because of how unusually mature and sophisticated she is for her age. He may even compliment her on her sexual prowess and say how much power she has over *him,* setting up the young victim so that she won't recognize what is happening to her. Even without a chronological age difference, some abusive men are drawn to women who have less life experience, knowledge, or self-confidence, and who will look up to the man as a teacher or mentor.

I have had quite a number of clients over the years who are attracted to women who are vulnerable because of recent traumatic experiences in their lives, including many who have started relationships by helping a woman break away from an abusive partner and then start to control or abuse her themselves. Some abusive men seek out a woman who comes from a troubled or abusive childhood, who has health problems, or who has suffered a recent severe loss, and present themselves as rescuers. Be alert for the man who seems to be attracted to power imbalances.

At the same time, I have observed that there are plenty of abusive men who are *not* particularly attracted to vulnerability or neediness in women and who are more drawn to tougher or more successful women. This style of abuser appears to feel that he has caught a bigger fish if he can reel in an accomplished, self-confident woman to dominate.

THE WARNING SIGNS OF ABUSE

He speaks disrespectfully about his former partners.

He is disrespectful toward you.

He does favors for you that you don't want or puts on such a show of generosity that it makes you uncomfortable.

He is controlling.

He is possessive.

Nothing is ever his fault.

He is self-centered.

He abuses drugs or alcohol.

He pressures you for sex.

He gets serious too quickly about the relationship.

He intimidates you when he's angry.

He has double standards.

He has negative attitudes toward women.

He treats you differently around other people.

He appears to be attracted to vulnerability.

No single one of the warning signs above is a sure sign of an abusive man, with the exception of physical intimidation. Many nonabusive men may exhibit a number of these behaviors to a limited degree. What, then, should a woman do to protect herself from having a relationship turn abusive?

Although there is no foolproof solution, the best plan is:

1. Make it clear to him *as soon as possible* which behaviors or attitudes are unacceptable to you and that you cannot be in a relationship with him if they continue.

2. If it happens again, stop seeing him for a substantial period of time. *Don't* keep seeing him with the warning that this time you "really mean it," because he will probably interpret that to mean that you don't.

3. If it happens a third time, or if he switches to other behaviors that are warning flags, chances are great that he has an abuse problem. If you give him too many chances, you are likely to regret it later. For further suggestions, see "Leaving an Abuser as a Way to Promote Change" in Chapter 14.

Finally, be aware that as an abuser begins his slide into abuse, he believes that *you* are the one who is changing. His perceptions work this way because he feels so justified in his actions that he can't imagine the problem might be with him. All he notices is that you don't seem to be living up to his image of the perfect, all-giving, deferential woman.

WHEN IS IT ABUSE?

Since abuse can sneak up on a woman, beginning with subtle control or disrespect that gains intensity over time, some burning questions emerge: How do I know when my partner is being abusive? Is there a distinct line that I can keep my eye on, so that I know when he has crossed it? How much is too much? Since nobody's perfect, how do I know the difference between a bad day when he's just being a jerk and a pattern that adds up to something more serious?

It's true that almost everyone does yell at one point or another in a relationship, and most people, male or female, call their partners a name from time to time, interrupt, or act selfish or insensitive. These behaviors are hurtful and worthy of criticism, but they aren't all abuse, and they don't all have the same psychological effects that abuse does. At the same time, all of these behaviors *are* abusive when they are part of a *pattern* of abuse. Being yelled at by a respectful partner feels bad, but it doesn't cause the same chilled, ugly atmosphere that an abuser's yells do.

The term *abuse* is about *power*; it means that a person is taking advantage of a power imbalance to exploit or control someone else. Wherever power imbalances exist, such as between men and women, or adults and children, or between rich and poor, some people will take advantage of those circumstances for their own purposes. (As I discuss in Chapter 13, partner abuse has been found not to exist in societies where males and females have equal power.) Thus the defining point of abuse is when the man starts to exercise power over the woman in a way that causes harm to her and creates a privileged status for him.

The lines where subtler kinds of mistreatment end and abuse begins include the following actions:

- *He retaliates against you for complaining about his behavior.*

Let's say your partner calls you a bitch one day. You are angry, and you let him know that you deeply dislike that word and don't ever want to be called that again. However, he responds to your grievance *by making a point of calling you a bitch more often.* Maybe he even gets a certain look in his eye now when he does it because he knows it gets under your skin. Similarly, you may say to your partner in an argument, "Stop yelling at me, I hate being yelled at," so he raises his voice *louder* and blames it on you. These are signs of abuse.

Another way he can retaliate against you for resisting his control is to switch into the role of victim. Suppose that you complain about being silenced by his constant interruptions during arguments. He then gets a huffy, hostile tone in his voice as if your objection were unfair to *him* and says sarcastically, "All right, I'll just listen and *you* talk," and acts as if you are oppressing him by calling him on his behavior. This is an effort to make you feel guilty for resisting his control and is the beginning of abuse.

And some men ridicule the woman when she complains of mistreatment, openly laughing at her or mimicking her. These behaviors remove all doubt about whether he is abusive.

Retaliation may not always be as clear and immediate as it is in these examples. But you can tell when your partner's behavior is designed to punish you for standing up to him, even if it doesn't come out until a couple of days later. He doesn't believe that you have the right to defy him, and he tries to hurt you so that next time you won't.

- *He tells you that your objections to his mistreatment are your own problem.*

When a woman attempts to set limits on controlling or insensitive behavior, an abuser wants her to doubt her perceptions, so he says things such as:

> *"You're too sensitive; every little thing bothers you. It shouldn't be any big deal."*
>
> *"Not everyone is all nicey-nice when they're angry like you want them to be."*
>
> *"Don't start talking to me like I'm abusive just because your ex-boyfriend (or your parents) abused you. You think everyone is abusing you."*
>
> *"You're just angry because you aren't getting your way, so you're saying I'm mistreating you."*

Through comments like these, the abuser can try to persuade you that: (1) you have unreasonable expectations for his behavior, and you should be willing to live with the things he does; (2) you are actually reacting to something else in your life, not to what he did; and (3) you are using your grievances as a power move against *him*. All of these tactics are forms of *discrediting* your complaints of mistreatment, which is abusive. His discrediting maneuvers reveal a core attitude, which he never explicitly states and may not even be aware of consciously himself: **"You have no right to object to how I treat you."** And you can't be in a fair and healthy relationship if you can't raise grievances.

- *He gives apologies that sound insincere or angry, and he demands that you accept them.*

The following exchange illustrates how this dynamic plays out:

CLAIRE: I still feel like you don't understand why I was upset by what you did. You haven't even apologized.

DANNY (Angry and loud):   All right, all right! I'm sorry, I'M SORRY!!

CLAIRE (Shaking her head):   You don't get it.

DANNY: What the fuck do you want from me?? I apologized already! What, you won't be satisfied until you have your pound of flesh??

CLAIRE: Your apology doesn't mean anything to me when you obviously aren't sorry.

DANNY: What do you mean I'm not sorry?? Don't tell me what I'm feeling, Little Ms. Analyst! You're not inside my head.

This interaction only serves to make Claire feel worse, of course, as Danny adds insults and crazy-making denial to whatever she was already upset about. Danny feels that Claire should be grateful for his apology, even though his tone communicated the opposite of his words; he in fact feels *entitled* to forgiveness, and he demands it. (He also considers it his prerogative to insist that she accept his version of reality, no matter how much it collides with everything she sees and hears; in this sense, he apparently sees her *mind* as part of what he has the right to control.)

- *He blames you for the impact of his behavior.*

Abuse counselors say of the abusive client: "When he looks at himself in the morning and sees his dirty face, he sets about washing the mirror." In other words, he becomes upset and accusatory when his partner exhibits the predictable effects of chronic mistreatment, and then he adds insult to injury by ridiculing her for feeling hurt by him. He even uses her emotional injuries as *excuses to mistreat her further.* If his verbal assaults cause her to lose interest in having sex with him, for example, he snarls accusingly, "You must be getting it somewhere else." If she is increasingly mistrustful of him because of his mistreatment of her, he says that her lack of trust is *causing her to perceive him as abusive,* reversing cause and effect in a mind-twisting way. If she is depressed or weepy one morning because he tore her apart verbally the night before, he says, "If you're going to be such a drag today, why don't you just go back to bed so I won't have to look at you?"

If your partner criticizes or puts you down for being badly affected by his mistreatment, that's abuse. Similarly, it's abuse when he uses the effects of his cruelty as an excuse, like a client I had who drove his partner away with his verbal assaults and then told her that her emotional distancing was *causing* his abuse, thus reversing cause and effect. He is kicking you when you're already down, and he knows it. Seek help for yourself quickly, as this kind of psychological assault can cause your emotional state to rapidly decline.

• *It's never the right time, or the right way, to bring things up.*

In any relationship, it makes sense to use some sensitivity in deciding when and how to tackle a difficult relationship issue. There are ways to word a grievance that avoid making it sound like a personal attack, and if you mix in some appreciation you increase the chance that your partner will hear you. But with an abuser, no way to bring up a complaint is the right way. You can wait until the calmest, most relaxed evening, prepare your partner with plenty of verbal stroking, express your grievance in mild language, but he still won't be willing to take it in.

Initial defensiveness or hostility toward a grievance is common even in nonabusive people. Sometimes you have to leave an argument and come back to it in a couple of hours, or the next day, and then you find your partner more prepared to take in what is bothering you. With an abuser, however, the passage of time doesn't help. He doesn't spend the intervening period digesting your comments and struggling to face what he did, the way a nonabusive person might. In fact he does the opposite, appearing to mentally build up his case against your complaint as if he were preparing to go before a judge.

• *He undermines your progress in life.*

Interference with your freedom or independence is abuse. If he causes you to lose a job or to drop out of a school program; discourages you from pursuing your dreams; causes damage to your relationships with friends or relatives; takes advantage of you financially and damages your economic progress or security; or tells you that you are incompetent at something you enjoy, such as writing, artwork, or business, as a way to get you to give it up, he is trying to undermine your independence.

• *He denies what he did.*

Some behaviors in a relationship can be matters of judgment; what one person calls a raised voice another might call yelling, and there is room for reasonable people to disagree. But other actions, such as calling someone a name or pounding a fist on the table, either happened or they didn't. So while a nonabusive partner might argue with you about how you are interpreting his behavior, the abuser denies his actions altogether.

- *He justifies his hurtful or frightening acts or says that you "made him do it."*

When you tell your partner that his yelling frightens you, for example, and he responds that he has every right to yell "because you're not listening to me," that's abuse. The abuser uses your behavior as an excuse for his own. He therefore refuses to commit unconditionally to stop using a degrading or intimidating behavior. Instead, he insists on setting up a quid pro quo, where he says he'll stop some form of abuse if you agree to give up something that bothers *him,* which often will be something that you have every right to do.

- *He touches you in anger or puts you in fear in other ways.*

Physical aggression by a man toward his partner is abuse, even if it happens *only once.* If he raises a fist; punches a hole in the wall; throws things at you; blocks your way; restrains you; grabs, pushes, or pokes you; or threatens to hurt you, that's physical abuse. He is creating fear and using your need for physical freedom and safety as a way to control you. Call a hot line as soon as possible if any of these things happens to you.

Sometimes a partner can frighten you inadvertently because he is unaware of how his actions affect you. For example, he might come from a family or culture where people yell loudly and wave their arms around during arguments, while those from your background are quiet and polite. The nonabusive man in these circumstances will be very concerned when you inform him that he is frightening you and will want to take steps to keep that from happening again—unconditionally.

Physical abuse is dangerous. Once it starts in a relationship, it can escalate over time to more serious assaults such as slapping, punching, or choking. Even if it doesn't, so-called "lower-level" physical abuse can frighten you, give your partner power over you, and start to affect your ability to manage your own life. Any form of physical intimidation is highly upsetting to children who are exposed to it. No assault in a relationship, however "minor," should be taken lightly.

I am often asked whether physical aggression by women toward men, such as a slap in the face, is abuse. The answer is: "It depends." Men typically experience women's shoves or slaps as annoying and infuriating rather than intimidating, so the long-term emotional effects are less damaging. It is rare to find a man who has gradually lost his freedom or self-esteem because of a woman's aggressiveness. I object to any form of physical aggression in relationships except for what is truly essential for self-defense, but I reserve the word *abuse* for situations of control or intimidation.

A woman *can* intimidate another woman, however, and a man can be placed in fear by his male partner. Most of what I have described about the thinking and the tactics of heterosexual abusers is also true of abusive gay men and lesbians. We look more at this issue in Chapter 6.

- *He coerces you into having sex or sexually assaults you.*

I have had clients who raped or sexually coerced their partners repeatedly over the course of the relationship but never once hit them. Sexual coercion or force in a relationship is abuse. Studies indicate that women who are raped by intimate partners suffer even deeper and longer-lasting effects than those who are raped by strangers or nonintimate acquaintances. If you have experienced sexual assault or chronic sexual pressure in your relationship, call an abuse hotline or a rape hotline, even if you don't feel that the term *rape* applies to what your partner did.

- *His controlling, disrespectful, or degrading behavior is a pattern.*

This item is as important as the others but requires the most judgment and ability to trust your instincts. When exactly does a behavior become a pattern? If it happens three times a year? If it happens once a week? There is no answer that applies to all actions or to all people. You will need to form your own conclusions about whether your partner's mistreatment of you has become repetitive.

- *You show signs of being abused.*

All of the other indicators of abuse discussed above involve examining what the man does and how he thinks. But it is equally important to look at *yourself,* examining such questions as:

Are you afraid of him?

Are you getting distant from friends or family because he makes those relationships difficult?

Is your level of energy and motivation declining, or do you feel depressed?

Is your self-opinion declining, so that you are always fighting to be good enough and to prove yourself?

Do you find yourself constantly preoccupied with the relationship and how to fix it?

Do you feel like you can't do anything right?

Do you feel like the problems in your relationship are all your fault?

Do you repeatedly leave arguments feeling like you've been messed with but can't figure out exactly why?

These are signs that you may be involved with an abusive partner.

You may notice that the above distinguishing features of abuse include little mention of *anger*. While chronic anger can be one warning sign of abusiveness, the two are sometimes quite separate. There are cool, calculating abusers who rarely explode in ire, for example, and at the same time some nonabusive men feel or express anger often. You might decide that you don't want to be with a partner who is angry all the time—I wouldn't care for it—but it isn't abuse in itself.

WHAT IF HE'S SORRY?

Almost every time that I speak on abuse, hands go up with the following two questions: (1) When an abuser acts remorseful, is he really? and (2) If he's really sorry, does that make him less likely to be abusive again?

QUESTION 10:
IS HE REALLY SORRY?

The good news is that remorse is often genuine; the bad news is that it rarely helps. To make sense out of this contradiction, we need to look first at a crucial aspect of what is going on inside an abuser: **Abusers have numerous contradictory attitudes and beliefs operating simultaneously in their minds.** A few examples of the typical contradictions include:

> *"Women are fragile and in need of protection **but** they need to be intimidated from time to time or they get out of hand."*

> *"My partner and I should have equal say over things **but** my decisions should rule when it comes to issues that are important to me."*

> *"I feel terrible about how I treated her **but** I should never have to feel bad in a relationship, no matter what I did."*

> *"I shouldn't raise my voice **but** I should have control over my partner, and sometimes I have to get loud to control her."*

> *"You should never hit a woman **but** sometimes a man has no other choice."*

When a man feels sorry for his abusive behavior, his regrets collide with his entitlement. The contradictory chatter inside his head sounds something like this:

> I feel bad that I said "fuck you" to her; that's not a good thing to say, especially in front of the children. I lost it, and I want my family to have an image of me as always being strong and in charge. I don't like for them to see me looking ugly the way I did in that argument; it hurts my self-esteem. But she called me "irresponsible"! How does she expect me to react when she says something like that? She can't talk to me that way. Now the children are going to think I was the bad guy, when she was the cause of it. If they start siding with her,

I'm going to let them know why I was mad. Now she's made me look really bad. Fuck her.

Let's follow the path that this man's internal dialogue takes. First, his remorse is not primarily focused on the way his verbal assault wounded his partner. What he feels bad about mostly is: (1) He damaged his image in other people's eyes; (2) he offended his own sense of how he would like to be; and (3) he feels he should be able to control his partner without resorting to abuse. From those thoughts he slides into blaming his outburst on his partner, which he feels entitled to do, and in this way rids himself of his feelings of guilt. By the end of his self-talk, he is holding his partner responsible for everything, including the effects that *he* has just had on their children. The abuser's self-focus and victim-blaming orientation tend to cause his remorse to fade in this way.

An abuser's show of emotion after early incidents of abuse can be dramatic: I have had clients who cry, beg their partners for forgiveness, and say, "You deserve so much better, I don't know why you are even with a jerk like me." His remorse can create the impression that he is reaching out for real intimacy, especially if you've never seen him looking so sad before. But in a day or two his guilt is vanquished, driven out by his internal excuse-making skills. The effects of the incident last much longer for the abused woman, of course, and pretty soon the abuser may be snapping at her: "What, aren't you over that *yet*? Don't dwell on it, for crying out loud. Let's put it behind us and move forward." His attitude is: "I'm over it, so why isn't she?"

Genuine remorse and theatricality are not mutually exclusive. Most abusers are truly sorry—though perhaps largely for themselves—while *also* playing up their emotions somewhat to win sympathy. A man's dramatic remorse shifts the center of attention back to him; his partner may almost forget his earlier bullying as compassion for his guilt and self-reproach washes over her. She may soon find herself reassuring him that she won't leave him, that she still loves him, that she doesn't think he's a terrible person. If they have children, she may find herself covering up what he did so that the children won't blame him, because she doesn't want him to feel even worse. He thus reaps soothing attention as a reward for his abusiveness, and his actions have the effect of keeping the family focused on his needs.

Remorse usually tends to decline as abusive incidents pile up. The genuine aspect fades as the abusive man grows accustomed to acting abusively and tuning out his partner's hurt feelings. The theatrical part fades as he becomes less concerned about losing the relationship, confident now that she is fully under his control and won't leave him.

The salient point about remorse, however, is that *it matters little whether it is genuine or not.* Clients who get very sorry after acts of abuse change at about the same rate as the ones who don't. The most regretful are sometimes the most self-centered, lamenting above all the injury they've done to their own self-image. They feel ashamed of having behaved like cruel dictators and want to revert quickly to the role of *benign* dictators, as if that somehow makes them much better people.

IF BEING SORRY AFTER AN INCIDENT DOESN'T HELP, WHAT WOULD?

The following steps could help prevent his next incident of abuse, in a way that apologies cannot:

- Giving you some extended room to be angry about what he did, rather than telling you that you've been angry too long or trying to stuff your angry feelings back down your throat

- Listening well to your perspective without interrupting, making excuses, or blaming his actions on you

- Making amends for anything he did, for example, by picking up anything that he threw, admitting to friends that he lied about you, or telling the children that his behavior was unacceptable and wasn't your fault

- Making unconditional agreements to immediately change behaviors

- Going to get help *without* you having to put a lot of pressure on him to do it

If he is willing to take all of these steps after an incident of mistreatment—and actually follow through on them—there's some chance that he may not be deeply abusive. Without such clear action, however, the abuse will return.

TAKE SELF-PROTECTIVE STEPS QUICKLY

Many women take a "wait and see" attitude when signs of abuse appear in a partner's behavior. They tell themselves: "It's so hard to leave him right now because I still love him. But if he gets worse, that will lessen my feelings for him, and then breaking up will be easier." This is a dangerous trap. The longer you are with an abuser, and the more destructive he becomes, the *harder* it can be to extricate yourself, for the following reasons:

- The more time he has to tear down your self-opinion, the more difficult it will be for you to believe that you deserve better treatment.

- The more time he has to hurt you emotionally, the more likely your energy and initiative are to diminish, so that it gets harder to muster the strength to get out.

- The more damage he does to your relationships with friends and family, the less support you will have for the difficult process of ending the relationship.

- The longer you have been living with his cycles of intermittent abuse and kind, loving treatment, the *more* attached you are likely to feel to him, through a process known as *traumatic bonding* (see Chapter 9).

For all of these reasons, act sooner rather than later.

At the same time, if you have already been in a relationship with an abuser for five years, or ten, or thirty, it is never too late to recover your rights and to get free. Help is available to you no matter how long your relationship has lasted and how deep the effects have been (see "Resources").

One final word of caution: If you do not have children with your abusive partner, *keep it that way.* Some women hope the arrival of a baby can cause an abuser to change his behaviors, but it can't. It won't make him settle down, become more responsible, or gain maturity. It won't stop his jealous accusations by convincing him that you are committed to him, nor will it get him to stop cheating on you. The presence of children in the home won't make him stop abusing you. Having children with an abusive partner will just make your life more stressful than it was before, as you begin to worry about the effects that his behavior is having on your children. And if you decide later that you do want to leave him, having children will make that choice much harder and will raise the possibility that he will threaten to seek custody of them (see Chapter 10). I have yet to encounter a case where the arrival of children solved a woman's problems with an abusive man, or even lessened them.

KEY POINTS TO REMEMBER

- The early warning signs of abuse are usually visible if you know what to look for.

- If the warning signs are there, act quickly either to set limits or to get out of the relationship. The more deeply you become involved with an abuser, the harder it is to get out.

- You do not cause your partner's slide into abusiveness, and you cannot stop it by figuring out what is bothering him or by increasing your ability to meet his needs. Emotional upset and unmet needs have little to do with abusiveness.

- Certain behaviors and attitudes are definitional of abuse, such as ridiculing your complaints of mistreatment, physically intimidating you, or sexually assaulting you. If any of these is present, abuse has already begun.

- Abused women aren't "codependent." It is abusers, not their partners, who create abusive relationships.

- Call a hotline for support, or use one of the resources listed in the back of this book, as soon as you start to have questions about abuse. Don't wait until you're certain.

6

The Abusive Man in Everyday Life

I feel like I'm going crazy.

Sometimes I can just tell it's one of those days; no matter what I do, I'm going to get it sooner or later.

He's a teddy bear underneath.

I never know what to expect; he can just turn on me, out of the blue.

I wouldn't call him an abuser. I mean, he can be really nice for weeks at a time.

I really love him.

OVER THE FIFTEEN YEARS I have worked with abusive men, I have spent many hundreds of hours on the telephone listening to the partners of my clients describe their lives. My job is to see my client through the woman's eyes, using my imagination to enter her home and absorb the atmosphere that he creates day in and day out. By assuming her perspective, I begin to see beneath my client's exterior.

At the same time, I don't see exactly the same man the abused woman sees. The circumstances under which I see him have several unusual aspects:

- It is safe for me to challenge and confront him, because I am sitting in a room full of witnesses, including my co-leader. In many cases, I have some power over the man because he is on probation, so a negative report from me could get him brought before a judge.

- I have names and descriptions for his tactics. He finds it difficult to confuse or intimidate me, or to make me feel bad about myself, because I keep pointing out his maneuvers and his motives. Abuse loses some of its power when you have names for its weapons.

- I don't have to live with this man, so he has few opportunities to retaliate against me for standing up to him.

- Some of the men in the group who are attempting to apply the concepts of the program may challenge the man on his attitudes and behaviors. These challenges from other abusers make it harder for him to blame everything on his partner, or on women in general.

I also learn about a man from seeing his reactions to discussions in his group. For example, he tends to express disapproval of other clients whose abuse is *different* from his—because he considers anything he wouldn't do to be "real" abuse—and while tending to express sympathy for and support of any fellow abuser who employs the *same* tactics or justifications that he does, turns to me to say: "But what do you expect the poor man to do given his circumstances?"

The abused woman and I thus try to form a team so that we can share our observations about the man and help each other to recognize patterns or dynamics. I am eager to learn *from* her about my client and at the same time eager to share *with* her any observations I have that might help her to protect herself or unravel what he is doing to her mind.

One of the earliest lessons I learned from abused women is that to understand abuse you can't look just at the explosions; you have to examine with equal care the spaces *between* the explosions. The dynamics of these periods tell us as much about the abuse as the rages or the thrown objects, as the disgusting name-calling or the jealous accusations. The abuser's thinking and behavior during the calmer periods are what cause his big eruptions that wound or frighten. In this chapter, we enter the mind of the abuser at various points in daily life to better understand what sparks his abusive actions.

THE ABUSIVE MAN IN ARGUMENTS

I will begin by examining in detail an argument between an abusive man and his partner, the kind that I hear about routinely from my clients and their partners. Jesse and Bea are walking along in their town. Jesse is sullen and clearly annoyed.

BEA: What's going on with you? I don't understand what you're upset about.

JESSE: I'm not upset; I just don't feel like talking right now. Why do you always have to read something into it? Can't I just be a little quiet sometimes? Not everybody likes to talk, talk, talk all the time just because you do.

BEA: I don't talk, talk, talk all the time. What do you mean by that? I just want to know what's bothering you.

JESSE: I just finished telling you, *nothing*'s bothering me . . . and give me a break that you don't talk all the time. When we were having dinner with my brother and his wife, I couldn't believe how you went on and on about your stupid journalism class. You're forty years old, for Christ sake; the world isn't excited about your fantasies of being famous. Grow up a little.

BEA: Fantasies of being famous? I'm trying to get a job, Jesse, because the travel agency jobs have all moved downtown. And I wasn't going on about it. They were *interested*; they were asking me a lot of questions about it—that's why we were on that subject for a while.

JESSE: Oh, yeah, they were real interested. They were being *polite* to you because you're so full of yourself. You're so naive you can't even tell when you're being patronized.

BEA: I don't believe this. That dinner was almost two weeks ago. Have you been brewing about it all this time?

JESSE: I don't brew, Bea, you're the one that brews. You love to get us confused. I'll see you later. I'm really not in the mood for this shit.

BEA: In the mood for what shit?? I haven't done anything! You've had it in for me since I arrived to meet you!

JESSE: You're yelling at me, Bea. You know I hate being yelled at. You need to get help; your emotions just fly off the handle. I'll see you later.

BEA: Where are you going?

JESSE: I'll walk home, thank you. You can take the car. I'd rather be alone.

BEA: It's going to take you more than a half hour to walk home, and it's freezing today.

JESSE: Oh, now suddenly you care about me so much. Up yours. Bye. (*Walks off.*)

The lives of abused women are full of these kinds of exchanges. Jesse didn't call Bea any degrading names; he didn't yell; he didn't hit her or threaten her. Bea will be in a tough spot when the time comes to explain to a friend how upset she is, because Jesse's behavior is hard to describe. What can she say? That he's sarcastic? That he holds on to things? That he's overly critical? A friend would respond: "Well, that sounds hard, but I wouldn't call it *abuse*." Yet, as Jesse walks away, Bea feels as if she has been slapped in the face.

WHAT IS GOING ON IN THIS ARGUMENT?

We will look first at what Jesse is *doing* and then examine how his *thinking* works. The first point to illuminate is:

THE ABUSER'S PROBLEM IS NOT THAT HE RESPONDS
INAPPROPRIATELY TO CONFLICT. HIS ABUSIVENESS IS OPERATING
PRIOR TO THE CONFLICT: IT USUALLY **CREATES** THE CONFLICT,
AND IT DETERMINES THE **SHAPE** THE CONFLICT TAKES.

Therapists often try to work with an abuser by analyzing his responses to disagreements and trying to get him to handle conflicts differently. But such an approach misses the point: His abusiveness was what caused the tension to begin with.

Jesse uses an array of conversational control tactics, as most abusers do:

- He denies being angry, although he obviously is, and instead of dealing with what is bothering him, he channels his energy into criticizing Bea about something else.

- He insults, belittles, and patronizes Bea in multiple ways, including saying that she likes to talk all the time and has fantasies of becoming famous, stating that she should "grow up," and telling her that she accuses him of stewing over things when it's actually her.

- He tells her that she is unaware that other people look down on her and don't take her seriously and calls her "naive."

- He criticizes her for raising her voice in response to his stream of insults.

- He tells her that *she* is mistreating *him.*

- He stomps off and plays the victim by putting himself in the position of having to take a long, cold walk home.

Bea is now left miserable—feeling like a scratching post that a cat has just sharpened its claws on. Part of why she is so shaken up by this experience is that she never knows when one of these verbal assaults is going to happen or what sets it off. On a different day she might have met Jesse to take him home and had a pleasant conversation with him about his workday. Thus she is left imagining that something bad must have happened to him at work and that he is taking it out on her—which may be true in a way but actually has little to do with what is happening.

So, what *is* going on? The story began two weeks earlier, when Jesse and Bea were out to dinner with Jesse's relatives. What we have just learned from their argument is that Jesse does not like Bea to be the center of attention for any length of time. Why not? There are a few reasons:

1. He considers it her job to play a supporting role to him. This is the same as the attitude that "behind every great man stands a woman." So if either of them is going to be the center of attention, it should be him, and if he is feeling like being quiet she should be, too, remaining in his shadow.

2. He is constantly focused on her faults, so he assumes everyone else is, too.

3. He doesn't like having her appear in public as smart, capable, and interesting, because that collides with his deeply held belief that she is irrational, incompetent, and worthy of being ignored—a view of her that he may want others to share with him.

4. He is afraid on some level that if she gets enough support for her strengths, she will leave him—and he's quite likely right.

Notice that numbers two and three are almost opposites: He assumes that she comes off badly, which embarrasses him, but he is also concerned that she may have come off very well, because then other people might see her as a capable person. He reacts strongly to both possibilities.

We also see the signs that Jesse finds Bea's journalism class threatening to his control over her. In fact, this is probably what he has been dwelling on most over the past two weeks, causing his grumpy mood. Abusive men are uncomfortable when they see signs of budding independence in their partners and often look for ways to undermine the woman's progress in the days ahead.

Returning now to the day of the argument, we can see that Jesse launches into attributing many of his own characteristics to Bea, saying that she is full of herself, that she dwells on grievances, that she yells, that she doesn't care about him. This behavior in abusers is sometimes mistakenly referred to as *projection,* a psychological process through which people attribute their own fears or flaws to those around them. But as we saw in Chapter 3, the process through which an abuser turns reality on its head is not quite the same as projection. Jesse perceives Bea to be yelling because one of his core values is that she's not supposed to get angry at him, no matter what he does. He thinks she doesn't care about him because in his mind she can't care about him unless she cares *only* about him, and not at all about herself or other people. He thinks she is full of herself because she sometimes gets excited about her own goals or activities, when he believes she should be most excited about what *he's* doing. He thinks she dwells on her grievances because she sometimes attempts to hold him accountable rather than letting him stick her with cleaning up his messes—literally and figuratively.

Jesse is also using projection as a control tactic. Part of why Jesse accuses Bea of doing all the selfish or abusive things that he does is to make it hard for her to get anywhere with her grievances. I have had many clients tell me: "Oh, I knew what I was saying about her wasn't true, but it's a way to really get to her." (It is surprising how common it is for abusers to admit—if they are caught off guard—to deliberate use of abusive and controlling behaviors.) For all of these reasons, saying simply that "he's projecting" doesn't adequately capture the reasons for an abuser's distorted accusations.

The final behavior we need to examine is Jesse's decision to take a long, cold walk home by himself. Why does he make himself a victim?

- He is drawn to making Bea feel sorry for him so that his feelings can remain the center of attention, crowding hers out. She will feel as though she shouldn't pursue her complaints about the ways in which he has just assaulted her verbally, because he is suffering so much.

- He also wants other people to feel sorry for him. He can describe to friends or relatives how the argument led to a miserable walk for him, and they will think: "The poor man."

And he will probably adjust the story to his advantage—abusers usually spruce up their accounts—perhaps saying that she was furious and drove off without him, and he was left to walk shivering all the way home. He doesn't consciously plan these maneuvers ahead of time, but experience has taught him on a deeper level that playing the victim increases the sympathy he receives.

- He may want her to worry about what other people will think. She won't want to come out looking like the mean one, so she'll take steps to smooth over the fight.

- On some level he enjoys walking alone for half an hour, wallowing in self-pity, because it helps him feel more justified about his recurring pattern of cruelty and undermining toward Bea. It's a way of reassuring himself that she's the bad one, not him. An abuser is a human being, and somewhere inside him, buried under thick layers of entitlement and disrespect, there is a heart that knows that what he is doing is wrong. This heart periodically tries to send a few beats up through the layers, so the abuser has to stomp them back down.

Each verbal battle with an abuser is a walk through a minefield, and each field is different. Jesse appears to be a mixture of the Water Torturer and the Victim, with a sprinkling of Mr. Right. Perhaps an argument on the same subject with the Drill Segreant or the Player would go quite differently. But, regardless of specific style, very little of what an abuser does in an argument is as irrational or emotional as it seems.

FOUR CRITICAL CHARACTERISTICS OF AN ABUSIVE ARGUMENT

You may find that each disagreement with your partner is unique and can start in any of a thousand ways, yet it can only arrive at four or five different endings—all of them bad. Your gnawing sensation of futility and inevitably is actually coming from the abusive man's thinking about verbal conflict. His outlook makes it impossible for an argument to proceed toward anything other than the fulfillment of his wishes—or toward nowhere at all. Four features stand out:

1. The abuser sees an argument as war.

His goal in a verbal conflict is not to negotiate different desires, understand each other's experiences, or think of mutually beneficial solutions. He wants only to *win*. Winning is measured by who talks the most, who makes the most devastating or "humorous" insults (none of which is funny to his partner), and who controls the final decision that comes out of the debate. He won't settle for anything other than victory. If he feels he has lost the argument, he may respond by making a tactical retreat and gathering his forces to strike again later.

Under this layer there is an even deeper stratum in many abusive men where we unearth his attitude that *the whole relationship is a war.* To this mind-set, relationships are dichotomous, and you're on either one end or the other: the dominator or the submitter, the champ or the chump, the cool man or the loser. He can imagine no other way.

2. She is always wrong in his eyes.

It is frustrating, and ultimately pointless, to argue with someone who is certain beyond the shadow of a doubt that his perspective is accurate and complete and that yours is wrong and stupid. Where can the conversation possibly go?

The question isn't whether he argues forcefully or not. Many non-abusive people express their opinions with tremendous conviction and emotion yet still allow themselves to be influenced by the other person's point of view. On the other hand, it isn't hard to tell when someone is refusing to grapple in good faith with your ideas and instead is just reaching for whatever stick he thinks will deal the heaviest blow to your side. When your partner says to you disparagingly, "Oh, the real reason why you complain about how I argue is that you can't deal with my having strong opinions," he's diverting attention from the tactics he uses. He is also reversing reality, which is that *he* can't accept *your* differences of opinion and doesn't want to let his thinking be influenced by yours. (And on the rare occasions when he does adopt your ideas, he may claim they were his to begin with.)

3. He has an array of control tactics in conflicts.

My clients have so many ways to bully their way through arguments that I couldn't possibly name them all, but the abuser's most common tactics are listed in the box below:

Sarcasm

Ridicule

Distorting what you say

Distorting what happened in an earlier interaction

Sulking

Accusing you of doing what he does,
or thinking the way he thinks

Using a tone of absolute certainty and
final authority—"defining reality"

Interrupting

Not listening, refusing to respond

Laughing out loud at your opinion or perspective

Turning your grievances around to use against you

Changing the subject to *his* grievances

Criticism that is harsh, undeserved, or frequent

Provoking guilt

Playing the victim

Smirking, rolling his eyes, contemptuous facial expressions

Yelling, out-shouting

Swearing

> Name-calling, insults, put-downs
>
> Walking out
>
> Towering over you
>
> Walking toward you in an intimidating way
>
> Blocking a doorway
>
> Other forms of physical intimidation,
> such as getting too close while he's angry
>
> Threatening to leave you
>
> Threatening to harm you

Conversational control tactics are aggravating no matter who uses them, but they are especially coercive and upsetting when used by an abusive man because of the surrounding context of emotional or physical intimidation. I have rarely met an abuser who didn't use a wide array of the above tactics in conflicts; if you consider an argument with a partner to be a war, why not use every weapon you can think of? The underlying mind-set makes the behaviors almost inevitable.

The abusive man wants particularly to *discredit* your perspective, especially your grievances. He may tell you, for example, that the "real" reasons why you complain about the way he treats you are:

- You don't want him to feel good about himself.

- You can't handle it if he has an opinion that differs from yours, if he is angry, or if he is right.

- You are too sensitive, you read too much into things, or you take things the wrong way.

- You were abused as a child or by a former partner, so you think everything is abuse.

These are all strategies he uses to avoid having to think seriously about your grievances, because then he might be obligated to change his behaviors or attitudes.

The abusive man's goal in a heated argument is in essence to get you to *stop thinking for yourself* and to *silence you,* because to him your opinions and complaints are obstacles to the imposition of his will as well as an affront to his sense of entitlement. **If you watch closely, you will begin to notice how many of his controlling behaviors are aimed ultimately at discrediting and silencing you.**

4. He makes sure to get his way—by one means or another.

The bottom line with an abuser in an argument is that he wants what he wants—today, tomorrow, and always—and he feels he has a right to it.

THE ABUSIVE MAN'S CYCLES

Life with an abuser can be a dizzying wave of exciting good times and painful periods of verbal, physical, or sexual assault. The longer the relationship lasts, the shorter and farther apart the positive periods tend to become. If you have been involved with an abusive partner for many years, the good periods may have stopped happening altogether, so that he is an unvarying source of misery.

Periods of relative calm are followed by a few days or weeks in which the abuser becomes increasingly irritable. As his tension builds, it takes less and less to set him off on a tirade of insults. His excuses for not carrying his weight mount up, and his criticism and displeasure seem constant. Many women tell me that they learn to read their partner's moods during this buildup and can sense when he is nearing an eruption. One day he finally hits his limit, often over the most trivial issue, and he bursts out with screaming, disgusting and hurtful put-downs, or frightening aggression. If he is a violent abuser, he turns himself loose to knock over chairs, hurl objects, punch holes in walls, or assault his partner directly, leaving her scared to death.

After he has purged himself, he typically acts ashamed or regretful about his cruelty or violence, at least in the early years of a relationship.

Then he may enter a period when he reminds you of the man you fell in love with—charming, attentive, funny, kind. His actions have the effect of drawing you into a repetitive traumatic cycle in which you hope each time that he is finally going to change for good. You then begin to see the signs of his next slow slide back into abuse, and your anxiety and confusion rise again.

Women commonly ask me: "What is going on inside his mind during this cycle? Why can't he just stay in the good period, what can I do to keep him there?" To answer these questions, let's look through his eyes during each phase:

• *The tension-building phase*

During this period, your partner is collecting negative points about you and squirreling them away for safekeeping. Every little thing that you have done wrong, each disappointment he has experienced, any way in which you have failed to live up to his image of the perfect selfless woman—all goes down as a black mark against your name.

Abusers nurse their grievances. One of my former colleagues referred to this habit as The Garden of Resentments, a process through which an abuser plants a minor complaint and then cultivates it carefully while it grows to tremendous dimensions, worthy of outrage and abuse. Jesse, for example, planted the dinner-table conversation in his Garden of Resentments and then harvested it two weeks later to throw in Bea's face, lumping it together with several other issues into one big ugly ball.

To defend against any complaints you attempt to express, the abuser stockpiles his collected grievances like weapons to protect his precious terrain of selfishness and irresponsibility. And some of his negativity about you is just plain habit. An abuser falls into a routine of walking around dwelling on his partner's purported faults. Since he considers you responsible for fixing everything for him, he logically chooses you as his dumping ground for all of life's normal frustrations and disappointments.

• *The eruption*

The abusive man tends to mentally collect resentments toward you until he feels that you deserve a punishment. Once he's ready to blow, the tiniest spark will ignite him. Occasionally an abused woman may decide to touch her partner off herself at this point, as scary as that is, because the fear of waiting to see what he will do and when he will do it is worse. The explosion of verbal or physical assault that results is horrible, but at least it's over.

After he blows, the abuser absolves himself of guilt by thinking of himself as having lost control, the victim of his partner's provocations or his own intolerable pain. Whereas at other times he may say that men are stronger and less emotional than women, he now switches, saying, "There is only so much a man can take," or "She really hurt my feelings, and I couldn't help going off." He may consider women's emotional reactions— such as breaking into tears—contemptible, even when they hurt no one, but when a man has powerful emotions, even violence may be excusable. Some of my most tough-guy clients unabashedly use their painful feelings to excuse their cruel behavior.

- *The "hearts and flowers" stage*

After the apologies are over, the abuser may enter a period of relative calm. He appears to have achieved a catharsis from opening up the bomb bays and raining abuse down on his partner. He feels rejuvenated and may speak the language of a fresh start, of steering the relationship in a new direction. Of course, there is nothing cathartic for his partner about being the target of his abuse (she feels worse with each cycle), but in the abuser's self-centered way he thinks she should feel better now because *he* feels better.

During this period, an abuser works to rebuild the bridge that his abusiveness just burned down. He wants to be back in his partner's good graces; he may want sex; and he seeks reassurance that she isn't going to leave him—or expose him. Cards and gifts are common in this phase; hence the name "hearts and flowers." The abusive man does not, however, want to look seriously at himself; he is merely looking to paste up some wallpaper to cover the holes he has made—figuratively or literally—and return to business as usual. The good period can't last because nothing has changed. His coercive habits, his double standards, his contempt, are all still there. The cycle is repeated because there is no reason why it wouldn't be.

Some abusive men don't follow a discernable cycle like the one I have just described. Your partner's abusive incidents may follow no pattern, so you can never guess what will happen next. I have had clients who seemed almost to get a thrill out of their own unpredictability, which further increased their power. Random abuse can be particularly deleterious psychologically to you and to your children.

A CLOSER LOOK AT THE GOOD PERIODS

When an alcohol abuser goes a month or two without a drink, we say the person is "on the wagon." The dry period is a break from the pattern and inspires some hope of a positive trend. But, with partner abuse, the periods when the man is being good—or at least not at his worst—are *not* really outside of his pattern. They are generally an integral aspect of his abusiveness, woven into the fabric of his thinking and behavior.

What functions do the good periods play? They perform several, including the following:

- His spurts of kindness and generosity help him to feel good about himself. He can persuade himself that you are the one who is messed up, "because look at me, I'm a great guy."

- You gradually feel warmer and more trusting toward him. The good periods are critical to hooking you back into the relationship, especially if he doesn't have another way to keep you from leaving, such as financial control or the threat of taking the children.

- While you are feeling more trusting, you expose more of your true feelings about different issues in your life and you show him more caring, which creates vulnerability that he can use later to control you (though he probably doesn't consciously plan to do this). During one of Jesse's bad periods, for example, Bea would probably protect herself by telling him that she was taking a journalism class "just to get the English credits toward my college degree." But during a more intimate period, she might open up about her dream of pursuing a career in journalism, and he would say it was a great idea. And still later, when he was back in abuse mode, he would be armed with knowledge about her inner life with which to hurt her, as we saw in their argument.

- He uses the good periods to shape his public image, making it harder for you to get people to believe that he's abusive.

I have not encountered any case, out of the roughly two thousand men I have worked with, in which one of an abuser's good periods has lasted into the long term, unless the man has also done deep work on his abusive attitudes. Being kind and loving usually just becomes a different approach to control and manipulation and gradually blends back into more overt abuse. I recognize how painful or frightening it can be for an abused woman to accept this reality, because those times of kindness, and the hope that comes with them, can feel like all you have left to hold on to, given how much he has taken away from you. But illusions of change also keep you trapped and can increase your feelings of helplessness or disappointment when he returns to his old ways. Real change looks very different from a typical good period—so different that you could scarcely mistake the two, as we will see in Chapter 14.

TEN REASONS TO STAY THE SAME

To answer the question "Why Does He Do That?" we have to examine the foundation on which abusive behaviors are based. On the first level are the abuser's attitudes, beliefs, and habits—the thinking that drives his behavior day in and day out, which we have been looking at. On the second level is the learning process by which some boys develop into abusive men or, in other words, where abusive values come from, which is the topic of Chapter 13.

There is also a third level, which is rarely mentioned in discussions of abuse but which is actually one of the most important dynamics: the *benefits* that an abuser gets that make his behavior *desirable* to him. In what ways is abusiveness rewarding? How does this destructive pattern get reinforced?

Consider the following scenario: Mom, Dad, and their children are having dinner on a Wednesday night. Dad is snappy and irritable, criticizing everybody during the meal, spreading his tension around like electricity. When he finishes eating, he leaves the table abruptly and heads out of the room. His ten-year-old daughter says, "Dad, where are you going? Wednesday is your night to wash the dishes." Upon hearing these words, Dad bursts into flames, screaming, "You upstart little shit, don't you dare try to tell me what to do! You'll be wearing a dish on your face!" He grabs a plate off the table, makes like he is going to throw it at her, and then turns away and smashes it on the floor. He knocks a chair over with his hand and storms out of the room. Mom and the children are left trembling; the daughter bursts into tears. Dad reappears in the doorway and yells that she'd better shut up, so she chokes off her tears, which causes her to shake even more violently. Without touching a soul, Dad has sent painful shock waves through the entire family.

We move ahead now to the following Wednesday. Dinner passes fairly normally, without the previous week's tension, but Dad still strolls out of the kitchen when he finishes eating. Does a family member remind him that it's his turn to wash the dishes? Of course not. It will be many, many months before anyone makes that mistake again. They quietly attend to the cleanup, or they squabble among themselves about who should do it, taking out their frustrations over Dad's unfairness and volatility on each other. Dad's scary behavior has created a context in which he won't have to do the dishes anytime he doesn't feel like it, and no one will dare take him to task for it.

Any incident of abusive behavior brings the abuser benefits just as this one did. **Over time, the man grows attached to his ballooning collection of comforts and privileges.** Here are some of the reasons why he may appear so determined not to stop bullying:

1. The intrinsic satisfaction of power and control

The abusive man gains power through his coercive and intimidating behaviors—a sensation that can create a potent, thrilling rush. The wielder of power feels important and effective and finds a momentary relief from life's normal distresses. It isn't the woman's pain that appeals to him; most abusers are not sadists. In fact, he has to go to some lengths to shield himself from his own natural tendency to empathize with her. The feeling that he *rules* is where the pleasure lies.

Yet the heady rush of power is the bare beginning of what the abuser gains through his mistreatment of his partner. If the rewards stopped here, I would find it much easier than I do to prevail upon my clients to change.

2. *Getting his way, especially when it matters to him the most*

A romantic partnership involves a never-ending series of negotiations between two people's differing needs, desires, and preferences. Many of the differences that have to be worked out are matters of tremendous importance to the emotional life of each partner, such as:

- Are we spending Christmas (or whatever holidays are most important to a particular couple) with my relatives, whom I enjoy, or with your relatives, who get on my nerves and don't seem to like me?

- Are we eating dinner tonight at my favorite restaurant, or at a place that I'm tired of and where the children seem to get wound up and irritating?

- Am I going to have to go alone to my office party, which makes me feel terrible, or are you going to come with me even though you would rather spend your evening doing almost anything else on earth?

It is important not to underestimate the impact of these kinds of day-to-day decisions. Your happiness in a relationship depends greatly on your ability to get your needs heard and taken seriously. If these decisions are taken over by an abusive or controlling partner, you experience disappointment after disappointment, the constant sacrificing of your needs. He, on the other hand, enjoys the luxury of a relationship where he rarely has to compromise, gets to do the things he enjoys, and skips the rest. He shows off his generosity when the stakes are low, so that friends will see what a swell guy he is.

The abuser ends up with the benefits of being in an intimate relationship without the sacrifices that normally come with the territory. That's a pretty privileged lifestyle.

3. Someone to take his problems out on

Have you ever suffered a sharp disappointment or a painful loss and found yourself looking for someone to blame? Have you, for example, ever been nasty to a store clerk when you were really upset about your job? Most people have an impulse to dump bad feelings on some undeserving person, as a way to relieve—temporarily—sadness or frustration. Certain days you may know that you just have to keep an eye on yourself so as not to bite someone's head off.

The abusive man doesn't bother to keep an eye on himself, however. In fact, he considers himself entitled to use his partner as a kind of human garbage dump where he can litter the ordinary pains and frustrations that life brings us. She is always an available target, she is easy to blame—since no partner is perfect—and she can't prevent him from dumping because he will get even worse if she tries. His excuse when he jettisons his distresses on to her is that his life is unusually painful—an unacceptable rationalization even if it were true, which it generally isn't.

4. Free labor from her; leisure and freedom for him

No abusive man does his share of the work in a relationship. He may take advantage of his partner's hard work keeping the house, preparing the meals, caring for the children, and managing the myriad details of life. Or, if he is one of the few abusers who carries his weight in these areas, then he exploits her emotionally instead, sucking her dry of attention, nurturing, and support, and returning only a trickle.

All this uncompensated labor from her means leisure for him. During the hours he spends talking about himself he is relieved of the work of listening. The long weekend days when she cares for the children are his opportunity to watch sports, go rock climbing, or write his novel. My clients don't make the connection that *someone* takes care of the work; they think of it as just mysteriously getting done and refer to women as "lazy." Yet on a deeper level the abuser seems to realize how hard his partner works, because he fights like hell not to have to share that burden. He is accustomed to his luxury and often talks exaggeratedly about his exhaustion to excuse staying on his rear end.

Studies have shown that a majority of women feel that their male partners don't contribute fairly to household responsibilities. However, a woman whose partner is not abusive at least has the option to put her foot down about her workload and insist that the man pick up the slack. With an abusive man, however, if you put your foot down he either ignores you or makes you pay.

The abuser comes and goes as he pleases, meets or ignores his responsibilities at his whim, and skips anything he finds too unpleasant. In fact, some abusers are rarely home at all, using the house only as a base for periodic refueling.

5. Being the center of attention, with priority given to his needs

When a woman's partner chronically mistreats her, what fills up her thoughts? Him, of course. She ponders how to soothe him so that he won't explode, how to improve herself in his eyes, how she might delicately raise a touchy issue with him. Little space remains for her to think about her own life, which suits the abuser; he wants her to be thinking about him. The abuser reaps cooperation and catering to his physical, emotional, and sexual needs. And if the couple has children, the entire family strives to enhance his good moods and fix his bad ones, in the hope that he won't start tearing pieces out of anyone. Consistently at the center of attention and getting his own way, the abuser can ensure that his emotional needs get met on his terms—a luxury he is loath to part with.

6. Financial control

Money is a leading cause of tension in modern relationships, at least in families with children. Financial choices have huge quality-of-life implications, including: Who gets to make the purchases that matter most to him or her; what kinds of preparations are made for the future, including retirement; what types of leisure activities and travel are engaged in; who gets to work; who gets to *not* work if he or she doesn't want to; and how the children's needs are met. To have your voice in these decisions taken away is a monumental denial of your rights and has long-term implications. On the flip side, the abuser who dominates these kinds of decisions extorts important benefits for himself, whether the family is low income or wealthy. One of the most common tactics I hear about, for example, is that the abuser manages to finagle dealings so that his name is on his partner's belongings—such as her house or her car—along with, *or instead of,* her name. In fact, I have had clients whose abuse was almost entirely economically based and who managed to take many thousands of dollars away from their partners, either openly or through playing financial tricks.

An abuser's history of economic exploitation tends to put him in a much better financial position than his partner if the relationship splits up. This imbalance makes it harder for her to leave him, especially if she has to find a way to support her children. He may also threaten to use his economic advantage to hire a lawyer and pursue custody, one of the single most terrifying prospects that can face an abused woman.

7. Ensuring that his career, education, or other goals are prioritized

Closely interwoven with financial control is the question of whose personal goals receive priority. If the abuser needs to be out several evenings studying for a certificate that will improve his job advancement potential, he's going to do it. If a career opportunity for him involves moving to a new state, he is likely to ignore the impact of his decision on his partner. Her own goals may also advance at times, but only as long as they don't interfere with his.

8. Public status of partner and/or father without the sacrifices

With his strong people-pleasing skills and his lively energy when under the public gaze, the abusive man is often thought of as an unusually fun and loving partner and a sweet, committed dad. He soaks up the smiles and appreciation he receives from relatives, neighbors, and people in the street who are unaware of his behavior in private.

9. The approval of his friends and relatives

An abuser often chooses friends who are supportive of abusive attitudes. On top of that, he may come from an abusive family; in fact, his father or stepfather may have been his key role model for how to treat female partners. If these are his social surroundings, he gets strokes for knowing how to control his partner, for "putting her in her place" from time to time, and for ridiculing her complaints about him. His friends and relatives may even bond with him on the basis of his view of women in general as being irrational, vindictive, or avaricious. For this man to renounce abuse, he would have to give up his cheerleading squad as well.

10. Double standards

An abusive man subtly or overtly imposes a system in which he is exempt from the rules and standards that he applies to you. He may allow himself to have occasional affairs, "because men have their needs," but if you so much as gaze at another man, you're a "whore." He may scream in arguments, but if you raise your voice, you're "hysterical." He may pick up one of your children by the ear, but if you grab your son and put him in time-out for punching you in the leg, you're a "child abuser." He can leave his schedule open and flexible while you have to account for your time. He can point out your faults, while setting himself above criticism, so that he doesn't have to deal with your complaints or be confronted with the effects of his selfish and destructive actions. The abusive man has the privilege of living by a special set of criteria that were designed just for him.

GLANCE BACK QUICKLY over this impressive collection of privileges. Is it any wonder that abusive men are reluctant to change? The benefits of abuse are a major social secret, rarely mentioned anywhere. Why? Largely because abusers are specialists in distracting our attention. They don't want anyone to notice how well this system is working for them (and usually don't even want to admit it to themselves). If we caught on, we would stop feeling sorry for them and instead start holding them accountable for their actions. As long as we see abusers as victims, or as out-of-control monsters, they will continue getting away with ruining lives. **If we want abusers to change, we will have to require them to give up the luxury of exploitation.**

When you are left feeling hurt or confused after a confrontation with your controlling partner, ask yourself: What was he trying to get out of what he just did? What is the ultimate benefit to him? Thinking through these questions can help you clear your head and identify his tactics.

Certainly the abusive man also *loses* a great deal through his abusive-

THE ABUSIVE MAN IN RELATIONSHIPS

ness. He loses the potential for genuine intimacy in his relationship, for example, and his capacity for compassion and empathy. But these are often not things that he values, so he may not feel their absence. And even if he would like greater intimacy, that wish is outweighed by his attachment to the benefits of abuse.

IS HE GOING TO GET VIOLENT?

An abusive man can be scary. Even if he never raises a hand or makes a threat, his partner may find herself wondering what he is capable of. She sees how ugly he can turn, sometimes out of the blue. His desire to crush her emotionally is palpable at times. He sometimes tears into her verbally with a cruelty that she could never have imagined earlier in their relationship. When a man shows himself capable of viciousness, it is natural, and in fact wise, to wonder if he will go even further. Abused women ask me over and over again: "Do you think my partner could get violent? Am I overreacting? I mean, he's not a *batterer* or something."

Before I take you through a list of points to consider in examining this issue, make a mental note of the following:

RESEARCH INDICATES THAT A WOMAN'S INTUITIVE SENSE OF WHETHER OR NOT HER PARTNER WILL BE VIOLENT TOWARD HER IS A SUBSTANTIALLY MORE ACCURATE PREDICTOR OF FUTURE VIOLENCE THAN ANY OTHER WARNING SIGN.

So listen closely to your inner voices above all.

When a woman tells me of her concerns about her partner's potential for violence, I first encourage her to pay close attention to her feelings. If he is scaring her, she should take her intuitive sense seriously, even if she doesn't believe his frightening behavior is intentional. Next, I want to learn more about what has already happened:

Has he ever trapped you in a room and not let you out?

Has he ever raised a fist as if he were going to hit you?

Has he ever thrown an object that hit you or nearly did?

Has he ever held you down or grabbed you to restrain you?

Has he ever shoved, poked, or grabbed you?

Has he ever threatened to hurt you?

If the answer to any of these questions is yes, then we can stop wondering whether he'll ever be violent; *he already has been.* In more than half of cases in which a woman tells me that her partner is verbally abusive, I discover that he is physically assaultive as well.

It is critical to use *common-sense—and legal—definitions of what constitute violence,* **not** *the abuser's definition.* An abuser minimizes his behavior by comparing himself to men who are worse than he is, whom he thinks of as "real" abusers. If he never threatens his partner, then to him threats define real abuse. If he only threatens but never actually hits, then real abusers are those who hit. Any abuser hides behind this mental process: If he hits her but never punches her with a closed fist . . . If he punches her but she has never had broken bones or been hospitalized . . . If he beats her up badly but afterward he apologizes and drives her to the hospital himself (as several clients of mine have done) . . . In the abuser's mind, *his* behavior is never truly violent.

A related mental process reveals itself when a client says to me, as many do: "I'm not like one of those guys who comes home and beats his wife *for no reason.*" In other words, if he had adequate justification, then it isn't violence. The abuser's thinking tends to wend its way inside of the woman, too, like a tapeworm. The partners of my clients say things to me, such as "I really pushed him too far," or "He's never hit me; he just shoves me sometimes," that almost certainly come from the abuser's indoctrination.

To steer clear of these distortions, we need to wrestle the definition of violence out of the hands of the abusers and implement a proper one of our own. *Violence* is behavior that does any of the following:

- Physically hurts or frightens you, or uses contact with your body to control or intimidate you

- Takes away your freedom of movement, such as by locking you in a room or refusing to let you out of a car

- Causes you to believe that you will be physically harmed

- Forces you to have sexual contact or other unwanted physical intimacy

Drawing on the above definition, we can answer important questions that arise:

Q: Is it violence if he tells me he will "kick the crap" out of me but he never does it?

A: Yes. Threats of bodily harm are physical abuse. The woman ducks or cowers, she runs out of the room, she goes into hiding with her children. There are emotional effects as well, of course, as physical abuse is by nature psychologically abusive.

Q: Is it violence if he pokes me?

A: Probably. Noncoercive men don't poke their partners in my experience. If it frightens you, causes you pain, controls you, or makes you start wondering what he will do next time, it's violence. Whether it will have these effects partly depends on what his history of past intimidation has been and on what his motives appeared to be in the specific incident. If he is repeatedly emotionally abusive, then a poke is definitely violent. In other words, context matters.

    The abuser will of course deny that he meant to intimidate his partner; he just "lost his cool" or "couldn't take it anymore." He may ridicule her for being so upset: "You call a poke *violent*?? That's *abuse*?? You're the most hysterical, melodramatic person in the world!" To me, this bullying response makes clear that he did indeed have power motives.

Q: I slapped him in the face, and he punched me and gave me a black eye. He says what he did was self-defense. Is he right?

A: No, it was revenge. My clients often report having hit their partners back "so that she'll see what it's like" or "to show her that she can't do that to me." That isn't self-defense, which means using the *minimal* amount of force needed to protect oneself. He uses her hitting him as an opening to let his violence show, thereby putting her on notice about what might happen in the future if she isn't careful. His payback is usually many times more injurious and intimidating than what she did to him, making his claims of self-defense even weaker; he believes that when he feels hurt by you, emotionally or physically, that gives him the right to do something far worse to you.

Q: He says that *I'm* violent, because I've slapped him or shoved him a couple of times. Is he right?

A: If your actions did not harm, frighten, or control him, they wouldn't fit my definition of violence. He labels you as violent in order to shift the focus to what *you* do wrong, which will just lock you more tightly in his grip. However, I do recommend that you not assault him again, as he might seize on it as an excuse to injure you seriously. Some women persuade themselves that they are holding their own by using violence too, saying, "I can take it, but I can also dish it out." But over time you will find that you are the one being controlled, hurt, and frightened. Besides, hitting a partner is just plain wrong, except in self-defense. Use your own behavior as a warning sign that you can't manage your abusive partner, and call an abuse hot line now.

QUESTION 11:
WILL HIS VERBAL ABUSE TURN TO VIOLENCE?

If your partner has not used any physical violence yet, how can you tell if he is likely to head in that direction? These are some of the rumblings that can tip you off that a violent storm may come some day:

- When he is mad at you, does he react by throwing things, punching doors, or kicking the car? Does he use violent gestures such as gnashing teeth, ripping at his clothes, or swinging his arms around in the air to show his rage? Have you been frightened when he does those things?

- Is he willing to take responsibility for those behaviors and agree to stop them, or does he justify them angrily?

- Can he hear you when you say that those behaviors frighten you, or does he throw the subject back on you, saying that you cause his behaviors, so it's your own problem if you're scared?

- Does he attempt to use his scary behaviors as bargaining chips, such as by saying that he won't punch walls if you will stop going out with your friends?

- Does he deny that he even engaged in the scary behaviors, such as claiming that a broken door was caused by somebody else or that you are making up or exaggerating what happened?

- Does he ever make veiled threats, such as "You don't want to see me mad," or "You don't know who you're messing with"?

- Is he severely verbally abusive? (Research studies indicate that the *best* behavioral predictor of which men will become violent to their partners is *their level of verbal abuse*.)

Although these questions can help you determine the degree of your partner's tendency to violence, it is important to contact a program for abused women regardless of your answers; the fact that you are even considering his potential for violence means that something is seriously wrong.

If your partner is hurting or scaring you, consider seeking legal protection. In many states, for example, you can seek a restraining order even if your partner has never hit or sexually assaulted you, as long as he has put you in fear. Some states offer a woman the option of obtaining an order that allows the man to continue residing in the home but that forbids him from behaving in frightening ways.

Some approaches to assessing how dangerous your partner may be are covered in "Leaving an Abuser Safely" in Chapter 9. The advantages and disadvantages of taking legal steps are discussed in "Should I Get a Restraining Order?" in Chapter 12.

RACIAL AND CULTURAL DIFFERENCES IN ABUSE

I find that the fundamental thinking and behavior of abusive men cut across racial and ethnic lines. The underlying goal of these abusers, whether conscious or not, is to control their female partners. They consider themselves entitled to demand service and to impose punishments when they feel that their needs are not being met. They look down on their partners as inferior to them, a view that often extends to their outlook on women in general.

At the same time, the particular *shape* that abusiveness takes can vary considerably among races and cultures. Abusers rely heavily on the forms of abuse that are most acceptable among men of their background. My white American clients, for example, tend to be extremely rigid about how their partners are allowed to argue or express anger. If the partner of one of these clients raises her voice, or swears, or refuses to shut up when told to do so, abuse is likely to follow. Clients from certain other cultures are more focused on precisely how their partners care for the house and prepare meals. Their social lives revolve around food, so they expect to be waited on like royalty with a warm, creative, and tasty dinner every night. If the man shows up two hours late without calling, the meal is *still* expected to be warm somehow, or else. I find that clients from certain countries stand out for their fanatical jealousy, which can lead verbally to ripping into their partners for speaking to a stranger on the street for ten minutes or for dancing one number with another man at a party. Abusive men from one region of the world commonly hit their children with belts, a behavior that meets with stern disapproval from abusers from other parts of the world, who in turn may horrify the first group by taking custody of their children away from the mothers.

Not only abusive behaviors but also the excuses and justifications that accompany them are formed partly by an abusive man's background. Men of one group may rely more on the excuse of having lost control of themselves, for example, whereas others admit that their behavior is a choice but justify it by saying that they have to resort to abuse to keep the family from spinning out of control.

As we will see in Chapter 13, abusiveness in relationships is a problem that is transmitted from generation to generation by cultural training and therefore takes a unique shape within each society. But for the women (and often children) who are the targets of this cruelty, the cultural variations don't necessarily change the quality of life very much. Abusiveness can be thought of as a recipe that involves a consistent set of ingredients: control, entitlement, disrespect, excuses, and justifications (including victim blaming)—elements that are always present, often accompanied by physical intimidation or violence. Abusive men tend to use a little more of one ingredient and a little less of another, substituting different tactics and excuses depending on their culture, allowing their partners certain rights and taking away others. But, despite the variations, the flavor of abuse remains pretty much the same. Abusers—and therefore their abused partners—have a tremendous amount in common across national and racial lines.

Is Abuse of Women Acceptable in Some Cultures?

I commonly run into the misconception that men from some national or ethnic groups behave much more abusively toward women than those in the mainstream of the United States and Canada. Social workers sometimes say to me, for example, "The family I am working with right now comes from one of those cultures where domestic violence is considered normal and acceptable." The reality, however, is that cultural approval for partner abuse is disturbingly high in our society, even among the privileged and educated (see Chapter 13), and our domestic-violence statistics, while not the worst in the world, are on the high end. The United States is the only industrialized nation that has failed to ratify the UN convention on eliminating discrimination against women, which specifically refers to violence against women as a form of discrimination. Pointing fingers at other countries can be a way to ignore the serious problems in our own.

In reality, abuse of women—and societal approval of it—is a widespread problem in the great majority of modern cultures. The only places where it has been found not to exist are among some tribal peoples who are highly disapproving of all forms of aggression and who give women and men equal or nearly equal power.

Abusive men from some national backgrounds are very explicit and direct about their cultural or religious rules, which can make their attitudes appear to be unusually bad. A man might say, for example, "God ordained that the man chastise the woman," or he might say threateningly to this partner, "Part of a wife's job is to give the man sex when he wants it." Do white American abusers think in these ways less than abusers of other cultures do? No. They do often hide their beliefs better and, by doing so, can create the impression of being more "enlightened." But the *directness* of a cultural message is not the same thing as its *strength*. I have worked with hundreds of nonwhite abusers from a spectrum of cultures and religions, with more than twenty different countries of origin among them, and I can assure you that my white, middle-class clients feel every bit as justified as the others and have attitudes toward women that are just as superior and disrespectful. As a product of white Anglo-Saxon Protestant culture, I am familiar with its centuries-old tradition of hiding its abuse of women under pretty packaging. Unwrapped, it doesn't look very different.

SOME SPECIFIC CULTURAL EXCUSES AND JUSTIFICATIONS

Certain culturally specific rationalizations used by abusive men can be particularly confusing to women. For example, I find it fairly common for an abusive man of color to believe that the racial discrimination he has faced in his life excuses his mistreatment of his partner. If you complain to him that he is abusing you, he may accuse you of betraying him as a man of color, saying that you are siding with the white culture that has already torn him down so much. Because racism does remain a harsh reality, he may succeed in making you feel guilty for criticizing him or for trying to leave him. If your background is the same as his, he applies a double standard of racial solidarity; in his mind he isn't betraying his racial group even though he is abusing a woman of color, yet he considers *you* disloyal when you complain of his treatment or denounce him. He's got reality turned around backward: The one who is betraying solidarity is him.

I have also had a few dozen clients over the years who belong to fundamentalist religious groups, usually Christian or Islamic fundamentalist or Orthodox Judaic. Abusive men from these groups tend to openly espouse a system in which women have next to no rights and a man is entitled to be the unquestioned ruler of the home. To make matters worse, these religious sects have greatly increased their political power around the globe over the past two decades. As a case in point, consider the growing influence of Christian fundamentalism in the United States. Women who live within these religious groups may feel especially trapped by abuse, since their resistance to domination is likely to be viewed as *evil* and the surrounding community may support or even revere the abuser. (Christian women living with abuse can find excellent guidance in *Keeping the Faith* by Marie Fortune. See "Resources.")

Some of my African-American clients claim that black women are too tough to abuse, and they may even claim to be victims of the women's violence. This claim is sometimes accompanied by descriptions of the black family as "matriarchal" or "female dominated." These exaggerations of cultural differences serve to cover up the fact that, according to the latest U.S. statistics, African-American woman are abused at roughly the same rate as white women. It is true, in my experience, that black women sometimes fight back more than white women against a physically violent abuser (though many white women fight back also), but they don't come out any less injured, frightened, or controlled.

Finally, men of some tribal cultures develop abusive behaviors toward women after they have had extensive contact with modern societies for the first time. Tribal women have sometimes reported, for example, that when television came to their geographic areas, domestic violence came with it, as their men began to learn the violent and male-dominant attitudes that characterize so much of modern culture. The tribal man thus may justify his abusiveness in terms of *progress* and *moving into the mainstream*, linking his ridicule of his partner to disparaging the overall tribal way of life, though some do the opposite, falsely claiming that tradition supports their oppressive behaviors.

WHILE I HAVE FOCUSED here on cultural differences and similarities among abusive men, there is another situation in which race and culture are very important to abuse: when the abuser is white American (or Canadian) but his partner is a woman of color or an immigrant. The abuser in such a relationship tends to use racism as an additional tactic to insult and control his partner. Women of color who have white abusers can face considerable bias from police, courts, or child protective services. Some specific resources for abused women of color—regardless of the race of the abusive man—are listed in the back of this book.

THE SAME-SEX ABUSER

Although most abusers are male and most abused partners are female, the reasons for this lopsided picture are social, not biological. Women sometimes abuse their lesbian partners, and men may be abused by their gay partners. The thinking that drives the behavior of lesbian and gay male abusers largely follows the patterns we have been examining. While it is true that some justifications used by heterosexual male abusers are not available to the gay or lesbian abuser—such as "I have the right to rule over you because I'm the man and you're the woman"—the same-sex abuser replaces these with others that can be as powerful. The abused lesbian or gay man therefore can get as badly ensnarled as the straight woman.

First, let's look at some of the things the same-sex abuser *can't* do as easily (I am going to call the abuser "she"):

- She won't be able to use sex-role expectations that are based on cultural or religious rules as easily as the straight male abuser can.

- She doesn't have as many social power advantages as a man who is involved with a woman does. (The straight male abuser can take advantage in multiple ways of the fact that we still live in "a man's world," despite recent societal changes.)

- She may not be able to use size and strength to intimidate as easily as most straight male abusers do. In fact, she may be smaller or appear to be less "tough" than her partner.

The same-sex abuser compensates for these gaps in several ways. I will offer just a few examples:

1. She may have an even deeper conviction than the straight male abuser that she couldn't possibly be abusive, no matter how cruel or even violent she gets, because abuse "doesn't happen" in same-sex relationships. She may sound so sure of herself on this point that she is able to convince her abused partner that what is happening is just normal relationship conflict.

2. She uses her partner's homosexuality against her. When she is angry, she may threaten to tell her partner's parents about their relationship or to call up her place of employment and "out" her, which could cause her to lose her job. If she is a violent abuser, she may tell her partner: "You think the police or the courts are going to help you when they know you're lesbian?" The gay male abuser may tell his partner: "The police are just going to laugh at you when you tell them you are afraid. They'll tell you to act like a man."

   The lesbian or gay male who is involved with a violent or threatening abuser does genuinely face discrimination from the police and courts, and the abuser knows this. In many states, for example, an abused person cannot obtain a restraining order to keep the abuser away if that person is of the same sex.

3. The same-sex abuser may get even more mileage out of playing the victim than the straight male abuser does. When a straight male goes around claiming that a woman is abusing him, he often meets with considerable skepticism—as well he should. But when we look at two people of the same sex, how are we to tell which one is abusing power? A quick glance won't give us the answer.

   The result is that a same-sex abuser can often convince people around her, and sometimes even her own partner, that *she* is the one being abused. When lesbians or gay men go to agencies for help with relationship abuse, it is not unheard of for the abuser to say that she is the victim *and* for the victim to say that she is the abuser! Sometimes the abuser succeeds in getting support and sympathy for quite a while before service providers catch on to the fact that they are assisting the wrong person.

4. The abuser can sometimes get her wider community to be silent about the abuse, because everyone is already struggling with the negative social image of homosexuality. Many lesbians and gay men feel, quite understandably, that awareness of abuse in same-sex relationships will be used by bigoted people as an excuse for further stereotyping and discrimination. And there's really no question that bigots will do exactly that. But silence is not the answer either, since it isolates and abandons abused lesbians and gay men and allows the abusers to go steamrolling forward over the lives of their partners.

The same-sex abuser may have had an extremely difficult life, and she may feel that anyone who labels her "abusive" is being unfair to her, given what she has gone through. She may have been banished from her family because of her homosexuality, barred from progressing in her career, or filled with secret shame during her adolescence. People in her social circle may have gone through similar trials and thus feel an instant sympathy for her excuses. But nonabusive lesbians and gay men have also endured oppressive experiences because of their sexuality. Same-sex abusers, like straight male abusers, seize any excuse they can to absolve themselves of responsibility for their actions and to elicit sympathy.

Ultimately, the thinking and actions of lesbian and gay male abusers are more similar to than different from those of other abusers. Later on, when we explore the social roots of abusiveness, it will become clear why all abusers follow more or less the same template.

KEY POINTS TO REMEMBER

- For the most part, an abusive man uses verbally aggressive tactics in an argument to *discredit* your statements and *silence* you. In short, he wants to avoid having to deal seriously with *your perspective* in the conflict.

- Arguments that seem to spin out of control "for no reason" actually are usually being used by the abusive man to achieve certain goals, although he may not always be conscious of his own motives. His actions and statements make far more sense than they appear to.

- An abusive man's good periods are an important and integrated aspect of his abuse, not something separate from it.

- Abusive men find abusiveness rewarding. The privileged position they gain is a central reason for their reluctance to change.

- Abusive men tend to be happy only when everything in the relationship is proceeding *on their terms*. This is a major reason for the severe mood swings that they so often exhibit from day to day.

- Violence is not just punches and slaps; it is anything that puts you in physical fear or that uses your body to control you.

- The styles of abusers vary by race, nationality, and sexual orientation. However, their commonalities far outweigh their differences.

- The turbulence, insecurity, and fear that your partner causes in daily life can make it hard to recognize his pattern of attitudes and behaviors. By taking a mental step back, you may begin to see recurring themes.

- Be cautious, and seek out assistance. You don't deserve to live like this, and you don't have to. Try to block his words out of your mind and believe in yourself. You can do it.

7

Abusive Men and Sex

He's not attracted to me anymore, which really hurts me.

It's easier sometimes to just give in.

He never hits me, but he did force me to have sex once.

*We both have an infection now, and he says it must have come from **me**, but I haven't had any affairs, so I know it's him.*

It seems like the only time we feel close is when we're making love.

LIBBY SCOWLED, the muscles in her face and neck tightening, as she described an abusive boyfriend she had left three years earlier. "Arnaldo never hit me, but he seemed to get a thrill out of being mysterious and terrifying. One day he described in graphic detail how he was going to torture and kill my cat, because he knew how precious my pets are to me. Another time he was giving me a massage, talking in this hypnotic, faraway tone, and he said, 'When I was in Green Beret training, I learned about a certain spot in a person's neck where, if you poke them hard and fast, you can paralyze them permanently.'" Libby found out later that Arnaldo had never been in the military. He had told other lies, too, like the one about his terminally ill grandmother who was going to leave him thirty thousand dollars. But his stories had all sounded so convincing. "He got me to support him for a year and to lend him a lot of money besides. I'm out five or six thousand dollars because of him." Resentment rang through her voice as she gained momentum. "I would be in such a different financial position right now if it hadn't been for him. And I bought it when he promised to pay me back any day, always saying that the money was just about to arrive. What a con artist!" And she told me how Arnaldo would harangue her about being too skinny, so that she became shameful of her body. I couldn't tell which was more potent inside of her, rage or grief.

Then, abruptly, Libby's face softened. A hint of a smile formed at the corners of her mouth, and her eyes shined lightly as she focused on an image inside her mind. "But there was one thing that wasn't like the rest with Arnaldo. Sex. Lovemaking with him was great. He was so completely *into* it. He would light candles and build the mood for a while. It would last a long time. He was so intense, and passionate. There was this drama around it that was so transporting. I have never experienced anything like it before. Or since, really. I wish I could capture just that one part of the relationship. The rest was awful."

Libby's story is not as unusual as you might think. When I interview partners of my clients, I always ask whether there has been any sexual mistreatment. It is not uncommon for me to hear the woman's voice lose its tension, as Libby's facial expression had, and hear her say with a certain lilt, "Oh, well, we've never had any problem in *that* area," followed by a contented and slightly embarrassed chuckle. In fact, memories of the better aspects of their sexual relationship can be part of why a woman who has left an abusive partner feels so tempted to give him another chance.

But there is also the other extreme. I have had clients whose only interest in sex was for domination and degradation. For the woman, being in bed with this style of abuser can be a nightmare. He wants sex when he wants it, the way he likes it, and with little attention to how she may feel or what her needs might be. Sexual episodes with him may feel like sexual assaults to her. As the partner of one of my clients said to me, "I don't even want to go into it. It's just ugly."

The sexually abusive man won't necessarily rape his partner in the literal sense of using physical force or threats of harm—though some do. Instead he may insult her when she declines his advances, call her names like "frigid" or "lesbian," or snarl accusingly, "You must be getting it somewhere else, since you never want to make it with me anymore." He may make her feel guilty about his sexual frustration, tell her that he feels like she doesn't love him anymore, or say that a man must have his needs met.

He may threaten infidelity: "Well, if you won't have sex with me, I can find plenty of women who will." And he may carry that threat out; many clients of mine have used affairs to punish their partners.

A woman named Cynthia recounted how her partner coerced her by using relentlessness: "If I don't want to have sex with Ernie, he just goes on and on, and he won't stop until I change my mind. He'll beg me, then he'll get crude and say I'm fucking someone else. Then it's nonstop insults. If I go to sleep, he wakes me up. Some nights I'm just exhausted after a while. So what do I do? Usually I finally give in. I can't stand to go through it. It ends up being better to just get it over with, even though it's awful, because then at least he lets me sleep."

When people think about forced sex, they picture physical assault. So when an abuser forces sex through pressure or manipulation or sleep deprivation, a woman doesn't know what to call it and may blame herself. Dozens of partners of my clients, including Cynthia, have said: "It's my own fault. I shouldn't give in to him." A woman can need some time and distance before she can come to realize that she was not responsibile for her partner's sexual mistreatment of her, before she can even name what he did. An ex-partner of one of my clients said to me, about two years after she and the abuser divorced, "Looking back on it now, I can see that I was raped over and over again for more than ten years." And she was realizing how destructive his actions had been to her soul. Studies show that *women whose partners abuse them sexually can have some of the greatest emotional difficulties, including depression, of any abused women.*

HOW MANY ABUSIVE MEN LOOK AT SEX

Arnaldo, the sexually amazing abuser, and Ernie, the sexually degrading abuser, are not as different as they may seem. Their underlying orientation toward sex is similar. One style of abusive man may behave in a sexually appropriate manner for the early period of a relationship, and then one night from hell he may broadside his partner with aggressive, degrading sex or even force her outright. The woman is left in shock, heartbroken and betrayed, feeling that her life has been turned upside down. A few of the women I've worked with have even told me of the anguish of being sexually assaulted on the night of their wedding or within a few days thereafter. With other abusive men the change may be gradual rather than abrupt, the early months of exciting and loving sexuality blending slowly into arm-twisting and ugliness. When we look inside the abuser's mind, we often find that dazzling lovemaking and spirit-murdering sexual aggression can actually be two aspects of the same mind-set.

Before I take you through the details and subtleties of how abusive men typically approach a range of sexual issues, I want to emphasize the underpinnings of the sexual mentality of many abusers, the foundation that often supports the rest of the structure.

1. IT'S FOR *HIM*.

The abuser's orientation toward sex is likely to be self-involved. Sex to him is primarily about meeting *his* needs. He may put some effort into creating pleasure for his partner, but probably not because her satisfaction, or sharing a mutual experience, is important to him. He is invested in having her reach orgasm so that he can see himself as a great lover. He wants to be erotic because he believes that his sexual prowess will enable him to dominate women. Of course, any lover gets some pride out of bringing pleasure to a partner. But to many abusive men, that's the *only* reason why the woman's satisfaction matters. Everything refers back to him.

An abusive man commonly rolls all of his emotional needs into one tremendous bundle, which he expects sex to be able to carry. He tends to have little real heart-to-heart connection with his partner, since a man cannot be truly close to a woman he is abusing. (Although his partner may feel very *attached* to him through traumatic bonding, and he may feel very *attached* to having her meet his various needs, attachment and closeness are two different things.) So he compensates for the lack of genuine intimacy by elevating sex to the highest plane, burdening it with the responsibility of providing for him all the emotional satisfaction that he is not receiving elsewhere in his relationship.

2. SHE OWES HIM SEX.

My clients commonly believe that a woman gives up her right to decline sex once she becomes seriously involved with a man. It's her responsibility to have sex with him to make him feel loved, to meet his sexual needs, or simply because that's her job. The specific point at which she loses her right to say no varies from abuser to abuser. For some, the gateway to sexual domination is the first time they have sex. In other words, she has the right to say no as long as she *always* says no, but the first time they actually make love, she forfeits her option to turn him down from that day forward. I find this particularly true of my younger clients. To other abusers, marriage is the moment when her body is transferred to his ownership. To still others, moving in together is the demarcation line.

A majority of my clients seem to believe that the woman loses her right to refuse him if the man determines that it has been "too long" since they have had sex. The definition of how many days without sex is too many differs for each abuser, but he watches his internal clock and expects access when the alarm goes off. Her decision not to have sex may be respected up to that moment, but then his entitlement tends to take over.

In a typical abusive inversion, my clients often attempt to convince me that they are the sexual victims in their relationships. As one man said: "My partner uses sex to control *me,* that's how women jerk men around. Women are the ones that really have the power over men because they know they have what we want the most, and they have the power to shut us out. My wife wants me to be her little puppy dog, begging and drooling and wagging my tail, that's the only way I'll get sex." The underlying attitude comes bursting out of his words: He believes his wife is keeping something of *his* away from him when she doesn't want intimate contact. He sees sexual rights to a woman as akin to mineral rights to land—and he owns them.

3. SEX IS A WAY TO ESTABLISH POWER AND DOMINANCE.

We have been looking at the abusive attitude that says: "We have sex because I have power over you." On the flip side of that outlook is an equally prevalent aspect of abusive thinking: "I have power over you because we have sex." In this respect his sexual actions are like those of a tomcat marking territory. Once he has "gone all the way" with a woman, he feels that he owns her, or at least owns a piece of her. Both the kinder and more cruel aspects of the sexuality of abusive men can spring from the use of sex to establish dominance.

One quarter or more of my clients cheat on their partners repeatedly. These men seem to get excitement from establishing their power over women in general, by demonstrating their ability to get sexual access. An abuser may get all this sex by creating an image of himself as a stupendous lover; by telling woman after woman that he is in love with her and that he is planning to leave his partner for her "as soon as I can break the news to her, but I just need a little time to let her down easy"; by using drugs or alcohol to impair a woman's ability to resist, or by force and intimidation. This man is heavily focused on "scoring," and the actual effect he has on the lives of these women, from broken promises to sexually transmitted infections, never seems to hit home for him.

Sexual access to lots of different women may not only make him feel powerful vis-à-vis women but also in relation to other men. If he feels competitive with men, he can demonstrate his superiority by having more notches in his belt, "bagging" women like deer. He may surround himself with men who share his view that high status in the pecking order accrues to those who can control or exploit the most women. (See "The Player" in Chapter 4.)

For those abusers who are not chronically unfaithful to their partners, this competition with men may still exist, perhaps taking the form of desiring to have the most beautiful or sexy partner and wanting other men to see how he owns and controls her. His partner may be flattered by his pride in her at first, but gradually she comes to feel that she is being used as a showpiece, with her humanity ignored.

4. HE SEES HER AS A SEX OBJECT.

An abuser who exhibits any one of the sexual attitudes described above—or all three—has to distance himself from his partner's thoughts and feelings in order to avoid guilty feelings about how he is using and wounding her sexually. One way he may do this is by seeing his partner as a sex object, as if she were a pornographic photo rather than a person, devoid of emotions or ambitions, free of any need for personal integrity or safety. This style of abusive man looks at his partner as a machine to be used for his sexual use. This depersonalizing of his partner can, in the long term, be as psychologically injurious to her as any of his other abusive behaviors. Partners of my clients sometimes tell me:

"He just makes me feel gross."

"I feel dirty and slimed on."

"He makes me feel cheap."

"The sexual stuff he does is what has really ruined my self-esteem."

"It's been years since I've had sex that really felt loving or voluntary. With him it seems more like he thinks he's winning a war or something. It's like an invasion. I hate it."

Dehumanization can be a sickening, horrible experience for the person at whom it is directed. If you are involved with a sexually exploitative partner, you may find that sex is sometimes, or perhaps always, a nightmare. Exploitative, rough, coercive, uncaring sex is similar to physical violence in its effects, and can be worse in many ways. And part of why it feels so degrading is that a woman can sense the fact that in her partner's mind she has ceased to exist as a human being.

Abusive men who have these kinds of attitudes of sexual ownership sometimes refuse to use birth control or to practice safe sex. I have had numerous clients, for example, who have conceived children through sexual assaults on their partners. The implications of these kinds of sexual abuse for a woman—and for her children—are very serious.

BACK TO MISTER AMAZING

Having laid out the worst aspects of the sexual mind-set of many abusive men, we now can go back to reexamine Arnaldo, the sexually exciting and engaging abuser. Ironically, part of why he is so sexually dynamic is that he is profoundly self-involved. He can create a vibrantly sensual lovemaking experience because of how engrossed he is in seeing himself as an awe-inspiring person. (This is connected to why severely self-centered people in general, not just abusive men, can often be charismatic and seductive.) When Mr. Amazing is lighting the candles, choosing the music, and using his soft, smooth voice to conjure the sexual mood, you may be thinking, "Wow, this is so amazingly deep, and here we are going through this together." But in reality the abuser is secretly off in a world by himself, engaged more with his fantasy than with you.

Mr. Amazing is enraptured for another reason: He finds possession enthralling. He feels like he is entering a magical realm where you belong to him totally, where he can be the ultimate master and you his unquestioning and contented slave. He craves, in short, a sexual partner with no mind or will of her own.

Finally, on some level he hopes that his ability to transport you sexually will tie you to him, so that he can have power over you in other, nonsexual ways. And, in some relationships, the abuser's belief in the power of his sexuality is self-fulfilling: if much of the rest of the time he acts cold or mean, the episodes of lovemaking can become the only experience you have of loving attention from him, and their addictive pull thus becomes greater. In this way he can draw you into being as dependent on sex as he is, although for a very different reason.

THE ABUSER WHO ISN'T INTERESTED IN SEX
(AT LEAST NOT ANYMORE)

Not every abusive man is pressuring or demanding with respect to sex. In fact, a substantial number of the partners of my clients complain of the opposite problem: The man has lost sexual interest almost completely, and the woman is feeling rejected and hungry for sex and affection. His drop in sexual energy can be propelled by several forces, including:

- A substantial proportion of abusive men are sexually shallow and so are only attracted to women with whom they have not had sex or to those they have been with only a few times. Your partner may not be interested in the kind of deep connection needed to sustain a lively sexual relationship over time and instead is off pursuing his latest fantasy of a great sexual relationship. His body may not be cheating yet, but his mind is.

- Similarly, he may be incapable of sustained sexual attraction to any woman who doesn't meet his exaggerated ideal. He may want a woman with perfect features and a flawless body, like the airbrushed models in magazines. He may lose interest rapidly in a real-life woman whose body changes over time (from childbearing, for example, or simply from age) or one who, on close examination, is revealed to have blemishes or imperfections, as any real human being does. He'll never find his dream girl because she doesn't exist, but he may pour a lot of his time and mental energy into the search—and into punishing you for not being her.

- He may be attracted primarily to sex involving domination, referred to by some researchers as *the sexualization of subordination.* As your relationship progresses, he may feel disappointed to discover that you don't fit his fantasy of a concubine—submissive and servile. There may be ways in which you stand up to him, refusing to relinquish certain aspects of your life or thoughts to his control. Some abusive men unfortunately have difficulty in achieving sexual arousal once they discover that a woman is determined to be her own person.

- He may be punishing you for some way you have challenged him, or for times when you have not felt like having sex with him. It is common for abusive men to withhold sex as a control tactic.

- If he is indeed having an affair, his energy for sex at home is bound to be siphoned off some. The chances that he is carrying a dangerous infection are also rising. If you have any concerns that your partner may be cheating on you, be sure to insist on safer sex practices. If requiring him to use safe sex feels dangerous to you because of how he may react, call a hotline for help right away.

- He may be addicted to drugs or alcohol. Some substance abusers lose their sex drive.

- He may be gay. A small number of my clients have eventually admitted to their partners, or to me, that they are primarily attracted to men. In a slightly larger but still small number of cases, the man never admits that he is gay, but the woman either catches him with a man or realizes that he spends most of his time at gay hangouts or with gay friends. Just because a man is gay doesn't mean that he can't be abusive to women. He may, for example, use a female partner as a window dressing to give him social respectability, diverting attention from his homosexuality. This is simply another example of how abusive men, straight or gay, tend to use women for selfish purposes.

- He may ration out sex as a way to gain power, sensing that you will try extra hard to keep him happy in hopes of getting him interested in lovemaking.

As I have discussed, abusive men tend to move between extremes, from loving and attentive to hateful and intimidating, from being overly involved in the minute details of your life to expressing no interest, from showing exclusive concern with what is good for you to being unboundedly selfish. The swing from electric sexual charge to loss of all sexual desire can increase his power just as the other highs and lows do.

SEX AS A CURE-ALL

A baffling question arises over and over again among the female partners of my clients: "Why does he want to have sex right after an incident in which he has been horrible to me? Sex is the *last* thing on my mind at that moment."

QUESTION 12:
WHY DOES HE WANT SEX AFTER ABUSING ME?

Contrary to what some abusive men seem to believe, women do not find abuse sexy. When a woman's partner calls her "bitch" or "whore," mocks her, or physically intimidates her, the image of entwining herself intimately with him recedes far from her mind. How can you "make love" after someone has just treated you in a way that feels more like hatred? Abusive men do not grasp how ugly they appear when acting cruel.

So why are *his* feelings so different? Does abuse turn him on? Perhaps. Some men do appear to find abuse arousing, probably because they associate sexuality with domination. But other reasons why he might want sex after mistreating you are more common, including:

- He is seeking a quick-fix for his abusive behavior. He feels that if you have sex together, it proves that his verbal degradation or his violence is not that serious, that you aren't hurt by what he did, and that everything is forgiven and forgotten.

- He wants to reassure himself that his abuse isn't going to cause you to pull away from him emotionally or sexually. In fact, pursuing sex after abuse can be an expression of the man's entitlement, as if to say, "Even if I'm mean to you, I should still get to have sexual access."

An incident of abuse leaves the abusive man with a bad taste in his mouth, which he wants to chase away quickly, and sex helps him do that. But the woman can't drive *her* anguish off so easily, as it runs much too deep. Unfortunately, the abuser's self-focus makes him unwilling to understand that difference.

SEX AS A WAY TO KEEP WOMEN DIVIDED

Some of my clients are the focal points of swirling wars among females who hate each other passionately. The man creates and feeds these battles by being sexually unfaithful, making promises to various women that he's going to pursue a long-term relationship with each one of them, bad-mouthing women to each other, getting women pregnant, and making them feel sorry for him. (See "The Player" in Chapter 4.) By getting women to channel their energy into fighting with each other, he escapes confrontation or accountability for his own actions and gets women to focus on meeting his needs and keeping him happy. Here are a couple of the approaches that clients of mine have used:

Chris and Donna

Chris makes his partner, Donna, insecure by frequently looking hard at other women or speaking flirtatiously with them and by spending a lot of time on phone calls for which he has odd explanations. He likes Donna to be aware that a lot of women are interested in him, so he drops suggestive comments from time to time. He pretends that he feels hostile toward these women, whom he accuses of "trying to tear us apart because they want to be with me." When Donna starts to hear rumors that he is sleeping around, and when one woman finally tells her outright that she has been having an affair with Chris, he tells Donna that these are lies designed to drive wedges between them. Donna spends a lot of time wondering whether Chris is really telling the truth and hating the women who are trying to take her man away from her.

Sam and Nancy

A few years into his relationship with Nancy, Sam has a secret affair for a couple of months with a woman named Zoe. He finally cuts off the affair and confesses to Nancy. He claims that Zoe seduced him and that he knew all along they shouldn't have been seeing each other, but he was afraid of hurting her because she seemed deeply depressed, so he kept postponing the decision to end it. "Zoe kept saying that she and I are right for each other, but I always knew it was just a fling and that I belong with you. She just wouldn't listen, though." He says that what finally prompted him to break things off with Zoe was her unkind comments about Nancy, which he quotes to her. Nancy becomes furious at Zoe upon hearing about her insults.

A year or so later, Nancy senses that Sam is drifting from her, including losing interest in sex. She snoops around a little and discovers that he is involved with Zoe again. She demands that Sam stop seeing her and he reluctantly agrees, but two months later he is involved with her again. "I don't know how to explain it," Sam says, "because I don't have feelings for her like I have for you. She just has some hold over me. It's a sexual thing I guess. I just can't seem to say no." Nancy comes increasingly to hate Zoe for ruining her relationship.

Meanwhile, Sam uses his tortured feelings about being "caught between two women" as an excuse for mounting abuse. For example, Nancy confronts him one day about lying to her and stealing her money. Sam responds by apologizing and explaining that he feels guilty and torn about his relationship with Zoe. He says that he stole the money to buy something for Zoe because she was so depressed that he was afraid she might try to hurt herself. Years go by, and he is still putting off making a clear choice between the two women, so their mutual bitterness is deep.

Over this period Sam's treatment of Nancy gets progressively worse, including one incident in which he knocks a table over onto her leg. He doesn't show any signs of using his abusive behaviors with Zoe, which makes Nancy hate her all the more. Zoe, meanwhile, goes around telling people: "Nancy treats Sam so badly; he is so hurt by her. He's told me all about how mean she is to him, and that's why he wants to be with me. The reason he has trouble divorcing her is that they go back a lot of years together and their families are friends of each other, but he's almost ready."

Both of the above scenarios involve an abusive man who keeps getting women to focus on each other's behavior rather than his. He relies partly on popular negative stereotypes of women, from which women themselves are not immune. Women are conditioned, for example, to see one another as catty, conniving, and eager to steal men from other women. Meanwhile he gets to remain a player, which is what he wants. On a couple of occasions, my colleagues and I have overheard clients in the waiting area joking and laughing about ways in which women fall for these machinations, as if their ability to get away with it reinforced their masculinity.

How to Stop This Routine

Women can interfere with these manipulations if they keep the following principles in mind:

1. An abusive man lies a lot. Don't believe what he tells you about what is happening in his relationships with other women, including what those women have supposedly said about you.

2. Communicate directly with other women as much as possible to compare stories about what he is saying and doing, so that he can't play you off against each other.

3. If a man cheats, that is 100 percent his own responsibility. Don't let him channel your anger toward the other woman as if he were the helpless victim of a seduction. Abusive men love to portray themselves as unable to control their hormonal urges, which is nonsense.

4. Apply the principle of "no third chances." When a man, especially an abusive one, cheats for the second time, that means that more affairs will follow, no matter what promises he may make.

5. Many women want to have a sexually intense partner, which is fine; men don't have to cheat to be sexy. Abusive men love to create the impression that their sexual wandering is a product of how passionate they are. But the reality is that sexual passion and faithfulness are entirely compatible. The reason he cheats is because he is a manipulator, not because he's sexy.

THE ROLE OF PORNOGRAPHY

In pornography that is geared toward heterosexual men, women are portrayed as very simple. They are always in the mood for sex, and they never say no. They have no sexual needs—or needs of any kind—of their own; all they seem to care about is the man's pleasure. They require no commitment, no sacrifice, and little money. When a man is finished with them, he turns off the video or closes the magazine, and they're gone. What could be easier?

Most pornographic images regrettably fit well with the abusive mindset. The woman is available and submissive. Reduced to a body, and usually further reduced to just her sexual organs, she is depersonalized. The man owns her, literally, because he owns the video or magazine or computer image. The woman is sometimes even depicted as being sexually excited by verbal abuse, roughness, violence, or even torture. Cartoons and jokes in pornography often insult or degrade women and their anatomy, or even make rape appear funny, feeding anti-female ways of thinking.

For many abusive men, pornography has shaped their sexuality since they were teenagers or even younger. It has helped to form their view of what women are like and what they ought to be. When a graduate of what I call "The Pornography School of Sexuality" discovers, for example, that his partner does not find a slap in the face arousing, he thinks that's evidence of something wrong with *her* sexually, not him. His mind-set is: The women in the magazines and videos all like it, so why don't you? A large percentage of abused women report that they have been pressured one or more times to behave like the women in pornography, often to the point of acting out a specific scenario that the man finds enticing but that she experiences as repulsive, frightening, or violent. Abusers thus sometimes directly model their sexual interests on stories or images from pornography.

Partners of my clients report to me on their efforts to set limits regarding the presence of pornography in the house, especially where children might get access to it. These women have good instincts. Abusive men absolutely need to be kept away from pornography, as it feeds the precise thinking that drives their abusiveness. Women who like to use pornography themselves should try to avoid doing so with an abusive partner.

I have received numerous reports over the years from women who have told me that they were being pressured or required by their abusive partners to watch pornography. This seems largely to be a strategy to break down the woman's resistance to performing certain sexual acts the man wants, although the actual effect is often to increase her repulsion rather than to create desire. Pornography tends to be filled with abuse of women, so his drive to make her watch it can also come from wanting to prove to her that his degrading treatment is normal.

WHAT ABOUT SEX THAT INVOLVES GAMES OF FORCE OR VIOLENCE?

Is all sex play that involves adopting roles of domination or force abusive, even if it's consensual? This is a highly controversial question among heterosexuals as well as lesbians and gay men. My opinion is that the answer is no. The key words, however, are *consensual* and *play*. For example, couples who play sex games involving force need to have a mutually established signal that means "I want you to stop for real," and that signal must be respected. If one partner gives the "stop" signal and the force doesn't immediately cease, what is occurring is sexual assault, not lovemaking.

Here is another critical point: *The meaning of what happens during sexual play is determined by the context of the relationship.* If partners are consistently kind to and respectful of each other in daily life, they can probably share kinky lovemaking without making either person feel unsafe or degraded. But in an abusive relationship these lines are too blurry. It's a stretch to call *any* sexual contact fully consensual when it takes place in an atmosphere of abuse; the woman is always having to gauge whether her partner will react abusively if she says no to a particular sex act, so her choices rarely feel truly free. Many abusers get a thrill out of taking sex play too far, to where it isn't play any more and causes genuine pain or fear. When the woman tells him later that she felt assaulted or raped, he may respond disparagingly, "We always play games like that. Come off it." When she tries to explain why the sex felt so bad, he isn't willing to listen, mostly because he *knows* it was not consensual this time, and he got a charge out of that.

When you are being mistreated in a relationship, stay away from force scenarios during lovemaking, even if the times when your partner does stay within appropriate limits are fun. Other times it isn't going to be fun at all. If you can say no to those games without running the risk of being attacked, do so. These kinds of games can only be played safely in a nonabusive relationship.

SEX AND DOUBLE STANDARDS

The double standards that are endemic to abusers can stand out sharply in the sexual arena. The most obvious one involves outside relationships. The abuser who has frequent affairs is often the same one who interrogates his partner about her movements and social contacts and goes ballistic when he has the slightest suspicion that she is developing any kind

of connection—sexual or otherwise—to another man. He may enjoy looking over other women from head to toe as he and his partner walk down
the street, but if she gives so much as a sidelong glance at a male, he
screams at her and calls her a "slut."

A popular justification for this double standard is that men have an
inherent need to be with many different women, whereas women want
to be monogamous. Over the years I have had many clients use such so-
ciobiological arguments with me, saying that from a genetics standpoint
males have reason to desire sex with as many different females as possible, while females succeed best—in evolutionary terms—if they choose
their partners carefully. You might call this the "human beings are basically baboons" argument. In reality, there are plenty of examples of stable
monogamy in nature. But these arguments are ultimately beside the
point; there is simply no excuse for double standards or for any other aspect of abuse. (I sometimes ask my clients, when they attempt to lead me
into this theoretical quagmire, "Do you cook your meat before you eat it?"
When they answer that of course they do, I say, "Isn't that awfully unnat-
ural? I've never seen any other animal doing such a peculiar thing." Human behavior can only be measured by human standards.)

My clients sometimes pressure their partners with the myth that men
can suffer physical pain or damage if they become sexually aroused and
are not satisfied. Of course, I have never heard them claim that this risk
applies to unsatisfied women.

A fair number of my clients have imposed an additional double standard, according to which the woman is expected to consent to sex any time
the man is in the mood, but she is never supposed to initiate sex herself.
As one partner of a client said to me: "If I'm in the mood, I have to make
sure not to let it show too much, because he shuts it off real fast if it's coming from me." Nothing could better illustrate the way in which an abuser's
approach to sex reflects his overall orientation toward power and control.
He wants to run the couple's sex life, and he doesn't want her needs inter-
fering with his fantasy in any way. He prefers the two-dimensional women
in the magazines, who never come to him asking for anything.

SEX AND VULNERABILITY

For most women (and perhaps for most nonabusive men as well) sex is an area of emotional vulnerability. An abuser's charm during the better periods of a relationship can lead his partner to open up to him about deeply personal and potentially painful issues. Sexual relations then add an additional layer of vulnerability, as the abuser learns about the woman's sexual likes and dislikes and about her previous sexual experiences. She may confide in him about some sexual victimization she suffered earlier in life, or about a period of promiscuity she went through, or about "hang-ups" or sexual difficulties that she has. The abusive man tends to make mental note of the highly personal knowledge he gains. At another phase in the relationship, when things turn ugly, his partner may find that her vulnerabilities are being thrown back on her. If she revealed to him earlier that she sometimes has difficulty reaching orgasm, he now may be throwing words like *frigid* and *cold fish* in her face. If she shared any discomfort regarding sex, he now will call her *uptight* and *repressed,* especially when she doesn't happen to like what *he* likes. (To the abuser, *sexual liberation* means the freedom to do whatever *he* wants.) If she told him about suffering child sexual abuse or previous experiences of rape, he now will characterize her as being permanently damaged by those violations or use her past to discredit her current grievances: "That's why you think I don't treat you well, because you were abused before. It's not me." In some of my cases the abuser has even spread private sexual information about his partner in public, including her sources of shame, thereby humiliating her and making it difficult for her to continue being around other people. Other of my clients have been careless or insensitive regarding the risk of pregnancy or of communicating sexually transmitted diseases, increasing the woman's sense of violation.

The shock to a woman of having her deepest vulnerabilities thrown back in her face by someone she has loved and trusted can cause a burning pain unlike any other. This is intimate psychological cruelty in one of its worst forms.

SEXUAL ASSAULT IS VIOLENCE

Over the years I occasionally have had clients who do not punch, slap, or physically hurt their partners but have repeatedly forced them to have sex through threats, intimidation, or physical force, including holding the woman down. The partner of this style of abuser sometimes says, "He was never violent to me," despite describing a degrading and debilitating history of coerced sex. But sexual assault *is* violence. An abuser who forces his partner to have any form of sexual relations against her will is physically battering her. There is a societal tendency not to recognize the violence present in sexual assault, which can make it more difficult for a woman to understand her own reactions and reach out for help. If you feel like you have been sexually violated by your abusive partner, trust your own perceptions and call an abuse or rape hotline (see "Resources").

Repeated studies have demonstrated that men who embrace certain key myths about rape are more likely to carry out a sexual assault. The misconceptions include the belief that women find rape arousing, that they provoke sexual assault with their style of dress or behavior, and that rapists lose control of themselves. These myths are easy for many abusive men to accept, because they are consistent with the other characteristics of an abusive outlook on female partners. It is not surprising, then, that the risk to an abused woman of being sexually assaulted by her partner is high. I also have had clients who use sexual assault to *punish* their partners, sometimes because of anger directly related to sex and sometimes not, including some who have raped their ex-partners for leaving them. The impact of such assaults can be devastating.

SEXUALITY IS a central arena in which the abuser's relationship to power is played out, including power over his partner's reproductive process. Although he may appear to keep his abusiveness separate from your sex life, closer examination of the dynamics of his conduct may persuade you that he carries his core attitude problems right into the bedroom with him. The subtle undercurrent of "sexualization of subordination" can take some time to identify. It is rare, unfortunately, for any aspect of an abuser's relationship with his partner to remain untouched by his entitlement and disrespect.

KEY POINTS TO REMEMBER

- The abuser often believes that the ultimate decision-making authority regarding sex rests with him. He may see his partner as his sexual possession.

- Sex with an abuser can be especially good, but it can also be a horror show. The two extremes actually result from similar attitudes in the abuser's mind-set regarding sex.

- The majority of abusers sexualize power, including some who find violence sexually exciting.

- Since sexuality is an area of particular vulnerability for most women, an abuser may use any of your sensitivities against you.

- If you feel uncomfortable about sexual interactions with your partner, listen carefully to your inner voice regarding what is good for you. An abusive man will try to tell you that your discomfort is your own problem rather than a product of his coercive, disrespectful, or humiliating sexual behavior.

- Women (and men) can heal from injurious sexual experiences, but healing is not likely to happen while abuse continues in the present. Attaining an abuse-free life is thus the first step to sexual wellness.

8

Abusive Men and Addiction

If I could just get him to stop drinking and smoking pot, the abuse would stop.

He's completely different when he's drinking—he turns mean.

He has stopped drinking, and now he says that I have a problem with alcohol.

I try really hard not to upset him, because when he gets mad he drinks.

He can be a terror when he doesn't have pot. He's a lot easier to deal with when he's stoned.

THE ROLE THAT ALCOHOL, drugs, and other addictions play in abusiveness has been greatly misunderstood. A majority of abusers are not addicts, and even those who do abuse substances mistreat their partners even when they are not under the influence. Abusive men who succeed in recovering from an addiction continue to abuse their partners, although sometimes there is a short break in their worst behaviors. Physically violent abusers sometimes refrain from violence for a substantial period of time when they get sober, but their psychologically abusive treatment continues or even worsens. *Addiction does not cause partner abuse, and recovery from addiction does not "cure" partner abuse.*

At the same time, a man's addictions can contribute in important ways to his cruelty or volatility. A drunk or drugged abuser tends to make his partner's life even more miserable than a sober one does. The trick is to separate fact from fiction, including the myths perpetrated by abusers themselves, regarding how addiction affects the abusive man and his partner.

NOT ALL SUBSTANCE ABUSERS ARE ABUSIVE PARTNERS

Part of how we know that partner abuse is not caused by substances is that many alcoholics and drug addicts are neither mean to nor controlling of their partners. Some alcoholics drink only late at night, or they drink away from home and return only to pass out. Some become passive and pathetic, not belligerent or domineering. A certain number even provide fairly responsibly for their families and take good care of their children, at least during the early years of their addiction. In such cases the man's substance abuse certainly causes serious problems for his partner and children, but the atmosphere differs sharply from that of a home where a partner abuser lives. And while substance abusers can be male or female, abusive partners are overwhelmingly male.

NOT ALL ABUSIVE PARTNERS ARE SUBSTANCE ABUSERS

We can further uncouple addiction from partner abuse by observing that a clear majority of partner abusers do not abuse alcohol or drugs or show other signs of addiction. Even if we restrict our discussion to physically violent abusers, I still find addiction present less than half of the time, and most researchers report similar observations.

In short, partner abuse and substance abuse are two separate problems. Both are rampant in the world today, so it is no surprise that they often turn up in the same person, along with dandruff, acne, college degrees, and various other noncausal factors.

ISN'T PARTNER ABUSE ITSELF A TYPE OF ADDICTION?

No. Partner abuse has its own causes and dynamics that are unrelated to addiction, although it also shares some features. In recent years some counseling programs have sprung up that claim to address substance addiction and partner abuse at the same time, but they are selling false hopes. A doctor theoretically may be able to develop specialties in both brain surgery and pelvic reconstruction—although it would be very difficult, given the complexities involved—but if he or she claims to perform *one* procedure that can solve a problem in *both* areas, you shouldn't buy it. The differences between abusing women and abusing substances are great enough that they have to be addressed in separate ways.

HOW PARTNER ABUSE AND ADDICTION ARE SIMILAR

The ways in which partner abuse resembles addiction include the following:

• *Escalation*

Alcoholics tend to find that they are drinking increasing amounts, or with increasing frequency, or both. This escalation is caused partly by *tolerance,* which means that the body adapts to the substance, so that more is required to have the same effect. "I can handle my alcohol" is essentially a short form for saying, "I have been drinking too much for a long time now, so it takes a lot to get me drunk." (Some addicts experience the opposite effect, so that smaller and smaller amounts can intoxicate them over time.) Substance abuse also escalates for other reasons, including the addict's increasing fear of facing reality the more time he or she has spent escaping it, and the mounting life problems that the addiction itself is creating, which gives the addict more things to need to escape *from.*

Partner abuse also tends to escalate, at least for the first few years of a relationship. One of the causes of mounting abuse is that the abuser gets frustrated by the effects of his own abusiveness, which he then uses as an excuse for more abuse. For example, you as the partner of an abuser may have become increasingly depressed over time (because chronic mistreatment is depressing), and now he gets angry about the ways in which your decreased energy make you cater to him less enthusiastically. Similarly, abuse may diminish your drive for sex, and then he is hurt and enraged about your lack of desire for him.

The concept of tolerance can also be applied to partner abuse, but with different implications. As an abusive man adapts to a certain degree of mistreatment of his partner, his feelings of guilt nag at him less and less, so he is then able to graduate to more serious acts. He becomes accustomed to a level of cruelty or aggression that would have been out of the question for him a few years earlier. In some cases the concept of tolerance also applies to the abused woman, when she becomes inured to his abusiveness and starts to stand up to him more. He then increases his abusiveness because he sees that it takes more to frighten or control her than it used to. This escalation is similar to the style of crowd control used by a military dictatorship, which shoots rubber bullets as long as they are adequate to disperse protestors but switches to live ammunition when the crowds stop running away from the rubber bullets.

However, many women (and their children) respond to the trauma of abuse by becoming easier to frighten rather than harder. A recent study of physical batterers found, for example, that about one-third of the men decreased their violence over time, because the women had become so frightened that the men could control them with scary words and glances, making actual assaults unnecessary.

- *Denial, minimization, and blaming*

Addicts and partner abusers share a capacity for convincing themselves that they don't have any problem and for hotly denying the problem to other people. An alcoholic may say that he drank "a couple of frosties" on a night when he had three forty-ounce beers and two shots, or insist that alcohol is not a problem for him because he never drinks liquor, although he throws back two cases of beer each weekend. The addict also follows the partner abuser's pattern in externalizing responsibility. In the world of substance abuse treatment, the expression *people, places, and things* is used to describe the addict's way of always finding someone or something to blame for drinking or drugging.

- *Choosing approving peers*

Substance abusers prefer to spend their time with other people who abuse substances or with those who at least accept the addiction without making an issue of it, and who will listen sympathetically to the addict's excuses for his behavior. Partner abusers make similar choices regarding their social circle. Their male friends tend to either abuse their own wives or girlfriends or else make comments about abuse that buy into excuse making and victim blaming. (In research terminology this is called *providing informational support for abuse.*) Their female friends may be mostly people who will accept their poor-me stories about being the victims of hysterical or mentally ill women.

• *Lying and manipulating*

Both partner abusers and addicts can have chronic problems with lying to cover up their problem, escape accountability, and get other people to clean up the messes they make. Partner abusers, however, use dishonesty and manipulation for the additional purpose of gaining power and control over their partners, which is a separate dynamic.

• *Lack of predictability*

Both partner abusers and substance abusers tend to keep their partners and children walking on eggshells, never knowing what is going to happen next. This dynamic helps to hook family members into hoping that he will change.

• *Defining roles for family members*

Both abusive men and addicts can set up family members to be cast in roles that serve the abuse scenario. One person may become the confronter, another the protector, and another the family scapegoat, whom the abuser uses as a place to lay all the blame for the problems that he himself is actually causing in the family.

• *High rates of returning to abuse after periods of apparent change*

Both groups have rampant problems with dropping out of treatment programs or with continuing to abuse even after "successful" completion of a program. Deep and lasting change comes only through an extended and painstaking series of steps, although the process of change for substance abusers is quite different from that for partner abusers.

How Partner Abuse and Addiction are Different

The ways in which partner abuse *differs from* addiction include the following:

- *Partner abusers don't "hit bottom."*

Substance abuse is self-destructive. Over time, the addict's life becomes increasingly unmanageable. He tends to have difficulty keeping jobs; his finances slide into disarray (partly due to the expense of his habit); his friendships decline. He may alienate himself from his relatives unless they are substance abusers themselves. This downward spiral can lead the addict to reach a nadir where his life is finally such a mess that he can no longer deny his problem. Alcoholics commonly attribute their entrance into recovery to such an experience of "hitting bottom."

Partner abuse, on the other hand, is not especially self-destructive, although it is profoundly destructive to *others*. A man can abuse women for twenty or thirty years and still have a stable job or professional career, keep his finances in good order, and remain popular with his friends and relatives. His self-esteem, his ability to sleep at night, his self-confidence, his physical health, all tend to hold just as steady as they would for a nonabusive man. One of the great sources of pain in the life of an abused woman is her sense of isolation and frustration because no one else seems to notice that anything is awry in her partner. *Her* life and her freedom may slide down the tubes because of what he is doing to her mind, but *his* life usually doesn't.

It is true that partner abusers lose intimacy because of their abuse, since true closeness and abuse are mutually exclusive. However, they rarely experience this as much of a loss. Either they find their intimacy through close emotional connections with friends or relatives, as many of my clients do, or they are people for whom intimacy is neither a goal nor a value (as is also true of many nonabusers). You can't miss something that you aren't interested in having.

In recent years, physically assaultive abusers are for the first time hitting bottom in one sense: They are occasionally experiencing unpleasant legal consequences for their actions. Unfortunately, most court systems still treat domestic abusers with special leniency (see Chapter 12), so the bottom seems to be a long way down.

- *Short-term versus long-term rewards*

Substance abuse can be highly rewarding. It brings quick, easy pleasure and relief from emotional distresses. It often provides camaraderie through entrance to a circle of friends whose social life revolves around seeking and enjoying intoxication. However, these rewards are usually short-lived. Over time, substance abuse causes the addict emotional distresses that are as great as the ones he or she was attempting to escape in the first place. Friendships based on substance abuse are shallow and are prone to tensions and ruptures due to financial resentments, paranoia, mutual irresponsibility, and many other factors. An alcoholic tends to drink more and more, not because of how well it is working but because of how poorly.

Partner abuse, on the other hand, can be rewarding to the abuser for many years, and potentially for a lifetime. In Chapter 6, we examined the multiple benefits that abusers gain through their behavior, none of which necessarily decreases over time. It is impossible to get partner abusers to change by trying to persuade them to look at the damage they are doing to their own lives (as I tried to do in my early years as an abuse counselor) because they perceive the gains as vastly outweighing the losses. Change in an abuser is primarily brought about when society succeeds in pressuring him into caring about the damage he is doing to *others*.

- *Societal approval for partner abuse is greater.*

Social supports for both substance abuse and partner abuse are regrettably high, but they are even stronger for the latter, as discussed in Chapter 13. Substance abuse receives the active promotion of alcohol advertising, which domestic abuse does not. But there is an array of writers and organizations that actively opposes improvements in legal and institutional responses to domestic abuse, whereas there are no parallel organized efforts to defend substance abuse. Television, movies, music videos, and other cultural outlets are replete with messages condoning partner abuse.

Because of these critical distinctions between partner abuse and addiction, programs and books that have attempted to address abusiveness based on an addiction model have failed badly. Batterers Anonymous groups, for example, are notorious for acting as support circles for abusers' excuses and justifications rather than as launching pads for change. Recovery programs generally address few or none of the central attitudes and habits that cause partner abuse.

PARTNER ABUSE DOESN'T GO AWAY WHEN AN ADDICT RECOVERS

QUESTION 13:
IF HE STOPS DRINKING, WILL HE STOP ABUSING ME?

Over the years, dozens of my clients have gone into recovery from addiction while they were participating in my program, sometimes because of pressure from me. No significant improvement has occurred as a result, except in those men who also worked seriously on their partner abuse issues. During the first several months of recovery, a man's harsh daily criticism and control sometimes soften, and any physical violence he was using may lessen or cease for a period, raising the hopes of the abused woman. She interprets this respite as confirmation that the addiction did indeed cause his abusiveness, but his behavior toward her gradually, or abruptly, reverts to being as destructive as it was while he was drinking, or nearly so.

Ironically, the man's backsliding tends to begin precisely *as his recovery from addiction starts to take solid hold.* The early period of recovery is all-consuming: The compulsion to drink is intense, so the alcoholic fights a daily internal battle, often holding on by a thread. He may be attending one or more substance abuse meetings per day, which occupy his time and maintain his focus. One result of this Herculean effort is that the man has little time, energy, or mental space to devote to controlling or manipulating his partner. He is entirely self-focused and absorbed. But when he starts to come out the other end of this white-knuckle process of early recovery, his energy and attention are redirected toward his partner, and his desire to bully her reemerges.

It is not uncommon for abusers to actually get *worse* when they are in recovery, partly because they may become irritable from not drinking and take it out on family members. Other abusers become more controlling when sober than they were while drunk, standing guard with eyes that are no longer clouded by alcohol.

Perhaps even more important is that an abuser's recovery program tends itself to become a weapon to use against his partner. Once he stops drinking, for example, he may turn around and insist that she is alcoholic too, even if she actually drinks moderately. He starts to criticize her for being "in denial" about her own drinking, a concept he has learned at his meetings and about which he now considers himself an expert. Insulting comments about her drinking habits and pressure on her to give up alcohol and join AA are likely to follow.

The abuser also can use specific concepts from AA against his partner. For example, AA encourages participants to review their own faults and misdeeds and make an inventory of them and discourages criticizing or focusing on the shortcomings of others, which is known as "taking someone else's inventory." The abuser turns this concept against his partner, so that any time she attempts to complain about his abusive behavior and how it affects her, he says to her, "You should work on your own issues instead of taking my inventory." Similarly, he uses the danger that he might drink as an excuse to control her. For example, when he is bothered by something she does, such as confront him about his bullying, he says, "You're getting me stressed, and you *know* I might drink if I get under too much stress." The accusation "You're threatening my sobriety!" becomes a new tool that the abuser uses to hammer and silence his partner. Abusers thus develop new excuses for abuse to make up for the fact that they no longer can blame it on being drunk.

The philosophy of twelve-step programs includes elements that could be valuable to abusers, but I find that my clients tend to ignore the principles that could help. For example, according to AA the alcoholic has a responsibility to make amends for all the damage he has done to other people while he was drinking. Abusers choose instead to take an almost opposite view, arguing that their partners should not raise grievances about past abuse, "because that was when I was drinking and I'm not like that anymore, so she should let go of the past." They think of recovery from addiction as a gigantic, self-awarded amnesty program that should cause their partners' resentments and mistrust to simply vanish.

Abusers in recovery can be just as committed to blaming their behavior on alcohol as they were while drinking. They choose to misinterpret the AA philosophy to mean that they were not responsible for their actions while they were drinking—which is *not* what AA proposes—and that therefore alcohol is a full and adequate explanation for all the cruelty and selfishness to which they have subjected women. Some of my clients use their recovery to try to escape their responsibilities, saying that they can't help with the children, get a job, or contribute in other ways, "because the program says I need to keep my focus on myself." In this way recovery can feed an abusive man's self-centeredness and excuse making. A woman who hears the abuser express these attitudes may find herself doubting that he is really changing, and her skepticism is well advised. Her partner may tell her, "You just have no faith in people" or "You don't believe anyone can change" (as if putting her down were the way to persuade her that he is no longer abusive!), but her instincts are correctly telling her that he is very much the same.

I have had clients who made significant changes from a *combination* of recovery from alcoholism *and* working seriously on taking responsibility for their abusiveness. Only then does an abuser's recovery from addiction become a significant step.

ALCOHOL HAS NO BIOLOGICAL CONNECTION TO ABUSE OR VIOLENCE

Alcohol does not directly make people belligerent, aggressive, or violent. There is evidence that certain chemicals can cause violent behavior—anabolic steroids, for example, or crack cocaine—but alcohol is not among them. In the human body, alcohol is actually a depressant, a substance that rarely causes aggression. Marijuana similarly has no biological action connected to abusiveness.

Alcohol and other substances thus contribute to partner abuse in two ways:

1. A man's beliefs about the effects of the substance will largely be borne out. If he believes that alcohol can make him aggressive, it will, as research has shown. On the other hand, if he doesn't attribute violence-causing powers to substances, he is unlikely to become aggressive even when severely intoxicated.

2. Alcohol provides an abuser with an *excuse* to freely act on his desires. After a few drinks, he turns himself loose to be as insulting or intimidating as he feels inclined to be, knowing that the next day he can say, "Hey, sorry about last night, I was really trashed," or even claim to have completely forgotten the incident, and his partner, his family, or even a judge will let him off the hook. (Courts tend to be especially lenient with abusers who blame their violence on a drinking problem.) And the alcohol is an excuse that *he* accepts, so he isn't kept awake at night with gnawing guilt about having hurt his partner.

I have had several physically violent clients admit that they made the decision to assault their partners *before* they had any alcohol in their systems. They went out, as a few of the men have put it, "to grease the wheels," drinking for a couple of hours before coming home to start a vicious, scary fight. The alcohol arms the abuser with an excuse and helps him to overcome any shame or embarrassment that might hold him back. Beware of the man who believes that drugging or drinking makes him violent. If he thinks it will, he'll be right.

WHAT ABOUT THE MAN WHO IS ABUSIVE *ONLY* WHEN HE DRINKS?

I could count on one hand the number of clients I have had whose abusiveness is entirely restricted to times of intoxication. However, I have worked with dozens of men whose *worst* incidents are accompanied by alcohol use but whose controlling and disrespectful behaviors are a pattern even when they are sober. These abusers tend to fit into one of the following categories:

1. *The verbally abusive man who escalates to physical violence or threats only when intoxicated:* When I ask the partner of such a man to describe his day-to-day behavior, she usually reports that he gets meaner and scarier when he's drinking but that his name-calling, disrespect, and selfishness are the same, whether he is drunk or sober. She tends to feel that his physically scary behaviors would stop if she could get him into recovery and that she could manage the rest of his abusive behaviors. This soothing hope is a false one for two reasons: (a) When this style of abuser gets sober, he gradually accustoms himself to using violence without the assistance of alcohol, usually over a period of one or two years; and (b) even if he is among the small number of exceptions to this rule, the woman usually discovers that his psychological abuse can be as destructive to her as his violence was, which tosses her back into having to figure out what to do.

2. *The verbal abuser who becomes even more cruel and degrading when drinking but doesn't escalate to violence:* He is doing the same thing that the physically assaultive abuser does: using alcohol as an excuse. If he gets sober, he gradually comes up with new excuses, including learning to use his recovery as an excuse, and life goes on more or less as before.

3. *The assaultive abuser who becomes even more violent when intoxicated:* I find this style the most common among substance-addicted partner abusers. When this abuser is not intoxicated, he mostly refrains from his scariest forms of violence, like punching, kicking, choking, or threatening to kill her. His partner may say, "He is only violent when he drinks," but she then goes on to tell me that he shoves or grabs her, walks toward her in menacing ways, is sexually rough, or uses other forms of physical intimidation or assault even when sober—behaviors that the abuser has succeeded in convincing her not to define as *violence.*

If your partner's behavior becomes much worse when he's intoxicated, you may tend to focus your attention on trying to manage his drinking, so that you never fully realize how abusive he is when he's sober. His substance-abuse problem can thereby create a huge diversion from critical issues.

Alcohol does not a change a person's fundamental *value system*. People's personalities when intoxicated, even though somewhat altered, still bear some relationship to who they are when sober. When you are drunk you may behave in ways that are silly or embarrassing; you might be overly familiar or tactlessly honest, or perhaps careless or forgetful. But do you knock over little old ladies for a laugh? Probably not. Do you sexually assault the clerk at the convenience store? Unlikely. People's conduct while intoxicated continues to be governed by their core foundation of beliefs and attitudes, even though there is some loosening of the structure. Alcohol encourages people to let loose what they have simmering below the surface.

ABUSERS MAKE CONSCIOUS CHOICES EVEN WHILE INTOXICATED

One of my first abusive clients, almost fifteen years ago now, was a physically assaultive husband named Max who worked for a utility company. He had gone out drinking after work one evening, and by the time he arrived at his front door he was "trashed." He told me that as soon as he came in the house, his wife, Lynn, began "nagging" him. He "saw red" and started to scream at her and soon was tearing into her with his fists. Max sheepishly recounted this event to me, going on to admit that he had torn off some of Lynn's clothes and had "partly" tied her to a chair. (I'm not sure how you "partly" tie someone to a chair; they are either tied or they're not.) As Max sat in my office, he seemed to be a likable, mild-mannered line worker. It was not easy to imagine what he must have looked like through Lynn's eyes that night.

I asked him to describe Lynn's injuries, and he told me that she had black-and-blue marks and welts up and down both of her legs. I inquired about any other injuries, and he said there were none. I was surprised, given the brutality of the attack. "Lynn had no bruises on her arms, or on her face? Why not?" Max's face changed shape, suddenly peering at me as if I must not be very bright, and he sputtered, "Oh, well, of course I wasn't going to do anything that would *show*."

Lynn confirmed to me later that Max had indeed been stumbling drunk that night. But had his inebriation caused him to lose control? Clearly not. He had remained focused on his desire to protect his own reputation and to avoid putting himself at risk of arrest, and so he had restricted Lynn's injuries to places where they would be covered by clothing the next day. He could scarcely be termed "out of control."

I could provide countless similar examples of the consciousness and decision making that my clients exhibit while drunk or on drugs. They may not choose their words quite as carefully, and they may not have perfect coordination of their movements, but they protect their self-interest: They avoid damaging their own prized belongings and usually don't let their friends and relatives see their most overt and cruel forms of verbal or physical abuse or anything that they feel wouldn't be adequately covered by the "I was drunk" excuse.

When I criticize my clients about their drunken abusiveness, they sometimes respond: "But I was in a blackout." However, a blackout is a memory disconnection that happens *after* a drunk person passes out, causing the person to no longer know what occurred upon awakening. The person was still conscious *during* the event. If you ask an extremely drunk but still-awake person what happened earlier that evening, he or she can tell you. Thus there is no such thing as being "in" a blackout; the loss of memory happens later.

Finally, even if substances could cause people to "lose control," the abusive man would still be responsible for his actions while intoxicated because he made the *choice* to impair himself with alcohol or drugs. A man's claim that he is not fully responsible for his mistreatment of his partner because he was drunk is simply another manifestation of the abusive mentality.

SUBSTANCES AS WEAPONS OF ABUSE

Oscar and Ellen

Oscar and Ellen were dining in a restaurant. Tension was mounting during the meal because of several relationship issues, mostly related to

Ellen's complaints of mistreatment by Oscar. Oscar, on the other hand, insisted that Ellen's complaints were all caused by her own hypersensitivity and desire to control *him*. Ellen was pinning her hopes for their relationship on persuading Oscar to deal with his alcohol problem. He had agreed at one point earlier in their relationship that he was indeed drinking too much, and he had maintained sobriety for nine months. His abusiveness toward her actually hadn't improved during that time, but she didn't see any other strategy to get him to change.

The argument at dinner that night focused on his economic abuse of her. Specifically, he had withdrawn $4,000—virtually the entirety of their savings—from their joint bank account and had bought an old BMW "for her." Ellen was angry that she hadn't been consulted, all the more so because she was pregnant with their first child and wanted the security of having some savings. Oscar responded by outdoing her anger, snapping through clenched teeth, "You never appreciate anything I do for you! Nothing is ever good enough for you! You just bitch, bitch, bitch!" He immediately proceeded to order a cocktail, which he knew would bother her. As soon as the waitress brought his drink, he looked Ellen in the eye, downed it in three gulps, and quickly ordered another. He set out to make himself rapidly drunk, and did. Ellen was then afraid to leave the restaurant with him, because she had been through numerous occasions on which he had combined alcohol and rage in a volatile mix that led to raised fists, pounded walls, thrown objects, and threats, leaving her cowering and trembling.

Among my clients, I have encountered numerous other ways that they have used substances as weapons, including:

- Stomping out to go driving while drunk, because he knows it will cause her to be upset and worried. This type of maneuver is particularly powerful if the couple has children and the family is dependent on the man's income for survival.

- Forcing her to assist him in running or dealing drugs, thereby putting her at risk of serious legal consequences, which he can use to control her further. (A large percentage of women who are in prison for drug- or alcohol-related charges, or for minor economic crimes such as forging checks, are serving time for crimes that either directly or indirectly were instigated by their abusive partners.)

- During periods when he is sober or clean, threatening to return to alcohol or drug use if she does not meet his demands or obey his orders, or claiming that her challenges of him are "threatening his sobriety."

- Blaming her for problems in his life that are really caused by his addiction.

- Pressuring and manipulating his partner into becoming substance-involved herself. He then uses her addiction to increase his power over her and to get other people to disbelieve her reports that he is abusive. This tactic is particularly common when the abuser has a substance-abuse problem himself, since he doesn't want his partner to be able to hold anything over him. But I have also had clients who kept their partners substance-involved while staying sober or using substances only moderately themselves.

Shane and Amanda

In one of my cases, an alcoholic woman named Amanda had entered sobriety several times, but her husband, Shane, would sabotage her progress each time by ridiculing her for being "dependent" on AA, telling her she was weak for not being able to stay away from alcohol on her own, "without a crutch." He would also go out and buy beer, telling her, "I just want to have a few on hand in case friends come over," but he never seemed to drink them. They would just sit in the refrigerator and in cabinets tempting her, and finally she would succumb.

Amanda eventually went into a detox center and didn't tell Shane where she was going, knowing that if she spoke with him she was likely to give in to the temptation to get back together with him. Shane left no stone unturned in his efforts to find out where she was and get a message to her. As of my last contact with the case, she had succeeded in staying away from him and as a result had regained custody of her children, which his abuse and her drinking had caused her to lose.

MUTUAL REINFORCEMENT OF ADDICTION AND PARTNER ABUSE

Notice that when a man uses substances as a weapon, he ends up contributing to his own problem with substances. Thus partner abuse can feed the problem of addiction, and not just vice versa. They are two separate issues, neither of which causes the other but which do help to keep each other stuck. A man's abusiveness strengthens his denial of his substance-abuse problem, as he can blame all of his life difficulties on his partner. His negative attitudes toward her allow him to easily dismiss concerns that she raises about his addiction. At the same time, the addiction fortifies his denial of his abusiveness, as he uses the substance as an excuse and as a weapon.

OTHER ADDICTIONS

I have worked with clients who have been addicted to gambling, cocaine, heroin, and prescription medications. Several have also claimed to be "sex addicts," but I don't buy this self-diagnosis from abusive men (for reasons that I covered in Chapter 4, under "The Player"). Any addiction can be a financial drain on a couple, contribute to the man's secretiveness, and encourage him to use his partner as a scapegoat. An abuser's addiction doesn't cause his abuse, but it does make his partner's life even more painful and complicated.

ENTITLEMENT AND ADDICTION

An abusive man typically believes that his use or abuse of substances is none of his partner's business. No matter how his addiction may lead him to abuse his partner economically (because he pours money into the substance and/or has trouble holding down a job) no matter how burdened she is with household responsibilities because he is out partying, no matter how much worse he may treat her while intoxicated, he nonetheless feels entitled to use substances as he chooses. If she criticizes him for his selfishness or confronts him with the effects that his partying has on her life, he feels justified in calling her a "nag" or a "bitch" or labeling her "controlling." In short, irresponsible use of alcohol or drugs is another one of the privileges that the abusive man may award himself, and he may use psychological or physical assaults to punish his partner for challenging it.

SUBSTANCE ABUSE BLOCKS SELF-EXAMINATION

While substance addiction does not cause a man to become abusive, it does ensure that the abusiveness *remains*. I have yet to see a substance-abusing client make significant and lasting improvements in his treatment of his partner unless he simultaneously deals with his addiction. In fact, I only give an alcoholic or drug addict about two months to get himself into recovery, and if he doesn't, I dismiss him from the abuser program; I don't want to give his partner false hopes, nor do I want to waste my program's time. Facing up to a problem with partner abuse, and changing it, is a profoundly complex and uncomfortable process that requires consistent commitment over a long period of time. It takes tremendous courage for a man to be honest with himself, to reevaluate his ways of thinking about his partner, and to accept how much emotional injury he has caused her. No active substance abuser is willing or able to take on this task.

Thus, although recovery from addiction is not sufficient to bring about change in a man's abusiveness, it is a *necessary prerequisite*. Only if he is willing to address *both* problems—and I have had a number of clients who have gotten serious about becoming both sober and respectful—can he stop being a source of pain and distress to his partner.

KEY POINTS TO REMEMBER

- Alcohol or drugs cannot make an abuser out of a man who is not abusive.

- Even while intoxicated, abusers continue to make choices about their actions based on their habits, attitudes, and self-interest.

- The primary role that addiction plays in partner abuse is as an excuse.

- Abusiveness and addiction are two distinct problems requiring separate solutions.

9

The Abusive Man
and Breaking Up

*Friends tell me that he's really not doing well since we split up.
I'm worried about him.*

*Last time I tried to leave him he scared me half to death.
Sometimes it seems like he could kill me.*

I don't want to take the children away from him; he's their father.

*He was okay with our breakup until he found out I was
dating somebody.*

VAN SPOKE WITH A RASPY, modulated voice that complemented his sadly
expressive blue eyes. His reddish-blond hair was always wrapped in a ban-
danna which, combined with his thick neck and upper arms, created a
biker image. But his language did not fit the tough-guy stereotype. He
spoke of his pain, of the need to face up to oneself, of the process of denial and acceptance. He appeared to be his own harshest critic, referring
frequently to his own selfishness, immaturity, and other "character flaws."
He stated openly that he was alcoholic and was attending at least one AA
meeting per day. He had not had a drink in almost eight months.

Van had, by his own description, nearly killed his partner Gail in a
beating nine months earlier. He would gaze at the floor and speak slowly
as he recalled this assault, the picture of remorse. "It was bad," he would
say. "Real bad. I'm lucky she's alive." He was arrested and spent that night
in jail, before his mother and brother bailed him out the next day. "I drank

nonstop for three weeks afterward, trying to blot out what I had done, and then I woke up one morning with bruises all over me from some fight I had been in, I don't even know where, and I haven't had a drink since. I finally accepted the fact that I wasn't going to be able to run from myself forever, and I was going to have to deal with what I had done to Gail." He did not join an abuser program until several months later, however, when he was required to do so by the court.

For weeks, Van was my star group member. He would challenge other men about their denial, about their efforts to blame their own behavior on their partners, about their need to take an honest and painful look at themselves. I pushed him a few times to stop using his alcoholism as an excuse for abusiveness and to examine more seriously his history of bullying of and violence toward Gail. He would react to my challenges with momentary irritation but then would soften and say, "I know I still have a lot of work left to do." In short, he seemed like an abusive man who was interested in doing the hard work involved in making real changes.

Van and Gail had been separated since the severe beating. They were speaking from time to time but not sleeping together. Van said he thought it would be a long time before Gail would trust him again, and he would have to give her space.

However, over a period of three or four months, Van began to realize that Gail was not taking a break from their relationship in order to rebuild her trust in him, as he had believed. She was getting herself unhooked. As it dawned on him that she was thinking seriously about closing the door permanently, he started a rapid backslide before my eyes. First, he surprised me one day by saying that Gail "should really give our relationship another chance." I was stunned. "Why on earth should a woman stay with a partner who gave her a beating that nearly killed her? I certainly wouldn't want to do it."

Van said, "The pain in our relationship wasn't all hers, you know. She hurt me a lot too." I asked if that somehow justified battering her. "No," he answered, "I'm not justifying it. I'm just saying it isn't like I was all bad and she was all good."

"And so that means she owes you another chance? How many times do you get to beat a woman up before she stops owing you?" To this, Van just muttered under his breath and lightly shook his head.

At the next session I focused more time on Van, because separation is a time when abusers can be particularly destructive. Since the previous session, he had received the definitive word from Gail that their relationship was over and that she was going to start dating, making it particularly important for us to try to influence his thought process. He plunged quickly into a homily about how hard he was working on himself in contrast to Gail, "who is going nowhere and who isn't dealing with *her* issues at all." I asked how Gail's progress was going to be assisted by getting back together with an abusive man. "Hey," he said, "I'm a lot better for her than those losers she's hanging around with now. Most of them are still drinking and acting totally immature."

Van's group was alarmed by his reversion, and members raced to try to get him back on track, pointing out to him that (1) he was claiming to have made great changes, but his entitled insistence that Gail owed him loyalty was evidence of an abuser who *wasn't* changing; (2) he was slipping back into minimizing how destructive his abusiveness and violence had been to Gail, to an extreme where he was convincing himself that he was a more constructive presence in her life than other people were; and (3) he was failing to accept the reality that a woman does not have to be "all good" in order to have the right to live free of abuse. I kept an additional thought to myself, which was that based on my conversation with her I was confident that Gail's life was not "going nowhere" and that her primary goal at that point was to heal from what *he* had done to her. When he made disparaging references to "her issues," he was ignoring the reality that her issues were 90 percent *him*. I remained silent on this point because I was concerned, given the state of mind he was in, that the better he understood her healing process, the more effectively he would take steps to sabotage it.

Van was not open to his group's feedback the way he had been in earlier months. His heels were dug in, as we could see in the digusted shaking of his head and the dismissive curl of his lip. The group had stumbled upon a core aspect of Van's entitlement—as tends to happen with each client sooner or later—and we weren't going to take it apart in a few short weeks. We hoped that we could reach him eventually though, for Van still had six months to go of the eleven the court had ordered him to spend in our program.

He never gave us the chance, unfortunately. Less than three weeks later, overwhelmed by his outraged entitlement, he approached Gail in a restaurant in front of numerous witnesses, called her a "fucking bitch," and walked off flashing her the finger. His verbal assault violated a restraining order barring him from approaching her, and since he was already on probation for his grave attack on her, he was jailed for a minimum of six months. Gail had little desire to see Van behind bars, but in this case his incarceration was a blessing, as it gave her an uninterrupted opportunity to move on with her life, which she did. (Later in this chapter we will look at strategies for getting away from a frightening relationship safely.)

WHAT AN ABUSER DOES IF YOU ARE LEAVING HIM

Breaking up with an abuser can be very hard to do. In fact, leaving a nonabusive partner is generally easier, contrary to what many people believe. Few abusers readily allow themselves to be left. When they feel a partner starting to get stronger, beginning to think for herself more, slipping out from under domination, abusers move to their endgame. Some of their more common maneuvers include:

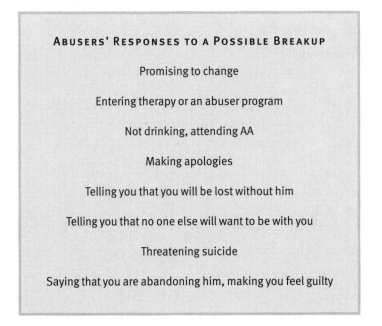

ABUSERS' RESPONSES TO A POSSIBLE BREAKUP

Promising to change

Entering therapy or an abuser program

Not drinking, attending AA

Making apologies

Telling you that you will be lost without him

Telling you that no one else will want to be with you

Threatening suicide

Saying that you are abandoning him, making you feel guilty

Threatening to kidnap or take custody of the children

Threatening to leave you homeless or with
no financial resources

Turning very nice

Getting other people to pressure you into
giving him another chance

Taking care of things that you have been complaining
about for a long time (e.g., finally fixing a hazardous
situation in the house, getting a job, agreeing that you
can go out with your friends)

Behaving in self-destructive ways so that you will worry
or feel sorry for him (e.g., not eating, drinking heavily,
skipping work, never talking to his friends)

Spreading rumors about you, trying to ruin
your friendships or reputation

Starting a new relationship/affair to make you
jealous or angry

Insisting that he already has changed

Spreading confidential information
about you to humiliate you

Threatening or assaulting anyone you try to start a new
relationship with, or anyone who is helping you

Getting you pregnant

Stalking you

Physically or sexually assaulting you

Trashing your house or car

Threatening to harm you or kill you

Each abuser uses a different mix of the above tactics, and some let go somewhat more easily than others. Strategies of control that appear contradictory may go hand in hand. For example, he may insist adamantly one day, "You should be able to tell that I've changed," and then call the next night to say, "If you don't give this relationship another chance, you're going to find out what I'm really capable of." One day on the phone he may tell you that his love for you will never die, but when his poetic language doesn't succeed in persuading you to meet him for a drink, he will abruptly switch to yelling: "I don't give a shit about you anyhow, so just let your life continue down the stinking hole it's in!" He doesn't care that these pieces don't fit together, because he is intently focused on a single desire: to get you back under his control.

He knows he used to be able to control you with charm, affection, and promises. He also remembers how well intimidation or aggression worked at other times. Now both of these tools are losing their effectiveness, so he tries to increase the voltages. He may switch erratically back and forth between the two like a doctor who cycles a patient through a range of antibiotics, trying to find the one that will get the infection under control. And the analogy is an apt one, because an abuser sees his (ex-) partner's growing strength and independence as a sickness rather than as the harbinger of health that it actually is.

Promises that an abuser makes during this period can be persuasive, especially if they are combined with sincere-sounding apologies or if he takes some concrete initiative such as quitting drinking, locating a therapist, or joining an abuser program. However, once he succeeds in getting you to reunite with him, he gradually plows his way back into the usual ruts, dropping counseling because he "can't afford it," saying he will go back to "a little" drinking because he can "handle it," and so forth. Before long, daily life has returned to its former contours.

My clients make flip-flopping statements during breakups about who is responsible for the dissolution of the relationship, bouncing between blaming everything on themselves and casting all fault on to the woman. Making it her fault is closer to their real thinking; the blaming of themselves is largely a way to win sympathy from other people, including abuse counselors, who can get drawn in by a theatrical show of pained guilt. And in an ironic twist, the more he says that the separation is his own fault, the more friends and relatives are tempted to pressure the woman to believe that he will change.

When one of my clients takes this *mea culpa* stance, I ask him to describe in detail how exactly his behavior drove his partner away. Eight times out of ten the man can give me only two or three examples, or none. In other words, he doesn't really believe that he is abusive, and my request for extensive specifics smokes him out. If he does manage to list a few things he did wrong, they often are far afield from the core of his destructiveness, as in comments like "I should have made her a higher priority; we didn't do things together enough," or they are actually backhanded remarks to get more digs in against her, such as, "I used to walk away from her because of the insane rages she goes into, but I should have realized that my leaving just made her feel even worse."

The volatile, abusive, and sometimes dangerous reactions that abusers can have when relationships draw to a close have often been considered, especially by psychologists, to be evidence of the man's "fear of abandonment." But women have fears of abandonment that are just as great as men's, yet they rarely stalk or kill their partners after a breakup. Not only that, but many abusers are vicious to their ex-partners *even when they do not desire a reunion or when they initiated the breakup themselves.* The clue to how an abuser handles separation lies in the same thinking that has been causing his controlling and abusive behavior throughout the relationship and that has driven his partner away from him.

How Abusers View Separation

Van's internal process, and the destructive behavior it led him to, captures the essence of how an abusive man perceives the ending of a relationship. Let's look at the central elements of his outlook:

"Abuse is no reason to end a relationship."

Van was unwilling to accept that his brutal mistreatment of Gail was adequate reason for her to leave him. Why? First, he believed that the pain Gail sometimes caused him during their relationship outweighed his abuse of her. If Van can convince himself that he has an even balance sheet, despite his severe physical assault, imagine how easily a purely psychological abuser can do so (even though the reality is that emotional abuse can do just as much damage).

Second, Van believed that it was unreasonable to expect a man to be nonabusive unless his partner *never* hurt his feelings or failed to cater to him. He felt that we were being unfair and unrealistic about a man's inherent nature, as if we were asking a tiger to be vegetarian. Without saying so directly, he revealed his attitude that a woman needs to accept the fact that a certain amount of abuse just comes with the territory of being involved with a man, unless she can be perfect.

"WHEN I PROMISE TO BE KINDER IN THE FUTURE, THAT SHOULD BE ENOUGH."

No matter how many times in the past Van had broken his promises to change, he still believed that *this time* Gail should see that he really meant it and should give him another chance. There was no limit in his mind to how many "other chances" he should get; he felt entitled to an endless series.

To make matters worse, Van felt that Gail was supposed to accept his rose-colored vision of the future even though he was simultaneously blaring loud warning signals that he *hadn't* changed. My clients demand forgiveness while continuing to insult, threaten, demand immediate responses, attend only to their own needs, and more. According to his mindset, she should believe that his abuse has stopped when *he* says it has stopped, regardless of what she sees in front of her own eyes.

"THERE IS NO LIMIT TO HOW MUCH SHE SHOULD BE WILLING TO 'WORK ON' OUR RELATIONSHIP."

The abuser feels entitled to end a relationship any time he feels like it, but he assigns no such privilege to his partner. Around breakup time, my clients grouse bitterly to me along the lines of:

"Nowadays, people just throw relationships in the trash as soon as it gets difficult. There's no commitment anymore to sticking it out and making it work."

"I guess our marriage vows didn't mean anything to her."

"She says she cares so much about our children, but it's no big deal to her if they have a broken home."

"She's prepared to just throw away everything we had because she's found some other guy."

No woman in any of my cases has ever left a man the first time he behaved abusively (not that doing so would be wrong). By the time she moves to end her relationship, she has usually lived with years of verbal abuse and control and has requested uncountable numbers of times that her partner stop cutting her down or frightening her. In most cases she has also requested that he stop drinking, or go to counseling, or talk to a clergyperson, or take some other step to get help. She has usually left him a few times, or at least started to leave, and then gotten back together with him. Don't any of these actions on her part count as demonstrating her commitment? Has she ever done enough, and gained the right to protect herself? In the abuser's mind, the answer is no.

Once again, the abuser's double standards rule the day. He doesn't consider his chronic verbal abuse, or even violence, to constitute a failure to "love and cherish," but her decision to move away for safety does. His affairs automatically deserve forgiveness, whereas any affairs *she* may have he considers proof of her low moral character and lack of caring. And his exposure of the children to his degrading and bullying of their mother doesn't keep him from awarding himself the title of Children's Protector, the one who wants to give them a "stable family life" while their "selfish" mother tries to split them apart.

"SHE IS STILL RESPONSIBLE FOR MY FEELINGS AND WELL-BEING."

In the abusive man's self-serving value system, the woman may be responsible for his needs and feelings even *after* she declares that she isn't his partner anymore. So if he loses his job, or his new fling doesn't work out, or his mother gets ill, he still feels entitled to have her take care of him emotionally. In particular, he tends to make her endlessly responsible for his hurt feelings from their relationship or from their breakup.

"THE RELATIONSHIP IS OVER WHEN I SAY IT'S OVER."

I repeatedly run into the following scenario: A new client in the abuse program is describing his most serious incident of abuse, as all participants are required to do, and he excuses his actions by saying, "It happened because I found out she was cheating on me." When I contact the woman, however, I find out that, although he may be right about her seeing another man, *she and my client were broken up at the time.* In other words, in the abuser's mind any relationship that she has is "an affair" if it happens during a period when *he* still wishes they were back together, because he feels entitled to determine when she can be free to see other people.

"SHE BELONGS TO ME."

The abuser's dehumanizing view of his partner as a personal possession can grow even uglier as a relationship draws to a close. I sometimes find it extraordinarily difficult to get a client to remember at this point that his partner is a human being with rights and feelings rather than an offending object to destroy. At worst, his efforts to reestablish his ownership may include following her and monitoring her movements, scaring people who try to assist her, threatening men she is interested in dating, kidnapping the children, and physically attacking her or people close to her. For abused women separation is a time of particularly high risk of homicide or attempted homicide, which can sometimes involve murderous assaults on her new boyfriend, her children, or on other people she cares about.

Numerous studies have found that mistreatment of women by abusers tends to continue for a substantial period after separation and commonly escalates to levels worse than those when the couple was together. Particularly common in postseparation is rape or other forms of sexual assault, which conveys a powerful message of ownership: *"You continue to be mine, and I retain my rights to your body until **I** decide otherwise."*

If you are concerned that your partner may be capable of extreme violence—even if he has not been violent in the past—take careful safety precautions (see "Leaving an Abuser Safely," page 225).

TRAUMATIC BONDING

One of the great tragedies of all forms of abuse is that the abused person can become emotionally dependent on the perpetrator through a process called *traumatic bonding*. The assaults that an abuser makes on the woman's self-opinion, his undermining of her progress in life, the wedges he drives between her and other people, the psychological effects left on her when he turns scary—all can combine to cause her to *need him* more and more. This is a bitter psychological irony. Child abuse works in the same way; in fact, children can become *more* strongly attached to abusive parents than to nonabusive ones. Survivors of hostage-taking situations or of torture can exhibit similar effects, attempting to protect their tormentors from legal consequences, insisting that the hostage takers actually had their best interests at heart or even describing them as kind and caring individuals—a phenomenon known as the *Stockholm syndrome*. I saw these dynamics illustrated by a young boy who got a shock from touching an electric fence and was so frightened by it that he grabbed on to the fence for security—and wouldn't let go as each successive shock increased his panic, until his sister was able to reach him and pull him off.

Almost no abuser is mean or frightening all the time. At least occasionally he is loving, gentle, and humorous and perhaps even capable of compassion and empathy. This intermittent, and usually unpredictable, kindness is critical to forming traumatic attachments. When a person, male or female, has suffered harsh, painful treatment over an extended period of time, he or she naturally feels a flood of love and gratitude toward anyone who brings relief, like the surge of affection one might feel for the hand that offers a glass of water on a scorching day. But in situations of abuse, *the rescuer and the tormentor are the very same person.* When a man stops screaming at his partner and calling her a "useless piece of shit," and instead offers to take her on a vacation, the typical emotional response is to feel *grateful* to him. When he keeps her awake badgering her for sex in the middle of the night and then finally quiets down and allows her to get some of the sleep that she so desperately craves, she feels a soothing peace from the relief of being left alone.

Your abusive partner's cycles of moving in and out of periods of cruelty can cause you to feel very close to him during those times when he is finally kind and loving. You can end up feeling that the nightmare of his abusiveness is an experience the two of you have *shared* and are escaping from together, a dangerous illusion that trauma can cause. I commonly hear an abused woman say about her partner, "He really knows me," or "No one understands me the way he does." This may be true, but the reason he seems to understand you well is that he has studied ways to manipulate your emotions and control your reactions. At times he may seem to grasp how badly he has hurt you, which can make you feel close to him, but it's another illusion; if he could really be empathic about the pain he has caused, he would stop abusing you for good.

Society has tended to label a woman "masochistic" or "joining with him in his sickness" for feeling grateful or attached to an abusive man. But, in fact, studies have shown that there is little gender difference in the traumatic bonding process and that males become as attached to their captors as women do.

The trauma of chronic abuse can also make a woman develop fears of being alone at night, anxiety about her competence to manage her life on her own, and feelings of isolation from other people, especially if the abuser has driven her apart from her friends or family. All of these effects of abuse can make it much more difficult to separate from an abusive partner than from a nonabusive one. The pull to reunify can therefore be great. Researchers have found that most abused women leave the abuser multiple times before finally being able to stay away for good. This prolonged process is largely due to the abuser's ongoing coercion and manipulation but also is caused by the trauma bonds he has engendered in his partner.

One exercise that can help you address this trap involves making a list of all the ways, including emotional ones, in which you feel dependent on your partner, then making another list of big or small steps you might take to begin to become more independent. These lists can guide you in focusing your energy in the directions you need to go.

WHY HE DOESN'T ACCEPT YOUR REQUEST
TO "TAKE A BREATHER"

Have you ever attempted to take a brief period of separation from your partner? Perhaps you had been considering getting out of your relationship but were afraid of your partner's reaction, so you asked for "a little time apart" instead of breaking up outright. Or maybe you weren't sure what you wanted to do and just craved some time away to consider where to go from here without having to deal daily with his bullying, criticism, and watching over you. You may have attempted to reassure him that the relationship wasn't ending, that you still wanted to "work on getting back together," but that you just needed a break. You probably requested that the two of you stay in separate places for a period of a few weeks or months and that you see each other little or not at all. You may have made other specific requests, such as not to speak at all, even by telephone, so that you could get a complete break. You may have asked for an agreement that you could each see other people during this period, or specifically requested the opposite. The great majority of the abused women I work with try at some point to get time out of the pressure cooker.

My clients, however, rarely honor their partners' requests. At the beginning the man presents himself as supporting the plan, saying, "I agree with her that we need some time apart to just let everything cool off, and then talk it over with level heads." But he doesn't think so for long. He soon starts cutting around the edges of the agreement. If she asked that he not call for a while, he sends a card. Then he calls on some pretext, perhaps a bill that has to be paid or an invitation for her from his sister, and throws in offhandedly, "So, how are you?" to try to get a conversation started. He may keep showing up "by coincidence" at places where she happens to be. He keeps chipping away at her resolve as much as he can, until she cracks and sees him. Once they are face-to-face, he pours on the sweetness and charm, reminiscent of his romantic persona in the early, glory days of the relationship, and sees if he can cajole or manipulate her into bed; he may sense that once they've had sex, she'll be hooked in again, a strategy that I have often seen my clients succeed with. One way or another, the woman never seems to end up getting the decompression time that she knew was indispensable to her well-being.

Why doesn't he allow the break to happen? On a conscious level he may simply miss her, but down deep he has other interests. He experiences the separation as a declaration by his partner that she is capable of surviving without him, that she is the best judge of what is good for her, that her needs shouldn't always take a backseat to his, that her *will* has force. These messages represent a powerful summary of everything that he *does not* want in his relationship, and he feels driven to move quickly to prove them false.

The abuser is afraid of what his partner may discover if she succeeds in getting a respite from his control. She may see how good it feels to live without put-downs and pressure. She may notice that there are other people in the world, both women and men, who respect her and treat her well, and may even observe that some of her female friends are treated as equals by their partners. She may start to think her own thoughts, without him there to monitor her reflections and channel them toward the views *he* wants her to have. Above all, she might discover how much better off she is without him. In short, he doesn't tolerate the break because on some level he senses that *it is too healthy and healing for the woman*. He wants her to hear his voice and see his face, because he believes he can destroy her resolve.

Does he think carefully through these concerns? Probably not entirely. He reacts largely on automatic, based on ruts in his thinking and behavior that have been deepening for years. And yet, I also keep observing how much more aware my clients are of their own strategies than you might expect; when they are upset with me, as they so often are, they often forget to keep their masks on, and they blurt out their honest thoughts and plans.

THE ABUSER WHO *WANTS* THE RELATIONSHIP TO END

What if your partner is the one who breaks off the relationship, or what if he's in complete agreement that you two don't belong together? The good news is that, if you don't have children with him, he may stay largely out of your hair. Perhaps he is interested in another woman or just wants to return to pursuing his fantasy of the dream girl who does everything for him and never challenges him. Or maybe something else altogether is occupying his mind.

I regret to say that even then peace is not an entirely sure thing (although I have not often heard of *physical* assaults by an abuser postseparation if he accepts the breakup, except in cases of ongoing conflicts over the children). Even the abusive man who is ready to be single again may still crave retaliation for all the ways he feels you hurt him, which in his distorted perceptual system may include all the times you defended yourself, questioned the superiority of his knowledge and judgment, or refused to simply be a carbon copy of him. So he may spread distorted stories about the history of your relationship or tell outright lies to try to turn people against you. Since he has to see himself as the more powerful one, he may declare that *he* broke things off while you "begged" him for another chance and that *you* "promised to change." These kinds of aftershocks of abusive behavior can be painful.

An abuser who accepts the end of the relationship, or even desires it, may nonetheless continue to try to settle old scores with you through the children, a matter we explore further in Chapter 10.

There are cases, of course, where the woman genuinely wants to continue the relationship and the abuser does not. My clients sometimes leave a woman to punish her. Women in this position can experience the abuser's departure as one final slap in the face following a long line of previous ones—figuratively or literally—that leaves her feeling even more humiliated and unlovable. Therefore it does not help an abused woman when people say to her: "What are you upset about? You're lucky to be rid of him." Anyone who wants to support an abused woman's recovery and empowerment needs to have room for both her sadness and her outrage about being left and to understand that his exit was just one more way she was walked on.

Abusers who take off often leave other damage in their wake besides the emotional or physical injuries to the woman. Debts, destroyed belongings, pregnancy, or traumatized children may be dumped in her lap. Communities that want to support abused women need to recognize that the abuser can create difficulties that endure long beyond his departure.

Leaving an Abuser Safely

Attempting to determine the level of risk that a particular abuser will become physically violent is a complex and imprecise process. If you are concerned that your partner may react destructively or violently to being left, listen carefully to your intuitions even if he has not been violent, or not extremely so, in the past. A recent study found that women's own predictions regarding future violence by their abusive partners were far more accurate than assessments based on any other factor.

Separation can be an especially risky time. I was close to a case recently in which a woman left a psychological abuser who became increasingly threatening and scary over the months after she left him, to the point where she went as far as making arrangements with relatives regarding who should care for her two children in the event of her death. And although he had never hit her during their relationship, he tragically did in fact kill her, hiding a block away from the courthouse to ambush her as she was leaving a hearing where she had obtained a restraining order against him, after which he committed suicide. (As a result of a brief speech I gave about this homicide death, I have come to know her heartbroken parents personally.)

Assessing the Potential Violence of an Abuser

The danger signs below can be useful whether or not you are currently thinking of leaving your partner. Some combination of these elements has been found to be present frequently—though not always—in cases where abusers have committed the most seriously violent acts. Pay attention to your own inner voice as you consider these indicators:

DANGER SIGNS IN ABUSIVE MEN

- He is extremely jealous and possessive.

- His violent behavior and threats have been escalating.

- He follows you, monitors your whereabouts, or stalks you in other ways.

- You are taking steps to end the relationship or have already done so.

- He was violent toward you during one or more of your pregnancies.

- He has been sexually violent toward you.

- He has threatened to kill you or hurt you badly, has choked you, or has threatened you with a weapon.

- He has access to weapons and is familiar with their use.

- He seems obsessed with you.

- He is depressed, suicidal, or shows signs of not caring what happens to him.

- He isn't close to anyone.

- He has a significant criminal history.

- He uses or threatens violence against other people.

- He abuses substances heavily.

- He has been abusive to children.

- His past violence toward you, or toward other partners, has been frequent or severe.

- He has killed or abused pets, or has used other terror tactics.

- He uses pornography.

- He exhibited extreme behaviors when you made previous attempts to leave.

- He is familiar with your routines, the addresses of your friends and relatives, the location of your workplace, or other personal information he can use to locate you.

There is, regrettably, no science to using these indicators. It would be misleading for me to say, for example, "Three to five 'yes' answers reflect moderate danger, six and up mean 'severe danger,'" or offer a similar interpretation, because the reality is not that simple. Some guides to assessing the risk of violence from abusers have created such "low-, moderate-, and high-risk" categories and by so doing can encourage women to underestimate the danger they are in by causing them to ignore their intuition. A small number of abusers who kill or severely injure their partners do so with *few or none* of the above elements known to be present, which is all the more reason to rely ultimately on your own "gut" feelings of how dangerous he is.

SAFETY PLANNING

The fact that you are even wondering how far your partner's abuse might go suggests to me that you have already seen aspects of him that are disquietingly mysterious or frightening. I urge you to seek assistance from a program for abused women (see "Resources") and to create a *strategic safety plan* with an abuse specialist through that program. Safety plans can involve two different sets of steps, one for increasing your safety while living with your partner and another for if and when you decide to leave him. Bear in mind that the process of leaving an abusive man can be risky, so if you are preparing for a breakup put some extra thought into the kinds of precautions that you can take. Specialists who work with abused women report that those women who succeed in leaving and staying away almost always have a plan before they go.

A safety plan while you are living with your abusive partner can include the following elements, among many others:

- Plan different escape routes from your house in case your partner becomes violent, and plan where you would go if you needed to stay away overnight.

- Hide spare car keys and important documents (birth certificates, health cards, bank cards) in places where they are safe and where you could grab them and leave quickly.

- Try to get out of dangerous places during arguments, such as leaving the kitchen where there are knives and other sharp objects the abuser could use to assault you.

- Obtain a private post office box or some other address you can use to receive confidential mail.

- Set code words with friends or relatives and with your children that indicate an emergency, and plan how they are to respond if you say the code word in person or over the telephone.

- Open a secret bank account so that you will have access to funds should you need to flee.

- Keep a working phone in a room with a door that locks so that you will be able to call for help in an emergency.

- Carry a cell phone.

- Obtain a firearm permit so that you can carry pepper spray.

- Stay away from drugs or alcohol yourself to make sure that your judgment is never impaired, and seek substance-abuse treatment for yourself if necessary.

- Call the abused women's hotline if you are afraid, and call the police if the danger is immediate.

After you leave your abusive partner, there are additional items you can add to your safety plan, a few of which include:

- Change the locks on your home.

- Inform neighbors of the danger and give them descriptions or photographs of the abuser and his car.

- Inform people at your workplace of the potential danger to you.

- Tell your children not to talk to the abuser and to seek assistance immediately if they see him.

- Advise the local police department of the risk to you, including any past threats or violence by your ex-partner, and ask what special services or protections might be available.

- Inform the children's schoolteachers and administrators of the risk, and provide them with a photograph of the abuser and other information, including a copy of your restraining order if you have one.

- Teach your children how to dial 911 from home and cell phones.

- Vary the routes that you and your children travel.

- If you plan to involve the court, such as by seeking a restraining order, contact a court advocate if one is available, and develop an additional safety plan with the advocate that specifically addresses how you can most safely use the court process. If you do obtain a restraining order, keep a copy on your person at all times and leave additional copies in your home, vehicles, and workplace.

These are selected examples of plans you can make, ideally with the assistance of an abuse specialist, to increase your safety and protect your children. You can call an abuse hotline and develop a safety plan without even providing your name or telephone number, ensuring your complete privacy. If you can go to the abused women's program and meet with an advocate face-to-face, all the better. I also strongly recommend the books *When Love Goes Wrong* and *It's My Life Now,* both listed in the "Resources" section, for any woman who is struggling to get safe from a frightening partner.

If you are afraid of your abusive partner it is important to make a safety plan *even if you do not plan to leave him at this point.* If he has demonstrated that he has a capacity for violence, or you suspect that he does, there is every reason to start planning *now* for how you will keep yourself and your children safe should a dangerous situation arise in the future.

Some psychologically abused women feel confident that their partners would never escalate to violence or threats. However, my experience is that most abusive men—though not all—do become physically frightening sooner or later, even if they never follow through with using violence. It makes sense for every abused woman to spend some time considering how she will respond if the unexpected happens.

If you are prepared to leave your relationship, safety planning becomes even more important. If you are afraid of your partner, don't tell him that you are breaking up with him until you have a clear plan and feel that you can inform him in a safe way. Then break all contact with him. Staying out of touch with an abusive ex-partner can be very difficult. The more afraid you are of him, the more tempted you may feel to check up on how he is doing, because in the past your safety may have depended on your constant awareness of his moods and readiness to respond to them. But making contact with him can be very dangerous as he may sound friendly and say that he just wants to see you for one final talk or to say good-bye, and then use that opportunity to attack you physically or sexually. I have been aware of a few cases where the man made an innocent-sounding excuse to get together "just once" and then murdered the woman for having left him. It is natural to have the hope of staying friends with an ex-partner, but this is rarely possible with an abusive man and is absolutely impossible with one who is physically dangerous to you. And if he doesn't choose to hurt you, he may lure you into becoming reinvolved with him instead.

ABUSED WOMEN WITH CHILDREN

Ending a relationship with an abusive man can be considerably more complicated for a woman with children, especially if the abuser is the children's legal father (biological or adoptive). The risk that the abuser will try to harm the children, turn them against you, or attempt to win custody of them through the legal system requires an additional strategic planning process. These issues are examined in detail in the next chapter.

If you do decide to flee abruptly, *take your children with you if you possibly can* and take their birth certificates, social security cards, and passports. Some women are in so much danger that they are forced to leave their children behind, but the abuser then may go to court for custody, saying that she "abandoned" them.

KEY POINTS TO REMEMBER

- When a breakup happens against an abuser's will, he may define his ex-partner's decision as a provocative declaration of independence and may go to war to prove that she belongs to him.

- Leaving an abuser is hard to do, but with time and planning you can succeed.

- As a relationship dissolves, and for a long while thereafter, an abused woman should be especially alert to her own safety and take steps to protect herself.

- After breaking up with an abusive man, wait at least a few months before becoming involved with a new partner. Taking time to heal emotionally from the abuse you have endured can be critical to helping you choose a nonabusive partner next time.

- Read *It's My Life Now* (see "Resources").

- Your life belongs to no one but you.

The Abusive
Man in
the World

Abusive Men as Parents

He's terrible to me, but he's a really good father.

He took no interest in the children until I left him, and then right away he filed for custody.

My children are freaked out and don't want to go on visitation with him, but the court won't listen to me.

I couldn't manage without him, because the children don't listen to me.

IT'S SATURDAY AFTERNOON, and excitement is high in the Turner family. Randy, who is eleven, and his big sister, Alex, thirteen, are getting ready to go with their parents to a big birthday bash for their twin cousins. Their mother, Helen, is helping them get their presents wrapped and choose what to wear, and periodically intervening to sort out quarrels between the two of them, which seem to erupt every few minutes. Tom, the father, is in the garage trying to fix Randy's dirt bike and is covered with grease. Helen's anxiety is mounting as the hour gets later, because Tom is doing nothing about getting ready to leave and keeps saying, "Get off my fucking back, I already told you I'd be ready on time. I can't drop this in the middle." Tensions between Randy and Alex are also escalating, and Randy finally jumps on Alex and starts punching her. Helen hears Alex screaming, goes running in to pull Randy off her, and in the process gets punched twice by Alex herself. Randy yells at her, "You always side with Alex, you bitch," and goes into his room and slams the door. Alex is crying hard and says to her mother, "You have to *do* something about him; I can't take it anymore. I swear, if he hits me one more time I'm going to *kill* him. He's out of control!"

Helen stays with Alex for a few minutes, then starts to put things into the car. The time to leave has passed. Tom finally comes in from the garage and starts to scrub his hands in a leisurely fashion. He then starts to look at the newspaper, and Helen snaps at him, "What are you *doing*? We need to go." Tom cuts her with a glare that makes her heart stop and says, "I was just seeing what time the game is on tonight. But since you mention it, maybe I *should* check out what else might be interesting." Then, with a cold sneer on his face, he takes the newspaper to the couch, puts up his feet, and begins to peruse the pages in earnest. Helen storms furiously upstairs. Ten minutes later Tom is still sitting on the couch. Helen calls to him, "We're already going to be nearly a half hour late; the children are afraid of missing the games."

Tom's lips form an icy smile, and he answers, "I guess you should have thought of that before deciding to give me a ration of your shit."

Helen yells, "Oh, you asshole!"

At this point Randy emerges from his room and starts down the stairs. "I see you're hysterical, as usual," he tosses flippantly at his mother as he goes. When he gets downstairs, he sees that his father is nowhere near ready to go, and he looks at the clock. He considers saying something but thinks better of it; he recognizes the signs of his father's anger, even when they are not outwardly obvious, and he doesn't want to make himself the target. So he goes back upstairs, tells Alex what is happening, and they both go looking for Helen, who is sitting crying on her bed.

Alex says urgently, "Come on, Mom, let's just go without Dad. The party's already started, we're missing it." Helen shakes her head no. Alex pleads, "Why not? Why can't we just go?"

Helen responds simply, "We're not going without him," not wanting to explain to the children how their father would make her pay if they did.

Randy then says, "Please go and apologize to him, Mom. You know that's all he's looking for, and then he'll get up and we can go."

Helen's tears stop, and her voice gets a hard edge. "I didn't *do* anything to him, Randy. Why don't you go ask *him* to apologize to *me*? What did *I* do?"

Randy's voice turns condescending, as if his mother is being stupid. "Right, Mom. When has Dad ever apologized for anything? Don't be ridiculous. I guess we can forget going to the party—that's basically what you're saying."

Then their father calls from downstairs, "Come on, let's get going." He has quietly put away his paper and cleaned himself up. Randy and Alex brighten and run off to grab their things. Helen can barely lift herself to her feet, feeling psychologically assaulted from all sides. She looks ashen for an hour or more afterward.

When they are almost out the door, Tom sees for the first time Alex's outfit, which he considers too sexy, and he barks at her, "You go right back upstairs, young lady, and put on something decent. You aren't going to the party looking like a prostitute."

Alex is on the verge of tears again, because she had been excited about what she was going to wear. "But Mom and I picked my clothes out together," she protests, a helpless whine in her voice. "She said I looked fine."

Tom glares at Helen, and his voice lays down the law: "If you aren't changed in two minutes, we're leaving and you're staying here!" Alex runs crying upstairs to throw on a different outfit.

In the car on the way to the party, Tom snaps out of his grumpiness, joking with the children. His humor includes cutting references to Helen's emotional outbursts and overanxiety, which are cleverly funny in their viciousness. The children can't help laughing, although Alex feels resentful toward both parents and guilty toward her mother even as she giggles. Helen is silent.

At the party, Tom acts as if nothing is wrong. Helen makes an excuse about being sick, since it is obvious to people that she is not herself. Tom is entertaining to both the adults and the children at the party, to the extent of giving each child a twirl around in the yard. Helen can see the impression that Tom makes on people and feels that it would be futile to attempt to describe to anyone what transpired before the party.

There are a few unfamiliar people at the party, to whom Tom introduces Alex as his "girlfriend," which he considers a charming joke. At one point he comments to some relatives on Alex's appearance, saying, "She's developing into quite an attractive young lady, isn't she?" Alex is nearby and feels humiliated. Tom sees her discomfort and says, "What, can't you take a compliment?" and there is laughter all around. He then gives her a hug, kisses her on the head, and tells his amused audience, "She's a great kid." Alex forces a smile.

When they get home from the party and the children are upstairs, Helen mentions to Tom that Randy hit Alex again that afternoon and that this time he hurt her. Tom responds, "Helen, welcome to the world. Siblings fight, okay? Or maybe you haven't *heard*, maybe that hasn't been on *Oprah* yet. Alex is two years older than Randy, and she's bigger. She loves to really play up being hurt, because she knows Mommy will come running and feel sorry for her, and it will be Big Bad Randy who's to blame, while Alex is all innocence. You're so naive."

Helen smarts from the series of barbs but forces herself to answer calmly, "I think we should talk to the school psychologist about it and get some suggestions."

Tom rises rapidly to his feet, instantly transformed as if he had just caught fire. He takes two steps toward Helen, pointing his finger and yelling, causing her heart to race. "You get those people in our business and you'll be sorry! You have no fucking idea what you are doing. You should use some damned judgment, you stupid idiot!" He stomps out to the garage, turns on the light, and goes back to work on Randy's bike, listening to the game on the radio. He does not come back in until after Helen has fallen asleep.

LIFE WITH AN ABUSER in the home can be as stressful and confusing for the children as it is for their mother. They watch the arguments; they feel the tension. When they hear screaming and name-calling, they worry about their parents' feelings. They have visions of the family splitting up; if the abuser is their father or a father figure, the prospect of separation is a dreaded one. If the abuser is physically scary, sometimes punching walls, knocking over chairs, or striking their mother, then a sharper kind of fear grips the children and may preoccupy them even during the calm periods in the home. Following incidents of abuse they may be wracked with guilt, feeling that they either caused their mother to be abused or should have found some way to have prevented it.

Witnessing incidents of abuse is just the beginning of what the chil-

dren endure, however. Abuse sends out shock waves that touch every aspect of family functioning. Hostility creeps into mothers' relationships
with their children, and siblings find themselves pitted against one other.
Factions form and shift. Children's feelings about each parent can swing
to extremes, from times of hating the abuser to periods of idealizing him
and blaming the mother for the fighting. Mothers struggle to keep their
relationships with their children strong in the face of the wedges driven in
by the abuser, and siblings find ways to support one another and offer protection. These wild cross-currents make family life turbulent.

(For simplicity, I refer in this chapter to the abuser as the children's
"father," but most of the themes I describe can apply equally to a stepfather or to a mother's live-in partner.)

WHY ABUSIVENESS SO OFTEN EXTENDS TO PARENTING ISSUES

QUESTION 14:
WHAT ARE ABUSIVE MEN LIKE AS FATHERS?

Although I have worked with some clients who draw sharp lines around
their mistreatment of their partners, so that their children neither see the
abusive dynamics nor get pulled into them, most abusers exhibit aspects
of their abusive mentality in their role as parents. There are various reasons why a man's abusiveness tends to affect his parenting choices, including the following:

1. Each important decision that parents make has an impact on
everyone in the family. Consider, for example, the decision that
many parents grapple with concerning whether a six-year-old is
ready to start first grade or should wait a year. Delaying a year
may mean another year during which the mother can't work
many hours outside the home, which affects the family finances.
The child may have to be up and out early to catch the bus,
which affects how much sleep the parents get. A younger sibling
may suddenly not have the first-grader at home as a playmate anymore and so may be moody and demanding of attention during

the day. How is an abuser likely to respond to this complex picture? He is likely to continue his usual tendency to consider his own judgment superior to his partner's and to be selfishly focused on how any changes will affect *him,* rather than on what works best for the family as a whole. Just because there are children involved, is his entire approach to decision making going to suddenly change? Not likely.

2. At the core of the abusive mind-set is the man's view of his partner as a personal possession. And if he sees her as his fiefdom, how likely is he to also see the children as being subject to his ultimate reign? Quite. If he is the children's legal father, he sees them as extensions of himself; otherwise he tends to see them as extensions of her. Either way, his mentality of ownership is likely to shape his parental actions.

3. It is next to impossible for the abuser to keep his treatment of the mother a complete secret from the children the way he does with other people, because they are almost always around. So he chooses instead to hook them into the patterns and dynamics of the abuse, manipulating their perceptions and trying to win their loyalty.

4. Children are a tempting weapon for an abuser to use against the mother. Nothing inflicts more pain on a caring parent, male or female, than hurting one of his or her children or causing damage to the parent-child relationship. Many abusers sense that they can gain more power by using the children against their partners than by any method other than the most overtly terrorizing assaults or threats. To their destructive mind-set, the children are just too tempting a tool of abuse to pass up.

REVISITING THE ABUSIVE MIND-SET: PARENTING IMPLICATIONS

I return now to the Turners, whom we met at the opening of this chapter, to look piece by piece at the dynamics that are being played out. The central elements of the abusive mind-set act as our guide:

CONTROL

From observing Tom's behavior, we learn one of his unspoken rules:

> "YOU DO NOT TELL ME TO HURRY UP. I GET TO TAKE
> AS LONG AS I PLEASE. IF YOU PRESSURE ME,
> I WILL PUNISH YOU BY TAKING A LOT LONGER."

Tom is not about to abandon his system of rules and punishments—which are fundamental to an abusive behavior pattern—just because the children are bearing the brunt of it. In fact, he is somewhat pleased that the punishment falls largely on them, because he knows that makes Helen feel even worse.

We also see Tom control Alex directly, ruling dictatorially over her clothing and *overruling* Helen's decision, thereby undermining her parental authority. He also seizes power over a process to which he has contributed nothing; if he wanted the right to have a say in what the children wore, he should have involved himself in the work of getting the family ready to go. The abuser does not believe, however, that his level of *authority* over the children should be in any way connected to his actual level of *effort* or *sacrifice* on their behalf, or to how much *knowledge* he actually has about who they are or what is going on in their lives. He considers it his right to make the ultimate determination of what is good for them even if he doesn't attend to their needs or even if he only contributes to those aspects of child care that he enjoys or that make him look like a great dad in public.

Like Tom, abusers tend to be authoritarian parents. They may not be involved that much of the time, but when they do step in, it's their way or the highway. My clients defend authoritarian parenting even though a large collection of psychological studies demonstrates that it's destructive: Children do best when parents are neither overly strict nor overly permissive, providing firm structure but also allowing for dialogue, respectful conflict, and compromise.

The abuser's coerciveness thus comes into his treatment *of* the children and his behavior *regarding* the children, including his bullying of decisions in which the mother should have an equal voice.

ENTITLEMENT

Tom doesn't accept that a couple's choice to have children requires major lifestyle changes and sacrifices. He'll work on Randy's dirt bike because he enjoys it, but whatever else needs to be done for the children is not his problem. Yet at the party he goes to great lengths to present himself as Mr. Dad, because he likes the *image* and *status* of fatherhood.

The selfishness and self-centeredness that his entitlement produces cause *role reversal* in his relationships with his children, in that he considers it their responsibility to meet *his* needs. Tom behaves flirtatiously with his teenage daughter at the birthday party, introducing her as his "girl-friend," commenting obliquely on her sexual development and kissing her in the midst of her embarrassment. The discomfort he causes Alex is obvious, but he can't be bothered to pay attention to that fact. He meets his own needs through the fantasy of having an attractive young partner while simultaneously taking pride as a parent in her attractiveness.

Children of abusers often find their father's attention and approval hard to come by. This scarcity has the effect of *increasing* his value in their eyes, as any attention from him feels special and exciting. Ironically, their mother can come to seem less important to them because they know they can count on her.

The abuser's entitled attitude that he should be above criticism makes it hard for his partner to intervene with him on her children's behalf. When Helen tries to get Tom to hurry up for the children's sake, he considers her efforts "a ration of shit" and punishes them all by deliberately taking even longer. Alex and Randy don't realize the price that their mother pays, and that they themselves pay, when she tries to stand up for them against him, so they wind up feeling that she doesn't care.

EXTERNALIZATION OF RESPONSIBILITY

Tom makes the children late for their party but then tells Helen it's her own fault. He also says that her overly sympathetic responses to Alex are the reason why the children's fights become a big deal. It never enters his mind that Randy's behavior toward females might be related to what he himself has modeled. Everything that goes wrong in the family is someone else's fault, usually Helen's.

Children who are exposed to the abuse of their mother often have trouble paying attention in school, get along poorly with their peers, or act out aggressively. In fact, they have been found to exhibit virtually every symptom that appears in children who are being abused directly. The abuser attributes all of these effects to the mother's poor parenting or to inherent weaknesses in the children.

When a family affected by partner abuse splits up, some children discover how much more pleasant life is without their father in the home and may choose to distance themselves from him. This can be a sign of emotional health and recovery. The abuser then often claims, predictably, that the mother is turning the children against him; in his mind, what else could it be?

MANIPULATIVENESS

As the Turner family drives off toward the party, Tom abruptly shifts into good humor, joking with the children and inducing them to bond with him against their mother. It is hard to stay angry at him when he is being playful. The children are ashamed of laughing at their mother—consciously for Alex, less so for Randy—but they are also drawn into an alliance with their father.

In certain ways children actually have an easier time living with an abusive parent who is mean all the time—at least then they know what they are dealing with and who is at fault. But the typical abuser is constantly changing faces, leaving his children confused and ambivalent and increasing the likelihood that they will identify with him in hopes of staying on his good side.

One critical category of manipulation involves the various tactics an abusive man may use to keep children from revealing to outsiders that their mother is being abused. Your partner may reward the children for maintaining secrecy or may make them feel that they would bring shame on the family, including themselves, if anyone were to find out. In some cases the man uses more overt pressure, including threats to enforce secret-keeping.

Children who do disclose the abuse going on at home sometimes suffer emotional or physical retaliation by the abuser. (Some children are also pressured by their mother not to tell, because she is afraid of what her partner will do to her or to them if word leaks out.) It is important to take steps to relieve any burden of secrecy that your children may be carrying, as I discuss at the end of this chapter.

SUPERIORITY, DISRESPECT

Tom openly ridicules Helen for being concerned with Randy's assaultiveness toward Alex. Her parenting is thus one of the things about which he abuses her. Children growing up in this atmosphere can gradually come to look down on their mother as a parent, having absorbed the abuser's messages that she is immature, irrational, illogical, and incompetent. Even those children who take their mother's side in most conflicts, as many daughters and some sons of abused women do, nonetheless can come to see her as inferior to other people and to themselves. Randy's behavior reveals this dynamic when he remarks condescendingly to his mother: "I see you're hysterical as usual." He has learned to see his mother through Tom's eyes.

POSSESSIVENESS

Tom treats Alex like an object that belongs to him. When he makes her change before the party, we might think, "He doesn't want his daughter to get sexualized at such a young age, which is good." But what we discover at the party is that he doesn't object to her sexualization, he just wants to be in control of it, and he wants it oriented toward *his* gratification. His demand that she not show off her body is not based on the viewpoint of a responsible parent but rather is more like the attitude of a jealous boyfriend.

Not all abusers perceive their children as owned objects, but many do. A man who already considers his partner a possession can find it easy to see his children the same way. But children are not *things,* and parents who see their children in an objectified way are likely to cause psychological harm because they don't perceive children as having rights.

PUBLIC IMAGE

It is confusing for children to see people responding to their abusive father as if he were a charming and entertaining person. What are Alex and Randy to make of how popular Tom is at the party? They are left to assume that his behavior at home is normal, which in turn means that they, and their mother, must be at fault.

THE ABUSIVE MAN AS CHILD ABUSER

Multiple studies have demonstrated that men who abuse their partners are far more likely than other men to abuse children. The extent of the risk to children from a particular abuser largely depends on the nature of his pattern of mistreatment toward their mother, although other factors such as his own childhood also can play an important role. The increased risks include the following.

PHYSICAL ABUSE

The abuser who is most likely to hit children is the one who is quite physically assaultive or threatening toward the mother. A battering partner is seven times more likely than a nonbattering man to physically abuse children, and the risk increases with the frequency of his violence toward the mother. However, there are also some abusers who hit the children but not the mother. The man in this category tends to be: (a) a particularly harsh and authoritarian parent, (b) a controlling and dictatorial partner, and, (c) a man who was physically abused by his own parents while he was growing up.

SEXUAL ABUSE

Incest perpetrators are similar to partner abusers in both their mentality and their tactics. They tend to be highly entitled, self-centered, and manipulative men who use children to meet their own emotional needs. Like Tom, they are often controlling toward their daughters (or sons) and view them as owned objects and tend to use seduction and sweetness to lure their victims in. In fact, Tom exhibits many of the warning signs of a sexually abusive father, including his apparent jealousy toward Alex and his penchant for giving a romantic and sexual tone to his interactions with her.

As in cases of physical abuse of children, multiple research studies have found that men who abuse their partners perpetrate incest at a much higher rate than do nonabusive men. These studies suggest that the incest perpetrator is not necessarily severely violent to the mother, but some degree of assault on her is common. The mentality and tactics of the incest perpetrator are very similar to those of the partner abuser, including self-centeredness and demands that his needs be catered to, manipulation, cultivation of a charming public persona, requiring the victim to keep the abuse secret, and others. Although the percentage of outright sexual abuse appears to be fairly low, even among abusive men, partners of my clients frequently raise concerns about subtler kinds of boundary violations and other sexually inappropriate behaviors along the lines of those exhibited by Tom at the party. A man who perceives his child as an owned object, as Tom did, is likely to disregard her rights to privacy or to integrity in her own body.

Boys are at some risk of being violated by abusive men as well, although most incest perpetrators choose to offend against a girl if one is available. Boys appear to be at particular risk when they are very young, while the vulnerability of girls remains steady and may even increase during adolescence.

PSYCHOLOGICAL ABUSE

Partners of my clients frequently share their distress with me over the mental cruelty the abuser visits upon the children. Name-calling, belittling, attacking their self-confidence, humiliating them in front of other people, shaming boys with regard to their masculinity, and insulting—or inappropriately complimenting—girls on the basis of their physical development and appearance are all common parenting behaviors among the abusive men in my groups. They tend to hurt their children's feelings further by failing to show up for important events, not following through on promises to take them on outings, or by showing no interest. Watching their children get rejected by their fathers in these ways is a source of pain for many of the abused women I speak with.

THE ABUSER AS ROLE MODEL

What are Randy and Alex learning from Tom's treatment of Helen and from the messages he gives them about her? Parents' statements and behaviors are probably the single greatest influence on the development of children's values and on how they perceive other people and themselves—at least as powerful as their parents' words (which sometimes convey opposite messages). Children exposed to partner abuse learn the following lessons from the dynamics they are caught in the middle of:

"THE TARGET OF ABUSE IS AT FAULT, NOT THE ABUSER."

Tom makes it clear to his children that Helen brings abuse upon herself by being too emotional, by questioning his decisions, or by being overly angry. Randy (and perhaps Alex as well) is likely to exhibit problems in how he treats other people, because he has been taught how to blame others, especially females, for his actions. Alex may believe that other people, especially males, have the right to mistreat her and that it is her own fault if they do.

"SATISFACTION IN LIFE COMES THROUGH CONTROLLING AND MANIPULATING OTHERS."

Tom's behavior communicates to his children that having power over other people is a desirable goal. The possibility that sharing, equality, cooperation, and mutual respect can lead to a fulfilling life may be beyond their conceptual reach. When the sons of abusers reach adolescence, for example, they commonly begin manipulating girls into relationships that are sexually or emotionally exploitative. They may lack empathy for their victims, having been conditioned by their fathers to shut themselves off to caring about the feelings of females.

"Boys and men should be in control, and females should submit to that control."

Unless they can find strong counter-examples among their friends or relatives, Alex and Randy run the risk of internalizing a rigid, abuse-prone view of what men and women inherently *are*. Children's parents are their first and most important source of sex-role definition and identification.

"Women are weak, incompetent, and illogical."

Tom is teaching his children—whether intentionally or not—to perceive women in the same degrading light that he casts on Helen. He reinforces these messages by treating Alex disrespectfully in public. Daughters of abusive men often have profound self-esteem problems. Why wouldn't they? Look at what the abuser is teaching them about how valuable and worthy of respect females are. Sons of abusive men in turn tend to be disparaging of and superior to girls and women, especially when the boys become old enough to begin dating.

"Mommies do the hard, constant, responsible daily work of parenting, while daddies step in to make the key decisions and share the fun times."

Alex and Randy are led to regard their mother as the brawn of the family operation and their father as the brains. They associate Helen with routine and structure, whereas they connect Tom with times that are special and exciting. Despite how grumpy he often is, Dad still comes out seeming like the fun parent; they notice how entertaining he is at the party, for example, while their mother is sullen and withdrawn.

"People that love you get to abuse you."

Children who grow up exposed to an abusive man's behavior learn that abuse is the price people pay if they want to receive love. This training can make it harder for children to recognize when they are being mistreated and to stand up for themselves.

As an abuser passes on his thinking to the next generation, he, in effect recruits his sons to the ranks of abusive men. He does not literally want his son to mistreat women—he doesn't believe he does so himself, after all—but he wants his son *to think as he thinks,* including adopting his same excuses and justifications, so the outcome is the same. And to a lesser extent he also recruits his daughters to join the ranks of abused women.

How Abusers Affect Mother-Child Relationships

Question 15:
Why is everyone in the family mad at each other instead of at him?

Tom's behavior drives wedges between the members of his family that expand over time. Many of the divisions he has sown are already bearing their poisonous fruit. How is he affecting Helen's relationships with her children? And how is he shaping—and distorting—how they view her?

Undermining Her Authority

It isn't hard for Alex and Randy to figure out where primary parental authority is vested in their family, because they see that Helen's decisions can be overruled. Children who detect such an imbalance learn to play one parent against the other and try to curry favor with the one who has the ultimate say. They also learn to defy the authority of the abused parent. Some abusive men further undermine the mother's authority by speaking badly about the mother to the children, characterizing her as crazy, alcoholic, or uncaring.

Even when a man does not directly undercut the mother's parenting as Tom does, his abuse undermines her authority *by its very nature.* Children who see or hear their father belittle their mother, silence her, walk away and ignore her, or physically intimidate her, learn that such behaviors toward her are both acceptable and effective. Most children of abused women are aware that their father does these things—even if the parents don't think they know—and they experiment with imitating his behaviors to see if it will help them get their way.

Children may also hope to win their father's approval by joining him in the abuse of their mother. This effort succeeds in some cases, but other abusers lay down the law quickly to establish that the privilege of disrespecting Mom belongs only to Dad. In this case the children may repress what they are learning until Mom and Dad split up; then, with the abuser out of the house, they let loose, re-creating his put-downs and intimidation of her, sometimes rapidly making themselves unmanageable.

Children of abusers absorb his expectations of constant catering from the mother. The son of an abused woman tends, for example, to become enraged at her for not waiting on him hand and foot, for pressing him to meet his responsibilities, or for challenging his inappropriate behaviors. His father is a direct model for his angry, verbally abusive responses in these particular circumstances.

INTERFERING WITH HER PARENTING

The evening after the birthday party, Tom forbids Helen to involve the school psychologist in addressing Randy's assaults on his sister. He doesn't say exactly what her punishment will be if she defies him, but she knows him well enough to not want to find out. She is thus forbidden to parent her children.

Dozens of abused women have complained to me of my clients' direct interference with their parenting. The most common complaint is that of being prevented from comforting a crying or frightened baby or young child. The men sometimes admit the interference openly. A recent client of mine, Jacob, told me that he was sick of the way his partner, Patricia, would pick up their eleven-month-old baby Willy when he cried and "fawn over him," and he blocked her from going into the baby's room. That was just the beginning. An older daughter of theirs was hospitalized for weeks in a city that was nearly two hours away with severe hepatitis. Patricia would rush to the hospital each night as soon as she got off work, visit briefly with her daughter, and then rush back home in hopes of seeing Willy before he fell asleep. However, if Patricia didn't make it back home by the nightly deadline that Jacob had set, Jacob *would not permit her* to go into Willy's room to see him, even if Willy was still awake. On at least one occasion the boy realized that Patricia was home and started yelling, "Mommy, Mommy!" and Jacob *still* blocked her from entering. His excuse to me? "I didn't set that deadline," he said. "We agreed to it mutually." (This would have been an unacceptable excuse even if it were true, but Patricia told me she never agreed to such a deadline.)

I think it is important to mention that Jacob never hit Patricia in their ten years together and that he was a college professor living in an unusually luxurious neighborhood. He provides a powerful illustration of the depth of the psychological cruelty an abuser can perpetrate with little or no physical violence and keep hidden behind the most impressive facade.

I SPEAK WITH some mothers who have developed psychiatric symptoms from being abused, such as nightmares, severe anxiety, or depression. Research studies have found that these conditions and related ones, including posttraumatic stress disorder, are not uncommon in women who have been abused by their partners. The abuser may have indoctrinated his children to perceive their abused mother as emotionally troubled, but he also may have actually *caused her* to become somewhat unstable. In either case, his behavior damages mother-child relationships, and it can take both time and outside assistance for mothers and children to reestablish a strong and trusting connection.

USING THE CHILDREN AS WEAPONS OF ABUSE

One of my clients many years ago was a mousy and mild-mannered young father named Wayne who characterized himself as a feminist. He was upset one morning about some things his wife, Nancy, had said to him before leaving the home, and he stormed around itching to make her really regret her words. He was looking in the refrigerator for milk for their ten-month-old baby when he came across a bottle from a few days earlier that had spoiled. He recognized the bottle immediately as the ultimate weapon and *proceeded to give the baby the spoiled milk to drink,* making him violently ill. Few other acts could have had an impact on Nancy as devastating as this one. The controlling effect was potent: Nancy was terrified for a long time after to defy Wayne or upset him in any way. She was also filled with anxiety as she left for work each morning.

Another client of mine described how he had told his wife during an argument, "If you don't shut up, you're going to be really sorry," and when she continued yelling at him, he went into their teenage daughter's closet and cut her prom dress to ribbons with a pair of scissors. The daughter's pain, I learned from the mother, was indescribable. Fueling this type of cruelty to children is the abuser's awareness that the mother's empathy for her children's emotional pain will hurt her more than anything he could do to her directly.

SHAPING THE CHILD'S PERCEPTIONS OF THE ABUSE

Many of my clients are skilled spin doctors, able to distract children's attention from what is before them and get them confused about the obvious. Consider the following scenario. A nasty argument breaks out between a mother and a father, with yelling and name-calling on both sides. Their children can barely follow what the fighting is about, partly because their stomachs are tied in knots from the tension. For the rest of the day, their mother is distant and depressed, snapping at them over trivial frustrations. Their father disappears for two or three hours, but when he turns up again he is in a good mood, joking and laughing with the children as if nothing had happened. (An abuser can naturally snap out of the bad effects of an abusive incident much more quickly than the abused woman can.) So which parent will seem to these children to have been responsible for shattering the calm of their home earlier? Probably the grouchy one. It is therefore not surprising that abusers are sometimes able to reverse their children's perceptions so that they see Mom as the volatile or unreasonable one despite the abuse they witness.

PLACING THE MOTHER IN A DOUBLE BIND

When Tom punishes Helen by deliberately making the children late, Randy and Alex become upset with *her* for not capitulating. They feel that if she would just cater to their father and manage his emotions they would get what they need, so they see her as the one who is hurting them. They know it's out of the question for him to do anything different. The abuser gets rewarded for his bullying behavior because the children give up on influencing his side of the equation and pour their energy into getting their mother to fix what's wrong.

Yet this is only half of the problem. On some other issue, Helen may give in to Tom precisely to avoid the kind of abuse and retaliation that resulted this time, and then the children will feel critical of her for *that*. They may say: "Why do you let Dad push you around like that? Why do you put up with that?" They may grumble: "When Dad is being mean to us, Mom doesn't do anything about it." Children of abused women thus feel angry and upset with their mother for *standing up* to the abuser and for *not standing up* to him. Their reactions in this regard are entirely understandable, but the mother can find herself in an impossible bind that leads to more distance and tension between her and her children.

Child protective services sometimes accuse an abused woman of "failing to protect" her children from exposure to an abusive man, without understanding the many efforts she may have made to keep them safe and the many tactics the abuser may have used to interfere with her parenting.

How Abusive Men Sow Divisions in Families

Randy and Alex are bitter adversaries one minute and loyal allies the next. They are like pebbles at the edge of the sea, with each wave of abuse toward their mother washing over them and changing their position in relation to each other. Randy's violence toward Alex is no surprise; boys who are exposed to the abuse of their mother are often disrespectful of and aggressive toward their peers, targeting females in particular for their hostility. Sons of abusers learn to look down on females, so they feel superior to their sisters and mothers and thus expect catering from them. Violence among siblings occurs at much higher rates in homes where there is partner abuse.

Abuse is inherently divisive; family members blame each other for the abuser's behavior because it is unsafe to blame him. If an incident of abuse began with an argument over one child's misbehavior, then an older sibling might say, "Daddy screamed at Mom and made her cry because he was mad that you were making so much noise. You should have listened to me when I told you to quiet down."

Tom contributes further to divisiveness through his *favoritism*: He treats Randy like a buddy and fixes his dirt bike, while ignoring Alex except when showing her off in public. Favoritism is rampant in the parenting of abusive men. They may favor boys over girls because of their own negative attitudes toward females. They favor children whom they see as siding with them and are rejecting of those who are sympathetic or protective of the mother. Children experience powerful emotional rewards from the abuser for distancing themselves from their mother and from any siblings who are allied with her.

My clients exhibit a range of other divisive tactics, including openly shaming children—especially boys—for being close to their mother, telling family members lies about each other, and making children feel like members of a special and superior club when they are part of his team. Finally, they use collective punishment, requiring all the children to pay a price for one child's behavior, which can be devastating in its ability to turn children against each other.

Why does an abuser sow divisions in these ways? One reason is that his power is decreased if the family remains unified. I have had a number of clients whose partners and children have consistently supported each other, and the client is always bitter about it, griping, "They've all turned against me," or, even more commonly, "She's brainwashed the children to be on her side." Many abusers take steps to avoid this outcome, using the principle of "divide and conquer": If people in the family are busy fighting with each other, attention is diverted from the man's cruelty or control.

RESILIENCE IN MOTHER-CHILD AND SIBLING RELATIONSHIPS

Almost miraculously, some family members of abusers manage to stay close to each other and unified. Several factors play a role in helping family relationships rebound from the effects of the abuser's behavior and grow strong:

1. *Access to good information about abuse:* When a mother receives assistance from a program for abused women, for example, she

has an easier time unraveling the convoluted dynamics of abuse, and then can assist her children to achieve greater clarity. It also helps her not blame her children for how they've been affected by the abuse.

2. *Access to children's services:* Many programs for abused women now offer free counseling for their children as well, and specialized counseling for children who have witnessed abuse is sometimes available through other sources such as hospitals or mental health centers. Family relationships benefit greatly when children get an opportunity to work through some of the dynamics we have been examining.

3. *Safety from the abuser:* Family members are more likely to stay by each other if their community stays by them, helping them to either leave the abuser or demand that he change. For the violent abuser, the police and courts can play a critical role in supporting the family, or they can drop the ball. The actions taken by family and juvenile courts can also be pivotal in protecting children from the effects of an abuser's behavior.

4. *Access to supportive community resources:* I have observed, for example, that children tend to do better simply by having the good fortune to live in a neighborhood where there are plenty of children to play with. If children have the opportunity to participate in sports, drama, or other activities that give them pleasure and help them feel good about themselves, they are less likely to channel their distress into hurting their siblings and their mother. Adults outside the family who devote attention to the children and engage them in activities can help them unhook themselves psychologically from the abuser, even without any direct mention of the abuse.

Support for the mother is as important as support for the children. Seek out a trustworthy friend or relative, and take the leap of talking about how you are being mistreated in your relationship. Breaking your isolation is critical to healing both you and your children.

5. *A mother who works hard at her parenting and gets help with it:* It is important for an abused mother to get community support and not to try to be a superhero. At the same time, there are helpful steps you can take. Try as hard as you can not to take your rage and frustration out on your children. Look for books or lectures about parenting and discipline strategies. Seek support for your parenting from friends and relatives, and try to be open to suggestions or constructive criticism from others. These are all extraordinary challenges for an abused mother; no one should blame you if you can't do all of these things, especially all at once. But I find that many abused women discover ways to be the best mothers they can under the circumstances, and their children feel the difference in the long run.

6. *An abuser who is a poor manipulator:* Some abusive men simply aren't as clever or persuasive in shaping the children's outlook, with the result that the children don't become as confused and ambivalent and cast less blame on to their mothers, their siblings, and themselves.

How Children Look at Their Abusive Fathers

In his children's eyes, the abuser is simultaneously hated and revered. They resent his bullying and selfishness but are attracted to his charm and power. They soak up the delicious moments when he is kind and attentive, partly because they may be so few. They may have an active fantasy life about getting big enough to stand up to him, and often dream of hurting him. If he is depressed or alcoholic, they worry about him. They observe that when their father is happy peace reigns in the family and that when he is unhappy he makes everyone else miserable, too, so they invest themselves in keeping him content. These many powerful mixed feelings are confusing and uncomfortable for children.

Children also are subject to traumatic bonding with the abuser, just as their mothers are, even if he does not abuse them directly. When child protective workers or custody evaluators assess a family in which there is partner abuse, they commonly conclude that the children are highly bonded to their father—as I find in their written reports—without examining whether or not that attachment is the result of trauma and manipulation rather than of extensive positive time spent together.

The abuser shapes how the children *and the mother* see him as a parent. It is common for a partner of one of my clients to say: "He treats me terribly, but he's a good father." But when I then ask detailed questions about the kinds of behaviors I have reviewed in this chapter, three times out of four the woman reports multiple important problems; she just hadn't been able to sort them out. You therefore may be finding that uncomfortable questions are arising for you about your own partner's parenting as you read along. When you are already struggling with how you are being treated yourself, it can be painful to consider that your children may be at risk of mistreatment as well. In the pages ahead, you will find suggestions for helping your children meet their own challenges.

THE ABUSER AS PARENT POSTSEPARATION

What happens to the parenting of abusers when couples split up? Some abusive men simply vanish from their children's lives, taking the attitude, "The children are her problem. If she wanted help with them, she should have treated me better. I don't want restrictions on my freedom." He thinks of having children as a reversible process, reminiscent of jokes about recovering one's virginity. He may pay little or no child support, and the children may not even receive birthday cards from him.

Children may actually fare better in the long term from having the abuser drop out of their lives rather than having him continue his manipulations and divisiveness for years, but these are both poor choices. When an abusive father disappears, children feel rejected and abandoned. In one of my current cases, the child keeps insisting that the reason for the disappearance of the father is "because he didn't like me," although the mother tells him that isn't so. Depending on their neighborhood or community, children also may suffer from the stigma of having a father who "ran off."

When abusive fathers stay involved, a different set of problems typically arise. First, the mother is generally the one who ended the relationship, and abusers do not take well to being left. They may use the children as weapons to retaliate against the mother or as pawns to try to get her back. I had a client named Nate, for example, who moved into an apartment when he and his wife separated and kept his new place as dingy and depressing as possible. He threw a bare mattress on the floor, put no pictures on the walls or rugs on the floors, and acquired little other furniture, although he could have afforded to make the place look decent. When the children came to visit him on weekends, they were shocked by his living conditions. He cried in front of them about how much he missed them and their mother and how bad it felt to be alone and outside of the family. He dressed sloppily, barely combed his hair, and rarely shaved, giving himself a pathetic mien. The children were crushed and could think of nothing other than their father's pain and loneliness. Naturally they began pressuring their mother to let him come back home.

Children can be used even more directly as weapons. A partner of one of my clients told me that she had left him about a year earlier but then got back together with him, "because he told me if I didn't let him back in the house he was going to sexually abuse our daughter." She had not reported this threat to a family court, because she assumed she would not be believed—family courts are widely reputed to treat women's sexual abuse allegations with strong disbelief.

Abused women have reported to me countless ways in which their ex-partners try to hurt or control them through the children, including:

- Pumping them for information about the mother's life, especially about new partners

- Returning them from visits dirty, unfed, or sleep-deprived

- Discussing with them the possibility of coming to live with him instead

- Continuing to drive wedges between them and their mother

- Undermining her authority by making his house a place where there are no rules or limits, permitting the children to eat whatever junk food they want, watch movies that are inappropriately violent or sexual, and ignore their homework, so that they chafe against normal discipline when they get back to her house

- Hurting the children psychologically, physically, or sexually in order to upset the mother

- Threatening to take the children away from her

- Seeking custody or increased visitation through the courts

- Insisting on taking the children for visitation only to leave them most of the time in someone else's care, usually his mother's or new partner's

Why He Uses the Children as Weapons Postseparation

What is going on in the abuser's mind as he hurts his ex-partner through the children?

1. He wants her to fail.

The last thing an abuser wants is for his partner to thrive after they split up, since that would prove that he was the problem. So he tries to make her parenting life as difficult as possible so that her life will stay stuck. She ends up feeling like she was never really permitted to leave him, feeling his presence around her all the time through his maneuvers involving the children. Many abusers cause more damage to mother-child relationships after separation than they did before.

2. He is losing most of his other avenues for getting at her.

Separation means that the abuser doesn't get his daily opportunities to control the woman and cut her down. He may still be able to get at her through various financial dealings, and he can stalk or assault her if he is willing to risk arrest. But the children become one of his only vehicles to keep a hook into her for the long term.

3. He considers the children his personal possessions.

While the abuser may believe that the *work* of raising children is his partner's responsibility, he assigns the *rights* regarding them to himself. He feels outraged postseparation that he is losing control not only of his ex-partner but of the children as well. This ownership mentality was illustrated neatly by a client of mine who went to court seeking sole legal custody but requesting that the mother retain physical custody; in other words, he wanted *her* to look after the child, but the right to make the decisions would be *his*. (Fortunately, his request was denied.)

An abusive father may go ballistic if his ex-partner begins a new relationship because, as clients often say to me: "I don't want another man around *my* children." In my experience, abused women often get involved with a more respectful man on the next go round, because their painful experience has taught them some signs of abuse to watch out for. Her children may then gravitate to the new man as if toward a magnet, thrilled to discover that they can get caring and appropriate male attention, a situation to which an abusive man may have a hostile reaction.

4. His perceptions of his ex-partner are highly distorted.

Many of my clients genuinely believe that they are doing what is best for their children by driving them away from their mother, because they have swallowed their own propaganda about how bad she is. An abuser strives to prove that his ex-partner is a poor mother by pointing to symptoms that are actually the effects that his cruelty has had on her: her depression, her emotional volatility, her difficulty managing the children's disrespect of her. He feels that *he* needs to save them from *her,* a stark and disturbing distortion.

DO ALL ABUSERS HARM THEIR CHILDREN EMOTIONALLY POSTSEPARATION?

Fortunately not. I have worked with abusers who have substantially more compassion for the children than they have for their partners and who do not use them as weapons postseparation. These men tend to be:

1. *The ones who behaved the most responsibly toward the children **prior to** separation:* The divorced or separated abuser who is kind to the children, cares for them responsibly, and does not try to damage their relationships with their mother is a man who was

also operating this way while the couple was together. He generally didn't degrade her right in front of the children and didn't abuse her during a pregnancy. He is usually less selfish and self-centered than the average abuser.

The parenting of abusive men rarely improves postseparation, unlike that of some nonabusive fathers. I have had clients who put on a big show of being nicer to their children and spending more time with them *because they were seeking custody,* or because they were trying to turn the children against their mother. These are not genuine improvements in parenting; once their campaign is over, win or lose, they revert to their old ways. The only question about an abuser's treatment of his children postseparation is "Will it stay the same or will it get worse?"

2. *The ones who are not intent upon settling old scores:* If he is willing to move on with life without having to punish you—or get back together with you—the picture for the children can brighten somewhat.

3. *The ones who do not use the legal system to pursue custody or increased visitation:* For a variety of reasons, many abusive men do not choose to use family courts as a venue for taking power over the woman and her children. Once the court becomes involved, the road to peace can be a long and painful one.

THE ABUSER IN FAMILY COURT

I have frequently served as a custody evaluator, or *guardian ad litem.* A custody evaluator is appointed by a court to investigate the children's circumstances in cases of divorce or separation and to make recommendations to the judge regarding custody and visitation. In my first case of this kind several years ago, a man named Kent was seeking to win custody of his three-year-old daughter from his ex-partner, Renée. Kent was in the military, so he did not have "flex-time" options; he told me that if he gained custody, his parenting plan was to put Tracy in day care forty hours a week. Tracy was currently in the full-time care of her mother. Kent was not critical of Renée's parenting; he said simply that he wanted Tracy to live with him because he could care for her even better. More important, he was offering to allow Renée liberal visitation, whereas Renée was restricting his contact with Tracy to a set schedule. "That way Tracy could have both parents," he said.

Kent informed me with audible outrage that Renée was accusing him of having been abusive, "but she has never provided one shred of evidence of her laughable allegations." He then went on, in response to my detailed questions, to describe *thirteen* different occasions on which he had *physically* assaulted Renée, including repeated incidents of pushing her down and one time when he kneed her so hard in the pelvic area that she got a large dark bruise. He claimed never to have punched or slapped her; apparently this is why he considered her reports of abuse such a joke.

That isn't all. Kent went on to tell me that he had participated only minimally in Tracy's care during her first year of life and not dramatically more during the subsequent two years. (Most abusers in custody disputes are craftier than Kent was. His entitlement was so severe that he didn't think I would see anything wrong with this picture.)

Why did Kent want to take a little girl out of the full-time care of a competent mother in order to put her into full-time day care? I was forced to conclude that he craved power over Renée, wanted contact with her and saw winning custody as the way to put the cards back in his hands.

Unfortunately, few custody evaluators or judges understand the nature of an abusive man's problem. If they find him likable, they assume the abuse allegations must be greatly exaggerated. And once they adopt that stance, it can become extraordinarily difficult to get them to listen carefully to what has gone on or to investigate the evidence.

The world of family courts, where legal struggles over custody and visitation take place, is a nightmare in the lives of many thousands of abused women across the United States and Canada. A woman who has overcome so many obstacles to finally free herself from abuse can suddenly find herself jerked back into the abuser's grip, because he is the legal father of her children and chooses to continue his abuse through the legal system.

The typical abusive man enters the court with self-assurance, assuming that court personnel will be malleable in his charming and manipulative hands. He typically tells lies chronically and comfortably. He looks and acts nothing like the social stereotype of an abuser and plays on the prevailing myths and prejudices concerning abuse. Imagine how Tom, the father in the scenario that opened this chapter, would appear in the courthouse; would anyone believe that he could be an abuser?

The Abuser's Tactics in Custody Disputes

Here are just a few of the strategies an abuser tends to use in custody and visitation disputes:

Taking Advantage of His Financial Position

Most men are in a better economic position than their ex-partners for at least the first few years following separation. This imbalance is greater for abusers because they may control and manipulate the finances while the couple is together and sometimes make dramatic attempts to destroy their partner economically as the relationship dissolves. An abuser can often afford to spend a great deal more than the woman on legal expenses, or he can get himself into a nice house to sway both the children and the custody evaluator. He may be able to completely ruin his ex-partner's financial position by dragging her back into court over and over again.

Asking for Psychological Evaluations

Most abusers do not show significant psychopathology on psychological tests, but their partners often do as a result of enduring years of abuse. The evaluating psychologist may report that the woman is depressed, hysterical, or vindictive; few evaluators take the abused woman's actual past experience or current circumstances into account. If she reports that she is being followed, for example, because the abuser is stalking her, she is likely to be labeled "paranoid" and her reports of abuse discredited on that basis. A psychologist's report on the abusive man may be based on a related set of misconceptions. I have read several evaluations that state that the man is unlikely to have perpetrated the reported acts of abuse because he is not mentally ill or because he doesn't show signs of aggressiveness in the evaluator's office. (On this erroneous basis, *most* abusive men could be declared to be victims of false accusations.) Unfortunately, many psychologists who take court appointments have been slow to accept that their standard array of theories and tests can lead to serious errors when applied to domestic-abuse cases.

Playing the Role of Peacemaker

A great number of my clients use a routine that goes like this: "There was a lot of fighting and bad feeling in our relationship, and I can understand that she is bitter about some things, but we need to put that all behind us for the good of the children. She is so focused on getting revenge against me that she is forgetting about the children's needs. That's why I'm asking for joint custody, so that the children would get lots of time with each of us, while she's asking for me to have only every other Saturday."

This piece of acting seeks to take advantage of the myth that women are more vindictive than men when relationships end (in the case of abuse, however, the reality is very much the opposite) and that men are frequently victims of false accusations of abuse by women who want to keep them away from their children. The abuser's goal with this and all other strategies is to get court personnel to disbelieve his ex-partner and ignore any evidence she presents.

Feigning Remorse over the Abuse

A surprising number of judges and custody evaluators consider a man's abuse of his partner irrelevant to custody and visitation decisions. They are either unaware or uninterested in the role that an abusive man plays as a role model for his children, the damage he can do to mother-child relationships, and the way he may use the children as weapons. So if an abuser says he regrets his verbal or physical assaults on the mother, that can be enough to manipulate court personnel into saying, "Let's leave all that in the past."

Confusing the Court with Crossaccusations

Most of my clients can lie persuasively, with soulful facial expressions, good eye contact, and colorful details. Court personnel have trouble believing that such a pleasant-seeming man could simply be inventing most or all of his accusations against the abused woman. In various cases of mine, court personnel have told me, "He accuses her of the same things, so I guess they abuse each other." In such cases, the court may accept his counteraccusations at face value, rather than look closely at the evidence.

Accusing Her of Trying to Turn the Children Against Him

Some abusive men do not succeed in turning children against their mother, and some don't even try. Children sometimes see the abuse for what it is and take whatever steps they can to protect themselves, each other, and their mother, including perhaps disclosing the abuser's treatment of her (or of them) to outsiders. The abusive man's typical response to this is to claim that the mother is turning the children against *him*. Some prominent psychologists have, unfortunately, contributed through their writings to the myth that it is unhealthy for children to distance themselves from an abusive father and that the mother is probably the cause of their desire to do so. Family courts tend to be unaware of how important it is to children not to be exposed to the negative role modeling of their abusive father and to his hostility and contempt toward their mother. Regrettably, a growing number of abusive men succeed in using such claims of "parental alienation" to win custody or ample unsupervised visitation, even in cases where there is extensive evidence that the man has abused not only the mother but the children as well.

The reality is that a mother who attempts to restrict her children's contact with the man who abused her is generally acting as an appropriate protective parent. She is also supporting healthy *self-protective* instincts in her children; children who are not supported or encouraged in this way to protect themselves from exposure to abuse will be at greater risk for accommodating abuse by others as they go through life.

I have noticed that charges of "parental alienation" are sometimes leveled against the most competent mothers, because of their strong and supportive bonds with their children—which the abuser terms *enmeshment* or *overdependence*—and because the children have learned to see through the abuser's facade and therefore choose to try to keep away from him.

Appealing to Popular Misconceptions

Several misleading arguments appear repeatedly in statements that abusers make during family court litigation. First is the claim that fathers are widely discriminated against by family courts in custody disputes. The research actually shows the opposite, that in fact fathers have been at a distinct advantage in custody battles in the United States since the late 1970s, when the maternal preference went out of vogue. Next often comes the myth that children of divorce fare better in joint custody, when the research shows overwhelmingly that they in fact do *worse*, except in those cases where their parents remain on good terms after the divorce and can co-parent cooperatively—which is almost impossible for a woman to do with an abusive ex-partner. Abusive men also assert falsely that there is a rampant problem of women's false allegations of abuse, that child support obligations are unfairly high, that domestic abuse is irrelevant to custody decisions, and that men are abused in relationships just as much as women.

THE SUCCESS OF these strategies relies heavily on the ignorance, and sometimes gender bias, of court personnel regarding women who disclose histories of partner abuse and on their stereotypes regarding men who are "just not the type" to be abusers. Prejudicial attitudes often take the place of careful investigation and consideration of the evidence. Unfortunately, family courts have generally not made the kinds of progress in recognizing and responding to domestic abuse that many other social institutions, such as the police and criminal courts, have (though serious work remains to be done in those arenas as well, as we see in Chapter 12).

MIXED SOCIAL MESSAGES TO ABUSED MOTHERS

What should a mother's role be in protecting her children from exposure to their father's abusiveness? Abused women can get caught in the profound societal ambivalence that exists regarding this question. While couples are together, professionals and other community members are highly critical of a mother who continues to live with an abusive man. They say things to her such as, "You are choosing your partner over your children," or "You must not care about what things are like for them." Child protection officials sometimes threaten to take a mother's children away from her for "failure to protect" if she won't leave a man who is abusing her. If she believes that the man has the potential to change, they are likely to say she is "in denial" or "unrealistic" for harboring such fantasies. These critics ignore the huge challenges she faces as a parent and how difficult it is to leave an abuser.

But when an abused mother *does* break up the relationship, society tends to do an abrupt about-face. Suddenly she hears from court officials and from other people:

> *"Well, maybe he abused* **you,** *but that's no reason to keep the children away from him. He is their father, after all."*

> *"Don't you think your own resentments are clouding your judgment about your children?"*

> *"Don't you believe that people ever change? Why don't you give him the benefit of the doubt?"*

In other words, a woman can be punished for exposing children to a man in one situation but then punished for *refusing to expose them to the same man* in another situation. And the second case is potentially even more dangerous than the first, because she is no longer able to keep an eye on what he does with the children or to prevent the postseparation escalation that is so common in abusive fathers.

Abused mothers are typically required by family courts across the United States and Canada to send their children on unsupervised visitation—or into custody—with their abusive fathers. When the children then begin to show predictable symptoms such as school behavior and attention problems, sleep disorders, unwillingness to respect their mother's authority, or emotional deterioration, court personnel and court-appointed evaluators commonly declare that these are normal reactions to divorce or that the children are actually responding to their *mother's* emotions rather than to their own. I have been involved in several cases where the abuser has physically or sexually abused the children in addition to abusing the mother, and the court *still* forced the mother to allow visitation with no professional supervision. Abused women across the continent report that it can become extraordinarily difficult to persuade the court to examine the evidence objectively once the mother has been labeled "vindictive" or "overemotional" or has been accused (however baselessly) of having influenced her children's statements.

The treatment that protective mothers so often receive at the hands of family courts is among the most shameful secrets of modern jurisprudence. This is the only social institution that I am aware of that so frequently *forbids mothers to protect their children from abuse.* Fortunately, over the past few years, women and men (including *many* nonabusive fathers) across the United States and Canada have been waking up to the severity of this problem with the result that there are multiple initiatives currently in motion to demand family court reform. I have been part of one such effort, assisting a well-funded organization that is preparing a human rights report for the international community on the revictimization of abused women and their children through custody and visitation litigation. (For more information, see "Battered Mothers Testimony Project" in the "Resources" section in the back of this book.)

PREPARING FOR CUSTODY BATTLES JUST IN CASE

If you have not experienced custody litigation, or at least not yet, please bear the following points in mind:

- It is important to keep records of your partner's abusive behaviors toward you or the children. If he writes scary or twisted letters to you, keep them. If friends or neighbors see him mistreat you or the children, ask them to describe in writing what they witnessed. If you have ever called the police, try to get a record of the call, whether they came or not. If he leaves abusive or threatening messages on your answering machine, keep a copy on tape.

- Seek legal representation if you can possibly afford it. If you have no resources, apply for a legal services attorney. In choosing an attorney, try to find one who is experienced in domestic abuse and who treats abused women with patience and respect. The fact that a lawyer is well known does not mean that he or she necessarily understands the issues involved in disputing custody or visitation with an abuser.

- Move cautiously. Avoid abruptly denying him visitation, for example, even if you have concerns about how your children are being affected. Courts can be quick to accuse women of trying to cut the children's father out of their lives even if she has good reason to be worried.

- Involve your children with a therapist if you can find a good one in your community. It is important to have professionals involved so that you are not the only one reporting the distress that your children's relationship with their father is causing them. In situations where it is just your word against his, he may be able to charm court personnel with his skillful lying and winning manner.

- If one of your children discloses to you sexual abuse by their father—which is an extraordinarily upsetting experience—it is especially important that you approach the court and your local child protection agency with as calm an appearance as you possibly can. If you get labeled as "hysterical about sexual abuse," no matter how justified your reactions, your reports may be discredited. If you are in this situation, read the excellent book *A Mother's Nightmare—Incest*, listed in "Resources," for further guidance on managing the legal system.

- Most abused women do succeed in keeping custody of their children. But the better you plan, the more likely you are to avoid a horrible surprise. For a free packet of information for abused women and their attorneys regarding custody and visitation litigation, call the Resource Center on Domestic Violence: Child Protection and Custody at 1–800–527–3223.

THE SUBJECT OF abusive men as parents, including their behavior in custody and visitation disputes, is a complex one; I have only touched the surface here. Readers who wish to pursue a more in-depth discussion should see my book *The Batterer as Parent: Addressing the Impact of Domestic Violence on Family Dynamics* (written with Dr. Jay Silverman), which addresses the full range of issues touched on in this chapter. Although that book focuses on the physically violent abuser, you will find that most of what we say applies to psychologically abusive men as well.

The more you are aware of how your children may be affected by their exposure to your partner's abuse of you, and to the problems in his style as a parent, the better able you will be to protect them from emotional harm. They need to know that you are a parent they can count on to be consistently kind and safe, since the abuser is unpredictable and at times intimidating. If they are giving you difficult behavioral challenges, are having some problems focusing their attention, or are prone to withdrawal or depression, bear in mind that these are all normal responses in children whose mothers are abused. Your patience and understanding are critical to them, including your ability to show them that you do not believe they are bad. Remember that growing up around an abusive father or stepfather is very confusing and anxiety producing for children even if he does not mistreat them directly.

Make your own healing—as well as your emotional and physical safety—a priority. Children of an abused woman can feel the difference when their mother starts to get help for herself and becomes more able to recognize abuse for what it is, blaming neither herself nor her children for the abusive man's behavior.

Here are some other actions you can take:

Insist on complete respect from your children. Children can absorb your partner's rude or bullying approach to you and begin to exhibit behaviors toward you that they have learned from him. Try to put a stop to this behavior as quickly as possible before it gets a chance to snowball. You may not be able to be firm with the children in front of your partner if he actively undermines you, but put your foot down as much as you can, especially when he isn't around.

Insist on respect for females in general. Your partner's control or abuse toward you creates an atmosphere in which negative attitudes toward females can grow like mold. Interrupt these whenever you see them appearing in your sons or daughters.

Confront your partner's undermining of your parenting. Unless you are afraid of how your partner will retaliate, name his undermining for what it is and demand that it stop.

Don't lie on your partner's behalf or cover for his behavior. You may feel that you should protect your children's image of your partner by making excuses for him, telling them what happened was your fault, or lying about what he did. Your relationships with your children will be damaged in the long run if your cover for him, however, and that is the outcome you most want to avoid. In addition, you increase their vulnerability to him if you encourage them to deny their own self-protective instincts. (However, you may need to lie to *him* to *protect them* sometimes.)

Be the best parent you can. As unfair as it is, the reality is that an abused woman has to be an outstanding parent in order to help her children process and heal from the abuse they have been exposed to. Draw on every resource you can, including parenting books and training courses, parent support groups, and play groups that may exist in your area. (For specific suggestions, see the "Resources" section in the back of this book.)

Consider leaving your relationship, at least for a while, if you can do so safely. One of the best ways to help children heal is for them to be free from witnessing abuse. As I discussed earlier, however, it is important to plan carefully in order to make it harder for your abusive partner to hurt the children through his visitation with them or through legal actions for custody.

If your partner has already succeeded in causing some distance in your relationships with your children, or has turned them against each other, it is still possible to heal those divisions and rebuild healthy connections. Make your relationships a priority and draw on counseling services in your community to help you work through the barriers that your abusive partner has erected. Encourage your children to talk about the upsetting interactions they have witnessed in the home, with the help of counselors if necessary; it is especially important to relieve any burden the children have felt to keep the abuse secret. Some abused women's programs have group counseling for children, which is an excellent environment in which they can break the secret about the abuse, gain insight into their own emotional reactions, and learn that the abusive man's behavior is neither their mother's fault nor their own.

Above all, don't give up. Healing ruptured relationships takes time and perseverance. In a case I am involved in currently in which the parents are divorced, the mother was on the verge of losing hope that she would ever be on good terms again with her teenage boy, who was allied with his abusive father and imitating his attitudes and behaviors—including threats of violence—toward the mother. But she persevered, despite many moments of despair over a three-year period, and now the boy has finally begun to recognize his father's bullying and manipulation and is gradually repairing his connection to his mother.

KEY POINTS TO REMEMBER

- An abuser in the home affects everybody.

- A good father does not abuse his children's mother.

- Abusers drive wedges between people, by accident or by design. Abused mothers and their children should seek support to heal as individuals and to heal their relationships with each other (see "About General Parenting Issues" in "Resources" in the back of this book).

- If you are preparing to leave an abuser with whom you have children, seek out legal advice regarding custody issues as soon as you can.

11

Abusive Men and Their Allies

I used to feel close to his mom, but now she seems to hate me.

I can't even call up our friends anymore, because they don't want to get in the middle.

Sometimes I feel like I must be the one who's messed up, because my own family sides with him.

I don't bother to call the police when he gets scary, because he's got buddies on the force who help him out.

The custody evaluator reported to the court that I'm hysterical and that the children should live with him.

IN EACH OF the following examples, all of which come from cases I have been involved in, something is happening that is very difficult to account for:

- A woman flees into hiding because she is terrified of her abusive husband. He looks everywhere for her and cannot track her down. When all else fails, he pays a visit to her parents. He tells them how sorry he is about how he treated their daughter and says he misses her terribly and is going to change. He cries and begs for her address, "just so that I can send her a letter and tell her how I feel," *and her parents give it to him.*

- A man joins an abuser program that has been denied certification by his state's Department of Public Health because it violates state regulations. While in the program, the man complains that his girlfriend sometimes hits him, too, and the counselor, who is a licensed psychologist, responds by *encouraging the abuser to get a restraining order against the abused woman.* The psychologist admits this openly to me.

- The daughter of a divorced abused woman discloses in explicit detail that she is being sexually abused by her father during visitation. The mother goes to court to request a professional evaluation of her daughter. The mother's sister arrives at court that day *with the abuser,* with whom she has now become friends despite the fact that she hated him before the divorce. The sister not only tells the judge that the sexual abuse allegations are lies but actually asks the judge to take custody of the girl away from the mother and give it to her. (Fortunately, the judge doesn't allow the sister to take the girl. The evaluation goes forward and winds up confirming the sexual abuse.)

- An abusive man's therapist assigns a psychological diagnosis to the abused woman *without having met her or even talked to her,* relying entirely on the man's descriptions of his partner, despite knowing that he is accused of abusing her.

- A mother flees with her children to a shelter for abused women because her house is vandalized. She can tell it was her physically abusive ex-husband who did it, and she takes the damage as a clear threat. Within several days of fleeing, she contacts the court-appointed custody evaluator to let him know where she is. The custody evaluator, however, shoots off a report to the court stating that the woman has no reason to be afraid of her husband, although she has told him of her partner's history of violence and threats, and recommends that the children be taken away from the mother and given to the father. He does not mention the woman's phone call to him from the shelter in his report. On the basis of the custody evaluator's report, all three children, including a girl who is only three years old, are sent to live at the abuser's home, and the mother is permitted only brief *supervised* visits, because she is now labeled a "flight risk."

How are abusive men able to attract allies to their cause? And why do some people become such enthusiastic, and at times vicious, agents of the abuser? To answer these questions we need to look not only at the mind-set of abusive men but also at the socially acceptable attitudes and styles of interaction that an abusive man can use to prevail upon other people to do his dirty work.

WHY THE ABUSIVE MAN SEEKS ALLIES

Controlling and intimidating a partner is not that easy. A man has a better chance of dominating a woman than vice versa, but it is still a challenge. Very few people willingly consent to having their rights systematically denied. The abusive man thus is faced repeatedly with the problem—from his perspective—of his partner's continued resistance to his control. Over time he gets tired of bullying her all by himself.

Certain other impediments can trip up the abuser. Changes in societal attitudes toward abuse, including improvements in some important laws and policies, are making it harder to get away with. The physically frightening or sexually assaultive abuser, for example, is much more likely to be arrested than he would have been ten or fifteen years ago. His partner now has the option of seeking a court order to keep him away from her.

Perhaps most important is that the *silence* surrounding abuse is being broken. In a current case of mine involving a psychological abuser, close friends of the woman sat her down one day and staged an "intervention," in which they supportively pressed her to recognize the impact her husband's abuse was having on her. Unlike the situation years ago, there are now various ways in which an abused woman can find assistance—or assistance can find her, as it did in this case.

In this context, an abuser has to work harder than ever to keep his partner blaming herself and to fend off helping hands that might reach her. One great way to keep people off of her side is to win them over to his side first. Besides, he feels that he *deserves* allies, because he considers himself the victim.

You may wonder why, if abusive men feel so justified in their actions, they distort their stories so much when seeking support. First, an abuser doesn't want to have to explain his worst behaviors—his outright cruelty, for example, or his violence—to people who might find those acts distasteful, and he may not feel confident that his justifications will be accepted. Second, he may carry some guilt or shame about his worst acts, as most abusers do; his desire to escape those feelings is part of why he looks for validation from other people, which relieves any nagging self-doubt. He considers his guilt feelings a weakness to be overcome. And, last, he may lie because he has convinced himself of his own distortions. The narcissistic abuser, for example, considers his fabrications real, which is one of the reasons why lie-detector tests are unreliable in cases of abuse (including child sexual abuse).

QUESTION 16:
HOW COME SO MANY PEOPLE SIDE WITH *HIM?*

The list of people an abuser can potentially persuade to act as his agents is a long one: friends, relatives, teachers, psychologists, clergypeople, police and judges, *her* relatives, and, following a breakup, his new partner. Let's take a look at several of these people from the abused woman's perspective, examining both how the abuser recruits them and why they are willing to be his front people.

THE ABUSER'S RELATIVES

"Sometimes he and his father rip into me together, putting me down and making fun of me. His dad is just like him."

"His uncle abuses his aunt and everybody in his family can tell, but they never say a word about it."

"He was arrested for pounding on my door when I had a restraining order against him, but his sister testified that he'd been over at her house that whole night, so he got off."

"His mother and I were good friends, but ever since he got arrested
*for hitting me she won't talk to me, as if **I** were the bad one."*

As these statements by partners of my clients illustrate, one fundamental
dynamic has changed little despite three decades of progress in social attitudes toward abuse: No one wants to believe that his or her own son or
brother is an abusive man. Parents don't want the finger pointed at them,
so they say: "*Our* child wouldn't abuse his partner. We brought him up
right." Allegations of abuse by the son can draw uncomfortable attention
to the dynamics of the previous generation; abusive men are three times
more likely than nonabusers to come from homes in which their father or
stepfather abused their mother. And if the father or stepfather is abusive,
he shares the son's entitled attitudes and victim-blaming tendencies.

Family loyalty and collective denial of family problems are powerful
binding agents. The abuser shapes his relatives' views of his partner over a
period of years. They have perhaps seen with their own eyes how she
"overreacts" to certain things he does in public, because with no idea of
what he has been doing to her behind closed doors, they can't accurately
judge her behavior. So they oppose abuse in the abstract, but they fight
fiercely for the abuser when he is their own.

THE ABUSED WOMAN'S RELATIVES AND FRIENDS

As if the support an abuser receives from his own relatives weren't bad
enough, I keep encountering cases where *the woman's relatives* also come
to his aid. At a conference I spoke at recently, a lawyer stood up to ask:
"Why do some of my clients find themselves in situations where their own
families are helping the abusers win custody?"

Every family has tensions within it, and abusers use their manipulative skills to take advantage of those rifts. In one case, for example, an
abuser named Ian heard that his ex-wife Tina had fallen out with her parents because they were upset that she had stopped attending church. Ian
made a point of starting to make a regular appearance at Sunday services
and one day found his way to "coincidentally" sit near Tina's relatives. He
engaged them in a conversation about his "concerns" about her loss of

faith and how bad he felt that Tina wasn't giving their children the benefits of consistent church attendance. He also slipped in a few assertions that he knew would bring to mind the kind of person who skips services, saying, "Our children tell me she's been drinking heavily and bringing a lot of different men around the house." Pretty soon a minor tiff had turned into a gigantic one.

It is uncomfortable for a woman to tell her family the details of her partner's abuse of her. She feels ashamed and wants to avoid having them ask: "Well, then, why are you with him?" But the abuser can take advantage of how much her family doesn't know. He is careful not to create the impression he's bad-mouthing her, while subtly planting his poisonous seeds. He might say, for example: "She's telling people now that I was *abusive* to her, and that really hurts me. It's gotten so I don't want to show my face places 'cause of what she's saying. I'm not keeping any secrets; I'll tell you right out that I did slap her one day, which I know is wrong. She has this thing about saying that my mother is a 'whore' 'cause she's been divorced twice, and that really gets to me, but I know I should have handled it differently."

When he leaves, her parents find themselves ruminating: "Gee, she didn't mention anything about insulting his mother in that incident. That makes it a little different. She can have quite a mouth on her, I've noticed that myself. He shouldn't slap her, but he's obviously feeling guilty about it now. And he's willing to admit that it's partly his fault, while she blames it all on him. She does that in conflicts with us sometimes; she doesn't realize it takes two to tango."

The part about the woman calling his mother a degrading name may never have even happened; my clients smoothly make up stories to cover their worst incidents. But whether or not he is telling the truth is almost beside the point; he is playing to the societal value, still widely held, that a man's abuse toward a woman is significantly less serious if she has behaved rudely herself.

There continues to be social pressure on women to "make the relationship work" and "find a way to hold the family together," regardless of abuse. Since so many people accept the misconception that abuse comes from bad relationship dynamics, they see the woman as sharing responsibility equally for "getting things to go better." Into this context steps the abuser, telling his partner's friends, "I still really want to work things out, but she isn't willing to try. I guess it isn't worth the effort to her. And she's refusing to look at her part in what went wrong; she puts it all on me."

What her family and friends may not know is that when an abused woman refuses to "look at her part" in the abuse, she has actually taken a powerful step out of self-blame and toward emotional recovery. She *doesn't* have any responsibility for his actions. Anyone who tries to get her to share responsibility is adopting the abuser's perspective.

Despite the challenges, many, many friends and relatives of abused women stay by them. Their presence is critical, for it is the level of loyalty, respect, patience, and support that an abused woman receives from her own friends and family that largely determines her ability to recover from abuse and stay free. (People wishing to support or assist an abused woman they care about should read *To Be an Anchor in the Storm* by Susan Brewster. See "Resources.")

THERAPISTS AND EVALUATORS

We need to take a large step back in time for a moment, to the early part of Freud's era, when modern psychology was born. In the 1890s, when Freud was in the dawn of his career, he was struck by how many of his female patients were revealing childhood incest victimization to him. Freud concluded that child sexual abuse was one of the major causes of emotional disturbances in adult women and wrote a brilliant and humane paper called "The Aetiology of Hysteria." However, rather than receiving acclaim from his colleagues for his ground-breaking insights, Freud met with scorn. He was ridiculed for believing that men of excellent reputation (most of his patients came from upstanding homes) could be perpetrators of incest.

Within a few years, Freud buckled under this heavy pressure and recanted his conclusions. In their place he proposed the "Oedipus complex," which became the foundation of modern psychology. According to this theory any young girl actually *desires* sexual contact with her father, because she wants to compete with her mother to be the most special person in his life. Freud used this construct to conclude that the episodes of incestuous abuse his clients had revealed to him *had never taken place*; they were simply fantasies of events the women had *wished for* when they were children and that the women had come to believe were real. This construct started a hundred-year history in the mental health field of blaming victims for the abuse perpetrated on them and outright discrediting of women's and children's reports of mistreatment by men.

Once abuse was denied in this way, the stage was set for some psychologists to take the view that any violent or sexually exploitative behaviors that couldn't be denied—because they were simply too obvious—should be considered *mutually* caused. Psychological literature is thus full of descriptions of young children who "seduce" adults into sexual encounters and of women whose "provocative" behavior causes men to become violent or sexually assaultive toward them.

I wish I could say that these theories have long since lost their influence, but I can't. A psychologist who is currently one of the most influential professionals nationally in the field of custody disputes writes that women provoke men's violence by "resisting their control" or by "attempting to leave." She promotes the Oedipus complex theory, including the claim that girls wish for sexual contact with their fathers. In her writing she makes the observation that young girls are often involved in "mutually seductive" relationships with their violent fathers, and it is on the basis of such "research" that some courts have set their protocols. The Freudian legacy thus remains strong.

Hoping to find that the mental health field was changing for the better, I recently reviewed the current catalogues for various graduate professional training programs in clinical and counseling psychology, including those from programs considered to be on the cutting edge. I was unable not only to locate a single course on any form of abuse, whether toward partners or children, but to locate any *reference* to abuse in the descriptions of courses on any other subject. I proceeded to call one of the schools that trains clinical psychologists and asked whether they ever offer any classes on abuse, and was told: "Well, if there is a particular interest in that subject among the students, they sometimes organize a student-led seminar."

The influence of the history of psychological thinking remains particularly potent in the field of custody evaluation, where mental health professionals routinely ignore or minimize allegations of partner abuse and child abuse, assume that women are hysterical and vindictive, and treat all problems as mutual in origin. Custody evaluators sometimes become fervent advocates for abusive men, joining them in accusing the women of alienating children from their fathers and refusing to consider the evidence of abuse.

Similar kinds of errors abound in the work of many individual and couples therapists. I've had couples counselors say to me, for example: "He just isn't the type to be abusive; he's so pleasant and insightful, and she's so *angry.*" Women speak to me with shocked voices of betrayal as they tell me how their couples therapist, or the abuser's individual therapist, or a therapist for one of their children, has become a vocal advocate for him and a harsh and superior critic of her. I have saved for years a letter that a psychologist wrote about one of my clients, a man who admitted to me that his wife was covered with blood and had broken bones when he was done beating her and that she could have died. The psychologist's letter ridiculed the system for labeling this man a "batterer," saying that he was too reasonable and insightful and should not be participating in my abuser program any further. The content of the letter indicated to me that the psychologist had neglected to ever ask the client to describe the brutal beating that he had been convicted of.

Outside the mainstream of psychological thinking there are many, many excellent practitioners and theorists, ones who take the impact of trauma and abuse seriously and who believe that most victims are telling the truth. The writings of theorists and practitioners such as Judith Herman, Bessel van der Kolk, Peter Jaffe, Angela Browne, John Myers, Susan Schechter, Anna Salter, Beverly James, and countless others serve to counter the hostility toward the oppressed of the prevailing professional atmosphere. I have come to know dozens of therapists who treat female clients with respect and play an empowering role in women's recovery from abuse. But psychologists who are trained in the area of trauma remain exceptional, and the battle to reform psychological thinking has just begun. Before selecting a therapist for yourself or for your child, be sure to interview possible choices carefully, exploring their knowledge of and values concerning trauma and abuse. As for conjoint counseling for you and your abusive partner, I recommend that you strictly avoid it, for reasons that we will see further ahead.

AN ABUSER'S NEW PARTNER AS HIS LEADING ALLY

Back in the first chapter, we met a man named Paul who had divorced his wife and was now seeing Laura. Laura felt terrible for Paul because he was such a sweet man and his ex-wife was accusing him of having abused her. Laura was determined to "be there" for Paul, and even hoping to help him win custody because his ex-wife was "out of control." Dozens of ex-partners of my clients have described how the abusive man's new partner takes on a role similar to Laura's: "His girlfriend is worse than he is. She talks to me like I'm dirt and she spreads bad things about me. I'd almost rather deal with him. I think she puts him up to some of the stuff he does. She's a bitch."

Perhaps his new partner really is a mean, hostile woman, but there is an equally good chance that she isn't. Look through her eyes for a moment. The abuser is re-creating the same dynamic he set up with you, beginning with loving, attentive treatment in the early months of dating. He speaks to her with downcast eyes that well up with tears as he recounts how mean and unreasonable you were and how you called him abusive whenever *he* refused to bow to *your* control. If you have children with him, his girlfriend's heart is bleeding because he cries in front of her about how much he misses them and says that you are keeping them away from him out of pure vindictiveness or out of a desire to turn them over to another man to be their dad. I currently have a case, for example, where the abusive father decided not to see his son for six months—he even put his decision in writing, in a document that I read—and then complained publicly that he was being denied visits. Paul has probably misled Laura in some similar ways. His girlfriend sees a kind, loving parent whose desire to maintain a relationship with his children is being thwarted; how could she not hate you?

He may remain on good behavior with his new girlfriend even longer than he did with you because he is motivated by his campaign against you. Of course, his other side will slip out sooner or later, but by that time he can blame it all on how badly you have hurt him. His girlfriend thus gets sucked into breaking her back trying to prove that she's a good woman—unlike you. She hopes that if she demonstrates her loyalty to him, he'll become loving and available to her once again, as he was at the beginning. So she wants to show him she is really there for him by joining with—or even outdoing—his hostility toward and blaming of you.

By the time his selfish and abusive side finally gets so bad that his new girlfriend can't rationalize it away any more, she's in pretty deep. She may even have married him by that time. For her to accept that he is an abuser, she would have to face what a terrible wrong she did to you, and that would be quite a bitter pill to swallow. So what tends to happen instead is that his new partner becomes angrier and angrier at *you* for the way she is being treated by him, believing that you "made him this way" by hurting him so badly.

A couple of years ago I worked with a woman who said to me, "I really hated his ex-girlfriend, but now I'm realizing he must have done the same stuff to her he's doing to me." Her guilt weighed heavily upon her. Women tend to need a long time before they can accept having been used in this way.

In the story of Paul and Laura we never meet Paul's ex-wife, but I have talked to two dozen or more women in her position among the ex-partners of my clients. It is difficult to capture the pain I hear in the voices of women whose abusive ex-partners are attempting to take their children away from them through the legal system, and the fact that they have a female ally helping them carry out that nefarious plan is almost too much to bear. The mothers ask me: "Does she realize what she is doing? Has she bothered to think about what it's like for a mother to be threatened with losing her children? What if he turns around years from now and does the same thing to her?"

At the same time, I believe it's important not to judge the new partner too harshly. I sometimes say to women, "You know how manipulative he can be, and he is sure to be feeding her carefully crafted distortions. I'm not saying you should excuse her actions, I'm just reminding you that the one behind it all is him, not her. If you pour energy into hating her, you are inadvertently serving his interests." We do, however, need to create a social ethic that makes it clear that anyone who chooses to go to bat for a man accused of abuse has a responsibility to get *all* the facts and not just the view that he promotes. The abuse of women is simply too rampant for anyone to assume that an allegation is false or exaggerated without checking it out very, very carefully.

Finally, I have had several cases in which the abuser's new partner was a man who became a gunner for the abuser against the abused woman just as a new female partner sometimes does. Some peer groups of gay men have negative attitudes toward women and become cheerleaders for abuse just as straight male peers can.

OTHER ABUSERS OF POWER AS ALLIES OF ABUSIVE MEN

You have undoubtedly come in contact at some point in your life with a person driven by a deep attraction to exercising power over others. Partner abusers have no monopoly on the desire to intimidate or manipulate, or on the skills for accumulating power and using it for selfish purposes or emotional gratification. Among professionals, for example—including those who are expected to respond constructively to abusers and their partners—there are some individuals who are motivated not by caring and respect but by hunger for control. Not everyone who enters police work wishes to be a public servant; there are those who look forward primarily to carrying a gun, pushing their weight around, and being above the law. I know many humane judges who take an interest in the challenges that people face and seek fair and practical responses. But I watch others who appear to get satisfaction out of insulting those who come before them, dismissing their concerns and perspectives, and acting with impunity. Among therapists there are plenty whose goal is teamwork, while others look down on their clients and speak condescendingly, making pronouncements about what each person "really" thinks, feels, and needs to do. There are custody evaluators who are eager to lend a hand through the painful process of divorce, but a tragically large number appears to be enamored with the power over the lives of men, women, and children that their custody recommendations give them.

People who are attracted to power and tend to abuse it have important common ground with a man who abuses women. For example, a dictatorial boss is bound to encounter some occasions when an employee finally gets fed up enough to swear at her, stomp out of the office, and quit. A manager who coerces his female subordinates into sexual contact with him may get reported for sexual harassment sooner or later. The abuser of power feels outraged when his or her victims attempt to defend themselves in these ways and considers them to be the unreasonable or aggressive ones. So it is not surprising that such a person, when looking at a woman who is complaining of abuse by a man, might have the following thoughts: "This woman is another one of those people who likes the role of victim. I know what they're like because I have to deal with them myself: They are never grateful no matter how much you do for them; they don't know their place; and everything turns into an accusation of mistreatment." The abuser of power thus may personalize the woman's resistance to oppression and feel a strong desire to retaliate on behalf of the abusive man, and in fact I have often observed this disturbing eagerness among some professionals to jump on abused women with both feet. Their statements have sometimes confirmed to me that they do indeed have the kind of thought process I have just described—coupled of course with the usual myths regarding women's hysterical exaggerations and their provocation of men's abuse.

A professional who is drawn to abusing power seems to have particularly strong reactions if the woman challenges his or her actions in any way or attempts to explain the effects the abuser has had on her. The underlying attitude sometimes appears to be: "How *dare* you continue to attempt to think for yourself when I am here before you with my obviously superior knowledge, status, judgment, and insight?" An abused woman can walk away from an interaction with such a professional feeling like she has just been beaten up, re-creating the ugliness of the verbal or physical abuse she has suffered from her partner. A number of abused women have said to me, for example, "The police came to my house one time after he pushed me around, but they were angry and insulting to me and kind of buddied up to him, and when I complained about how they were treating me they told me if I didn't shut up they would arrest *me*." I have been involved in cases where some judges and custody evaluators—both male and female—go out of their way to discredit and demean women who report abuse and request protection for themselves or their children, and if the woman protests the professional response they explode into verbally abusing her or retaliating against her. In this way the mentality and tactics of certain professionals can closely parallel those of abusers, and the result is revictimization of the woman.

In some institutions whose own power dynamics have tended to fall badly on abused women in these ways, such as police departments, courts, and child protective services, social pressure has brought about the creation of positions for abused women's advocates or domestic-violence specialists whose job it is to make sure that the abused woman is not re-victimized by the system that should be there to protect her rights. If you are involved with one of these systems, find out whether an abuse special-ist is on staff and, if so, request to bring that person into your case.

ATTORNEYS

Some attorneys for abusers are in a class by themselves. I have rarely seen anyone become as vicious and unprincipled in the role of coabuser of a man's partner as certain lawyers do. Woman after woman has described to me the way her heart begins to race when she sees the abuser's attorney at court or the jolt she feels when court papers prepared by the attorney arrive at her home.

An abuser or accused abuser of course has the right to legal represen-tation, as anyone does. But does offering proper legal counsel mean that the attorney needs to insult and deride the woman, make far-fetched ac-cusations against her, treat every allegation made by the man as gospel truth, and even lie at times to promote his goals? Of course not. However, such conduct is disturbingly widespread among certain defense attorneys who represent accused abusers as well as among some family law attor-neys handling custody and visitation cases. Some of this behavior appears to be motivated by economics: Attorneys can build a successful practice if word gets around that they specialize in representing accused abusers. Abusers love it when they hear that a certain attorney has a reputation for "really going for the woman's jugular," since that ruthless orientation is in keeping with their own. Women are sometimes as traumatized by their ex-partner's attorney as they were by him.

There is an urgent need for the creation of legal standards for attor-neys who represent accused abusers, so that a sharp line is drawn be-tween giving a man a proper chance to have his side heard in court, which is his legal right, and acting as a weapon of the man's abuse, allowing him to cause financial and psychological damage that would have been impos-sible for him without the lawyer's assistance.

THE MYTH OF NEUTRALITY

It is not possible to be truly balanced in one's views of an abuser and an abused woman. As Dr. Judith Herman explains eloquently in her master-work *Trauma and Recovery,* "neutrality" actually serves the interests of the perpetrator much more than those of the victim and so is not neutral. Although an abuser prefers to have you wholeheartedly on his side, he will settle contentedly for your decision to take a middle stance. To him, that means you see the couple's problems as partly her fault and partly his fault, which means it isn't abuse.

I was speaking with a person one day who was describing the abusive relationship of a man and woman, both of whom were friends of hers. "They each want me to side with them," she explained to me, "but I refuse to take sides. They have to work out their own dynamics. I have let both of them know that I'm there for them. If I openly supported her, he would just dig his heels in harder." She added, "People need to avoid the tempta-tion to choose up teams" in a tone that indicated that she considered her-self to be of superior maturity because of her neutrality.

In reality, to remain neutral is to collude with the abusive man, whether or not that is your goal. If you are aware of chronic or severe mis-treatment and do not speak out against it, your silence communicates im-plicitly that you see nothing unacceptable taking place. Abusers interpret silence as approval, or at least as forgiveness. To abused women, mean-while, the silence means that no one will help—just what her partner wants her to believe. Anyone who chooses to quietly look the other way therefore unwittingly becomes the abuser's ally.

Breaking the silence does not necessarily mean criticizing or con-fronting the abuser regarding his behavior. It certainly doesn't mean going to him with anything you have learned *from her,* because the abuser will retaliate against her for talking about his behavior to other people. It does mean telling the abused woman privately that you don't like the way he is treating her and that she doesn't deserve it, no matter what she has done. And if you see or hear violence or threats, it means calling the police.

How Society Adopts the Abuser's Perspective

Almost anyone can become an ally of an abusive man by inadvertently adopting his perspective. People usually don't even notice that they are supporting abusive thinking, or they wouldn't do it. Let's examine some of the most common forms of accidental support:

- *The person who says to the abused woman: "You should show him some compassion even if he has done bad things. Don't forget that he's a human being too."*

I have almost never worked with an abused woman who overlooked her partner's humanity. The problem is the reverse: *He* forgets *her* humanity. Acknowledging his abusiveness and speaking forcefully and honestly about how he has hurt her is indispensable to her recovery. It is the *abuser's* perspective that she is being mean to him by speaking bluntly about the damage he has done. To suggest to her that his need for compassion should come before her right to live free from abuse is consistent with the abuser's outlook. I have repeatedly seen the tendency among friends and acquaintances of an abused woman to feel that it is their responsibility to make sure that she realizes *what a good person he really is inside*—in other words, to stay focused on his needs rather than on her own, which is a mistake. People who wish to help an abused woman should instead be telling her what a good person *she* is.

- *The person who says to her: "But he's the father of your children."*

The abusive man uses the children to entrap the woman in the relationship, saying that she is depriving them of a father by splitting up the family. But *he* is the one who is keeping those children from having the father they need, by forcing them to grow up with a father who abuses their mother. Children need an abuse-free home.

- *The person who says to her: "You made a commitment, and now you need to stick with it through hard times."*

The abusive man believes that chronic mistreatment, overt disrespect, intimidation, and even violence are not good enough reasons for a woman to want to stay away from a man. When people say to her, "You made your bed; now lie in it," they are supporting the abuser's value system.

• *The person who says to her: "You are claiming to be a helpless victim."*

If the abuser could hear these words being spoken to his partner, he would jump for joy. He may have said the very same thing to her. The abuser's perspective is that the woman exaggerates the hurtfulness of his conduct because she *wants* the status of victim, attributing to her the maneuvers that he is actually fond of using himself. When an abused woman tries to tell you how bad things are, listen.

• *The person who says: "These abuse activists are anti-male."*

How is it anti-male to be against abuse? Are we supposed to pretend we don't notice that the overwhelming majority of abusers are male? This accusation parallels the abuser's words to his partner: "The reason you think I'm abusive is because you have a problem with men!" One of the best counters to this piece of side-tracking is to point out how many men are active in combating the abuse of women. Remember also that abused women are the sisters, daughters, mothers, and friends of men; men's lives *are* affected by abuse, because it happens to women we know and care about.

I HAVE GIVEN just a few of the dozens of examples I have encountered of how people take on the abuser's view of his abuse. When you hear these kinds of statements, draw the speaker's attention to the fact that he or she is making the abuser's arguments for him. Most people don't want to carry his banner and will drop it quickly once you show them what is in their hands.

It is impossible for a community to stop abuse while continuing to assist or ignore abusers at the same time. *Protecting or enabling an abuser is as morally repugnant as the abuse itself.* This critical concept needs to become firmly embedded in our culture. Colluding with abuse abandons the abused woman and her children, and ultimately abandons the *abuser* as well, since it keeps him from ever dealing with his problem. In particular we have to bring to light the actions of those powerful, well-trained professionals who choose to join the abuser in his goals and tactics. If we can erode the ability of abusers to gain allies, they will stand alone, and alone they are easier to stop.

It often falls to the abused woman herself, unfortunately, to try to educate the people around her whose help and support she needs, so that they will understand the dynamics of abuse and stop supporting the abusive man. Much of why an abuser is so able to recruit allies, besides his own manipulativeness and charm, is his skill in playing on people's ignorance and misconceptions and often on their negative attitudes toward women. As difficult as it is to take on, you will often find yourself having to be your own best advocate, arguing forcefully against the range of ways in which your society's values may buy into the abusive man's outlook, in order to gain the kind of strong backing that you deserve from all those around you.

KEY POINTS TO REMEMBER

- When people take a neutral stand between you and your abusive partner, they are in effect supporting him and abandoning you, no matter how much they may claim otherwise.

- People cannot claim to be opposed to partner abuse while assisting their own son, brother, friend, or partner in his abusiveness toward a woman.

- Everyone should be very, very cautious in accepting a man's claim that he has been wrongly accused of abuse or violence. The great majority of allegations of abuse—though not all— are substantially accurate. And an abuser almost never "seems like the type."

- The argument that "he is a human being, too, and he deserves emotional support" should not be used as an excuse to support a man's *abusiveness*. Our society should not buy into the abusive man's claim that holding him accountable is an act of cruelty.

12

The Abusive Man
and the Legal System

He's on probation for hitting me, but he acts like it's a big joke.

He's been arrested four times, but he always gets off.

I called the police and reported that he violated the restraining order, but they said since he didn't get violent or threatening this time, the violation is too minor for them to do anything about it.

The D.A. wants me to testify, but there's no way I'm going in that courthouse again. Last time his defense attorney humiliated me; it's just not worth it.

The judge told me that we should go to couples counseling to work on our relationship issues.

He's been sending me scary letters from jail. What should I do?

LURKING BENEATH THE SURFACE of most women's experience of abuse is *fear*: fear of what he will do if you stand up to him; fear of how he will react if he finds out you've been spending time with your friends, whom he hates; fear of what he might do to one of your children; fear that he will get you pregnant again; fear of how he may retaliate if you try to leave him.

Sometimes a woman can describe to me what she is afraid of, because her partner's bullying and cruelty follow a pattern. You may dread his insults and his rage or his contempt and disgust. If he is violent, you may get shaky when images go through your mind of his twisted, hate-filled face as he slams his fists. At times it may seem like he could kill you—and he may threaten to.

In other cases, the fear is unnameable. You might find yourself saying to a friend: "I don't know *what* he'll do; there's no way to tell with him, but he'll do *something,* and it's going to be bad." Waiting for the punishment can be even harder when you don't know what it will be. Even the abuser who has never used violence knows that there can always be a first time—and he may well be aware that you know that too. So he looks for ways, perhaps explicit or perhaps enigmatic, to remind you not to "push him too far," because you won't want to see what happens.

The impact of fear accumulates over time. The twentieth time a loved one scares you is not the same as the first. You become enraged, or para-lyzed, or numb, or all of those at the same time. You feel like it's harder and harder to figure out what to do.

If your partner is physically frightening or sexually assaultive, one op-tion you can consider to gain protection for your rights and safety is to use the legal system. You can call the police to report an assault or a threat, or go to a court and ask for a restraining order (which also may be known as a "protective order" or "peace bond"). The restraining order may require the abuser to move out of the house, even if it is in his name; to stay away from you; or to have no contact with you of any kind, depending on what arrangement you feel you need.

The first time a woman considers involving the police or courts in her relationship, something inside her rebels. This is a man she loves, or at least once loved, with whom she has a history, with whom she has shared the highs and lows of moments of physical or emotional intimacy, with whom she may have children. She thinks to herself incredulously, *I am go-ing to get a court order against this man? I am going to call the police and let them arrest him? I am going to cause him to have a criminal record, or per-haps even go to jail??* She shuts these preposterous-seeming possibilities out of her mind. *Relationship problems are solved by talking, or by seeking counseling, or by taking some time apart,* she tells herself, *not by using laws and judges and police departments.*

But if the woman's partner continues to frighten her—and it is unusual for scary behavior to stop once it rears its head—sooner or later she finds herself feeling that the situation has gone beyond what she can handle herself. The step of reaching out for legal help then stops seeming so farfetched.

Or she may become involved with the legal system without making the choice. Neighbors, bystanders, or her own children may call the police during a scary incident. Neighbors are much less likely nowadays to put their hands over their ears and pretend that nothing is happening; the traditional belief that domestic violence is a "private matter" is rapidly fading. Schools now teach children how to use 911 and sometimes even explain to children that they have a right to safety inside their homes, not just outside.

A woman who faces purely verbal or economic abuse from her partner, without the elements of physical assault, sexual assault, or physical intimidation, generally does not have recourse to the police or courts under current laws. The impact on her of her partner's behavior may be severe nonetheless, but she will need to seek other sources of support, beginning with the nearest program for abused women.

QUESTION 17:
HOW COME HE KEEPS GETTING AWAY WITH IT?

THE DIFFERENT PLAYERS IN THE LEGAL SYSTEM

A call to the police or a visit to the court to seek a restraining order is a courageous and potentially empowering step. But an abused woman can also encounter some nasty surprises. Although the legal system is supposed to be her friend and protector, sometimes public officials seem to forget their job. Legal responses to abuse involve many players, each of whom has the potential to help the woman—or to drop the ball. When police are called to your home, they have a responsibility to make sure that you and your children are safe and to arrest the abuser if he has been violent or threatening. If he has violated a restraining order, the police should take him away even if he "only committed a technical violation" of the order or has some "good reason" for being there, such as asserting that you called him up and asked him to come over, or that he just wanted to drop off gifts for the children.

If the police do not arrest the abuser, or were never called, responsibility next falls to the court to file a charge. If you report to the court that you were assaulted or threatened, or that your partner broke a restraining order, *your word is evidence*. Courts can, and do, file charges on the basis of victim reports alone, but tragically they can be reluctant to do so in cases of domestic abuse or sexual assault. Courts reserve a special skepticism toward women who complain of abuse by a partner, and disparaging biases against females are still the rule of the day in some courts—even among female employees.

If the court does file a charge, the baton then passes to the district attorney. His or her job is to take the crime just as seriously as if it had been committed by a stranger and to pursue a conviction just as assiduously. The fact that the accused is your partner should make no difference or should actually lead the prosecutor to consider the offense *more* dangerous. Negotiations between the prosecutor and the abuser that fail to address the central issue of abuse—such as agreeing to reduce the charges if the abuser sees a therapist, or dropping the charges because the couple has split up "so it's not an issue anymore"—have no place here. But they sometimes creep in.

Next comes the judge, who not only makes sentencing decisions but, unless there is a jury trial, also is the one ruling on the man's guilt or innocence. Will the judge apply the same standards of proof used for other cases, or will he or she require a higher standard for domestic violence or sexual assault cases? Studies have shown that it is harder to convince judges and juries to convict in abuse cases, because of prejudices against the complainants as well as misconceptions about what "type" of man would commit such a crime.

A judge is also the one who grants or denies a restraining order to protect the woman. Some judges listen carefully to plaintiffs' concerns, whereas others assume that women are lying and exaggerating. A remarkable number of judges grant restraining orders *to abusers* to use against their victims or grant mutual orders, which validate the abuser's claim that his partner shares responsibility for causing his scary behavior.

And finally comes the probation department at the court. It is rare for an abuser to spend time in jail unless he is on his third or fourth *conviction*, which typically would mean five or ten or more *arrests*. So his probation officer becomes the person who determines whether or not the abuser feels the bite of consequences or is left to coast. I have worked with probation officers who send abusers an unequivocal message: "Domestic abuse is a serious offense. I will not permit you to get away with blaming your victim in any way, and it is up to you to do some serious work on yourself." But I have also worked with many others who buddy up to the abuser with a wink and a nod, who bond with him in the belief that there exists an anti-male bias in the court system and who signal him that he needn't take the abuser program seriously by saying things such as: "Just show up to your required number of group meetings and we'll get you right off probation."

The front doors of police departments and courthouses sometimes open into cold and adversarial worlds. Police and courts may have little training in how to respond to a person who has suffered chronic or terrifying abuse. Even if they don't say or do anything unkind, their brusque, businesslike manner can feel like an icy slap in the face to a woman who seeks relief from psychological assault and intimidation at home. And too often, regrettably, they share the abuser's attitudes. I could not possibly count the number of women who have said to me: "I wish those people down at the court could live my life for a day and see what it's like."

On the other hand a kind word, a useful pamphlet, some patient listening can touch an abused woman deeply. Increasingly I hear women say: "The police who came were so nice to me: They talked to me in private and asked me what happened, and they told me about programs where I could get help," or "The judge said not to hesitate to come back if there were more problems or if I needed additional protection." When an abused woman encounters humane, intelligent responses from officials who are informed on the subject of abuse, not only is her external freedom promoted but her inner feelings are validated, helping to keep her spirit alive. She walks away thinking, *Maybe everything isn't the way he says it is. Maybe some people do care. Maybe I'm not so bad as to deserve being torn down all the time. Maybe he can't fool everybody."* And the budding belief that life *can* be filled with something other than cruelty and superiority grows a little stronger inside her.

In the pages ahead, we will look at how the abuser views and maneuvers through the legal system, trying to prevent his partner from receiving empowering assistance and striving to avoid accountability. Armed with this awareness, both individuals and communities are in a better position to press the police, courts, and prosecutors to do their jobs properly and become part of the solution rather than part of the problem of abuse.

HOW THE ABUSER THINKS ABOUT LAWS AND CONSEQUENCES

My clients support laws that prohibit domestic abuse—as long as they are applied only to other men. Each one has a mental image of what a "real abuser" is like, and it isn't him. In his mind, the "real abuser" is more violent and scary than he is and has a partner who is "a nice lady" who doesn't deserve abuse. Dozens of my clients have said to me: "I'm not like those guys who come home and abuse their partners for no reason, you know." A man who minimizes and excuses his abuse in these ways is shocked when the police arrest him or when a court orders him to vacate his home. He feels outraged at the unfairness of the system. He thinks, *With all those horrible batterers out there, why are they coming after* me? *This is ridiculous!*

Since he can't accept the idea that he is abusive, he has to find something wrong with everyone else—another example of the abuser seeing his dirty face and washing the mirror. His thinking is rife with distortions, including the following:

* *"She really exaggerated what I did."*

His first line of mental defense is to impugn her honesty and accuse her of being calculating: "She told the police I *punched her in the face*, because she knew that would make me look like a real bad guy. I only slapped her, and no harder than she slaps me." My response to such statements is to say that just because she remembers the incident differently doesn't mean her version is wrong and his is right; in fact, abused women typically have memories of what occurred that are clearer and more accurate than those of the abuser, because of the hyperalert manner in which people react to any danger. And even if this time he is technically right that his hand was open, what difference does it make? He obviously hit her hard enough to make her *think* that she was punched, so he is not a candidate for my sympathy. Besides, even if it was a slap, that's enough to hurt a woman and put her in fear.

- *"The judge didn't even want to hear about what **she** did. In court the man is automatically wrong, so the woman can do whatever she wants."*

The abuser feels justified in using intimidation "when it's really called for," so he gets frustrated if he finds that court officials do not find his excuses about her behavior compelling or don't even want to hear them. He feels that if the court is going to take action against him for intimidating her, then it should simultaneously crack down on *her* for hanging around with friends of hers whom he dislikes, talking back to him when he tells her to shut up, fighting back physically when he is assaulting or threatening her, or whatever his grievances may be.

- *"The system is controlled by women."*

Every aspect of the multipronged legal system even today is dominated by males: police, prosecutors, judges, probation officers. In addition, the state legislatures that make the laws are still disproportionately male. So how does the abuser come to the far-fetched conclusion that women are somehow lurking in the shadows, pulling strings to cause him to suffer consequences for his actions when he thinks there shouldn't be any? This absurd leap occurs for two reasons. One is that he already has well-entrenched habits of blaming women for his own behavior. So when society sends him the message that he is responsible for what he does, he just widens the scope of his blame-projecting machine to target *all* women. The second is that if he didn't blame women, he would have to accept the fact that a large proportion of *men* are opposed to what he is doing. Cultural values are changing, slowly but surely, and abusers cannot always count on other men to back them up anymore—a fact that makes them feel betrayed so they close their eyes to it.

- *"I've never experienced any consequences for my abuse before. It isn't going to suddenly happen now."*

Once the abuser recovers from his initial shock at legal intrusion into his private domain, he falls back on one of his core assumptions, which is that he can get away with it. He starts manipulating court officials the same way he manipulates his partner and the people around her. Unfortunately, his sense of invulnerability is not as deluded as it may seem; abusers slide by in ways that can be startling to watch. And the abuser who coasts through court is often worse than he would have been had he never been arrested; he feels that his belief that nothing can stick to him has been confirmed, and he feels vindicated before the world, with the result that his abusive behavior may escalate.

- *"Nothing is going to stop me."*

This last attitude is less pervasive, belonging to that minority of abusers who are unimpressed by legal consequences and who will stop at nothing to maintain their control of their partners. This style of man finds ways to be abusive and controlling even from jail, either sending letters or relaying messages through friends to keep her frightened. Jail doesn't convince him that he has done anything wrong; it just sharpens his appetite for revenge. Abused women, and the communities that support them, need to be alert to the need to take additional steps to prepare for the eventual release of the hell-bent abuser.

Keep the above attitudes in mind as we observe the abuser's approach to the various legal situations he faces; his moves follow predictably from this thinking.

When the Police Come to the Door

Anyone who believes that abusers lose control of themselves should peer through the window when the police enter a home. Hundreds of women have told me: "It's as if he could flick a switch. The police arrive, and he's suddenly cool as a cucumber. Meanwhile, I'm freaking out, so of course they think something is wrong with *me*. They don't believe he could settle down that fast." If abusers truly had tremendous problems managing their anger, if they were as emotionally vulnerable or deeply injured from childhood as they often maintain, they wouldn't be able to shut themselves off like a faucet as soon as a cop knocks on the door.

Abusers tell stories to the police of hard luck and misunderstanding, of unstable or drunk women and helpless, well-intentioned men who are trying to fend off disaster. The most common routines are variations on the following themes:

- *"It was just a verbal argument, there was no hitting."*

He hopes that the police will ignore any signs of chairs knocked over, plates smashed, or scratches on her arms (or his). He assumes his partner will be too scared to tell the truth or that she'll feel responsible for protecting him.

- *"She was hitting me over and over again while I tried to get out of the apartment, and all I did was push her out of my way so I could get out."*

How many women want to keep an enraged man trapped indoors? Not many, unless perhaps the man is threatening to commit suicide or to attack one of her friends or relatives. In the rare cases where a client of mine is telling the truth that his egress was blocked, he still had other options besides assault, including going out the back door. I've never yet had a man tell me that he was unable to get to the phone to call for assistance, for example, in the way that has happened to hundreds of the female partners of my clients.

Countless clients of mine claim self-defense as an excuse, but then they admit that they were not frightened or injured by their partners nor was the woman able to successfully control their movements or keep them from saying whatever they wanted. It's payback, not self-defense. Among the two thousand clients I have had, I can think of only one who genuinely had a problem with serious violence on his wife's part that was not a reaction to violence, and even he was not especially afraid of her.

- *"She was drunk and was going out to drive, and I was just trying to get the keys away from her."*

This excuse is a tricky one, because abused women sometimes do develop alcohol or drug problems, usually because of the abuser's behavior. However, her addiction is no excuse to abuse her further. Unfortunately, if a woman is visibly intoxicated when the police come, they may feel inclined to believe the abuser and discredit her. If I ask a few questions, though, I usually find out that the reason she was trying to leave the house was that he had been on a mounting verbal rampage that day, and she was trying to get away from a physical assault that she could tell was coming soon.

- *"She said that if I didn't give her more money, she'd call the police and say that I hit her."*

I have heard this story from so many of my clients that I find myself wondering if they are all graduates of the same Abuse Academy. I have yet to encounter a case in which there turned out to be any truth to this claim, even when the man was asserting at first that he had witnesses.

- *"I just stepped in to protect our child from her abuse."*

Again, a situation in which a nonabusive man had to take physical steps to protect a child from an assaultive mother could truly arise, but he would do so by removing the child, not by assaulting the mother.

Carrying false allegations of domestic violence all the way through to a conviction is extraordinarily hard to do. If a vindictive woman really wants to stick it to a man, there are ways to do it that are more satisfying, less time consuming, and far less prone to failure. There isn't the slightest evidence that rates of false allegations for domestic abuse are higher than for any other kind of crime. In fact, research suggests that they may be lower.

When an abuser is accused of violating a restraining order, he has another set of explanations ready, including:

- *"It's just a coincidence that we were there at the same time. I had no idea she would be present."*

In determining the legitimacy of this excuse, I have noticed that men who are determined to obey their restraining orders always seem to find ways to stay away from the woman, whereas other abusers seem to "just by accident" keep violating the order over and over again.

- *"I didn't realize I wasn't allowed to even send a letter."*

Even when this excuse is true, it shows the man's contempt for both his partner and for the court, since it means he didn't bother to read the order. And he doesn't need an attorney to analyze the statement **"Do not contact the plaintiff."**

- *"I just called to speak to the children because I miss them terribly.
  I haven't had visitation with them in two months."*

No excuse pulls heartstrings down at the police department and court-house quite the way this one does. Several of my clients who have used this excuse actually did have visitation rights but were *choosing* not to use them because they didn't like the terms. They stated: "If I can only see them one afternoon a week, or if I have to see them with a supervisor, I'm not go-ing to see them at all." So much for the devoted fathers they claim to be.

Even in cases where the mother or the court has indeed denied the abuser visitation, he knows perfectly well what he is doing when he calls the home and the feelings of fear and invasion it will cause the mother. If his concern for his children is as profound as he claims, he can prove it by doing what his children need from him the most—deal seriously with his abuse problem.

WHEN THE POLICE go to a home on a domestic-abuse call, the woman sometimes scrambles to cover for her abusive partner. Consider her posi-tion: She knows that in a few minutes the police will leave her house and she will remain there alone, either with the abuser or without him. If the police do arrest him, it is only a matter of time until he is released—and angrier than ever. She calculates that her safest position is beside her partner; if she teams up with him, he might not rip her to pieces when the police car disappears up the street. Even if she called for help herself, she wasn't necessarily looking for an arrest; most women call to get a scary ex-perience to stop. They want the police to calm the man down and typi-cally would like him removed from the home for the night. But jail, even just for a day or two? Few women would want to see that happen unless they have suffered a long history of abuse by him.

At the same time, women are noticeably more likely to tell the truth to the police than they were fifteen years ago. Although the abuser may say, "You put me in jail!", the reality is that he put *himself* there, and an in-creasing number of people are beginning to understand this crucial point. Why should you have to suffer abuse to protect *him* from the pain or humiliation of being locked up? He knows what he needs to change in order to keep the police from being called the next time. It's on him.

I am not recommending that you stand by idly while the police arrest your partner if you fear that he may kill you when he gets out. Every woman has to make her own decisions based on what she knows about the status of her own safety; you are the expert on your own partner. You may know from your experience that the legal system is not going to be able to control his behavior and that you will have to seek alternate strategies for safety, such as planning an escape.

SHOULD I GET A RESTRAINING ORDER?

Throughout almost all of the United States and Canada, a woman who is being physically abused, sexually assaulted, or physically threatened by an intimate partner or ex-partner has the option to seek an order of protection from a court to keep the abuser away from her. (Purely psychological abuse without these elements of threat or assault is generally not covered under the laws governing protective orders.) In some areas there are important gaps in eligibility, however, such as states where a woman cannot get an order against a lesbian partner who is abusing her or cannot get an order if she has never lived with or been married to the abuser. There are also places where, regrettably, the woman is required to pay a substantial fee in order to obtain the order. Call either the courthouse or your local program for abused women to find out whether you are eligible to seek an order and what the process is for obtaining one.

The question of whether and when to obtain a restraining order is a complex one that no one can answer for you. Consider the following points in making your decision:

1. Is he afraid of the police, courts, or jail? If he is, the restraining order may keep him away from you. But if he has no fear, the order may incite him to get scarier than ever. I have had clients who responded to a restraining order as a red flag waved in front of a bull.

2. Is your main concern that he will intimidate you, attempt to hit you, or hassle you verbally, or are you afraid he will do something

even more serious, such as attempt to kill you? Restraining orders can be helpful for stopping harassment and nonlethal assault but may not be worth a great deal in stopping an abuser whose intentions are murderous. If you fear the worst, it is important to take multiple steps to protect your safety (see "Safety Planning" in Chapter 9), which can include a restraining order *as one aspect of a larger plan,* and even then *only if you think it will contribute to your safety.*

3. Are the police and courts in your area supportive? Are they likely to take serious action if he violates the order? Will they believe you if you report a violation to them? A restraining order can do more harm than good if the legal system is not prepared to back you up.

I have seen cases where restraining orders have contributed greatly to women's safety and peace of mind and have helped immeasurably in women's efforts to move on with their lives and be free. But each abusive man is different. I have been involved in cases where the woman regretted getting the order because it made her life even scarier. If possible, speak with an advocate for abused women *before* making a decision about seeking an order. And whether or not you choose to request a restraining order, also make sure to take *other* steps to protect your safety. A restraining order should be one part of a larger safety plan (see "Leaving an Abuser Safely" in Chapter 9).

IF THEY DO ARREST HIM, WHAT THEN?

Once an abuser is released from jail following arraignment, he typically devotes his efforts to achieving the following goals: (1) persuading the woman to drop the charges and not to testify if charges do proceed; and (2) receiving the lightest possible consequence from the court.

One of my early clients, a large biker named Phil, introduced me to many of the tactics that predominate during this period. He joined my abuser group voluntarily following an arrest for assaulting his girlfriend, Betty. He was fairly unpleasant in the early weeks of his participation, because of his arrogance and his "I don't give a damn about anything" posture. But he softened as the weeks went by and began to make appropriate comments to other group members about their abuse. Betty reported that she was seeing a side of Phil that had disappeared for several years: He was calmer, he was listening to her more when she talked, and he was walking away from arguments instead of frightening her. Even more important to her was that he had stopped by her sister's house one afternoon and made an effort to begin mending fences after two years of refusing to talk to her and insisting that she was a "bitch." And Betty was happy to hear that his attendance at and participation in our program were good.

Two things had happened, however, that left Betty confused. One day they had gotten into a tense argument, which had been uncommon lately, and he had yelled at her: "I have all these court hassles now because you decided to go and call the fucking police on me." This jab didn't seem to be consistent with the remorse he was showing on other days. However, he apologized the next day and referred to his own behavior as "backsliding." A couple of weeks later, in another tense exchange, he said to Betty in a low growl, "If you go forward with testifying against me, you are going to be really sorry." Later he insisted that he had just meant that she would feel guilty for treating him "like a criminal," but Betty continued to feel that he had meant something more.

By the date of his hearing, Phil had put more than three good months together in a row. Betty reported this change in him to the judge, and Phil described his involvement in our program, saying that he had accepted that he had a problem he needed to work on. The judge was impressed that Phil had gotten into counseling on his own initiative without waiting for the court to mandate his attendance. The charges were dismissed.

Phil and Betty walked down the courthouse steps together before heading off toward their separate cars. As they parted, Phil gave a smile that looked more like a sneer and said, "Well, I guess that's it for Mr. Nice Guy." And he meant it. He never set foot in his abuser group again and overnight reverted to his habitual mistreatment of Betty.

After watching a steady trickle of clients in our program follow in Phil's footsteps, we finally adopted a policy of not allowing men to join our program between an arrest and the date of the court disposition. We didn't want to be another tool used by abusers to manipulate their partners and escape legal consequences.

Women often berate themselves for not following through with prosecution. A woman may say to me: "What an idiot I was. I don't know why the hell I believed his promises. I should have gone ahead and testified. Now look at the mess I'm in." If you have had occasion to dump on yourself in this fashion, stop for a moment and consider: Why is it your fault that he is so persuasive, that he knows so well how to muddle your mind, that he has collected information over the years about your vulnerabilities and knows how to play them? How are you to blame for how manipulative he is? The reason it takes so long to figure out an abuser is that he knows how to keep himself hidden in constantly shifting shadows. If abusers were so easy to figure out, there would be no abused women.

In counties where abused women find a court system that is well trained in abuse and sensitive to their circumstances, and where victim advocates are actively involved, 80 percent or more go forward with testifying. If you can't stand dealing with a system that doesn't understand your needs, that isn't a shortcoming of yours. Also, remember that your decision to drop a restraining order or criminal charges doesn't mean you can't try again to use legal protections in the future (although you may encounter prejudice against you from the police or the courts if you have started actions and dropped them in the past).

THE COURT HANDS DOWN A SENTENCE

My physically violent clients seem to have nine lives when it comes to staying out of jail. Through dozens of interactions I have had over the years with probation officers, magistrates, prosecutors, and judges, it has become clear to me that courts have been regrettably slow to free themselves of the beliefs that any man is "bound to lose it sooner or later if his wife pushes him far enough," that "alcohol is what really causes partner abuse," or that "women frequently exaggerate partner abuse out of hysteria or vindictiveness." These persistent attitudes can dovetail with the abusive man's native ability to lie convincingly and elicit sympathy.

Sentences for the violence that men do to their wives or girlfriends are shorter on average than those they receive for assaults on strangers, even though partner violence causes more serious injuries and deaths than male-on-male fights do. Courts don't want to send abusers to jail, because they consider them a special class of offenders who deserve unusual compassion and because they often accept victim-blaming justifications for men's violence.

Old attitudes die hard. A few years ago, a judge approached me after a judicial training session I had given and said, "All right, I understand about these men who beat their partners black and blue, who punch them in the face and put them in the hospital. But how about the guy who just gives his wife a push or a shove once in a while? I can't treat him like he's a *batterer*. You didn't explain what judges should do in those cases." I attempted to explain how shocking and intimidating a man's shove can be to a woman, but I could tell his mind was already closed.

I've seen judges who were worse than this one, who seem angrier at the woman for reporting the violence than they are at the man for perpetrating it. But I have worked with others who look carefully at the evidence, listen respectfully to all parties, and make a decision based on fact instead of prejudice. In cases where the man is found guilty, they speak to him in strong terms about the seriousness of his offense, reject his excuses, and impose a punishment that fits the crime.

I have spoken with judges who like to give an abuser a strong verbal admonition *instead of* imposing some sanctions, in the belief that a stern warning from a judge can make an abuser realize that he has to stop. But in reality, the man considers the judge's lecture a joke if no sentence comes with it. He puts on a chastised expression for the court but then smiles all the way home, smug and empowered. I see the emboldening effects of such court dates on my clients.

I am not an advocate of long sentences for abusers, however. Abusers spend much of their time in jail brooding over their grievances against the abused women and plotting their revenge. Men's jails do not help them to overcome their oppressive attitudes toward women; in fact, they are among the more anti-female environments on the planet. Yet courts are going to have to overcome their reluctance to send abusers to jail if they ever want them to sit up and take notice. A *short* jail sentence, combined with a long postjail period of probation and participation in an abuser program, can provide powerful motivation for an abuser to deal with his problem. Jail time involving at least a few weekends—so that the man can continue bringing in income for his family—should be imposed on his *first* conviction for any offense related to domestic abuse. Each subsequent offense should lead to a longer sentence and a higher fine than the previous one, following the principle of "staircased" sentencing that is often applied to drunk driving. Unfortunately, this type of approach is rare at present.

An important part of the sentence for any man convicted of domestic abuse should be an extended period—not less than a year—of participation in a specialized abuser program. The abuser program cannot be replaced by psychotherapy or anger management, as those services are not designed to address the range of behaviors that make up abuse and the core attitudes that drive them (see Chapter 3). In Chapter 14, we will examine how a competent abuser program works and how to evaluate the strengths and weaknesses of a particular program in your area.

THE ABUSER ON PROBATION

I used to supervise an excellent young abuse counselor named Patrick. He was fiery and courageous, but both he and the group clients were always aware of his youth—he was twenty-three and looked about nineteen—and his small size. We assumed that sooner or later one of the more violent abusers would try to intimidate him. Sure enough, one day when Patrick was laying down the law with a client about his disruptive behavior in the group, the man demanded that Patrick "step outside" so that they could fight. His body posture demonstrated how much he relished the opportunity to use his fists. Patrick politely declined the offer, however, and told the abuser to leave the room. The client considered his options and decided to storm out without hitting anyone.

We reported the incident to the court and waited to see how quickly this man would be jailed for threatening the counselor at his court-mandated abuse program. Imagine our astonishment when we heard from the chief probation officer two weeks later that she had called the man in to give him "some strong talk" and then had instructed him to *enroll in another abuser program*. In other words, his "consequence" was that he got out of completing our program. I had a similar experience with the same court in a case where we suspected that one of our clients was abusing his prescription pain medication. We requested permission to speak to the prescribing doctor, but the client refused. His probation officer was soon ringing my telephone and sputtering angrily that a client's prescription medication was none of our business. The probation officer then proceeded to declare to me unabashedly that *his* pain medication was prescribed *by the same doctor.* (No wonder he didn't want us examining the matter too closely.)

My clients have no problem figuring out whether or not their probation officers consider domestic abuse a serious crime. Each man tries out his excuses and justifications to see how fertile the ground is; the more space the probation officer gives him for whining and victim blaming, the less strict he knows the supervision will be. The probation officer's attitude regarding domestic violence is, in turn, largely a reflection of the tone set by the chief probation officer, just as I have observed to be true in police departments. When I work with courts that have pro-victim probation departments, the majority of men they refer cooperate with my program and complete all the requirements. But when the sympathies of the probation department lie primarily with the abuser—as seemed to be true in the court described above—the men present recurring behavior, attitude, and attendance problems, and I have to keep kicking guys out of the program for noncooperation. Why? Because they have already figured out that getting terminated isn't likely to lead to serious consequences at that court, so they would rather not put up with an abuser program that challenges them.

When an abuser finds that he can manipulate or bond with his probation officer, he not only paints a twisted picture of the abused woman but also employs his divide-and-conquer strategy with respect to the abuser program. "I *know* what I did was wrong," he says, "and I really want to work on myself. But over at the abuse group they don't help us change; they just tell us that we're terrible people and everything we say is wrong. They just hate men over there, and they take it out on us." The probation officer then calls me to relay the man's complaint. My response has always been: "Come over some night and sit in on two or three of our groups. You'll see for yourself what we offer." One probation officer did in fact visit a few groups and then started attending regularly once per month. He caught on quickly to what a patient and educational approach we actually take with abusers, and he became impossible to manipulate after that.

The abuser's distortions regarding the abuser program follow the same lines of his thinking about his partner. If I tell a loquacious client that he can't dominate the entire group discussion and needs to be quiet for a while, he tells his probation officer, "The counselors say we can only listen and we're not allowed to talk at all." If I set limits on a man's disruptiveness in the group, he turns in his seat, drops his head like a victim, and says sarcastically, "Right, I get it: We're always wrong, and the women are always right." If I terminate a man from the program after three warnings for inappropriate behavior, he says, "If we don't tell you exactly what you want to hear, you kick us out, and you don't give anyone a second chance." His twisted reports on our statements provide important glimpses into how he discredits his partner at home—and why she may feel so angry, frustrated, and ready to scream.

EFFORTS TO BOND

As the abuser encounters each new player in the legal system, he tries to make a personal connection. With men he relies on "male bonding," making jokes about women or seeking sympathy based on anti-female stereotypes. With women he experiments with flattery and flirtatiousness, or tries to learn private details of people's lives so that he can show concern with statements such as: "I heard your daughter has been sick. How is she doing?" The unspoken message running through these efforts is: "See, I'm not an abuser, I'm just a likable, ordinary person like you, and I want to be your friend." My clients attempt to run the same routines at the abuser program, so I come to know them well.

USING THE LEGAL SYSTEM FOR HIS OWN PURPOSES

Over the fifteen years I have worked with abusive men, I have seen my clients become increasingly shrewd at getting the police and the courts to work on their behalf. Abused women are arrested much more commonly than when I began, as abusers have learned to use their own injuries from a fight to support claims of victimization. I find that the more violent an abusive man is, the more likely he is to come out of a fight with some injuries of his own, as his terrified partner kicks, swings her arms, and scratches in her efforts to get away from him. But some police take a look at the abuser's injuries and say: "Well, we're going to arrest her, because he's got scratches."

Abusers have also learned to rush to the court for restraining orders before their partners get a chance to do so and sometimes scoop up custody of their children in the process. It would be difficult to find anyone more self-satisfied than the man who repeatedly assaults his partner verbally or physically and then has the pleasure of handing her a court order that bars *her* from the residence. And of course the shock to the woman of discovering that the court has kicked her when she was already down can propel her several more yards in the direction of resignation and bitterness. But, fortunately, the story need not end there for the abused woman.

SURVIVING THE LEGAL SYSTEM

Despite the confidence and superiority of abusers and the regressive attitudes of some police and court officials that still persist, tremendous progress has been made in the legal system's response to domestic abuse. Hundreds of thousands of women per year succeed in obtaining orders of protection from courts, and a large proportion of those orders accomplish what the woman is seeking: restoration of her safety and a desperately needed break from the abuser. Many states now mandate the police to arrest abusers in domestic-abuse cases, and district attorneys often are diligent in pursuing convictions.

If you choose to use the police or courts for protection—or if you are cast into the legal system because of a call made by a neighbor or relative—here are some principles to tuck away in your survival kit:

- *Ask for help, ask for help, ask for help.*

I can't say it enough. Dealing with the police and courts can leave you feeling isolated, afraid, and disempowered. Some women decide, after getting a taste of this cold and sometimes hostile system, that they will never reach out for official assistance again. One antidote is to draw upon every resource available to you. Is there a program for abused women near you that provides advocates to accompany women to court? Does the county employ victim/witness advocates, and are they available at the courthouse? Is there a friend or relative who could accompany you to request a restraining order? Does your police department have a specially trained domestic-violence officer with whom you could discuss your case? Remember, anyone who specializes in "domestic violence" is there to help you deal with a scary or intimidating partner, even if he has never hit you. Involve as many of these people in your case as possible; emotional and logistical support can make an immense difference.

- *Cooperate with the prosecution unless it is too dangerous for you to do so.*

Multiple studies have demonstrated that abusers who are prosecuted are more likely to stop their violence than those who are not. If your partner suddenly seems serious about changing, it is not a reason to drop legal action; on the contrary, it is another reason to *continue* it. Court involvement will help give him the structure and incentives he needs to carry through with his good intentions. Without that extra push, an abuser's thoughts of change almost always fade with time.

Some women say to me: "But if I go forward with testifying, he is going to be furious, and then he'll never be willing to look at his problem." This is a common misconception: You cannot get an abuser to change by begging or pleading. The only abusers who change are the ones who become willing to accept the consequences of their actions; if he is unrelentingly angry about prosecution, you can be 100 percent sure that he wouldn't have worked on himself anyhow. You also may be concerned that a criminal conviction will burden him with a humiliating stigma and make it harder for him to find jobs in the future. However, few employers do criminal record checks, and even fewer turn down a man because of an offense related to domestic abuse. As for the stigma, he needs it; he may seem to have snapped out of his denial for the moment, but you will be surprised by how quickly he leaps back into it once the threat of court action has passed.

• *Avoid dropping a restraining order.*

Stay away from your partner until the court order expires, even if you are missing him very much and he seems like a completely different person. Courts unfortunately often develop prejudices against women who seek restraining orders and then drop them, just as police and prosecutors can look negatively upon a woman who does not want to go through with testifying. I understand the fear you may have that he will do something extreme if you don't back off, the challenge of surviving without his financial support (especially if you have children), the pressure you may be getting from other people to give him another chance, and numerous other weights on your shoulders. But courts sometimes do not consider these issues and can be reluctant to assist a woman the next time she reaches out for help. Stick with it through the whole period unless your situation becomes too dangerous.

• *Don't give up prematurely.*

Most police departments have some officers who handle domestic abuse cases well and some who don't, just as most courts have judges who hold abusers accountable and others who let them skate. Just because things went badly this time doesn't mean they always will. Some abusers get sick of dealing with the legal system after awhile, and some public officials decide to finally take action if a case erupts in front of them enough times.

There are exceptions to what I have just said, however. You may know for a fact that in your community legal recourse is stacked against you. If the abuser is on the police force or has close buddies who are, calling 911 can make things worse rather than better. If the abuser is a judge—and I have talked to a few women who were in this sad circumstance—relief may not be available at the courthouse. There is a point at which it does make sense to scrap the legal system and start considering what other strategies you might try. Begin always with a call to an abuse hotline.

- *Advocate for yourself.*

If the abuser is on probation, ask for a face-to-face meeting with the probation officer; it will make it harder for your partner to paint a distorted picture of you and may make the probation officer feel responsible for your safety. If the prosecutor is considering a plea bargain, demand to be included in the process of negotiation, so that your needs are considered before any deal is made. If the abuser is mandated to attend an abuser program, communicate frequently with the abuser program and make sure that they are on your side, not his. (Chapter 14 offers guidelines for determining whether or not a particular abuser program is a good one.)

THE LEGAL SYSTEM cannot solve the problem of abuse by itself, but, when it is working properly it can be an important ally in defending your rights. The better that you and anyone attempting to help you understand the abuser's tricks for turning the legal process to his advantage, the better you can pressure the system to hold him accountable.

KEY POINTS TO REMEMBER

- Abusers rarely change if they aren't forced to suffer any consequences. A man should be required to complete an abuser program *in conjunction with,* not *instead of,* legal consequences.

- Many abusers see the legal system as another opportunity for manipulation. Whether or not he succeeds in that approach will depend largely on how well trained the crucial public officials are on the subject of abuse—and on how many of them think as he does.

- A woman who wants the legal system to help protect her rights needs to seek out assistance for herself and to be prepared to advocate for her own needs and interests. Her first call should be to a program for abused women.

- The legal system will tend not to contribute well to your safety unless you use it *in conjunction with* other self-protective steps (see "Safety Planning" in Chapter 9).

- Any form of physical aggression, including a push, poke, shove, or threat, is illegal in most states and provinces. You do not need to wait until you are severely injured to seek police assistance.

- There is no such thing as a "minor" violation of a law or a court order by an abusive man. If the legal system does not hold him accountable, he will escalate to more serious violations under the assumption that the system does not mean what it says.

Changing the Abusive Man

13

The Making of
an Abusive Man

We pass a magazine rack, and he points at the cover of Cosmo *and says, "Why don't you look like that?"*

His favorite song is that Guns N' Roses one: "I used to love her, but I had to kill her." He puts it on all the time.

His dad treats his mom the same way he treats me.

You should see the way he and his buddies talk about women, like they're pieces of meat.

Once upon a time, there was a boy who grew up with a happy dream. He was told when he was very young—as soon as he was old enough to understand *anything*, really—that a beautiful piece of land out on the edge of town was in trust for him. When he was grown up, it would be his very own and was sure to bring him great contentment. His family and other relatives often described the land to him in terms that made it sound like a fairy world, paradise on earth. They did not tell him precisely when it would be his but implied that it would be when he was around age sixteen or twenty.

In his mid-teens, the boy began to visit the property and take walks on it, dreaming of owning it. Two or three years later, he felt the time had come to take it on. However, by then he had noticed some disturbing things: From time to time, he would observe people hiking or picnicking on his acres, and when he told them not to come there without his permission, they refused to leave and insisted that the land was public! When he questioned his relatives about this, they reassured him that there was no claim to the land but his.

In his late adolescence and early twenties, he became increasingly frustrated about the failure of the townspeople to respect his ownership. He first tried to manage the problem through compromise. He set aside a small section of the property as a public picnic area and even spent his own money to put up some tables. On the remainder of the land he put up "No Trespassing" signs and expected people to stay off. But, to his amazement, town residents showed no signs of gratitude for his concession; instead they continued to help themselves to the enjoyment of the full area.

The boy finally could tolerate the intrusions on his birthright no longer. He began screaming and swearing at people who trespassed and in this way succeeded in driving many of them away. The few who were not cowed by him became targets of his physical assaults. And when even his aggression did not completely clear the area, he bought a gun and began firing at people just to frighten them, not actually to shoot them. The townspeople came to the conclusion that the young man was insane.

One particularly courageous local resident decided to spend a day searching through the town real estate records and was able to establish what a number of people had suspected all along: The property was indeed public. The claim made by the boy's family on his behalf was the product of legend and misconception, without any basis in the documentary record.

When the boy was confronted with this evidence, his ire only grew. He was convinced that the townspeople had conspired to alter the records and that they were out to deprive him of his most cherished dream. For several years after, his behavior remained erratic; at times it seemed that he had accepted having been misled during his childhood, but then he would erupt again in efforts to regain control of the land through lawsuits, creating booby traps on the land to injure visitors and employing any other strategy he could think of. His relatives encouraged him to maintain his belligerence, telling him, "Don't let them take away what is yours." Years went by before he was able to accept the fact that his dream would never be realized and that he would have to learn to share the land. Over that period he went through a painful, though ultimately freeing, process of gradually accepting how badly misled he had been and how destructive his behavior had been as a result.

IN ORDER TO know how to foster change in abusive men, individuals and communities need to understand not only how abusive thinking *works,* which has been my focus so far, but also *where it comes from.* Overcoming the scourge of relationship abuse demands attention to the root causes of the problem.

The story I have just told is a metaphor for the childhood social process that produces an abuser. As I have explained in earlier chapters, abusiveness has little to do with psychological problems and everything to do with values and beliefs. Where do a boy's values about partner relationships come from? The sources are many. The most important ones include the family he grows up in, his neighborhood, the television he watches and books he reads, jokes he hears, messages that he receives from the toys he is given, and his most influential adult role models. His role models are important not just for which behaviors they exhibit to the boy but also for which values they teach him in words and what expectations they instill in him for the future. In sum, a boy's values develop from the full range of his experiences within his *culture.*

Each boy's socialization is unique. Even two siblings close in age do not learn identical values. Culture is thus transmitted on a *continuum.* In a culture that is fairly religious, for example, some children will grow up to be devout believers; others will reject the faith completely; and most will fall in with the average level of religious observance for their community. Where a child will land on this continuum partly depends on how strong a set of messages he or she receives from the social environment and partly on his or her personal predispositions. The family rebel, for example, might become an atheist, while the child who is most focused on pleasing the parents might become even more religious than they are.

How a Boy Learns Abuse

Children begin at a very young age—certainly by the time they are three and probably sooner—to absorb the rules and traditions of their culture. This learning continues throughout their childhood and adolescence. The family in which children grow up is usually the strongest influence, at least for their first few years, but it is only one among many. Children's sense of proper and improper ways to behave, their moral perceptions of right and wrong, and their beliefs about sex roles are brought to them by television and videos, popular songs, children's books, and jokes. They observe behaviors that are modeled by friends and relatives, including adults to whom they are close. They watch to see which behaviors get rewarded—by making people popular, for example—as opposed to those that are condemned. By age four or five they start to express curiosity about laws and police, both of which play an important role in shaping their moral sense. During their adolescence, young people have increasing access to the wider culture, with less and less filtering by adults, and are subject to the rapidly growing influence of their peers. Even after reaching adulthood, people continue to read the social messages that surround them in the culture and to adjust their values and beliefs in response to what is socially acceptable.

QUESTION 18:
WHERE DID HE LEARN TO BE THAT WAY?

Let's look now at how society influences the development of a boy or a young man's attitude toward abuse. Some of what I describe here dates back many hundreds of years, while other messages are more recent arrivals on the cultural scene. I give examples from child-oriented culture, such as children's books and movies, and others from adult culture, which trickle down to children from the models they observe of adult behavior and from what adults tell them directly about right and wrong.

• *Laws and the legal system have colluded with the abuse of women.*

Until well into the 1800s, it was expressly legal for a man in the English-speaking world to physically abuse his wife. She had no recourse to the police or the courts, and, if she chose to divorce him because of his abusiveness, he was legally entitled to custody of their children. In the late nineteenth century some legal consequences were finally legislated for some of the most extreme beatings of women, but they were rarely enforced *until the 1970s* and were not enforced consistently at all until the 1990s! For hundreds and perhaps thousands of years the domestic assault of women has been considered a necessary tool for a man to maintain order and discipline in his home, to make sure that his superior intelligence rules, and to avoid the mushrooming of the hysterical, short-sighted, and naive qualities that men widely attribute to women. It was only with the women's movement of the 1960s and 1970s, and especially with the work of those activists focusing specifically on battering and sexual assault, that the intimate oppression of women began to be taken seriously as a crime.

This legal history plays an important role in shaping today's cultural views among males—and females—about the abuse of women. It is likely to take a number of generations to overcome the accumulated impact of hundreds of years of destructive social attitudes. The culture that shaped these laws, and was in turn shaped by them, is reflected in people's continued willingness to blame women for "provoking" abuse, to feel sorry for men who face legal consequences for intimate violence, and to be highly skeptical of women's reports of abuse. These are all attitudes that children can absorb from the behaviors and comments of the adults around them.

Children also notice responses by the legal system. A boy who grows up in a home where his father assaults his mother may observe over the years that his father never seems to get in any serious trouble, indicating to him that his father's behavior is not viewed as wrong by the community. (In fact, any male who is older than ten or fifteen years of age today is unlikely to have ever seen his father prosecuted for domestic violence, since such prosecution was uncommon before 1990). When a woman asks me, "Why does a physically abusive man believe he can get away with it?", I have to answer that until very recently he *could,* and even now legal consequences are less serious for men who assault partners than for those who assault strangers. This historical condoning of the physical abuse of women has also played a critical role in making it difficult to address and overcome emotional abuse, as it has created an atmosphere of impunity regarding men's conduct in partner relationships.

- *Religious beliefs have often condoned the abuse of women.*

The most influential religious scriptures in the world today, including the Bible, the Torah, the Koran, and major Buddhist and Hindu writings, explicitly instruct women to submit to male domination. Genesis, for example, includes the following passage: "Unto the woman He said, I will greatly multiply thy sorrow and thy conception; in sorrow thou shalt bring forth children: and thy desire *shall be* to thy husband, and he shall rule over thee." I have had numerous clients over the years who explicitly rely on quotations from scripture to justify their abuse of their partners. Similarly, religious prohibitions against divorce have entrapped women in abusive marriages. The book *When Love Goes Wrong* (see "Resources"), published in 1985, describes a study of conservative Protestant clergy that reported that 21 percent said that no amount of abuse would justify a woman's leaving her husband, and 26 percent agreed with the statement "a wife should submit to her husband and trust that God would honor her action by either stopping the abuse or giving her the strength to endure it."

Children who are raised in a faith tradition are commonly taught that the rules of their religion are the ultimate guide to right and wrong, superior even to civil law. A boy's early religious training can be formative in the development of his image of appropriate behaviors in intimate relationships, the status of women, and the entitlements of men. If the more destructive aspects of his religious background are the ones that are given the most emphasis in his family or community, some dangerous seeds may have been sown.

- *Popular performers both reflect and shape social attitudes.*

The white rapper Eminem won a Grammy Award while I was writing this book. At the time of his award, one of his newest popular songs was "Kim," the name of Eminem's wife. The song begins with the singer putting his baby daughter to bed and then preparing to murder his wife for being with another man. He tells his wife, "If you move I'll beat the shit out of you," and informs her that he has already murdered their four-year-old son. He then tells his wife he is going to drive away with her in the car, leaving the baby at home alone, and then will bring her home dead in the trunk. Kim's voice (as performed by Eminem) is audible off and on throughout the song, screaming with terror. At times she pleads with him not to hurt her. He describes to her how he is going to make it look as if she is the one who killed their son and that he killed her in self-defense, so that he'll get away with it. Kim screams for help, then is audibly choked to death, as Eminem screams, "Bleed, bitch, bleed! Bleed!" The murder is followed by the sound of a body being dragged across dry leaves, thrown into the trunk of a car, and closed in.

Even more horrible than Eminem's decision to record this song glorifying the murder of a woman and child is the fact that it did not stop him from receiving a Grammy. What is a teen boy or a young man to conclude about our culture from this award? I believe I can safely say that a singer who openly promoted the killing of Jews, or blacks, or people in wheelchairs would be considered ineligible for a Grammy. But not so, unfortunately, for encouraging the brutal and premeditated murder of one's wife and child, complete with a plan for how to escape consequences for it.

And, unfortunately, Eminem has plenty of company. The extremely popular Guns 'n' Roses recorded a song that goes: "I used to love her / But I had to kill her / I had to put her six feet under / And I can still hear her complain." The singer (Axl Rose) goes on to sing that he knew he would miss her so he buried her in the backyard. This song supports a common attitude among physical abusers that women's complaints are what provoke men to violence. Another outstanding example is the comedian Andrew Dice Clay, whose repertoire of "jokes" about the beating and sexual assault of females has filled performance halls across the country. Fans of these kinds of performers have been known to state defensively, "Come on, it's just humor." But humor is actually one of the powerful ways a culture passes on its values. If a man is already inclined toward abuse because of his earlier training or experience, he can find validation in such performances and distance himself even further from empathy for his partners. In one abuse case that I was involved in, the man used to play the above Guns 'n' Roses song on the stereo repeatedly and tell his wife that this was what was going to happen to her, laughing about it. But in the context of verbal assault and physical fear that he created, what was a joke to him was a blood-curdling threat to his partner.

- *Popular plays and movies romanticize abuse of women.*

Several years ago I saw the play *Frankie and Johnny Got Married* in Boston. The story line goes like this: Johnny is in love with Frankie and knows that she is the right woman for him. One evening he comes to her apartment to express his love and convince her to get involved with him. She is not interested, and tells him so. Johnny then begins a relentless pressure campaign that lasts for the remainder of the play. He criticizes her and puts her down, telling her that her fears of intimacy and commitment are the reasons why she avoids being with him. He lets her know that, whatever knowledge she may have about who she is and what she needs, his judgment is better. Frankie remains unimpressed.

So Johnny's coercion escalates. At one point Frankie, who is exhausted after hours of this pressure, attempts to go to sleep, but Johnny blocks her path to the bedroom, grabbing her arms. She then goes to the kitchen and makes herself a sandwich, figuring that if she can't sleep she might at least eat. It is not to be, however, because Johnny grabs the plate away from her and heaves it into the sink, sandwich and all.

Exasperated, Frankie orders Johnny to leave her apartment. He refuses. She threatens to call the police to remove him, to which he replies with words to the effect of: "Go ahead, bring them over. In an hour they will have released me, and I'll be back on your fire escape. Sooner or later you're going to have to deal with me."

So now that Frankie has discovered that she can't succeed in having *any* of her rights respected at all, what happens next? Lo and behold, she has an epiphany! A life-changing breakthrough! In a flash, she overcomes her fear of deep connection—it turns out Johnny was right about her fear of intimacy as well as everything else—and she falls enraptured into his arms. Frankie and Johnny are in love. *The curtain falls.* (Presumably Frankie is now permitted to eat and sleep, though we have no way to say for sure.)

The most astounding part of the evening was still to come, however. To my amazement, the roughly two hundred and fifty well-educated, economically privileged adults who were packed into their Huntington Theater Company seats rose in a roar of delighted applause, smiling from ear to ear. Not a person in the auditorium remained seated—except me. I had been working with abusers for over five years at this point and knew perfectly well what we had been witnessing. No one else seemed to notice anything amiss in the physical grabbing, sleep and food deprivation, threats, superiority, and other forms of coercion we had just watched. Was Frankie reluctant to be with Johnny because she feared intimacy? Or could it perhaps have been because he was arrogant, coercive, and physically violent? Who *wouldn't* fear intimacy with this bully? One ought to.

The messages to young men, intentional or not, are that coercion and even a degree of physical violence and intimidation are compatible with deep love and that a man can know better than a woman what is good for her. The attitudes that drive the behavior of many of my clients were woven throughout this play. And if a young boy doesn't see this play—most of the audience was adult—he nonetheless is influenced by the attitudes that his parents bring home with them from the theater.

- *A boy's early training about sex roles and about relationships can feed abuse.*

At least until quite recently, a boy has tended to learn from the most tender age that when he reaches young adulthood he will have a wife or girlfriend who will do *everything* for him and make him a happy man. His partner will belong to him. Her top responsibility will be to provide love and nurturing, while his key contribution will be to fill the role of "the brains of the operation," using his wisdom and strength to guide the family. Tightly interwoven with these expectations are other messages he is likely to receive about females. He may learn that boys are superior to girls, particularly if he grows up around men who exhibit that attitude. (In many families, there is no worse insult you can give to a boy than to say, "You're acting like a girl.") When he is old enough to know about sex, he may learn that the most valuable thing about females is their capacity to give sexual pleasure to males. Depending on what his father or stepfather is like, what kinds of peers he chooses in his teen years, or what kinds of music he listens to, he may learn that, when a female partner does not defer to him, he can use verbal degradation or even physical intimidation to punish her and ensure better cooperation in the future.

Studies have found that nearly half of abusive men grow up in homes where their father or stepfather is an abuser. Home is a critical learning ground for values and sex-role expectations. Boys are at risk to absorb the abuser's attitude through his words and actions (see Chapter 10). Even if the dad never explicitly says that females are inferior, for example, or that the man should have the last word in an argument, his behavior can get the message across.

The sex-role expectations to which boys and men have historically been subjected are captured powerfully by an article called "The Good Wife's Guide," from a 1955 issue of *Housekeeping Monthly* that includes such instructions as "Don't ask him questions about his actions or question his judgment or integrity. Remember, he is the master of the house and as such will always exercise his will with fairness and truthfulness," and "Don't complain if he's late home for dinner or even if he stays out all night. Count this minor compared to what he might have gone through that day." The wife is further encouraged to make sure the children are quiet when he gets home, to keep the house perfectly orderly and clean, and not to complain if her husband goes out for evening entertainment without her, because she needs to "understand his world of strain and pressure." Our society's sex-role attitudes have certainly progressed greatly over the past fifty years, yet the expectations laid out in this article are precisely the ones I find in many of my abusive clients to this day; cultural values that run this deep take generations to unearth and dispose of.

- *Some messages in media oriented toward children and teens support abuse by men.*

In a book in the popular Berenstain Bears series for children called *Trouble with Homework,* both the mother and the children cower when Father becomes angry. (It's on the cover.) At one point he knocks over a chair and clenches his fists above his head. At the end of the story, the children have pleased Dad by doing what he wanted, and Mom smiles happily to see them cuddled up with Dad on the couch. In *Bedtime for Francis,* by Russel Hoban, the father threatens Francis that he will spank her if she does not stop asking for help with her fear of the dark, and she falls asleep alone with the fear of how the spanking would hurt.

Fairy tales also sometimes support the abusive mentality. In *Beauty and the Beast,* for example, the beast is cruel to the woman and isolates her from the world, but she loves him anyhow, and her love ultimately transforms him into a good man—the precise myth that keeps some women entrapped in their abusive relationships. In *The Little Mermaid,* Ariel chooses to *give up her voice*—literally—in order to live on land so that she can marry the man she loves. A woman with no voice is the dream girl of many abusive men.

Even movies that are aimed at children and teens commonly include messages that condone abuse of females. In a recent Jim Carrey film, for example, a man sits down in a park next to a strange woman who is nursing her baby and then suddenly pushes the baby away from the woman and begins to suck her breast himself. This sexual assault is presented as humorous.

Music videos and computer games have become the predominant sources of cultural training for children and teenagers. In the world of MTV and VH1, many of the sex-role messages are worse than ever, with males aggressive and in control and the value of females restricted to their sexual allure. As was exposed in a recent documentary broadcast on MTV, pornographers are frequently being hired to make music videos, which predictably leads to portrayals of women that make them look like they exist for men to use.

Some music videos show abuse explicitly. In one, for example, a man stalks a woman throughout the song as she repeatedly tries to escape him, including one part in which she dives into a car to get away and he pulls open another door and jumps in after her. At the end of the video, she gives up and *falls in love* with him. The message thus is not only that stalking proves how much he loves her but also that the stalker was actually doing *what was best* for her. Women in music videos never mean "no" when they say it, and when they run away, they really want to be chased and caught. What could more perfectly capture the abusive mentality?

- *Pornographic videos, magazines, and web sites are learning grounds.*

As a boy enters his teen years, he is likely to encounter another powerful shaper of his outlook on females and how to treat them: pornography. Most pornographic movies, magazines, and web sites can function as training manuals for abusers, whether they intend to or not, teaching that women are unworthy of respect and valuable only as sex objects for men. The Internet has made access to pornography much easier—and free— for teenage boys; a recent study found, for example, that one in four teenage boys has experienced exposure to unwanted sexual material, most commonly through Internet solicitations. A great deal of mainstream pornographic material—not just so-called "hard core"—contains stories and images showing the abuse of both women and children as sexy, sometimes including presentations of rape as erotic. The harm to teens from looking at pornography has little to do with its sexual explicitness and everything to do with the *attitudes* it teaches toward women, relationships, sexual assault, and abuse. Spend some time looking at pornography yourself—if you can stand it—and think about the messages it is sending to young people and especially to boys.

I learned of a recent case in an upper-class suburb involving a group of middle school–aged boys who were in the habit of spending hours each day after school watching pornography on their computers. One day they went from this activity to a party where they succeeded in pressuring several girls—with an average age of twelve—into performing group oral sex on them, inspired by something they had watched at a web site. Parents found out about what happened and a scandal ensued, but the community still did not seem to recognize the critical influence of the images to which the boys were being exposed.

- *Boys often learn that they are not responsible for their actions.*

Boys' aggressiveness is increasingly being treated as a *medical* problem, particularly in schools, a trend that has led to the diagnosing and medicating of boys whose problem may really be that they have been traumatized and influenced by exposure to violence and abuse at home. Treating these boys as though they have a chemical problem not only overlooks the distress they are in but also reinforces their belief that they are "out of control" or "sick," rather than helping them to recognize that they are making bad choices based on destructive values. I have sometimes heard adults telling girls that they should be flattered by boys' invasive or aggressive behavior "because it means they really like you," an approach that prepares both boys and girls to confuse love with abuse and socializes girls to feel helpless.

In most media coverage of bullying and school violence, including highly publicized school murders such as Columbine, reporters have overlooked the gender issues. Headlines have described these events as "kids killing kids," when close to 100 percent of them have involved *boys* killing kids. In some cases it has been revealed that the killings were related to boys' hostility toward females, including one case in which the two boys who went on a murderous rampage said afterward that they had done it because they were angry that their girlfriends had broken up with them. But the urgent need to confront the anti-female attitudes among these boys was never mentioned as a strategy for preventing future school violence.

- *When culture and home experience dovetail, each reinforces the other.*

If a boy grows up in a home where his mother is abused, hearing a song like Eminem's "Kim" could leave a deep imprint on him. He may well feel that society is giving its public stamp of approval to the mistreatment of women he has witnessed at home. The likelihood that he will blame his mother for what happens to her and begin to copy the abuser's behavior increases with each pro-abuse message he absorbs from his surroundings. My counseling experience persuades me that the men who are most likely to grow up to abuse women are probably those who grow up with an abuser as an important role model and who *also* get especially heavy doses of destructive cultural training. But also be aware: Half or more of my clients do *not* come from homes in which a man modeled abuse of women. The cultural influences I have discussed above are sufficient *in themselves* to prepare a boy to become an abusive man. It is therefore essential to teach boys to respect women and think critically about the societal messages to which they are exposed.

Many sons of abused women whom I have known, including police officers, writers, therapists, and activists, have dedicated their lives to *opposing* the abuse of women. The example set by these men shows that a boy's family influences are only the beginning of the story and that he can make the choice to channel his childhood distress into constructive action—if he learns about alternative ways of thinking and acting.

LET'S RETURN NOW to our growing boy. From a combination of different cultural influences, he develops an image of his future, which he carries within him. He pictures a woman who is beautiful, alluring, and focused entirely on meeting his needs—one who has no needs of her own that might require sacrifice or effort on his part. She will belong to him and cater to him, and he will be free to disrespect her when he sees fit. In his mind this picture may illustrate the word *partner,* but a more accurate word for the image he is developing might be *servant.*

When this boy gets involved in actual—as opposed to imagined—dating, especially as he reaches an age where his relationships become more serious, his childhood fantasy life collides with the real-life young woman he is seeing. She defies him on occasion. She has other people in her life who are important to her rather than making him her exclusive focus. She demands from time to time that he take an interest in her as a person. She doesn't always accept his opinions as accurate and superior to hers. She may even attempt at some point to break up with him, as if she were not his personal possession. The boy doesn't believe that he is demanding anything unreasonable; he seeks only what he considers his due. In fact, our young man feels like he gives his girlfriend more freedom than a lot of other guys do, just as the boy in our opening story felt generous for providing a public picnic area on "his" land. And, like that boy's reaction to the "trespassers," he becomes increasingly frustrated, erratic, and coercive as he tries to regain control over his partner. His first sexual experiences are likely to be a result of his pressuring a girl steadily until she gives in, so that sexual coercion becomes one of his earliest relationship habits. He may even start to appear mentally ill, as did the young man who began firing at hikers, but in fact his behavior is largely logical and rational, given what his key social influences have led him to believe. Above all, he feels that *his* rights are the ones being denied—which is precisely the attitude of almost all of my clients when they begin my program. The abusive man feels cheated, ripped off, and wronged, because his sense of entitlement is so badly distorting his perceptions of right and wrong.

In sum, an abuser can be thought of not as a man who is a "deviant," but rather as one who learned his society's lessons *too* well, swallowing them whole. He followed too carefully the signposts his culture put out for him marking the path to manhood—at least with respect to relationships with women.

THE CULTURAL EXCUSE

My abusive clients sometimes become aware of these ways in which society has shaped their values and, sticking closely to their long-standing abusive habits, seize this insight as a new excuse. Instead of saying "I was drunk " or "I was abused as a child," they rise to a new level of sophistication in escaping responsibility, declaring, "I did it because I learned entitled expectations and the devaluing of females." I respond by telling the client that he is putting old wine in a new bottle. "The number-one lesson you seem to have learned," I say, "is how to make excuses for abusing women. And I see that you're still practicing it." Abusive men do need to learn about social influences, but not in a way that gives them yet another means of letting themselves off the hook.

ABUSE AS A FORM OF OPPRESSION

A home where a woman is abused is a small-scale model of much larger oppressive systems that work in remarkably similar ways. Many of the excuses an abusive man uses for verbally tearing his partner to shreds are the same ones that a power-mad boss uses for humiliating his or her employees. The abusive man's ability to convince himself that his domination of you is for your own good is paralleled by the dictator who says, "People in this country are too primitive for democracy." The divide-and-conquer strategies used by abusers are reminiscent of a corporate head who tries to break the labor union by giving certain groups of workers favored treatment. The making of an abuser is thus not necessarily restricted to the specific values his society teaches him about men's relationships with women; without realizing it he may also apply attitudes and tactics from *other* forms of oppression that he has been exposed to as a boy or as a young adult and that he has learned to justify or even admire.

If you look at any oppressive organization or system, from a racist country club up to a military government, you will find most of the same behaviors and justifications by the powerful that I have described in this book. The tactics of control, the intimidation of victims who try to protest, the undermining of efforts at independence, the negative distortions about the victims in order to cast blame upon them, the careful cultivation of the public image of the oppressors—all are present, along with many other parallels. The people in power generally tell lies while simultaneously working hard to silence the voices of the people who are being dominated and to stop them from thinking, just as the abusive man strives to do. And the bottom line is the same: Oppressive systems stay in existence because the people in power enjoy the luxury of their position and become unwilling to give up the privileges they win through taking advantage of other people and keeping them down. In short, *the abusive mentality is the mentality of oppression.*

The connection among different kinds of power abuses can add greatly to the stress experienced by an abused woman. If you already face discrimination as a woman of color or if you are a low-income woman or a lesbian, you may feel overwhelmed at times by how similar the control and abuse from your partner feel to other forms of oppression you have endured. Some abusive men even deliberately take advantage of their partner's social vulnerabilities. I have had several clients, for example, whose partners are undocumented immigrants whom they have threatened to have deported if the women ever disclose the abuse. In some geographical areas you can find supportive services for specific groups of abused women, such as immigrants or lesbians, or locate agencies where there are staff people from your background who understand the additional challenges you face. (See "Resources.")

WHEN WE STEP BACK and gaze upon the broad panorama of social influences on a boy's development, we can see that it's really no great wonder that he may learn the patterns of abuse. What he isn't taught by the cultural messages around him that specifically support the abuse of women he can learn from the tactics of other abusers of power and from the blaming of other victims. In fact, the greater surprise is that so many boys do *not* grow up to abuse women. There must not be anything inherently abusive or power-hungry about men, or it would be impossible for so many to refuse to follow the path where their cultural training is propelling them. One of the best-known male crusaders against the abuse of women, a man with whom I have had the good fortune to work, grew up in a home where his mother was physically beaten. He could have modeled himself after his father, but he didn't. He chose instead to think critically about his experience and take the opposite road. Many of the influential leaders of the movement against the abuse of women in the

United States, Canada, and other countries are male, including men who have mentored me in my work.

The oppressive mentality can be taken apart and replaced with a new consciousness. The composer of "Amazing Grace," you may have heard, was a slave trader who repented of his cruelty and became an abolitionist. Abusive men can learn respect and equality—if we insist that they do so. But they won't make those changes unless they are subjected to tremendous pressure, because their cultural values as well as their privileges are pushing them so hard to stay the same.

There has never been a better time than the present to apply that pressure, to demand that abusers accept responsibility for the destruction they cause. We live in a period of mounting international pressure for the respect of human rights for *everyone,* of insistence on the recognition of the worth and dignity of each person, male or female, young or old, wealthy or poor, and of whatever color. The current context is probably the most hopeful one there has ever been for putting an end to the abuse of women, and to the range of abuses of power that follow its pattern. Resistance never disappears; it waits in the shadows, sometimes for many years, and then eventually sprouts again. You may have gone through dark times when you felt, "I just can't fight this anymore, I give up," yet you rebound after a while to try again to recover your rights. And one day you will succeed.

KEY POINTS TO REMEMBER

- An abuser is not born; he is made.

- In order to bring about change in an abuser, we have to reshape his attitude toward power and exploitation.

- Abusive behavior is reinforced by multiple societal messages, some of which are specific to the abuse of women and some of which reflect the overall culture of oppression.

- Your courageous resistance to partner abuse—and you *have* stood up for yourself (and your children) in many ways, whether you realize it or not—is a gift to everyone, because all forms of abuse are intertwined.

14

The Process of Change

Since he started going to therapy, he's gotten more self-centered than ever.

I think this time he's really sorry.

He's usually very closed off to his feelings, so it gives me hope that he's finally opening up a little.

*Our couples counselor says we **both** have to be willing to change.*

Do you think he can change? I'm not sure how long I should wait around to see whether he will or not.

MY FIFTEEN YEARS OF WORKING day in and day out with abusive men have left me certain of one thing: There are no shortcuts to change, no magical overnight transformations, no easy ways out. Change is difficult, uncomfortable work. My job as a counselor is to dive into the elaborate tangle that makes up an abuser's thinking and assist the man to untie the knots. The project is not hopeless—if the man is willing to work hard— but it is complex and painstaking. For him, remaining abusive is in many ways easier than stepping out of his pattern. Yet there are some men who decide to dig down inside of themselves, root out the values that drive their abusive behavior, and develop a truly new way of interacting with a female partner. The challenge for an abused woman is to learn how to tell whether her partner is serious about overcoming his abusiveness.

The first challenge with an abusive man is to motivate him to work on himself. Because he becomes attached to the many rewards that his controlling and intimidating behaviors bring him, he is highly reluctant to make significant changes in his way of operating in a relationship. This reluctance cannot be overcome through gentle persuasion, pleading, or cajoling by the woman. I am sorry to say that I have never once seen such approaches succeed. The men who make significant progress in my program are the ones who know that their partners will definitely leave them unless they change, and the ones on probation who have a tough probation officer who demands that they really confront their abusiveness. In other words, the initial impetus to change is always *extrinsic* rather than self-motivated. Even when a man does feel genuinely sorry for the ways his behavior has hurt his partner, I have never seen his remorse alone suffice to get him to become a serious client. *After* a few months of deep work in the program, some men do start to develop intrinsic reasons for change, such as starting to feel real empathy for their partners' feelings, developing awareness of how their behavior has been harming their children, or even sometimes realizing that they themselves enjoy life more when they aren't abusive, despite all the privileges of abuse they have to give up. But it takes a long time for an abusive man to get to that point.

As I discussed in the Introduction, the majority of abusive men do not make deep and lasting changes even in a high-quality abuser program. However, if even a minority become nonabusive, or at least significantly less abusive, the job is worth doing. At least as important is that the program can help the abused woman develop clarity about her abuser's patterns and manipulations and can share insights with her. For example, an abusive man's underlying attitudes tend to leap out of him in the heat of debates and confrontations in his group, and the counselor can then assist the woman in identifying the thinking that is driving his behavior. Follow-up surveys by abuser programs have found that the support that the counselors give to *her* tends to be the aspect of the program that the woman finds most valuable. (These surveys indicate that an abuser program that is not focused on supporting the abused woman and that does not consider serving *her* to be its primary responsibility is severely limiting what it can accomplish and may even be contributing to her difficulties.)

For an abusive man to make genuine progress he needs to go through a complex and critical set of steps. To give my clients a road map of the process of change, I tell them the following story:

There once was a man whose neighbors had a large and beautiful maple tree growing behind their house. It gave shade in the hot summers, turned stunning colors of fire in the fall as it dropped its leaves, and stood against the winter snow as a magnificent wooden sculpture. But the man hated his neighbors' tree, because the shade that it cast into his yard made his grass grow poorly and stunted his vegetable garden, which was his passion. He pressured the neighbors repeatedly to either cut the tree down or prune it drastically, and their response was always the same: "You are free to cut any branches that stick out over your property, but beyond that we are going to leave the tree alone, because it is beautiful and we love it. We are sorry about the shade it casts on your side, but that is what trees do."

One summer the neighbors went away on vacation for a week, and the man decided to rid himself of his aggravation. He took a chainsaw and cut their tree to the ground, making careful cuts so that the tree would not fall on the neighbor's house and destroy it but also directing it away from his own yard, so he wouldn't have to clean it up. Then he walked home, fully satisfied if perhaps a little afraid. The next day he took his chainsaw, threw it in the dump, and prepared himself to deny having any idea who had brought the giant down, even though the truth would be obvious.

There was only one hole in his plan: He didn't realize how popular his neighbors were, and he didn't know how unbearable it would be to have the entire local population turn against him, to the point where no one would even look at him or talk to him. So the day finally came when the man realized his life would be wrecked for good unless he dealt with his destructive and selfish act. What steps did he have to take in order to set things right?

THE STEPS TO ACCEPTING RESPONSIBILITY

1. He had to *admit,* and *admit fully,* that he cut down the tree. He dreaded looking at people and saying, "Yeah, it was me"—even though they already knew—but he had to do it. He had to stop claiming that the neighbors had cut the tree down themselves so

that they could blame him and turn everyone against him. And when he did admit his act, he also had to acknowledge what an old and impressive tree he had killed, rather than try to save face by insisting that it had been small and ugly.

2. He had to admit that he had cut it down *on purpose,* that his actions were a *choice.* He couldn't claim that he had been so drunk or enraged that he didn't know what he was doing. He couldn't say, "Well, I just meant to put a little cut into the trunk as a warning to them, but I accidentally cut too far and the tree fell down." In short, he had to *stop making excuses.* Furthermore, he had to admit that he had *goals* that he tried to further through his destructive behavior; he needed to be honest about his *motives.*

3. He had to acknowledge that what he did was *wrong.* This meant that he had to *stop blaming* the neighbors and playing up how victimized he had been by the shade. He had to make a sincere, heartfelt apology.

4. He had to *accept the neighbors' right to be angry* about what he did, which meant that he had to be willing to *truly acknowledge the effects of his actions.* He had to take in the anguish he had caused. He had to stop asserting that they were "making too big a deal over one stupid tree" and that "it happened a long time ago and they should be over it by now." Although apologizing was important, he also had to accept that saying he was sorry was only the beginning and that it meant nothing unless he also looked seriously at the damage he had done.

5. He had to *accept the consequences of his actions.* First, he had to provide reasonable monetary damage for the value of the destroyed tree. He then needed to plead guilty to the criminal charges, so that the neighbors would not have to go through the ordeal of testifying against him. He had to stop seeking sympathy from people for the problems he himself had caused, along the lines of: "Poor me, I had to pay out all this money that I can't afford because of their tree when the only reason I cut it down was because they were wrecking my yard with it."

CHANGING THE ABUSIVE MAN

6. He had to devote *long-term and serious effort* toward setting right what he had done. No amount of money can replace a mature tree; there's no way to erase the effects of such a destructive act. The man therefore had to make amends. He needed to buy as large and healthy a young tree as he could find in a nursery and to plant it carefully behind the neighbors' house. What's more, he had to water the tree, protect it from deer, watch it for diseases, and fertilize it as necessary *for years*. A young tree takes a long time to securely establish itself.

7. He had to *lay aside demands for forgiveness.* He had to recognize that even if he sincerely were to take all of the steps I have described, the neighbors might still be left with pain, hurt, and bitterness, and the man had no right to tell them how long their bad feelings should last, especially since he was the cause. People might be nicer to him now that he had stopped denying what he did, but they wouldn't necessarily ever like him. The neighbors might never want to be his friends—and why should they be? If they did decide to be friendly with him at some point, he should see their forgiveness as an act of kindness and *not* as his due for replacing the tree.

8. He had to *treat the neighbors consistently well* from that point forward. He couldn't decide to stick it to them five years later by cutting down a rosebush, for example, and then say, "Okay, I messed up, but shouldn't I get credit for the five years that I've been good? You can't expect me to be perfect." Asking someone not to cut down the neighbors' flowers is not the same thing as expecting perfection.

9. He had to *relinquish his negative view* of his neighbors. He had to stop speaking badly about them to other people and accept that most—perhaps even all—of what he disliked about them actually had to do with their responses to the damage he had done and their refusal to be bullied by him. He had been the creator of their hostility toward him.

As I go over each of these responsibilities with my clients, I ask them if they have any disagreements. They concur that each of the above steps is fair and necessary—as long as we are talking about trees and neighbors. However, as soon as I start to go back through the story, reviewing how each piece applies to a man who has abused his partner, my clients begin backpedaling. They are reluctant to do the serious work of change, feeling that it would be easier to throw a new blanket over the moldy mattress and carry on with life as usual.

How These Steps Apply to Abuse

The box below summarizes how the steps in the tree story apply to an abusive man's process of change.

Steps to Change

1. *Admit fully to his history of psychological, sexual, and physical abusiveness toward any current or past partners whom he has abused.* Denial and minimizing need to stop, including discrediting your memory of what happened. He can't change if he is continuing to cover up, to others or to himself, important parts of what he has done.

2. *Acknowledge that the abuse was wrong, unconditionally.* He needs to identify the justifications he has tended to use, including the various ways that he may have blamed you, and to talk in detail about why his behaviors were unacceptable without slipping back into defending them.

3. *Acknowledge that his behavior was a choice, not a loss of control.* For example, he needs to recognize that there is a moment during each incident at which he gives himself permission to become abusive and that he chooses how far to let himself go.

4. *Recognize the effects his abuse has had on you and on your children, and show empathy for those.* He needs to talk *in detail* about the short- and long-term impact that

---

his abuse has had, including fear, loss of trust, anger, and loss of freedom and other rights. And he needs to do this without reverting to feeling sorry for himself or talking about how hard the experience has been for *him*.

5. *Identify in detail his pattern of controlling behaviors and entitled attitudes.* He needs to speak in detail about the day-to-day tactics of abuse he has used. Equally important, he must be able to identify his underlying beliefs and values that have driven those behaviors, such as considering himself entitled to constant attention, looking down on you as inferior, or believing that men aren't responsible for their actions if "provoked" by a partner.

6. *Develop respectful behaviors and attitudes to replace the abusive ones he is stopping.* You can look for examples such as improving how well he listens to you during conflicts and at other times, carrying his weight of household responsibilities and child care, and supporting your independence. He has to demonstrate that he has come to accept the fact that you have *rights* and that they are equal to his.

7. *Reevaluate his distorted image of you, replacing it with a more positive and empathic view.* He has to recognize that he has had mental habits of focusing on and exaggerating his grievances against you and his perceptions of your weaknesses and to begin instead to compliment you and pay attention to your strengths and abilities.

8. *Make amends for the damage he has done.* He has to develop a sense that he has a *debt* to you and to your children as a result of his abusiveness. He can start to make up somewhat for his actions by being consistently

kind and supportive, putting his own needs on the back burner for a couple of years, talking with people whom he has misled in regard to the abuse and admitting to them that he lied, paying for objects that he has damaged, and many other steps related to cleaning up the emotional and literal messes that his behaviors have caused. (At the same time, he needs to accept that he may never be able to fully compensate you.)

9. *Accept the consequences of his actions.* He should stop whining about, or blaming you for, problems that are the result of his abuse, such as your loss of desire to be sexual with him, the children's tendency to prefer you, or the fact that he is on probation.

10. *Commit to not repeating his abusive behaviors and honor that commitment.* He should not place any conditions on his improvement, such as saying that he won't call you names as long as you don't raise your voice to him. If he does backslide, he cannot justify his abusive behaviors by saying, "But I've done great for five months; you can't expect me to be perfect," as if a good period earned him chips to spend on occasional abuse.

11. *Accept the need to give up his privileges and do so.* This means saying good-bye to double standards, to flirting with other women, to taking off with his friends all weekend while you look after the children, and to being allowed to express anger while you are not.

12. *Accept that overcoming abusiveness is likely to be a life-long process.* He at no time can claim that his work is done by saying to you, "I've changed but you haven't," or complain that he is sick of hearing about his abuse and control and that "it's time to get past all that." He needs to come to terms with the fact that he will probably need

> to be working on his issues for good and that you may
> feel the effects of what he has done for many years.
>
> 13. *Be willing to be accountable for his actions, both past and future.* His attitude that he is above reproach has to be replaced by a willingness to accept feedback and criticism, to be honest about any backsliding, and to be answerable for what he does and how it affects you and your children.

Abusive men don't make lasting changes if they skip any of the above steps, and some are easier than others. Most of my clients find it fairly easy to apologize, for example. In fact, an abuser may weave apologies into his pattern of abuse, so that when he says "I'm sorry," it becomes another weapon in his hand. His unspoken rule may be that once he has apologized, no matter how cursorily or devoid of sincerity, his partner must be satisfied; she is not to make any further effort to show her feelings about his mistreatment, nor may she demand that he fix anything. If she tries to say anything more about the incident, he jumps right back into abuse mode, yelling such things as, "I already *told* you I was sorry! Now shut up about it!"

But even a genuine and sincere apology is only a starting point. Many of my clients make it through the first three steps: They admit to a substantial portion of their abuse; they agree that their actions resulted from choice rather than loss of control; and they apologize. Then they dig in their heels at that point. An abuser's sense of entitlement is like a rude, arrogant voice screaming inside his head. It yells at him: "You've given up too much already; don't budge another inch. They already talked you into saying your abuse is all your own fault when you know she's at least half to blame because of the shit that she does. She should be *grateful* to you for apologizing; that wasn't easy to do. She's lucky you've gone this far; a lot of guys would tell her to go screw, you know." And the voice drags him back into the mud that he had finally taken a couple of baby steps out of.

Step number four, for example, demands that the abusive man accept his partner's right to be angry. He actually has to take seriously the furious things that she says and *think about them* rather than using her emotional pitch as an excuse to stuff her opinions back down her throat as he has normally done. When I explain this step, my clients at first look at me as though I had an eye in the middle of my forehead. "I should do what?? When she is yelling at me, I'm supposed to just sit there and *take it*??" To which I reply, "More than that, actually. You should reflect on the points she is making and respond to them in a thoughtful way." And then we begin practicing exactly that in the group; I ask them for examples of their partners' angry statements and then guide them through understanding why their partners are furious and accepting their right to feel that way.

The steps go on. Steps six and seven require that he make up for what he has done, that he actually has incurred a *debt* because of his abuse. Step eight says that he has to change his behavior in the future, not just say he's sorry for the past, and he has to stop his abusiveness *completely* and *for good*. In other words, he is truly going to have to deal with the attitudes that are driving his bullying and disrespect of his partner. Step eleven requires him to give up the privileges that his abusiveness has won him. As we go through each of these steps, some clients choose to struggle through, as hard as the process is, while others throw in the towel and resume their abusive behaviors.

The Abuser's Outlook on Change

To guide my clients through the work of overcoming abusiveness, I have to keep in mind the fact that they bring their usual habits, attitudes, and manipulations to the process of change itself. This is why a woman finds herself feeling like she is riding a roller coaster while her partner claims to have changed. Here are some of the attitudes that abusers commonly exhibit when their partners, or a court, or an abuse program begin demanding that they stop:

• *"The change game is just like the rest of the routine."*

Abusers can turn their manipulative skills to creating an appearance of change. This was the style we saw in Chapter 1 with Carl, who put on such a show of developing insights at his abuser group but whose treatment of Peggy was as verbally cruel as ever and was rapidly heading back toward physical violence. I couldn't count the number of clients who come into groups of mine when they are separated from their partners and hoping for a reconciliation, or barred from the house with a restraining order and trying to get permission to return, who then vanish from the abuser program the moment they get what they want. A man may say to his partner, "I am learning so much from the abuse groups, and if you let me move back in I'll work even harder at the program," but as soon as his bags are unpacked, the excuses begin: The program is too expensive; he doesn't need it anymore; he doesn't feel comfortable being in a room with "real abusers" because he's not like them, "you and I have just had a few little problems."

- *"I can stop abuse by learning nonabusive ways to control and manipulate my partner."*

I hear this (mostly unconscious) attitude in the voice of the client who says to me: "I thought you were going to be giving me tools to help me manage my partner's crazy behavior. But you aren't helping me with that at all." His expression *crazy behavior* is a code phrase for any way in which she stands up to him, expresses anger, or insists on maintaining a separate identity rather than just conforming to exactly what he wants her to be. A large percentage of men who join abuser programs quit within the first few weeks. They make various excuses at home, but the true reason is that they discover that the program expects them to start treating their partners with respect when they were hoping to just learn kinder, gentler approaches to running the show.

- *"Change is a bargaining chip."*

An abuser often tries to use the promise of change to cut deals, since he believes that his partner's behaviors are just as wrong as his: "I'll agree not to call you 'bitch' anymore if you don't bug me to help clean up the children's mess when I'm trying to watch the game. I won't call you 'slut' or 'whore' if you give up talking to your male friends. I won't push you up against the wall if you drop your side of an argument whenever you see that I'm really upset." To him, these seem like fair deals, but in reality they require a woman to sacrifice her rights and freedom in return for not being abused—a coercive bargain that is in itself abusive.

- *"I don't mind changing some of what I do as long as I don't have to give up the attitudes and behaviors that are most precious to me."*

At some point during the first few months that a man is in my program, I usually stumble upon the core of his privilege, like a rear bunker on his terrain. He may abandon a few of his forward positions, but this fortification is where he surrounds himself with sandbags and settles in for protracted war. A client may agree to stop constantly interrupting his partner and dominating arguments, for example, but when I tell him that he needs to be doing his share of child care, even during football season, he draws the line. If being a respectful partner requires actually rising off of his behind, he'd rather be abusive. Another client may consent to stop spending all of his family's money on himself, but if I tell him that he also has to give up his chronic pattern of having affairs, he decides the losses have become too great, and he quits.

An abuser who does not relinquish his core entitlements will not remain nonabusive. This may be the single most-overlooked point regarding abusers and change. The progress that such a man appears to be making is an illusion. If he reserves the right to bully his partner to protect even one specific privilege, he is keeping the abuse option open. And if he keeps it open, he will gradually revert to using it more and more, until his prior range of controlling behaviors has been restored to its full glory.

Abusers attach themselves tightly to their privileges and come to find the prospect of having equal rights and responsibilities, living on the same plane as their partners, almost unbearable. They resent women who require them to change and persuade themselves that they are victims of unfair treatment because they are losing their lopsided luxuries. But they can't change unless they are willing to relinquish that special status—one of the key pieces of work they have to do in an abuser program.

FOR ME TO BE ABLE TO help an abusive man change, I have to guide him past the points where he gets stuck. I explain to him that he is going to feel some guilt, for example, and that his sense of entitlement will make him want to backslide when the guilty feelings come up. I have to alert him when he starts trying to cut deals to preserve aspects of his abusive behavior and when he reverts to blaming his partner or feeling sorry for himself. I have to help him become aware of his real motives for abusive behavior. Above all, I have to confront his lack of empathy for his partner and children, pressing him to get in touch with the feelings of those he has harmed; it is my job to take away the abusive man's privilege of turning his eyes away from the damage he has done. If the man is willing to persist through this long and difficult process, the potential for real change begins.

How to Assess an Abuser's Claims of Change

QUESTION 19:
How can I tell if he's really changing?

No one is in a better position than the abused woman herself to distinguish genuine progress from window dressing. A woman may call me after her partner has been in my program for a few weeks, her voice edged with anxiety and hope, to ask: "So, how is he doing? Do you think the program is working?" She's counting on the abuse expert to look deeply into her partner's eyes and read his potential. But I can't do it. I have to push the umpiring back to her.

You are the only one who can judge your partner's change. There are men who join my group and become model clients, getting the right answers and showing the appropriate emotions, yet when I talk to their partners I find out that life at home is business as usual or maybe has gotten a little worse. And I work with other men who are cantankerous during meetings, but the report I receive from the front lines is that their treatment of their partners is noticeably improved. What the client shows *me* matters little.

There are two main principles to keep in mind when deciding how much potential an abuser has to become a kind, respectful partner in the long run:

1. He cannot change unless he deals deeply with his entitled and superior attitudes. No superficial changes that he may make offer any real hope for the future.

2. It makes no difference how *nice* he is being to you, since almost all abusers have nice periods. What matters is how *respectful* and *noncoercive* he chooses to become.

Holding on to these fundamental points, you can use the following guide to help you identify changes that show promise of being genuine. We are looking for "yes" answers to these questions:

Has he learned to treat your opinions with respect, even when they differ strongly from his?

YES _____   NO _____

Is he accepting your right to express anger to him, especially when it involves his history of mistreating you?

YES _____   NO _____

Is he respecting your right to freedom and independence? Does that include refraining from all interference with your friendships and giving up the demand to always know where you are and whom you are with?

YES _____   NO _____

Has he stopped making excuses for his treatment of you, including not using your behavior as an excuse for his?

YES _____   NO _____

Is he being respectful about sex, applying no pressure and engaging in no guilt trips?

YES _____   NO _____

Has he stopped cheating or flirting with other women, or using other behaviors that keep you anxious that he will stray?

YES _____   NO _____

Does he listen to your side in arguments without interrupting, and then make a serious effort to respond thoughtfully to your points, even if he doesn't like them?

YES _____   NO _____

Have you been free to raise your grievances, new or old, without retaliation from him?

YES _____ NO _____

Has he stopped talking about his abuse as if it were an accident and begun to acknowledge that he used it to control you?

YES _____ NO _____

Is he actually responding to your grievances and doing something about them (for example, changing the way he behaves toward your children)?

YES _____ NO _____

Has he greatly reduced or eliminated his use of controlling behaviors (such as sarcasm, rolling his eyes, loud disgusted sighs, talking over you, using the voice of ultimate authority, and other demonstrations of disrespect or superiority) during conversations and arguments?

YES _____ NO _____

When he does slip back into controlling behavior, does he take you seriously when you complain about it and keep working on improving?

YES _____ NO _____

Is he being consistent and responsible in his behavior, taking into account how his actions affect you without having to be constantly reminded?

YES _____ NO _____

Is he acting noticeably less demanding, selfish, and self-centered?

YES _____ NO _____

Is he being fair and responsible about money, including allowing you to keep your own assets in your own name?

YES _____ NO _____

Has he stopped any behaviors that you find threatening or intimidating?

YES _____ NO _____

Has he significantly expanded his contribution to household and child-rearing responsibilities and stopped taking your domestic work for granted or treating you like a servant?

YES _____ NO _____

Has he begun supporting your strengths rather than striving to undermine them?

YES _____ NO _____

Have you had any major angry arguments with him in which he has shown a new willingness to conduct himself nonabusively?

YES _____ NO _____

"No" answers to any of the above questions are signs of work that your partner still needs to do. If he is committed to changing, he will take you seriously when you voice your continued concerns and he will acknowledge that he needs to continue working on his attitudes and habits. On the other hand, if he is impatient with or critical of you for not being satisfied with the gestures of change he has already made, that is a sign that his overt abusive behaviors will be coming back before long. My experience with abusive men is that small or even medium-level improvements generally slip away over time; the man who actually maintains his progress is usually the one who changes completely even though that process tends to take considerable time. Thus, when you are attempting to preserve a relationship with a man who has abused you, you need to some extent to hold him to an even higher standard than you would a nonabusive partner.

Sometimes when a woman reports to me that her abusive partner has been doing better, it turns out that he hasn't been doing anything at all. He isn't swearing at her or scaring her, but he also isn't spending time with her, talking to her, or showing her any affection. He's avoiding abusiveness simply by disconnecting from the relationship. As a partner of one of my clients said to me: "It's like he's got two gears: angry and neutral."

Distancing himself can be worse than avoidance; it can be a way to punish you for putting your foot down about the way he treats you. A certain number of my clients leave their partners once they realize that their abuse really isn't going to be tolerated anymore. But the more typical approach is to remain physically present but to retool the machinery to churn out passive aggression instead of open hostility. He learns how to hurt her through what he *doesn't* do instead of through what he does.

The previous questions can help you to distinguish between genuine change and an abusive man's usual pattern of going through a "good" period. If your partner is truly on the road to renouncing abuse, you will notice a dramatic difference in him. Partners of my successful clients say that they feel almost as though they were living with a different person and that now they sense a deeper change that involves a real shift in attitudes rather than just his usual use of superficial sweetness to smooth things over.

CLEAR SIGNS OF AN ABUSER WHO *ISN'T* CHANGING

Your partner can make several statements or behave in several ways that clearly indicate he *isn't* making progress:

- He says he can change only if you change too.

- He says he can change only if you "help" him change, by giving him emotional support, reassurance, and forgiveness, and by spending a lot of time with him. This often means that he wants you to abandon any plans you had to take a break from seeing him.

- He criticizes you for not realizing how much he has changed.

- He criticizes you for not trusting that his change will last.

- He criticizes you for considering him capable of behaving abusively even though *he in fact has done so in the past* (or has *threatened to*) as if you should know that he "would never do something like that," even though he has.

- He reminds you about the bad things he would have done in the past but isn't doing anymore, which amounts to a subtle threat.

- He tells you that you are taking too long to make up your mind, that he can't "wait forever," as a way to pressure you not to take the time you need to collect yourself and to assess how much he's really willing to change.

- He says, "I'm changing, I'm changing," but you don't feel it.

BE STRAIGHT WITH YOURSELF

To use good judgment and make wise decisions about the prospects for change in your abusive partner, you need to be honest *with yourself*. Because you love him, or you have children with him, or leaving him would be difficult for other reasons, you may be sorely tempted to get overly hopeful about small concessions that he finally makes. If he doesn't budge for five years, or twenty years, and then he finally moves an inch, your exhaustion can make you think, *Hey! An inch! That's progress!* You may wish to overlook all the glaring signs indicating that his basic attitudes and strategies remain intact. Beware of his deception and your own self-deception. I have heard such heart-rending sadness in the voices of many dozens of abused women who have said to me: "I wish I could somehow recover all those years I wasted waiting around for him to deal with his issues." Save yourself that sadness if you can, by insisting on nothing less than complete respect.

THE ABUSER IN COUPLES THERAPY

Attempting to address abuse through couples therapy is like wrenching a nut the wrong way; it just gets even harder to undo than it was before. Couples therapy is designed to tackle issues that are *mutual*. It can be effective for overcoming barriers to communication, for untangling the childhood issues that each partner brings to a relationship, or for building intimacy. But you can't accomplish any of these goals in the context of abuse. There can be no positive communication when one person doesn't respect the other and strives to avoid equality. You can't take the leaps of vulnerability involved in working through early emotional injuries while you are feeling emotionally unsafe—because you *are* emotionally unsafe. And if you succeed in achieving greater intimacy with your abusive partner, you will soon get hurt even worse than before because greater closeness means greater vulnerability for you.

Couples counseling sends both the abuser and the abused woman the wrong message. The abuser learns that his partner is "pushing his buttons" and "touching him off" and that she needs to adjust her behavior to avoid getting him so upset. This is precisely what he has been claiming all along. Change in abusers comes only from the reverse process, from completely stepping out of the notion that his partner plays *any* role in causing his abuse of her. An abuser also has to stop focusing on his feelings and his partner's behavior, and look instead at *her feelings* and *his behavior.* Couples counseling allows him to stay stuck in the former. In fact, to some therapists, feelings are all that matters, and reality is more or less irrelevant. In this context, a therapist may turn to you and say, "But *he* feels abused by *you,* too." Unfortunately, the more an abusive man is convinced that his grievances are more or less equal to yours, the less the chance that he will ever overcome his attitudes.

The message to you from couples counseling is: "You can make your abusive partner behave better toward you by changing how *you* behave toward *him.*" Such a message is, frankly, fraudulent. *Abuse is not caused by bad relationship dynamics.* You can't manage your partner's abusiveness by changing your behavior, but he wants you to think that you can. He says, or leads you to believe, that "if you stop doing the things that upset me, and take better care of my needs, I will become a nonabusive partner." It never materializes. And even if it worked, even if you could stop his abusiveness by catering to his every whim, is that a healthy way to live? If the way you behave in the relationship is a response to the threat of abuse, are you a voluntary participant? If you have issues you would like to work on with a couples counselor, wait until your partner has been *completely abuse-free* for two years. Then you might be able to work on some of the problems that truly are mutual ones.

A professional book I recently read offers a powerful example of how couples therapy works with an abuser. The therapist made an agreement with the couple that the man would avoid his scary behaviors and in return the woman would stop making her friends such an important part of her life "because her friendships were causing so much tension in the marriage." The therapist had, in effect, assisted the man in using the threat of violence to get his way, cutting his partner off from social connections and sources of support that were important to her. What the therapist portrayed as a voluntary agreement was actually coercion, although the authors of the book showed no signs of realizing this.

Couples counseling can end up being a big setback for the abused woman. The more she insists that her partner's cruelty or intimidation needs to be addressed, the more she may find the therapist looking down at her, saying, "It seems like you are determined to put all the blame on him and are refusing to look at your part in this." The therapist thereby inadvertently echoes the abuser's attitude, and the woman is forced to deal with yet another context in which she has to defend herself, which is the last thing she needs. I have been involved in many cases where the therapist and the abuser ended up as a sort of tag team, and the abused woman limped away from yet another psychological assault. Most therapists in such circumstances are well intentioned but fail to understand the dynamics of abuse and allow the abuser to shape their perceptions.

The therapist's reassuring presence in the room can give you the courage to open up to your partner in ways that you wouldn't normally feel safe to do. But this isn't necessarily positive; an abuser can retaliate for a woman's frank statements during couples sessions. Later, when he is screaming at you, "You humiliated me in front of the therapist, you made me look like the bad guy, you told things that were too private!" and delivering a nonstop diatribe, you may regret your decision to open up.

Irene, an abused woman who tells her own story in public and has appeared on several panels with me, shares the following account: She had been in couples counseling for about six months with her husband, Quentin, when one day the therapist decided it was time to get the ball rolling. He said, "These session have gradually stopped going anywhere, and I think I know why. Irene, you're not opening up very much, and I think you need to take more emotional risks." Irene felt that the therapist was right; she *had* been exposing very little week to week. So she decided to take the plunge. She told the therapist about Quentin's abuse of her, which included considerable physical violence and the downward emotional spiral she had been in as a result. Quentin appeared moved and shaken, his eyes reddening as if he might cry at any moment. "I have really been in denial about my violence," he told the therapist, "and I haven't been facing how badly it has been affecting Irene." The therapist felt that a crucial barrier to progress had been overcome. "Now," he declared, "I think your couples work can begin to yield results for you."

On the drive home from the session, Quentin kept one hand on the steering wheel. In the other hand he clutched a large handful of Irene's hair as he repeatedly slammed her head into the dashboard, screaming, "I told you to never fucking talk to anyone about that, you bitch! You promised me! You're a fucking liar!" and similar insults in a nonstop rant. After hearing Irene's account, I was careful to never again underestimate the risk to an abused woman of conjoint therapy.

If couples counseling is the only type of help your partner is willing to get—because he wants to make sure that he can blame the problem on you—you may think, *Well, it's better than not getting any counseling at all. And maybe the therapist will see the things he does and convince him to get help.* But even if the therapist were to confront him, which is uncommon, he would just say: "You turned the therapist against me"—the same way he handles any other challenges.

Some couples therapists have said to me: "Before I work with a couple whose relationship has involved abuse, I insist on clear agreements that there won't be any abuse while they are in therapy with me and no paybacks for anything that gets said in a session." Such agreements are meaningless, unfortunately, because abusers feel no obligation to honor them; *virtually every abuser I've ever worked with feels entitled to break his word if he has "good enough reason,"* which includes any time that he is really upset by his partner. Increasingly, therapists across the United States and Canada are refusing to engage in couples or family sessions with an abuser, which is the responsible course of action.

THE ABUSIVE MAN IN INDIVIDUAL THERAPY

The more psychotherapy a client of mine has participated in, the more impossible I usually find it is to work with him. The highly "therapized" abuser tends to be slick, condescending, and manipulative. He uses the psychological concepts he has learned to dissect his partner's flaws and dismiss her perceptions of abuse. He takes responsibility for nothing that he does; he moves in a world where there are only unfortunate dynamics, miscommunications, symbolic acts. He expects to be rewarded for his emotional openness, handled gingerly because of his "vulnerability," colluded with in skirting the damage he has done, and congratulated for his insight. Many years ago, a violent abuser in my program shared the following with us: "From working in therapy on my issues about anger toward my mother, I realized that when I punched my wife, it wasn't really her I was hitting. It was my mother!" He sat back, ready for us to express our approval of his self-awareness. My colleague peered through his glasses at the man, unimpressed by this revelation. "No," he said, "you were hitting your wife."

I have yet to meet an abuser who has made any meaningful and lasting changes in his behavior toward female partners through therapy, regardless of how much "insight"—most of it false—that he may have gained. The fact is that if an abuser finds a particularly skilled therapist and if the therapy is especially successful, when he is finished he will be a happy, well-adjusted *abuser*—good news for him, perhaps, but not such good news for his partner. Psychotherapy can be very valuable for the issues it is devised to address, but partner abuse is not one of them; an abusive man needs to be in a specialized program, as we will see.

THE ABUSER PROGRAM

Bringing about change in an abuser generally requires four elements: (1) consequences, (2) education, (3) confrontation, and (4) accountability. Consequences, the first item on the list, are manifested primarily through the abuser's experience of losing his relationship (at least temporarily if not permanently), or through the legal system if he has committed any abuse-related crimes, such as threats or assaults. He may also experience consequences in the form of ciriticism or disapproval from other people in his life.

The abuser program has responsibility for items two and three, providing the abusive man with education about abuse and confronting him with his attitudes and excuses. A high-quality abuser program is entirely different from therapy. The critical distinctions include:

- Therapy focuses on the man's feelings and gives him empathy and support, no matter how unreasonable the attitudes that are giving rise to those feelings. An abuser program, on the other hand, focuses on his *thinking*. The feelings that the abuser program discusses are primarily his partner's and his children's, not his.

- Therapy involves few rules, or none, governing what the man is allowed to do during the period he is in therapy. The abuser program requires the man to refrain from all physical violence and threats and to work seriously on reducing his verbal aggression and other forms of psychological abuse, or he can't stay in the program.

- An abusive man's therapist usually will not speak to the abused woman, whereas the counselor of a high-quality abuser program always does.

- Therapy typically will not address any of the central causes of abusiveness, including entitlement, coercive control, disrespect, superiority, selfishness, or victim blaming. An abuser program is expected to cover all of these issues and in fact to make them its primary focus.

- An abuser program is expected to provide the man with education about abuse, to counsel him on how to apply those concepts to his own life, and to confront his abusive attitudes and excuses. It is rare for therapy to do any of these things.

At the same time, an abuser program possesses no more magic than anyone else. The man who makes major life changes as a result of attending an abuser program is the one who *chooses to work the program,* not the one who sits back and waits for the program to "help" him, expecting service as he usually does. The successful client neither fights his counselors every step of the way, telling them what ignorant idiots they are, nor kisses up to them unctuously while claiming that the program has caused him to see the light. Rather, he comes weekly with a seriousness of purpose, practices what he is told, and tries to face up to the damage he has done.

I regret to say that a majority of abusers choose not to do the work. It isn't that they *can't* change (any abuser who doesn't have a major mental illness can change) but that they decide they don't wish to. They run a sort of cost-benefit analysis in their heads and decide that the rewards of remaining in control of their partners outweigh the costs. They decide that to consider seriously the perspective their counselors are presenting to them is just too uncomfortable and difficult and offends their arrogant sense of certainty about everything—at least, about everything having to do with relationships and the particular women they are with.

Later in this chapter I offer some suggestions on how you can increase the likelihood that your partner will be among those who do overcome their abusiveness. Bear in mind, though, that the ultimate choice is his; the saying "You can lead a horse to water but you can't make him drink" applies particularly well here.

How Do I Know If His Abuser Program Is a Good One?

The first test of the quality of an abuser program is whether the main goal of the staff members appears to be helping *you* or helping *him.* In a responsible program the abused woman is considered the primary client. The only "assistance" they should be offering to the man is to educate and challenge him about his abusive attitudes and behaviors. *He,* on the other hand, may have numerous other goals—to get back together with you, to get more visitation with the children or reduce his child support payments, to escape criminal charges—but the program has no business assisting him with any of these; the last thing an abused woman needs is more people helping her abuser to work against her.

Those in charge of an abuser program *should* do the following:

- Contact you quickly after your partner enters the program.
  In this call, they should ask you to give a history of his abusive

behavior and of any substance abuse, and tell you where to go for abused women's services.

- Warn you that only a minority of abusers make lasting changes and that a few actually get *worse* from participating in an abuser program.

- Tell you the rules he has to follow to be in the program.

- Describe to you the topics that will be covered in his group meetings and give you as much detail about those sessions as you request.

- Give you any information you request about his attendance and the attitudes he expresses in the program, and about *any specific statements he makes in group* that you would like to know. They should not be promising him any confidentiality *with respect to you.*

- Devote most sessions at the program to discussing the core attitudinal and behavioral issues of abuse (as covered in Chapter 3).

Furthermore, you should be given a copy of any written reports generated by the program about the abuser, such as court reports. These reports should include:

- A full description of all the abuse that your partner has admitted to while in the program, including psychological abuse, sexual coercion, or violence

- Any steps toward change that he has failed to make (see the box earlier in this chapter)

There are various signs you can watch for that indicate an abuser program is *ineffective*:

- Counselors fail to contact you or to tell you the limitations of what counseling is likely to accomplish.

- They tell you that they think he is really changing and that he is doing very well in the program. (They should know that what *you* see is what matters, not what *they* see; lots of abusers put on a good show at the abuser program.)

- They try to involve you in couples counseling, suggest that you drop your restraining order, encourage you to communicate with your partner, or advocate for his interests in any way.

- They relay messages to you from him.

- Their group meetings seem to spend too much time teaching him to identify his feelings, to apply conflict-resolution skills, to manage his anger better, or to deal with other issues that do not affect his underlying beliefs.

- Their written reports are vague, do not address the steps to change (see the box earlier in this chapter), or give an overly rosy image of his prospects for change without describing the steps he still has left to take.

I know how hard it is for a woman to get her partner to attend an abuser program. After she's finally succeeded in that campaign, I wish I could tell her that a cure is sure to follow, but it isn't. A large proportion of abusers would rather stay stuck in their old ruts. I consider myself an excellent counselor for abusive men; I am patient with them, approaching them as an educator rather than as a harsh critic. At the same time, I can detect manipulation; I know what their issues are, and I don't allow them to fool me. I have worked with colleagues whom I believe to be even more skilled than I, and from whom I have learned volumes. But even the very best counselors give the same report: It is more common for abusers to stay the same or get worse than it is for them to make the kinds of changes that bring qualitative improvements in the lives of their partners and children. A responsible abuser program encourages clients who are doing serious work but always mixes caution with its optimism.

If your partner or ex-partner joins an abuser program, I recommend that you examine the program's literature carefully, ask lots of questions, and advocate for yourself to make sure the program does the kind of work with the man that you know needs to be done. At the same time, keep your own life moving forward, focusing on your own healing process, *not* on the man's process of change. Waiting around for him to get serious about developing respect for you could be a long stall in your own growth and development. Don't sell yourself short.

CREATING A CONTEXT FOR CHANGE

An abuser doesn't change because he feels guilty or gets sober or finds God. He doesn't change after seeing the fear in his children's eyes or feeling them drift away from him. It doesn't suddenly dawn on him that his partner deserves better treatment. Because of his self-focus, combined with the many rewards he gets from controlling you, an abuser changes only when he feels he has to, so the most important element in creating a context for change in an abuser is placing him in a situation where he has no other choice. Otherwise, it is highly unlikely that he will ever change his abusive behavior.

Once an abuser has made substantial improvements, his motivation to *sustain* those changes sometimes does become more internal. But the initial impetus is always external. Either his partner demands change and threatens to leave him or a court demands change and threatens to jail him. I have never seen a client make a serious effort to confront his abusiveness unless somebody required him to do the work. The abuser who truly enters counseling voluntarily, with no one holding anything over his head, quits within a few sessions, unless he finds a counselor he can manipulate.

QUESTION 20:
HOW CAN I HELP MY ABUSIVE PARTNER CHANGE?

Creating a context for change also involves these elements:

1. Establishing *consequences* for him for continued abusiveness. You may be able to use the legal system to impose sanctions if your partner's style of abuse is physically violent or threatening,

or involves sexual assaults. Leaving him is another good consequence for him, perhaps even better than legal intervention, depending on who he is and how well the police and courts work where you live. *To get an abuser to change, you have to either prepare to leave him—if you can do so safely—or use the police and courts, or both.*

2. Making clear to him what your *expectations* are for his treatment of you, including specifically what you are willing to live with and what you are not.

3. Focusing on your own healing and strength, so that he senses that he if he doesn't change, you are ready to move on.

You cannot, I am sorry to say, get an abuser to work on himself by pleading, soothing, gently leading, getting friends to persuade him, or using any other nonconfrontational method. I have watched hundreds of women attempt such an approach without success. The way you can help him change is to demand that he do so, and settle for nothing less.

It is also impossible to persuade an abusive man to change by convincing him that *he* would benefit, because he perceives the benefits of controlling his partner as vastly outweighing the losses. This is part of why so many men initially take steps to change their abusive behavior but then return to their old ways. There is another reason why appealing to his self-interest doesn't work: The abusive man's belief that his own needs should come ahead of his partner's is at the core of his problem. Therefore when anyone, including therapists, tells an abusive man that he should change because that's what's best for *him,* they are inadvertently feeding his selfish focus on himself: *You can't simultaneously contribute to a problem and solve it.* Those abusive men who make lasting changes are the ones who do so because they realize how badly they are hurting their partners and children—in other words, because they learn to care about what is good for *others* in the family and develop empathy, instead of caring only about themselves.

LEAVING AN ABUSER AS A WAY TO PROMOTE CHANGE

Breaking up with an abusive man, or even deciding to take some time apart, needs to be done with caution, as I discussed in "Leaving an Abuser Safely" in Chapter 9. But if you feel you can leave, doing so may help provide the impetus your partner needs to look at his behavior. If you are separating with the hope that you might get back together in the future, consider the following suggestions:

- Be very clear about what kind of contact you want to have with your partner during the separation, if any. *It is generally best to have none at all.* If you keep talking to him or seeing him from time to time, you will find it much harder to keep your own thinking clear, because you will tend to miss him even more intensely, feel sorry for him, and get drawn in by his promises and his charm. Occasional contact is bad for *him,* too, not just for you; it feeds his denial of his problem, encouraging him to assume that he can use his usual manipulations to avoid dealing with himself.

  If you feel that you do want to permit some contact, consider the specifics. Can he call you, or do you want to be the only one to initiate contact? Can he send letters? If you are going to see each other in person, where, when, and how often?

- Once you make up your mind about the above questions, be explicit with your partner about your wishes for contact and let him know that *you expect your wishes to be respected.* Tell him that if he is serious about changing, the first way he can demonstrate that to you is by giving you the space you are asking for.

- Stay away from him for as long as you can stand it. Get support during this period from friends, relatives, your religious community, or anyone else you can trust to help you stay strong. Attend counseling or a support group at a program for abused women if there is one in your area, even if your partner has never been violent. Give yourself as much time as possible to heal emotionally and to clear your mind.

  The separation needs to be long enough to make him really

THE PROCESS OF CHANGE

uncomfortable—enough to motivate him to change. Part of what creates discomfort for him is the dawning realization that maybe you really could live without him. A separation that is too short, on the other hand, will serve in his mind as proof that you *can't* stand to be on your own, so he will think he can get away with anything. Try to prepare yourself for the possibility that he will start to date someone else during your separation. This is a common move, used to test your strength and get you to lose your resolve and start seeing him again. His new relationship is not very likely to last, so just try to sweat it out.

- If you decide to get back together with him, be clear with yourself and with him about what the rules are for his behavior. The *first* time he violates one of those rules—and it is likely that he will—it is of critical importance to *take another period of separation*. Your partner does not believe that you will go through with setting limits on his conduct. You need to prove him wrong. He may test you the first day you move back in together, or he may wait two years. But the day will probably come, so have your response ready.

- The next separation should be longer than the first in order to give your partner a clear message and to motivate him to change. If during the first break you spoke to him occasionally, this time permit no contact at all for a few months. As always, focus on making yourself stronger. Pursue new friendships, get exercise, do artwork, or engage in whatever activity you love the most and that helps you feel that your life is moving forward. If you are drinking too much or have developed other problems, seek out the help you need and deserve. The more space you get from abuse, the less willing you will be to endure it and the harder it will be for your (ex-)partner to con you.

  Have you ever noticed that people sometimes quit a job soon after returning from a vacation? We all have a higher tolerance for frustrating or unhealthy situations in our lives when they are constant, but when we get a little time away and then come back, that taste of freedom changes our perspective. What had been a dull ache turns into a sharp pain and becomes unbearable. The same can happen to an abused woman. If you give yourself a long enough taste of life without being cut down all the time, you may reach a point where you find yourself thinking, *Go back to that? For what? Maybe I'll never stop loving him, but at least I can love him from a distance where he can't hurt me.*

- If he doesn't get serious about stopping his mistreatment of you, you will come to a day when you feel ready to end the relationship for good. This may seem inconceivable to you now, however, so just keep moving forward with your life. Focus on yourself as much as possible, pursuing your own goals and filling your life with the activities you enjoy and find satisfying. Trying too hard to get your partner to change is a dead-end street. To do so keeps you wrapped up in the dynamics of abuse, because an abuser *wants* you to be preoccupied with him. Only permit him to occupy your thoughts for a portion of the day and then reserve the lion's share of your mental space for yourself.

The only time an abusive man will deal with his issues enough to become someone you can live with is when you prove to him, and to yourself, that you are capable of living without him. And once you succeed in doing so, you may very well decide that living without him is what you would rather do. Keep an open mind, and make sure you are not clipping your own wings on top of the clipping that he has given them. Sometimes I work with a woman who is among the fortunate ones whose partners do make deep changes, but she finds that his change has ceased to matter, because she has simply outgrown him. The fundamental principle, then, is to do what is best for *you*.

WHICH ABUSERS ARE MOST LIKELY TO CHANGE?

Prediction is difficult. I have had clients who were stellar participants in group and whose partners reported good progress in the early months, but who dive-bombed later on, rushing back to their worst behaviors as if reuniting with dear old friends. On the other hand, I have worked with men who were ornery during group meetings, who were slow and stubborn about taking in the concepts, yet who months later stood out for having done some of the most serious work on themselves of anyone in the program.

I have noticed some recurring themes among those abusers whose changes go the deepest and last the longest, however:

- His close friends and relatives recognize that he is abusive and tell him that he needs to deal with it. They support the abused woman instead of supporting him. I have a much more difficult time with the abuser whose friends and family back up his excuses and encourage his disrespect for the woman.

- He is lower than others on the scale of self-centeredness. He tends to show signs early on of having more empathy than other clients do for the pain he has caused his partner, and his empathy seems more genuine and less theatrical. The highly self-referential, arrogant abuser, on the other hand, believes that he is above criticism and considers his own opinions and insights to be the last word on the planet. So who is going to be able to persuade him that he has been cruel and selfish?

- His partner gets the most unreserved, unequivocal support from her friends and relatives, her religious community, and from the legal system if she needs it. The more consistently she receives the message that the abuse is in no way her fault and that her community intends to stand behind her 100 percent, the stronger and safer she feels to settle for nothing less than fully respectful treatment from her partner or ex-partner.

- He joins a high-quality abuser program and stays for a long time— about two years.

But, even in cases where all of these conditions are met, his progress still depends on whether or not he decides to carefully and seriously take each of the steps to change.

KEY POINTS TO REMEMBER

- You can't make or even help an abusive man change. All you can do is create the context for change, and the rest is up to him.

- You are the best judge of whether or not he is truly developing respect for you and for your rights. Don't put anyone else's opinions ahead of your own.

- Change in an abusive man is not vague; it is highly specific. Use the information in this chapter to measure for yourself whether he is getting down to the real work of change or whether he is trying to fly by with the usual nods and winks.

- An abusive man won't change by "working on his anger," unless he also does the more difficult work of changing his entitled attitudes.

- Make your own recovery, and that of your children, your top priority.

- Abusiveness is like poison ivy, with its extensive and entrenched root system. You can't eradicate it by lopping off the superficial signs. It has to come out by the roots, which are the man's attitudes and beliefs regarding partner relationships.

15

Creating an Abuse-free World

I've joined a support group. It feels so good to talk to people who get it.

I met this guy at work who said that my partner's behavior is abuse.

I'm so grateful for my friends and family; they really have been there for me.

I told my son that the next time he calls a girl "bitch," he's grounded.

My daughter's teacher asked me if everything is okay at home. I lied and said, "Yes," but it's actually really nice that somebody noticed.

PARTNER ABUSE is a cyclone that leaves a swath of destruction behind it as it rips through the lives of women and children: destroyed self-confidence, loss of freedom, stalled progress, fear, bitterness, economic ruin, humiliation, heartbreak, physical injury, ugly custody battles, isolation, wedges driven between mothers and their children, confusion, mistrust between siblings, secrets, lies.

No woman should have to live this way. Neither should her children. But there are other lives that are also affected, because for every abused woman, there are friends and relatives who suffer, too, from their worry and pain over what they see happening to her. Some of those who approach me to share their anguish are men who are groping desperately for clues to how they can assist their daughters and sisters and mothers who they see being sliced to ribbons a day at a time. In fact, it is unusual for me to talk to anyone, male or female, whose life has not been saddened at some point by an abusive man.

In recent years, in my public presentations, I have increasingly addressed the effects on children who are exposed to partner abuse. While writing this book I spoke at a training session for police officers, where a young cop who was built to intimidate—about as wide as he was tall—came up to me privately during a break and said, "All this stuff you are talking about went on in my family growing up. My old man was just like what you describe, always controlling, scaring everybody. And he drove me and my mom apart, just like you said. But we all saw through him when we got older, and me and my mom are close now." I told him how happy I was that he had become a police officer, so that when a family calls for help, they might be sent a cop who can see through the children's eyes and remember that they are victims too.

We all have a stake in ending abuse, if not for ourselves, then for our loved ones who may be targets or bystanders or who may find themselves mired in an abusive relationship someday. Anyone who chooses to can play an important role in chasing this scourge out of our homes, our communities, and our nations.

Abuse is a solvable problem. We know where it comes from; we know why abusers are reluctant to change; and we know what it takes to make abuse stop. Abusers specialize in creating mystery and intrigue, but when we clear the smoke away we are left with an obvious moral wrong and a straightforward task to set it right. All that is required is the clarity of our minds and the will of our communities.

Throughout this book, I have been putting forth my suggestions to abused women about steps that they can take to make sense out of what is occurring, to seek safety, and to set their own healing in motion. I have a few more words of advice for them, but most of this chapter is directed at *everyone*—male or female, survivor of abuse or not, young or old—who is interested in helping to end abuse.

WHAT THE ABUSED WOMAN CAN DO

My primary message to you is this: An abuser distorts the life and mind of his abused partner, so that she becomes focused on him. The main way out of the abuse vortex, therefore, is to reorient your thinking so that you devote your attention to yourself and to your children. I hope this book has helped to solve some puzzles for you about what is going on in your partner's mind. Now see if you can stop puzzling about him and turn your energy toward moving yourself forward on your chosen course.

Most of this chapter talks about the ways in which people can transform the attitudes toward abuse that prevail in their communities. Please don't concern yourself with these suggestions unless you are sure you are ready for them. If you jump from trying to take care of your own abusive relationship to trying to take care of other abused women, you may forget that you deserve caretaking for yourself. Let other people take on the world for now and just be the "hero of your own life," as one book refers to abused women. Taking action in your community against the abuse of women may be an empowering and healing activity for you, but not if you take it on too soon. You'll know when you're ready.

I have woven practical ideas through all of the previous chapters. I would like to leave you with just a few more thoughts:

- Get support for yourself no matter how. Find someone somewhere who can understand what you are going through, who can be trusted with confidences, and who can help you hold on to your sense of reality. *Reach out.*

- Keep a journal to document your experience, so that when your partner is making you crazy with mind games or with sudden "good" behavior, you can look back through your writings and remember who you really are and what he really does.

- Stay away from people who aren't good for you, who don't understand, who say things that push you down into self-blame.

- Do anything you can think of that's good for you, that nurtures your soul. Even women who have extraordinarily controlling partners often can find some ruse that will free them long enough to work out, take a class, go for a walk, or just get some time alone to think.

- Keep your abusive partner out of your head as much as you can. Use this book to help you understand what he is doing; naming and understanding is power. If you can understand how he thinks, you can avoid absorbing his thinking yourself and prevent him from crawling inside your head.

- Don't blame yourself when you don't reach your goals right away, when, for instance, you break down and get back together with him. Just pull yourself together and try again. You will succeed eventually, perhaps even on your very next attempt.

How to Support an Abused Woman

QUESTION 21:
How can I help my daughter, sister, or friend who is being abused?

If you would like to make a significant difference in the life of an abused woman you care about, keep the following principle fresh in your mind: *Your goal is to be the complete opposite of what the abuser is.*

THE ABUSER: Pressures her severely

SO YOU SHOULD: Be patient. Remember that it takes time for an abused woman to sort out her confusion and figure out how to handle her situation. It is not helpful for her to try to follow *your* timetable for when she should stand up to her partner, leave him, call the police, or whatever step you want her to take. You need to respect her judgment regarding when she is ready to take action—something the abuser never does.

THE ABUSER: Talks down to her

SO YOU SHOULD: Address her as an equal. Avoid all traces of condescension or superior knowledge in your voice. This caution applies just as much or more to professionals. If you speak to an abused woman as if you are smarter or wiser than she is, or as if she is going through something that could never happen to *you,* then you inadvertently confirm exactly what the abuser has been telling her, which is that she is beneath him. Remember, your actions speak louder than your words.

THE ABUSER: Thinks he knows what is good for her better than she does

SO YOU SHOULD: Treat her as the expert on her own life. Don't assume that you know what she needs to do. I have sometimes given abused women suggestions that I thought were exactly right but turned out to be terrible for that particular situation. Ask *her* what she thinks might work and, *without pressuring her,* offer suggestions, respecting her explanations for why certain courses of action would not be helpful. Don't tell her what to do.

THE ABUSER: Dominates conversations

SO YOU SHOULD: Listen more and talk less. The temptation may be great to convince her what a "jerk" he is, to analyze his motives, to give speeches covering entire chapters of this book. But talking too much inadvertently communicates to her that your thoughts are more important than hers, which is exactly how the abuser treats her. If you want her to value her own feelings and opinions, then you have to show her that *you* value them.

THE ABUSER: Believes he has the right to control her life

SO YOU SHOULD: Respect her right to self-determination. She is entitled to make decisions that are not exactly what you would choose, including the decision to stay with her abusive partner or to return to him after a separation. You can't convince a woman that her life belongs to her if you are simultaneously acting like it belongs to you. Stay by her even when she makes choices that you don't like.

THE ABUSER: Assumes he understands her children and their needs better than she does

SO YOU SHOULD: Assume that she is a competent, caring mother. Remember that there is no simple way to determine what is best for the children of an abused woman. Even if she leaves the abuser, the children's problems are not necessarily over, and sometimes abusers actually create *worse* difficulties for the children postseparation than before. You cannot help her to find the best path for her children unless you have a realistic grasp of the complicated set of choices that face her.

THE ABUSER: Thinks *for* her

SO YOU SHOULD: Think *with* her. Don't assume the role of teacher or rescuer. Instead, join forces with her as a respectful and equal team member.

Notice that being the opposite of the abuser does not simply mean *saying* the opposite of what he says. If he beseeches her with, "Don't leave me, don't leave me," and you stand on the other side badgering her with, "Leave him, leave him," she will feel that you're much like him; you are both pressuring her to accept your judgment of what she should do. Neither of you is asking the empowering question, "What do *you* want to do?"

DEALING WITH YOUR OWN FRUSTRATIONS

Because empowerment and recovery for an abused woman can be a long process, people who want to be there for her tend to go through periods when their patience wears thin. They are tempted to aim their frustration at the woman herself, saying, "Well, if you put such a low value on yourself as to choose to be abused, I can't keep hanging around," or "If you care about him more than you care about your children, you're as sick as he is." I understand why you feel irritated, but it doesn't make sense to put her down. The message you send with such an outburst is that you think she is causing herself to be abused, which is just what the abuser is telling her. And the last thing you want to do is support his message.

One of the biggest mistakes made by people who wish to help an abused woman is to measure success by whether or not she leaves her abusive partner. If the woman feels unable or unready to end her relationship, or if she does separate for a period but then goes back to him, people who have attempted to help tend to feel that their effort failed and often channel this frustration into blaming the abused woman. A better measure of success for the person helping is how well you have respected the woman's right to run her own life—which the abusive man does not do—and how well you have helped her to think of strategies to increase her safety. If you stay focused on these goals you will feel less frustrated as a helper and will be a more valuable resource for the woman.

Here is a mental exercise you can do to help you through your impatience. Think about your own life for a moment, and consider some problem that has been difficult for you to solve. Perhaps you have had difficulty finding a job you really like; perhaps you have a weight problem or some other health problem; perhaps you wish to quit smoking; perhaps you are unhappy in your current relationship or unhappy being single. Now think about a time when friends or relatives were jumping in to tell you what you should do about the challenge facing you. How much did that help? Did they gloss over the complexities, making solutions sound simpler than they really are? Did they become impatient when you were reluctant to take the steps that they proposed? How did their impatience feel to you?

Other people's problems almost always appear simpler than our own. Sentences that start with "If I were you, I would . . ." rarely help. When people start to impose their solutions on me, for example, I feel the desire to respond: "If you are such an expert on how I should wend my way through life's obstacles, why are there still important sources of unhappiness in *your* life? Why haven't you made everything perfect for yourself?" No life situation is as simple as it may appear from the outside.

When your frustration is about to get the best of you, seek support for yourself. Talk to someone you care about. Share how painful it is to be unable to instantly pluck the abused woman from her thorny trap, which of course is what you wish you could do, as do I. Tell about the rage you feel toward the man who is abusing her. Then prepare yourself to go back and be patient and loving with the woman you are trying to help. Abused women tell me over and over again that nothing has mattered more to their progress toward safety and recovery than the love and support of friends, relatives, and respectful professionals.

One more word of caution: I observe that many people are eager to find *something* wrong with an abused woman, because if they can't, they are confronted with the uncomfortable reality that any woman can be abused. The urge to find fault in her interferes with your ability to help her—and ultimately colludes with the abusive man.

WHAT IF SHE DOESN'T BELIEVE SHE IS BEING ABUSED?

Family and friends of an abused woman sometimes ask me how they can get her to realize that her partner is an abuser. They complain: "She always makes excuses for him. She has these ideas about how to make him get better, like by helping him find a less stressful job, that obviously aren't going to work. And she blames herself, saying that she's the one who sets him off a lot of times. She's in a lot of denial."

She may actually be more aware of the abuse than she is willing to say. Her shame, and her fear that other people will pressure or criticize her, may make her pretend she doesn't see. If she has been with her partner for a long time, or if he is especially scary or crazy-making, she may be experiencing traumatic bonding (see Chapter 9). Or she may believe that her partner is right—that her behavior really is the root of their difficulties, not his. In any event, you will not be able to "make her" see her partner's abusiveness any more than she can "make him" see it. I wish I could say otherwise, because I know how difficult it is for an abused woman's loved ones to accept the limits on what they can do.

Here are a few steps you *can* take, however:

- Tell her that you don't like the way she is being treated and that you don't think she deserves it.

- Tell her you love her and that you think she is a good person.

- Ask her to read this book. You also might hand her one of the other books listed under "Resources" in the back of this one.

- Ask her if she would be willing to make plans with you for ways to respond to specific situations of abuse as they arise. See, for example, if she would agree to call you the next time her partner starts to yell at her. Offer to pay for her to spend the night at a hotel the next time he gets scary. Ask whether she could make an excuse to come and visit you on her own for a week over the summer, so that she might get a chance to clear her head a bit. You may think of other alternatives of your own.

- If you ever think she is in danger at a particular moment—if, for example, she calls you in the midst of violence or threats— call the police in her area and tell them what is happening.

- Call her or write her often, even if she never seems to return calls, unless she asks you not to (which would indicate that he punishes her for being in contact with people).

- Treat her consistently well. She'll feel the difference between what you do and what he does.

- Encourage her to call a program for abused women "just to talk." She does not need to give them her name or her telephone number, and she doesn't even have to believe that she is being abused. She can call for support and reality checks and just to describe her struggles in her relationship. The first call to a women's program sometimes breaks the ice so that it gets easier for her to reach out for help again.

You may wonder why I stated earlier that abuse is a solvable problem, yet now I am saying that you sometimes will have to watch and wait. To say that we can end abuse in our communities does not mean that we can rescue each individual abused woman right this minute. To help your friend or relative achieve an abuse-free life may take some time. To achieve an abuse-free society will take a lot of effort on many levels, as we will see.

Finally, do yourself one great favor: Read *To Be an Anchor in the Storm,* a wonderful book that has been written precisely for the loved ones of abused women (see "Resources") and is filled with wisdom from cover to cover.

REACHING THE ABUSER

If I were asked to select one salient characteristic of my abusive clients, an aspect of their nature that stands out above all the others, I would choose this one: They feel profoundly justified. Every effort to reach an abuser must be based on the antidote to this attitude: *Abuse is wrong; you are responsible for your own actions; no excuse is acceptable; the damage you are doing is incalculable; your problem is yours alone to solve.*

Who has the opportunity to have an impact on an abuser's thinking, and what can they do?

FRIENDS AND FAMILY

You are the front line. You have a better chance of turning around an abuser's attitude than everyone else—the abused woman, a therapist, an abuser program, the courts—put together. You are the hardest ones to discredit. He dismisses the others on the list with a wave of his hand, because they are "crazy" or "liars" or "hysterical" or "anti-male." But when his loved ones criticize him, he is likely to experience some uncertainty for the first time.

Here are some guidelines to follow:

1. When someone you care about is accused of abuse, don't tell yourself that it can't possibly be true. Unfortunately, when an abuser complains to his relatives in an outraged voice, "My partner accuses me of being *abusive,*" they generally jump blindly to his side. They shake their head in disgust and outrage, and respond: "How could she *say* that about you? What a bitch!" Nobody asks any questions.

Instead of falling prey to this knee-jerk reaction, begin by finding out all you can. What exactly does he do that she finds abusive? How does she say she is affected by him? What does she want him to do differently? He will respond to these questions by making her sound ridiculous. He may say, for example, "She says that if I'm ever grouchy or in a bad mood, that's abuse. Every time she doesn't get her way, she labels me an abuser." Keep pressing him about what her perspective is. Ask him to give examples of specific interactions. Refuse to jump on his bandwagon. Show him that you are reserving judgment.

Next, have a private conversation with his partner. Tell her that he has revealed that she feels abused and that you would like to know what her concerns are. She may tell you very little, depending on how much she feels she can trust you. But if she does open up, you are likely to find that she doesn't come out sounding like a crazy bully the way he would like you to believe her to be. When a woman complains of abuse, the great majority of the time she has valid and important complaints about how her partner is treating her.

2. Don't repeat to him confidences she has shared with you unless she gives you clear permission. You may be persuaded that he isn't the type to retaliate, but she knows better. Ask her which issues or events are safe for you to bring up with him and which ones are not. To the extent that she gives you the go-ahead, press him to think carefully about her complaints and to make the improvements in his behavior that she is requesting.

3. Don't ignore events you witness directly. It is awkward to address a loved one's conduct toward his partner, but silence implies acceptance. Talk to each of them separately, raising your concerns about his behavior.

4. Follow up, especially with her. Find a moment to ask her privately whether or not the problem is persistent, and what kind of help she could use.

I understand and value the loyalty of family members to each other. There is a natural temptation to speak out forcefully against abuse until the man whose behavior is under the microscope is one of our own, and then we switch sides. But we can't have it both ways. Abuse won't stop until people stop making exceptions for their own brothers and sons and friends.

Supporting a woman against a man's abusiveness does not necessarily mean taking her side in every conflict in their relationship. They may have huge issues between them that are a tangled mess—collisions about finances or child rearing or choices of friends—in addition to the abuse. When you challenge a loved one about mistreating his partner, he will say: "You are siding with her; she's turned you against me." Respond to these distortions by saying: "I am not against *you*; I am against your hurtful behavior. I'm not saying that she's right about every issue between you. What I am saying is that you won't be able to work out any of those other differences unless you first deal with your abuse problem. As long as you keep bullying her, *you* are the number-one problem."

Nothing would work faster to end the abuse of women than having the friends and family of abusive men stop enabling them. And that begins, in turn, with making sure that you listen carefully and respectfully to her side of the story—something the abusive man never does.

THERAPISTS, CLERGYPEOPLE, AND OTHER COUNSELORS

While an abused woman may sometimes approach a counselor and describe her struggle straightforwardly, an abuser speaks in terms that are less direct. He seeks help not because he senses that he is abusive but because he is tired of the tension in his home or is afraid that his relationship is going to split up. He will not typically volunteer the fact that he swears, tears his partner down, or frightens her. If he is physically violent, he will almost certainly make no spontaneous mention of that fact. However, he may give various hints. Some common ones include:

> *"I have a bad temper, and I lose my cool sometimes."*

> *"My girlfriend claims that I don't treat her right."*

"My partner is always making eyes at other men."

"My wife attacked me, so I had to defend myself, and she got hurt."

None of these statements is proof of abuse in itself, but each one is adequate cause for serious concern and should be treated as an indication that the counselor needs to ask many questions about the man's behavior and his partner's perspective.

I recommend that counselors use tremendous caution in accepting a man's claim that he has been falsely accused of abuse or that he is the victim of a violent or controlling woman. You could easily become an unwitting source of support and justification for his psychological—or physical—assaults on his partner. Remain neutral until you have learned a great deal about his circumstances and attitudes.

When you are concerned that a man might have an abuse problem, ask him to talk in detail about his partner's perspective and feelings about various aspects of her life, including her view of conflicts with him. The abuser will typically have difficulty looking through her eyes with sympathy and detail, *especially* with respect to her grievances against him. The more he ridicules and trivializes her point of view, the greater reason you have to believe that the problem lies with him. At the same time, if you keep asking what *she* would say, you will find that you often get critical clues to what his behavior and attitude problems are.

Whether or not you suspect abuse, it is always valuable to provide some basic education to any male about partner abuse. Give some examples of abusive behaviors, describe their destructive impact on women and children, and explain that a man is entirely responsible for his own actions. If you hear him use other people's behavior as an excuse for his own or if he blames stress or alcohol, point out that he is rationalizing his mistreatment of his partner. If he admits to abuse at any point, encourage him to contact an abuser program.

POLICE, PROSECUTORS, JUDGES, AND PROBATION OFFICERS

Various guidelines for law enforcement personnel are included in Chapter 12. I will review just three critical points here: (1) Abusers need to suffer consequences for their actions now, not just receive warnings of future sanctions, which have little impact on abusers. (2) He can't overcome his abuse problem by dealing with anything other than the abuse. Working on stress or anger management, alcoholism, or relationship dynamics will have little or no impact on a man's abusiveness. (3) Criticism from people in positions of authority can sometimes have the greatest impact of any fallout that abusers experience. On the other hand, language from professionals that excuses or minimizes abuse, or that attributes responsibility partly to the victim—as in the case of a probation officer who says to a man: "You and your wife really need to work out your issues and stop abusing each other"—makes an important contribution to *enabling* the abuser.

Communities

Any community group or agency can help reach abusive men by prominently displaying posters against abuse and disseminating brochures and other literature. Bear in mind that materials that prominently feature words such as *abuse* or *violence* can be useful in getting the attention of abused women, but abusers tend to think, *That isn't me they're talking to.* Instead, use simple questions and descriptions, such as:

> *"Do you have a problem with your temper?"*
>
> *"Has your wife or girlfriend ever complained of being afraid of you?"*
>
> *"Do you sometimes swear or call her names?"*
>
> *"Do you ever blame your behavior on your partner?"*

The smaller print should explain that there is no excuse for a man to insult, frighten, isolate, or lie to his partner, *even if he feels that she does the same things.* Descriptions of laws and potential legal consequences are helpful, including the fact that he can be arrested for pushing, poking, restraining, or threatening his partner, even if he does not hit her. Few men are aware of this possibility, and abusers are shocked when they get arrested for such "lower-level" violence. If your area has a high-quality abuser program include the telephone number, but remember that few abusers follow through on counseling unless someone demands it of them. The main purpose of your posters and pamphlets is to educate abusers and potential abusers about *community values.*

An abuser rejects at first what he hears from any of these sources. But when positive social messages begin to line up, that's another matter. I have occasionally had physically abusive clients, for example, who have been criticized by the arresting officer, then prosecuted fully, then criticized by the judge—in addition to having a sentence imposed—then criticized by the probation officer, and then finally confronted in an abuser program. This man may also see a program on television about abuse or read a pamphlet in the waiting room of a doctor's office. His own mother or brother may tell him that he needs to stop bullying his partner. If all these different voices reinforce each other, saying that he is responsible for his own actions, refusing to let him blame the victim, breaking the silence about the pain he is causing, and insisting that the responsibility to change rests on his shoulders alone, the abuser's vast sense of entitlement starts to shrink. I have watched it happen. Here is where change can begin.

REMEMBERING THE CHILDREN

Amid the screaming and insults, behind the cascade of accusations and counteraccusations, lost in our panic as we see a woman being repeatedly psychologically hammered or physically beaten, we can forget that the abuser has other victims too. The children can become invisible. The police who go on a domestic abuse call sometimes have been known to forget to even ask whether there are children in the home. These children recede into the corners, trying to keep themselves safe, and may remain unnoticed until they are old enough to try to jump in to protect their mothers.

As is true with almost every approach to abuse, we have to begin by breaking the silence. Ask the mother privately how she feels her children are being affected by the man's behavior and by the tension it creates. Does he abuse her in front of them? How do they react? What are her concerns about them? What does she feel they need? (Remember, think *with* her, not *for* her.)

Break secrecy with the children as well. Let them know that you are aware of what is happening and that you care about their feelings. Ask:

"How are things going at home for you?"

"Is it hard for you when your parents argue?"

"What happens when they get mad at each other?"

"Does anyone at your house ever hurt any one else's feelings, or frighten anyone?"

"Would you like to tell me about that?"

Even if the child answers no to all of your inquiries, you have demonstrated that he or she matters to you and that you understand that the abuse—without calling it that—can be hurtful or frightening. Then leave the door open to future communication by saying: "You can tell me about your life at home any time you want. It's okay to talk about it. Children can get upset sometimes when their parents argue."

Notice that I recommend using soft terms that neither name abuse nor assign responsibility for it until you find out how much the child knows. This language is important to avoid alerting children to painful dynamics of which they may not be aware. This guideline should be *reversed,* however, if the child does disclose abuse directly to you or if you know that he or she has directly witnessed explicit verbal or physical abuse toward the mother. Then it becomes important *not* to use neutral terms; children of abused women already feel that they themselves and their mothers are at least partly at fault, and you do not want to reinforce those hurtful misconceptions. So once the secret is out, avoid even-handed language such as *the problems between your parents* or *the mean things they sometimes do to each other.*

Children do need to hear the following messages:

- *"It's not your fault if someone in the family says mean things or hurts someone."*

- *"It's not your mother's fault if someone treats her badly."*

- *"No one should ever blame you for being mean to you or hurting you."*

- *"A child can't really protect his or her mother, and it isn't the child's job."*

The term *abuse* doesn't mean anything to children younger than ten or twelve but may be useful in speaking with teenagers. In general, descriptions work better than labels.

If the abuser is the children's father or father figure, take particular caution not to speak badly of him as a person but only to name and criticize his *actions*. Children do not want to hear that their dad is mean, selfish, or bad. In cases where the abuser is dangerous, it is helpful to discuss the risks with the children, both to help them protect themselves and to validate their reality. However, even a violent, dangerous abuser is a human being, and children tend to be acutely tuned in to the humanity of anyone they know well. Don't talk about him as if he were a monster. You can say, for example, "Your dad has a problem that makes him unsafe sometimes, doesn't he?" These are terms that make sense to children.

Those community members who work with the children of abused women in a professional capacity, such as teachers, police officers, therapists, or court employees, can increase their effectiveness by being sensitive to the family dynamics that partner abuse creates and by remembering how manipulative abusers can be. Too many children of abused women are labeled "ADD" or "ADHD" and given medication instead of receiving the assistance they need. Children need us to take an interest in their predicament, help them to learn positive values, and support their crucial connection to their mothers.

INFLUENCING YOUR COMMUNITY'S RESPONSE TO ABUSE

One-on-one approaches to overcoming abuse work well only when the wider community pulls together to create an environment in which the victims are supported and the abusers held accountable. You can play a role in making your community an abuse-free zone, a haven where abused women know that they can count on complete support and where abusers know that they will not succeed in gaining sympathy for their excuses or in avoiding the consequences of their actions.

Here are just a few of the many steps you can take:

- Offer to help your local program for abused women as a volunteer, fund-raiser, public speaker, or board member. These programs are always short of both help and funds, because the number of abused women needing assistance is so tragically high. Many programs offer free or low-cost training for volunteers.

- Get involved with an abuser program if there is one in your area. You can be trained to be a counselor for abusers or to be an advocate for abused women within the abuser program. Use your influence to guide the program to keep improving the support it offers abused women and their children and the quality of education and counseling it provides the abusers. If no local program exists, contact one of the abuser programs listed in "Resources" in the back of this book for guidance in starting one up.

- Join or start an organization devoted to education and activism regarding the abuse of women. Such groups distribute literature, hold protests, promote more effective laws, sponsor artistic projects related to domestic abuse, and take many, many other forms of courageous and creative action to end abuse. Your local program for abused women may have a "social action" or similarly named committee, but efforts to promote social change are sometimes more effective when they come out of a separate organization that is not trying simultaneously to provide services.

- Bring programs into your school system that teach respect and equality for females and that make children aware of relationship abuse.

- Join your local domestic abuse task force, or start one if none exists. An effective task force (or "roundtable") includes representatives from as many community institutions as possible that deal with families affected by abuse. Invite therapists, clergypeople, school personnel, police, personnel from the district attorney's office, and court personnel as well as staff from programs for abused women and for abusers. Such task forces have been multiplying rapidly over the past ten years, with countless laudable accomplishments in coordinating services, launching new programs, and educating the public.

• Help to get services going in your area for children of abused women, especially counseling groups. Press therapists who work with children to educate themselves on the issue of partner abuse and its effects on children who are exposed to it. Participate in public education efforts regarding the reinjuring of abused women and their children through custody and visitation litigation. For more information on all of these suggestions, see "Resources" at the back of this book.

• Join educational efforts in secondary schools regarding abuse in teen dating relationships, in order to stop abuse before it starts. (See the section on teen issues in "Resources".)

• Advocate for expanded welfare benefits and other forms of public economic support for abused women. The cuts in public assistance over the past decade have often made it much more difficult for abused women to leave their partners, especially if they have children. Women can't leave abusive men if they are economically trapped.

• Protest TV and print media portrayals that glorify abuse and sexual assault or that blame victims, including news coverage.

• If you are a former abused woman who is no longer with her abuser, consider telling your story in public. There is a tremendous need for women who have had personal experience with abuse to go to social service agencies, schools, police departments, and other groups and help people to grasp more deeply what abuse looks like and what tremors it sends through so many lives. I have often seen professionals and other community members transformed by hearing the account of a real-life woman who has lived with psychological or physical assault.

- Support women who are survivors of abuse to take leadership in your community, and make sure that they are represented on all task forces and policy-making bodies addressing domestic abuse.

CHANGING THE CULTURE

Abuse is the product of a mentality that excuses and condones bullying and exploitation, that promotes superiority and disrespect, and that casts responsibility on to the oppressed. All efforts to end the abuse of women ultimately have to return to this question: How do we change societal values so that women's right to live free of insults, invasion, disempowerment, and intimidation is respected?

One way is simply to declare out loud to people in your life that women *have* these rights unconditionally. Much of modern society remains regrettably unclear on this point. I still hear: "Well, he shouldn't have called her a 'slut,' but she did dance all night with another man." I hear: "He did keep hassling her at her job even when she told him to stay away, but he was *heartbroken* over their breakup." I hear: "He did use some force in having sex with her, but she had really led him on to believe that they were going all the way that night." You can influence your friends, your religious group, your bowling club, your relatives by having the courage to stand up and say: "Abuse of a woman is wrong—period."

Next, put on pressure against songs, videos, "humor," and other media that aid and abet abusers. The flood of complaints regarding Eminem's Grammy award succeeded in pressuring CBS to run a public-service announcement about domestic abuse during the broadcast and led the Grammy's president to read an antiviolence statement from the podium. A stream of complaints flowed into Simon & Schuster for distributing a video game in which the object was for the male character to successfully rape a female, who was a tied-up Native American woman. When the public decries the cultural agents that teach or excuse abuse, the culture receives another strong push in the right direction.

Refuse to go along with jokes that insult or degrade women. If you are a man, your refusal to fall in step with destructive jokes and comments can be especially powerful. When someone tells you, "It's just a joke," answer by asking, "How do you think an abuser reacts when he hears this joke? Do you think it helps him realize the harm he is doing? Or do you think that his sense of justification gets even more solid than it was?"

Encourage the women in your life—your friends, sisters, mothers, daughters—to insist on dignity and respect, to have faith in themselves, to be proud. Expect boys and men to be respectful, kind, and responsible, and don't settle for less. Again, men have a particularly important role to play in cultural change. When a father tells his son, "I don't want to hear you saying bad things about girls," or "No, I'm not going to let you have a 'boys only' birthday party, that's prejudiced," the boy sits up and takes notice. The "Resources" section includes some organizations that are particularly involved in helping men take leadership against the abuse of women. Vocal leadership by men makes it much more difficult for abusers to claim that the battle over abuse is one between men and women rather than between abusers and everyone else.

Finally, promote alternatives to abuse and oppression by recognizing how intertwined different forms of abuse and mistreatment are. The opposite of arrogantly defining reality is listening respectfully to each person's perspective. The opposite of placing yourself above other people is seeing them as equals. The opposite of establishing a hierarchy in which the top few people lounge comfortably while everyone else gets squashed is sharing resources. The opposite of madly scrambling to the top, whether it's the top of the corporate ladder, the top of the softball league, or the top of the household pecking order, is building communities devoted to cooperation and support, where everyone wins. To consider a world without relationship abuse is to open up to even more profound possibilities, to the potential for human beings to live in harmony with each other and with their natural environment.

Anger and conflict are *not* the problem; they are normal aspects of life. Abuse doesn't come from people's inability to resolve conflicts but from one person's decision to claim a higher status than another. So while it is valuable, for example, to teach nonviolent conflict-resolution skills to elementary school students—a popular initiative nowadays—such efforts contribute little by themselves to ending abuse. Teaching equality, teaching a deep respect for all human beings—these are more complicated undertakings, but they are the ones that count.

Some people may feel that I am unrealistic to believe in a world that is free of abuse. But words like *unrealistic, naive,* and *impractical* come from voices of superiority who use them as put-downs to get people to stop thinking for themselves. Abuse *does* affect us all. If you haven't been involved with an abusive partner yourself, even if no woman that you love has ever suffered chronic mistreatment, the quality of your life is still dragged down, your horizons still circumscribed, by the existence of abuse and the culture that drives it. The voice of abuse takes so many different forms. You can hear it each time a child's dreams are shot down by an adult who thinks he or she knows it all. It rings in the ears of anyone who has ever been ridiculed for crying. It echoes through the mind of each person who has dared to put a name to his or her own mistreatment, or to the cruelty directed toward someone else, and then has been derided with stinging words such as *sissy* or *mama's boy* or *hysterical* or thousands of others.

If you choose to believe that your life could be free of abuse, or that the whole world could be, you will be taunted by similar voices, some originating inside your own head. Some people feel threatened by the concept that abuse is a solvable problem, because if it is, there's no excuse for not solving it. Abusers and their allies are reluctant to face up to the damage they have done, make amends, and live differently in the future, so they may choose to insult those who address the problem of abuse. But the taunts and invalidation will not stop you, nor will they stop the rest of us, because the world has come too far to go back. There are millions of people who have taken stands against partner abuse across the globe and are now unwilling to retreat, just like the woman who gets a taste of life without the abuser and then can't live under his control anymore, because the taste of freedom and equality is too sweet.

KEY POINTS TO REMEMBER

- Once we tear the cover of excuses, distortions, and manipulations off of abusers, they suddenly find abuse much harder to get away with.

- If Mothers Against Drunk Driving can change the culture's indifference to alcohol-related automotive deaths, we can change the culture's attitude toward partner abuse.

- Everyone has a role to play in ending abuse.

- If you are trying to assist an abused woman, get help and support for *yourself* as well (see "Resources").

- All forms of chronic mistreatment in the world are interwoven. When we take one apart, all the rest start to unravel as well.

Resources

BELOW YOU WILL FIND a wide collection of books, videos, websites, and organizations. These resources offer support, guidance, and inspiration to abused women, to loved ones wishing to help them, and to community members interested in addressing the wider problem of abuse and violence in our society. Many of the resources listed below refer to physical violence in their titles or descriptions, but they are nonetheless *all* relevant to women who have experienced verbal, economic, or sexual coercion by a partner, regardless of whether actual assaults or threats have been involved. If you do not have Web access and are interested in pursuing some of the Internet resources listed here, try your public library—many libraries offer free time on computers connected to the Internet.

FOR WOMEN OF ALL BACKGROUNDS

- National Domestic Violence Hotline for the United States and Canada: 1-800-799-SAFE.

Call this number to receive a referral to the closest hotline in your area for abused women. *The use of this number is not restricted to women who have experienced physical violence:* Women and teens are welcome to call with any issue regarding verbal abuse or control in a relationship, or just because something is happening in their relationship that is making them uncomfortable.

- Rape, Abuse, and Incest National Network Hotline (Rain): 1-800-656-4673.

Call this number if you have been sexually assaulted or sexually abused by your partner or ex-partner (or by anyone else), and you will be connected immediately to the sexual assault hotline closest to you.

- *When Love Goes Wrong: What to Do When You Can't Do Anything Right,* by Ann Jones and Susan Schechter (HarperPerennial).

This is the essential book for women who are seeking guidance on how to cope with a controlling partner and how to move toward freedom and recovery. It is practical, down-to-earth, and accurate, and it covers in detail a wide range of issues that women face.

- *It's **My** Life Now: Starting Over After an Abusive Relationship or Domestic Violence,* by Meg Kennedy Dugan and Roger Hock (Routledge).

Despite the title, this book is equally valuable for women who are still involved with an angry or controlling partner and for those who have left. This is a wonderful, warm, compassionate book by authors who deeply understand both emotional and physical abuse.

- *The Verbally Abusive Relationship: How to Recognize It and How to Respond,* by Patricia Evans (Bob Adams).

Evans's book takes the reader through the details of verbally abusive tactics in relationships, and it explains how to understand their effects on you. The author offers terrific insight and practical advice. (The book contains a couple of the common misconceptions about the psychology of abusers, but this is a very minor drawback compared to its many strengths.)

- *Into the Light: A Guide for Battered Women,* by Leslie Cantrelli (Chas. Franklin Press).

This booklet is short and simple, with accurate information and good advice. This is a great resource for a woman who does not have the time or energy for the longer books listed above, or who wants to have quick inspiration handy.

- *Not to People Like Us: Hidden Abuse in Upscale Marriages,* by Susan Weitzman (Basic Books).

A valuable exposé of abuse among the wealthy, with important guidance for abused women. Weitzman's descriptions of abusive men are accurate and helpful (though a couple of the myths slip in). I recommend this book highly.

For Teenagers and Their Parents

- *What Parents Need to Know About Dating Violence,* by Barrie Levy and Patricia Occhiuzzo Giggam (Seal Press).

The essential book for parents who are concerned that their daughters or sons may be involved in abusive dating relationships. Compassionate, insightful, and highly practical, written by people who grasp the wide range of anxieties and challenges that parents face.

- *In Love and Danger—A Teen's Guide to Breaking Free of Abusive Relationships,* by Barrie Levy (Seal Press).

A guide for the teenager herself in responding to an abusive or controlling partner, written in just the right tone and language to reach adolescents—an excellent book. It's out of print, so look for it used or at the library, or try to find it online.

For Women of Color

- *Chain Chain Change: For Black Women in Abusive Relationships,* by Evelyn C. White (Seal Press).

This excellent book remains the key reading resource for any African American woman who is involved with a controlling or abusive partner. It provides general information combined with guidance that is specific to the black woman's experience, and it includes a section that speaks to abused black lesbians.

- *Mejor Sola Que Mal Acompañada: For the Latina in an Abusive Relationship,* by Myrna Zambrano (Seal Press).

Zambrano's book for Latina women in abusive relationships is available in a bilingual edition, making it readable for women who use either Spanish or English as their primary language. This excellent resource speaks to the cultural context in which Latinas live, and it offers specific validation and recommendations.

- *Black Eyes All of the Time: Intimate Violence, Aboriginal Women, and the Justice System,* by Anne McGillivray and Brenda Comaskey (University of Toronto).

The experience of abused indigenous (native) women is told largely in their own voices in this wonderful and groundbreaking volume. Although there are a few portions where the writers use some difficult academic language, the great majority of the book is highly accessible and moving.

- Mending the Sacred Hoop
  202 E. Superior St.
  Duluth MN 55802
  (218) 722-2781
  www.duluth-model.org, then select "Mending the Sacred Hoop"

This project of Minnesota Program Development focuses on addressing the abuse of women in tribal cultures.

- Institute on Domestic Violence in the African American Community
  University of Minnesota School of Social Work
  290 Peters Hall
  1404 Gortner Ave.
  St. Paul MN 55108-6142
  (877) 643-8222
  www.dvinstitute.org

This organization's website includes resources for abused women themselves, while also reaching out to policy makers, researchers, and other concerned community members.

- National Latino Alliance for the Elimination of Domestic Violence
  P.O. Box 22086
  Ft. Washington Station
  New York NY 10032
  (646) 672-1404
  www.dvalianza.org

Mostly oriented toward research and policy. Extensive listings.

- Asian and Pacific Islander Institute on Domestic Violence
  942 Market St., Suite 200
  San Francisco CA 94102
  (415) 954-9964
  www.apiahf.org, then select "Programs," then select the Institute.

FOR LESBIANS

- *Naming the Violence: Speaking Out About Lesbian Battering,* edited by Kerry Lobel (Seal Press).

Regrettably, this 1986 book is out of print, but you can find it through a library, a used-book store, or online. The personal stories of many abused lesbians are shared here to help you to identify the problem and know that you are not alone.

- *Woman-to-Woman Sexual Violence: Does She Call It Rape?,* by Lori Girshick (Northeastern University Press).

With the stories of survivors of sexual assaults by same-sex partners woven through, this book reports on an important survey and helps bring to light a seldom-examined aspect of intimate partner abuse.

- *Lesbians Talk: Violent Relationships,* by Joelle Taylor and Tracy Chandler (Scarlet Press).

This is a short book that draws from the voices of women themselves to describe the problem of abuse in lesbian relationships and offers solutions.

- *Same-Sex Domestic Violence: Strategies for Change,* by Beth Leventhal and Sandra Lundy (Sage Publications).

This well-written and insightful book offers guidance to community members who want to address the needs of abused lesbians and gay men, explaining the structuring of service provision and the overcoming of institutional barriers.

- On the Web, try going to Gayscape and doing a search for "domestic violence"— many listings are available for organizations, publications, and websites.

FOR IMMIGRANT AND REFUGEE WOMEN

- Family Violence Prevention Fund
383 Rhode Island St., Suite 304
San Francisco CA 94103-5133
(415) 252-8900
www.endabuse.org, then select "Immigrant Women," then select "Help Is Available"

FVPF helps abused immigrant women to get information about their rights and options and to find referrals to programs in their area.

- NOW Legal Defense and Education Fund
Immigrant Women's Project
1522 K St., NW, Suite 550
Washington DC 20005
(202) 326-0040
www.nowldef.org, then select "Issues," then select "Immigrant Women"

- National Lawyers Guild
National Immigration Project
14 Beacon St., Suite 602
Boston MA 02108

(617) 227-9727

www.nlg.org, then select "National Immigration Project," then select "Domestic Violence"

ABOUT CHILDREN OF ABUSED WOMEN

- *Childhood Experiences of Domestic Violence,* by Caroline McGee (Jessica Kingsley).

Although this is a professional book, it is very readable and compassionate. McGee understands the challenges an abused mother faces. Told largely in the words of mothers and children themselves, this is the single best introduction I have found to the experiences of children exposed to an abusive man, with extensive guidance for how to effectively assist them to safety and recovery.

- *The Batterer as Parent: Addressing the Impact of Domestic Violence on Family Dynamics,* by Lundy Bancroft and Jay Silverman (Sage Publications).

Although this professional book focuses on physically abusive men, the great majority of what we cover applies to verbally abusive and controlling men as well. We explain how an abusive man can affect the relationships between a mother and her children and between siblings, and how abusers may try to continue their control through the children postseparation. Abused mothers, including those involved in the family court system, report finding this book both validating and helpful.

- *Children Who See Too Much: Lessons From the Child Witness to Violence Project,* by Betsy McAlister Groves (Beacon Press).

This book is for parents or professionals who are assisting children who have been exposed to serious physical violence, including domestic violence, to help them understand children's emotional reactions and their recovery needs. It is brief but very clear and helpful.

ABOUT CHILD CUSTODY, DIVORCE, AND CHILD SUPPORT

- Resource Center on Domestic Violence: Child Protection and Custody, operated by the National Council of Juvenile and Family Court Judges. 1-800-527-3223.

The Resource Center offers a free packet of information for abused women in custody and visitation litigation. It does not become involved in specific cases or provide legal advice. The Center also offers a book called *Managing Your Divorce* that helps women prepare for the process of resolving child custody, visitation, and child support.

- *Women and Children Last: Custody Disputes and the Family "Justice" System,* by Georgina Taylor, Jan Barnsley, and Penny Goldsmith of the Vancouver (BC) Custody and Access Support and Advocacy Association.

This excellent book prepares abused mothers for the difficult emotional and legal challenges of family court litigation, to help increase their ability to keep their children safe and maintain custody. Advocates and concerned community members can also benefit from the explanations of how the family court system works and why abused women can find the environment so hostile. (For ordering information, call Vancouver Status of Women at (604) 255-6554.)

- The Battered Mothers Testimony Project: A Human Rights Report on Child Custody and Domestic Violence.

This activist project interviewed forty abused women about their experiences of being revictimized by family courts through the abuser's use of custody and visitation litigation, and also interviewed numerous judges, custody evaluators, and advocates. The project report, which exposes these systemic abuses as violations of women's internationally recognized human rights, is available from: Publication Office, Wellesley Centers for Women, Wellesley College, (781) 283-2510, or at www.wcwonline.org.

- "Small Justice: Little Justice in America's Family Courts," a video by Garland Waller of Boston University.

This one-hour video documents three cases in which abused women faced systematic mistreatment by family courts as they attempted to protect their children from domestic violence and sexual abuse. This well-made and carefully researched film is an important resource for community members working for court reforms. (Available from Intermedia, 1-800-553-8336)

- *Divorced from Justice: The Abuse of Women and Children by Divorce Lawyers and Judges,* by Karen Winner (Regan Books).

This is another book that is out of print, but you can find it at libraries, used-book stores, or online. The stories are painful ones, and this makes the book heavy reading, but Winner offers crucial advice to women and to anyone who is trying to help them, and she also gives important suggestions to people interested in working for court reform.

- *The Hostage Child: Sex Abuse Allegations in Custody Disputes,* by Leora Rosen and Michelle Etlin (Indiana University Press).

An eye-opening education for people interested in working toward family court reform, this book documents the obstacles that abused women can encounter while attempting to protect their children from abuse, even in cases where extensive evidence exists. (I don't recommend this book for abused women to read themselves if they are currently involved in litigation—it's very frightening, and most cases don't go as badly as the ones presented here.)

- National Child Support Enforcement Association
  444 North Capitol St., Suite 414
  Washington DC 20001-1512
  (202) 624-8180
  www.ncsea.org

NCSEA provides information on child support collection, with links to specific child support resources in your geographical area.

FOR MOTHERS OF SEXUALLY ABUSED CHILDREN

- *A Mother's Nightmare—Incest: A Practical Legal Guide for Parents and Professionals,* by John E. B. Myers (Sage Publications).

Written by a smart and compassionate attorney, this is a critical book for any woman who has reason to suspect that her child has been sexually abused by the child's father or stepfather, whether or not the child has explicitly disclosed.

ABOUT GENERAL PARENTING ISSUES

The books listed in this section are general parenting guides, full of tremendous practical help and insight. I have found all of these titles to be terrific. However, two words of caution: First, these books tend not to address the impact on children of exposure to a man who abuses their mother, including the role that abuse plays in as much as half of divorces. Second, with the exception of *Real Boys*, these books do not offer detailed guidance to parents who have a gay or lesbian teen (though *Reviving Ophelia* touches on the issue briefly).

You can also find additional parenting resources in your phone book, such as parental stress hotline numbers, Parent's Anonymous, and various kinds of parent education classes, or do an Internet search for "Parent Education."

- *How to Talk So Kids Will Listen and Listen So Kids Will Talk,* by Adele Faber and Elaine Mazlish (Avon).

- *Siblings Without Rivalry,* by Adele Faber and Elaine Mazlish (Avon).

- *The Courage to Raise Good Men,* by Olga Silverstein and Beth Rashbaum (Penguin). Consider this book a *must read* for any parent of a son, especially if that son has been exposed to a man who mistreats the son's mother.

- *Reviving Ophelia: Saving the Selves of Adolescent Girls,* by Mary Pipher (Grosset/Putnam).

- *Real Boys: Rescuing Our Sons from the Myths of Boyhood,* by William Pollack (Random House).

- *How to Mother a Successful Daughter,* by Nicky Marone (Three Rivers).

- *How to Father a Successful Daughter,* by Nicky Marone (Fawcett Crest).

FOR WOMEN INVOLVED WITH LAW ENFORCEMENT OFFICERS

- Spouse Abuse by Law Enforcement (SABLE)
  Life Span
  P.O. Box 445
  Des Plaines IA 60016
  (847) 824-0382
  www.policedv.com

SABLE offers a booklet called *Police Domestic Violence: A Handbook for Victims* for $5 (including shipping) from the above address.

FOR WOMEN IN FAITH COMMUNITIES

- Minnesota Center Against Violence and Abuse
  www.mincava.umn.edu, then select "Faith Response"

This website offers many readings and resources regarding the abuse of Christian, Jewish, and Islamic women, and a collection of interfaith writings and organizations. A terrific resource for women whose spiritual or religious involvement is an important part of their lives.

- *Keeping the Faith: Guidance for Christian Women Facing Abuse,* by Marie Fortune (Harper San Francisco).

Fortune offers clarity, advice, and validation, along with new interpretations of scriptural texts, to help abused Christian women escape entrapment and draw strength from their spiritual beliefs. (I am not currently aware of similar books for women of other faiths, but you may find one, as new resources on abuse appear every day.)

About Abusive Men

The organizations listed here offer literature, videos, and training for people interested in starting or improving counseling programs for men who abuse women.

- Emerge: Counseling and Education to End Domestic Violence
  2380 Massachusetts Ave., Suite 101
  Cambridge MA 02140
  (617) 547-9879
  www.emergedv.com

- Domestic Abuse Intervention Project
  206 West Fourth St.
  Duluth MN 55806
  (218) 722-2781
  www.duluth-model.org

For Those Assisting Abused Women

- *To Be an Anchor in the Storm: A Guide for Families and Friends of Abused Women,* by Susan Brewster (Ballantine Books).

An outstandingly caring, practical, and wise book for the loved ones of an abused woman. If you are trying to assist a woman who is in a bad relationship, *read this book.* It will help you to feel better *and* make you a much more effective helper. (However, one word of caution: A section at the end of the book on reporting child abuse contains information that I find ill-advised. Before you involve child protective services with a mother you care about, call a program for abused women in your area and seek advice about whether and how to make a child-abuse report.)

- *Safety Planning with Battered Women,* by Jill Davies, Eleanor Lyon, and Diane Monti-Catania (Sage Publications).

This is a professional book, but it is very readable and helpful for anyone who wants to understand what is really involved when a woman is considering leaving an abusive partner, and it provides guidance for how to help a woman be safer *even if she can't leave or doesn't want to.* The authors talk about much more than just safety planning—they address the full range of practical realities that abused women face in a way that I have found in no other book.

- *Trauma and Recovery,* by Judith Herman (Basic Books).

Dr. Herman's book is the bible of trauma, especially for those kinds of traumatic experiences for which the society tends to blame the victim or deny the reality of her/his experience. An outstandingly brilliant work.

ABOUT OVERCOMING PARTNER ABUSE IN COMMUNITIES

- National Coalition Against Domestic Violence
1532 16th St., NW
Washington DC 20036
(202) 745-1211
www.ncadv.org

Join this organization to support policy and service development to benefit abused women and their children NCADV also has various resources that you can order (at a discount if you are a member) and listings of other sources of information.

- *Next Time She'll Be Dead: Battering and How to Stop It,* by Ann Jones (Beacon Press).

This terrific work elucidates the cultural influences and institutional actions that support abuse and gives to-the-point suggestions for concerned community members on how to end the abuse of women.

- *Rural Woman Battering and the Justice System: An Ethnography,* by Neil Websdale (Sage Publications).

This excellent book describes the special challenges faced by abused women who live far from large population centers, who may be very isolated and may face local communities that are not supportive of escaping abuse. Groundbreaking and insightful, with concrete strategies for how agencies and institutions can better serve abused women in rural areas.

- *Coordinating Community Responses to Domestic Violence: Lessons from the Duluth Model,* edited by Melanie Shepard and Ellen Pence (Sage Publications).

Detailed guidance on how to draw from the United States's premier model of collaborative work in communities to assist abused women, hold abusers accountable, and change community values about partner abuse.

- *Pornography: The Production and Consumption of Inequality,* by Gail Dines, Robert Jensen, and Ann Russo (Routledge).

This highly readable book provides the most reasonable and persuasive explanations that I have encountered of how pornography can shape men's ways of perceiving and interacting with women, and of the various excuses that groups and individuals use to avoid looking at the damage that pornography can do.

- "Dream Worlds II," a video by the Media Education Foundation.

This powerful and disturbing video reveals the attitudes toward women that are taught by today's music videos. Available from MEF, 26 Center St., Northampton MA 01060, 1-800-897-0089, www.mediaed.org.

- "Tough Guise," a video by the Media Education Foundation.

This widely acclaimed video created by Jackson Katz shows how popular portrayals of masculinity force boys and men into unhealthy roles and teach males to be abusive toward females. (See ordering information under previous listing.)

- Transforming Communities
734 A St.
San Rafael CA 94901-3923

(415) 457-2464
www.transformcommunities.org

Transforming Communities has a tremendous collection of resources and ideas for how to combat the abuse of women and children.

FOR MALE ALLIES

Many opportunities exist for men who want to be active in stopping the abuse of women, and more appear every day. Below are just a few examples.

- Men Overcoming Violence
  1385 Mission St., Suite 300
  San Francisco CA 94103
  (415) 626-MOVE [6683]
  www.menovercomingviolence.org

Public speakers, counseling groups, and opportunities for activism.

- Men Can Stop Rape
  P.O. Box 57144
  Washington DC 20037
  (202) 265-6530
  www.mencanstoprape.org

MCSR describes its mission as being "to promote gender equity and build men's capacity to be strong without being violent." Many programs, including outreach to youth and education on teen-dating violence.

- Family Violence Prevention Fund
  www.endabuse.org

Information is available on the FVPF website about their program "Coaching Boys Into Men" (with a brochure that you can download), and a new initiative for reaching out to boys called "Teach Early" has recently been launched. (The FVPF website is also full of information and resources on many aspects of partner abuse, including guidebooks for health-care providers and many other materials.)

- Men's Initiative for Jane Doe
  14 Beacon St., Suite 507
  Boston MA 02108
  (617) 248-0922
  www.menscampaign.org

A new project that offers various ideas for how men can get involved as allies to abused women.

You can also visit the Campus Outreach Services website at www.campusoutreach services.com: go to "Resources," and then select "Men Against Violence Against Women Organizations," and you will be provided with descriptions and links for *twenty* different men's groups around the country that are focused on stopping the abuse of women.

Index